KAPLAN PUBLISHING

AF773966

EXCITING EXTRA ONLINE RESOURCES INCLUDED

Kaplan Publishing are constantly finding new ways to make a difference to your studies and our exciting online resources really do offer something different to ACCA students looking for exam success.

THIS COMPLETE TEXT COMES WITH FREE EN-gage ONLINE RESOURCES SO THAT YOU CAN STUDY ANYTIME, ANYWHERE

Having purchased this Complete Text, you have access to the following online study materials:

- An online version of the Text which allows you to click in and out of the expandable content and view the answers to the Test Your Understanding exercises
- Fixed Online Tests with instant answers
- Test History and Results to allow you to track your performance
- Interim Assessments including Questions and Answers

How to access your online resources

- **Kaplan Financial students** will already have a Kaplan EN-gage account and these extra resources will be available to you online. You do not need to register again, as this process was completed when you enrolled. If you are having problems accessing online materials, please ask your course administrator.
- **If you purchased through Kaplan Flexible Learning or via the Kaplan Publishing website** you will automatically receive an e-mail invitation to Kaplan EN-gage online. Please register your details using this e-mail to gain access to your content. If you do not receive the e-mail or book content, please contact Kaplan Flexible Learning.
- **If you are already a registered Kaplan EN-gage user** go to www.EN-gage.co.uk and log in. Select the 'add a book' feature and enter the ISBN number of this book and the unique pass key at the bottom of this card. Then click 'finished' or 'add another book'. You may add as many books as you have purchased from this screen.
- **If you are a new Kaplan EN-gage user** register at www.EN-gage.co.uk and click on the link contained in the e-mail we sent you to activate your account. Then select the 'add a book' feature, enter the ISBN number of this book and the unique pass key at the bottom of this card. Then click 'finished' or 'add another book'.

EN-gage

Your Code and Information

This code can only be used once for the registration of one book online. This registration will expire when the final sittings for the examinations covered by this book have taken place. Please allow one hour from the time you submitted your book details for us to process your request.

Please scratch the film to access your Engage code

Please be aware that this code is case-sensitive and you will need to include the dashes within the passcode, but not when entering the ISBN. For further technical support, please visit www.EN-gage.co.uk

ACCA

Paper F5

Performance Management

Complete Text

British library cataloguing-in-publication data

A catalogue record for this book is available from the British Library.

Published by:
Kaplan Publishing UK
Unit 2 The Business Centre
Molly Millars Lane
Wokingham
Berkshire
RG41 2QZ

ISBN: 978-0-85732-280-7

The text in this material and any others made available by any Kaplan Group company does not amount to advice on a particular matter and should not be taken as such. No reliance should be placed on the content as the basis for any investment or other decision or in connection with any advice given to third parties. Please consult your appropriate professional adviser as necessary. Kaplan Publishing Limited and all other Kaplan group companies expressly disclaim all liability to any person in respect of any losses or other claims, whether direct, indirect, incidental, consequential or otherwise arising in relation to the use of such materials.

Printed and bound by CPI Group (UK) Ltd, Croydon, CR0 4YY.

Acknowledgements

We are grateful to the Association of Chartered Certified Accountants and the Chartered Institute of Management Accountants for permission to reproduce past examination questions. The answers have been prepared by Kaplan Publishing.

Contents

chapter
Intro

Paper Introduction

How to Use the Materials

These Kaplan Publishing learning materials have been carefully designed to make your learning experience as easy as possible and to give you the best chances of success in your examinations.

The product range contains a number of features to help you in the study process. They include:

(1) Detailed study guide and syllabus objectives

(2) Description of the examination

(3) Study skills and revision guidance

(4) Complete text or essential text

(5) Question practice

The sections on the study guide, the syllabus objectives, the examination and study skills should all be read before you commence your studies. They are designed to familiarise you with the nature and content of the examination and give you tips on how to best to approach your learning.

The **complete text or essential text** comprises the main learning materials and gives guidance as to the importance of topics and where other related resources can be found. Each chapter includes:

- The **learning objectives** contained in each chapter, which have been carefully mapped to the examining body's own syllabus learning objectives or outcomes. You should use these to check you have a clear understanding of all the topics on which you might be assessed in the examination.
- The **chapter diagram** provides a visual reference for the content in the chapter, giving an overview of the topics and how they link together.
- The **content** for each topic area commences with a brief explanation or definition to put the topic into context before covering the topic in detail. You should follow your studying of the content with a review of the illustration/s. These are worked examples which will help you to understand better how to apply the content for the topic.
- **Test your understanding** sections provide an opportunity to assess your understanding of the key topics by applying what you have learned to short questions. Answers can be found at the back of each chapter.

- **Summary diagrams** complete each chapter to show the important links between topics and the overall content of the paper. These diagrams should be used to check that you have covered and understood the core topics before moving on.
- **Question practice** is provided at the back of each text.

Icon Explanations

Definition - Key definitions that you will need to learn from the core content.

Key Point - Identifies topics that are key to success and are often examined.

Expandable Text - Expandable text provides you with additional information about a topic area and may help you gain a better understanding of the core content. Essential text users can access this additional content on-line (read it where you need further guidance or skip over when you are happy with the topic)

Illustration - Worked examples help you understand the core content better.

Test Your Understanding - Exercises for you to complete to ensure that you have understood the topics just learned.

Tricky topic - When reviewing these areas care should be taken and all illustrations and test your understanding exercises should be completed to ensure that the topic is understood.

On-line subscribers

Our on-line resources are designed to increase the flexibility of your learning materials and provide you with immediate feedback on how your studies are progressing.

If you are subscribed to our on-line resources you will find:

(1) On-line referenceware: reproduces your Complete or Essential Text on-line, giving you anytime, anywhere access.

(2) On-line testing: provides you with additional on-line objective testing so you can practice what you have learned further.

(3) On-line performance management: immediate access to your on-line testing results. Review your performance by key topics and chart your achievement through the course relative to your peer group.

Ask your local customer services staff if you are not already a subscriber and wish to join.

Syllabus

Syllabus objectives

We have reproduced the ACCA's syllabus below, showing where the objectives are explored within this book. Within the chapters, we have broken down the extensive information found in the syllabus into easily digestible and relevant sections, called Content Objectives. These correspond to the objectives at the beginning of each chapter.

Syllabus learning objective and Chapter references

A SPECIALIST COST AND MANAGEMENT ACCOUNTING TECHNIQUES

1 Activity-based costing

(a) Identify appropriate cost drivers under ABC.[1] **Ch. 1**

(b) Calculate costs per driver and per unit using ABC.[2] **Ch. 1**

(c) Compare ABC and traditional methods of overhead absorption based on production units, labour hours or machine hours.[2] **Ch. 1**

2 Target costing

(a) Derive a target cost in manufacturing and service industries.[2] **Ch. 1**

(b) Explain the difficulties of using target costing in service industries.[2] **Ch. 1**

(c) Suggest how a target cost gap might be closed.[2] **Ch. 1**

3 Life-cycle costing

(a) Identify the costs involved at different stages of the lifecycle.[2] **Ch. 1**

(b) Derive a life cycle cost in manufacturing and service industries. **Ch. 1**

(c) Identify the benefits of life cycle costing. **Ch. 1**

4 Throughput accounting

(a) Calculate and interpret a throughput accounting ratio (TPAR).[2] **Ch. 1**

(b) Suggest how a TPAR could be improved.[2] **Ch. 1**

(c) Apply throughput accounting to a multi-product decision making problem.[2] **Ch. 1**

5 Environmental accounting

(a) Discuss the issues business face in the management of environmental costs. **Ch. 1**

(b) Describe the different methods a business may use to account for its environmental costs. **Ch. 1**

B DECISION-MAKING TECHNIQUES

1 Relevant cost analysis

(a) Explain the concept of relevant costing. **Ch. 5**

(b) Identify and calculate relevant costs for a specific decision situations from given data. **Ch. 5**

(c) Explain and apply the concept of opportunity costs. **Ch. 5**

2 Cost volume profit analysis

(a) Explain the nature of CVP analysis. **Ch. 2**

(b) Calculate and interpret breakeven point and margin of safety. **Ch. 2**

(c) Calculate the contribution to sales ratio, in single and multi-product situations, and demonstrate an understanding of its use. **Ch. 2**

(d) Calculate target profit or revenue in single and multi-product situations, and demonstrate an understanding of its use. **Ch. 2**

(e) Prepare break even charts and profit volume charts and interpret the information contained within each, including multi-product situations. **Ch. 2**

(f) Discuss the limitations of CVP analysis for planning and decision making. **Ch. 2**

3 Limiting factors

(a) Identify limiting factors in a scarce resource situation and select an appropriate technique. **Ch.3**

(b) Determine the optimal production plan where an organisation is restricted by a single limiting factor, including within the context of "make" or "buy" decisions. **Ch.3**

(c) Formulate and solve multiple scarce resource problem both graphically and using simultaneous equations as appropriate. **Ch.3**

(d) Explain and calculate shadow prices (dual prices) and discuss their implications on decision-making and performance management. **Ch.3**

(e) Calculate slack and explain the implications of the existence of slack for decision-making and performance management.(Excluding simplex and sensitivity to changes in objective functions.) **Ch.3**

4 Pricing decisions

(a) Explain the factors that influence the pricing of a product or service. [2] **Ch.4**

(b) Explain the price elasticity of demand.[1] **Ch. 4**

(c) Derive and manipulate a straight line demand equation. Derive an equation for the total cost function (including volume-based discounts). [2] **Ch. 4**

(d) Evaluate a decision to increase production and sales levels considering incremental costs, incremental revenues and other factors. [2] **Ch. 4**

(e) Determine prices and output levels for profit maximisation using the demand based approach to pricing (both tabular and algebraic methods) **Ch. 4**

(f) Explain different price strategies, including: [2] **Ch. 4**

(i) all forms of cost plus

(ii) skimming

(iii) penetration

(iv) complementary product

(v) product-line

(vi) volume discounting

(vii) discrimination

(viii) relevant cost.

(g) Calculate a price from a given strategy using cost plus and relevant cost.[2] **Ch. 4**

5 Make-or-buy and other short-term decisions

(a) Explain the issues surrounding make vs buy and outsourcing decisions [2]**Ch. 5**

(b) Calculate and compare 'make' costs with 'buy-in' costs.[2] **Ch. 5**

(c) Compare in-house costs and outsource costs of completing tasks and consider other issues surrounding this decision.[2] **Ch. 5**

(d) Apply relevant costing principles in situations involving make or buy in, shut down, one-off contracts and the further processing of joint products. [2] **Ch. 5**

6 Dealing with risk and uncertainty in decision making

(a) Suggest research techniques to reduce uncertainty, e.g. focus groups, market research.[2] **Ch. 6**

(b) Explain the use of simulation, expected values and sensitivity.[1] **Ch. 6**

(c) Apply expected values and sensitivity to decision making problems. [2] **Ch. 6**

(d) Apply the techniques of maximax, maximin, and minimax regret to decision making problems including the production of profit tables. [2] **Ch. 6**

(e) Calculate the value of perfect information and the value of imperfect information. **Ch. 6**

C BUDGETING

1 Objectives

(a) Outline the objectives of a budgetary control system.[2] **Ch. 7**

(b) Explain how corporate and divisional objectives may differ and can be reconciled.[2] **Ch. 7**

(c) Identify and resolve conflicting objectives and explain implications.[2] **Ch. 7**

2 Budgetary systems

(a) Explain how budgetary systems fit within the performance hierarchy. [2] **Ch. 8**

(b) Select and explain appropriate budgetary systems for an organisation (systems to include: top down, bottom up, rolling, zero base, activity base, incremental and feed-forward control).[2] **Ch. 8**

(c) Describe the information used in budget systems and the sources of the information needed.[2] **Ch. 8**

(d) Explain the difficulties of changing a budgetary system.[2] **Ch. 8**

(e) Explain how budget systems can deal with uncertainty in the environment.[2] **Ch. 8**

3 Types of budget

(a) Indicate the usefulness and problems with different budget types (zero base, activity based, incremental, master, functional, flexible).[2] **Ch. 8**

(b) Explain the difficulties of changing the type of budget used.[2] **Ch. 8**

4 Quantitative analysis in budgeting

(a) Analyse fixed and variable cost elements from total cost data (high/low and regression).[2] **Ch. 9**

(b) Explain the use of forecasting techniques. (Techniques: time series, simple average growth models and estimates based on judgement and experience.) Predict a future value from provided time series analysis data using both additive and proportional data.[2] **Ch. 9**

(c) Estimate the learning effect and apply the learning curve to a budgetary problem. This includes calculations on steady states.[2] **Ch. 9**

(d) Discuss the reservations with the learning curve.[2] **Ch. 9**

(e) Apply expected values and explain the problems and benefits.[2] **Ch. 9**

(f) Explain the benefits and dangers inherent in using spreadsheets in budgeting.[1] **Ch. 9**

5 Behavioural aspects of budgeting

(a) Identify the factors which influence behaviour.[2] **Ch. 7**

(b) Discuss the issues surrounding setting the difficulty level for a budget.[2] **Ch. 7**

(c) Explain the benefits and difficulties of the participation of employees in the negotiation of targets.[2] **Ch. 7**

D STANDARD COSTING AND VARIANCES ANALYSIS

1 Budgeting and standard costing

(a) Explain the use of standard costs.[2] **Ch. 10**

(b) Outline the methods used to derive standard costs and discuss the different types of costs possible.[2] **Ch. 10**

(c) Explain the importance of flexing budgets in performance management. [2] **Ch. 10**

(d) Prepare budgets and standards that allow for waste and idle time.[2] **Ch. 10**

(e) Explain and apply the principle of controllability in the performance management system.[2] **Ch. 10**

(f) Prepare a flexed budget and comment on its usefulness.[2] **Ch. 10**

2 Basic variances and operating statements

(a) Calculate, identify the cause of and interpret basic variances:[1] **Ch. 10**
   (i) sales price and volume
   (ii) materials total, price and usage
   (iii) labour total, rate and efficiency
   (iv) variable overhead total, expenditure and efficiency
   (v) fixed overhead total, expenditure and, where appropriate, volume, capacity and efficiency.

(b) Explain the effect on labour variances where the learning curve has been used in the budget process.[2] **Ch. 10**

(c) Produce full operating statements in both a marginal cost and full absorption costing environment, reconciling actual profit to budgeted profit.[2] **Ch. 10**

(d) Calculate the effect of idle time and waste on variances including where idle time has been budgeted for.[2] **Ch. 10**

(e) Explain the possible causes of idle time and waste and suggest methods of control.[2] **Ch. 10**

(f) Calculate, using a simple situation, ABC based variances.[2] **Ch. 10**

(g) Explain the different methods available for deciding whether or not to investigate a variance cause. **Ch. 10**

3 Material mix and yield variances

(a) Calculate, identify the cause of and explain mix and yield variances.[2] **Ch. 11**

(b) Explain the wider issues involved in changing mix e.g. cost, quality and performance measurement issues.[2] **Ch. 11**

(c) Identify and explain the interrelationship between price, mix and yield.[2] **Ch. 11**

(d) Suggest and justify alternative methods of controlling production processes.[2] **Ch. 11**

4 Sales mix and quantity variances

(a) Calculate, identify the cause of, and explain sales mix and quantity variances **Ch. 11**

(b) Identify and explain the relationship of the sales volume variances with the sales mix and quantity variances **Ch. 11**

5 Planning and operational variances

(a) Calculate a revised budget.[2] **Ch. 11**

(b) Identify and explain those factors that could and could not be allowed to revise an original budget.[2] **Ch. 11**

(c) Calculate planning and operational variances for sales (including market size and market share) materials and labour.[2] **Ch. 11**

(d) Explain and resolve the manipulation issues in revising budgets.[2] **Ch. 11**

6 Behavioural aspects of standard costing

(a) Describe the dysfunctional nature of some variances in the modern environment of JIT and TQM.[2] **Ch. 11**

(b) Discuss the behavioural problems resulting from using standard costs in rapidly changing environments.[2] **Ch. 11**

(c) Discuss the effect that variances have on staff motivation and action.[2] **Ch. 11**

E PERFORMANCE MEASUREMENT AND CONTROL

1 The scope of performance measurement

(a) Describe and calculate and interpret financial performance indicators (FPIs) for profitability, liquidity and risk in both manufacturing and service businesses. Suggest methods to improve these measures.[2] **Ch. 12**

(b) Describe, calculate and interpret non-financial performance indicators (NFPIs) and suggest methods to improve the performance indicated.[2] **Ch. 12**

(c) Explain the causes and problems created by short-termism and financial manipulation of results and suggest methods to encourage a long-term view.[2] **Ch. 12**

(d) Explain and interpret the Balanced Scorecard, and the Building Block model proposed by Fitzgerald and Moon.[2] **Ch. 11**

(e) Discuss the difficulties of target setting in qualitative areas.[2] **Ch. 12**

2 Divisional performance and transfer pricing

(a) Explain the basis for setting a transfer price using variable cost, full cost and the principles behind allowing for intermediate markets.[2] **Ch. 13**

(b) Explain how transfer prices can distort the performance assessment of divisions and decisions made.[2] **Ch. 13**

(c) Explain the meaning of, and calculate, Return on Investment (ROI) and Residual Income (RI), and discuss their shortcomings.[2] **Ch. 13**

(d) Compare divisional performance and recognise the problems of doing so.[2] **Ch. 13**

3 Performance analysis in not-for-profit organisations and the public sector

(a) Comment on the problems of having non-quantifiable objectives in performance management.[2] **Ch. 14**

(b) Explain how performance could be measured in these sectors.[2] **Ch. 14**

(c) Comment on the problems of having multiple objectives in these sectors.[2] **Ch. 14**

(d) Outline Value for Money (VFM) as a public sector objective.[1] **Ch. 14**

4 External considerations and behavioural aspects

(a) Explain the need to allow for external considerations in performance management. (External considerations to include stakeholders, market conditions and allowance for competitors.)[2] **Ch. 12**

(b) Suggest ways in which external considerations could be allowed for in performance management.[2] **Ch. Ch. 12**

(c) Interpret performance in the light of external considerations.[2] **Ch. 12**

(d) Identify and explain the behaviour aspects of performance management.[2] **Ch. 12**

The superscript numbers in square brackets indicate the intellectual depth at which the subject area could be assessed within the examination. Level 1 (knowledge and comprehension) broadly equates with the Knowledge module, Level 2 (application and analysis) with the Skills module and Level 3 (synthesis and evaluation) to the Professional level. However, lower level skills can continue to be assessed as you progress through each module and level.

The examination

Paper F5, Performance management, seeks to examine candidates' understanding of how to manage the performance of a business.

The paper builds on the knowledge acquired in Paper F2, Management Accounting, and prepares those candidates who will decide to go on to study Paper P5, Advanced performance management, at the Professional level.

There will be calculation and discursive elements to the paper. Generally the paper will seek to draw questions from as many of the syllabus sections as possible.

	Number of marks
Five compulsory questions worth 20 marks each	**100**
Total time allowed: 3 hours	

Paper-based examination tips

Spend the first few minutes of the examination **reading the paper** and planning your answers. During the reading time you may annotate the question paper but not write in the answer booklet. In particular you should use this time to ensure that you understand the requirements, highlighting key verbs, consider which parts of the syllabus are relevant and plan key calculations.

Divide the time you spend on questions in proportion to the marks on offer. One suggestion **for this examination** is to allocate 1.8 minutes to each mark available, so a 20-mark question should be completed in approximately 36 minutes.

Spend the last **five minutes** reading through your answers and **making any additions or corrections**.

If you **get completely stuck** with a question, leave space in your answer book and **return to it later**.

If you do not understand what a question is asking, state your assumptions. Even if you do not answer in precisely the way the examiner hoped, you should be given some credit, if your assumptions are reasonable.

You should do everything you can to make things easy for the marker. The marker will find it easier to identify the points you have made if your answers are legible.

Case studies: Most questions will be based on specific scenarios. To construct a good answer first identify the areas in which there are problems, outline the main principles / theories you are going to use to answer the question, and then apply the principles / theories to the case. It is essential that you tailor your comments to the scenario given.

Essay questions: Some questions may contain short essay-style requirements. Your answer should have a clear structure. It should contain a brief introduction, a main section and a conclusion. Be concise. It is better to write a little about a lot of different points than a great deal about one or two points.

Computations: It is essential to include all your workings in your answers. Many computational questions require the use of a standard format. Be sure you know these formats thoroughly before the exam and use the layouts that you see in the answers given in this book and in model answers.

Reports, memos and other documents: some questions ask you to present your answer in the form of a report or a memo or other document. So use the correct format - there could be easy marks to gain here.

Study skills and revision guidance

This section aims to give guidance on how to study for your ACCA exams and to give ideas on how to improve your existing study techniques.

Preparing to study

Set your objectives

Before starting to study decide what you want to achieve - the type of pass you wish to obtain. This will decide the level of commitment and time you need to dedicate to your studies.

Devise a study plan

Determine which times of the week you will study.

Split these times into sessions of at least one hour for study of new material. Any shorter periods could be used for revision or practice.

Put the times you plan to study onto a study plan for the weeks from now until the exam and set yourself targets for each period of study - in your sessions make sure you cover the course, course assignments and revision.

If you are studying for more than one paper at a time, try to vary your subjects as this can help you to keep interested and see subjects as part of wider knowledge.

When working through your course, compare your progress with your plan and, if necessary, re-plan your work (perhaps including extra sessions) or, if you are ahead, do some extra revision/practice questions.

Effective studying

Active reading

You are not expected to learn the text by rote, rather, you must understand what you are reading and be able to use it to pass the exam and develop good practice. A good technique to use is SQ3Rs - Survey, Question, Read, Recall, Review:

(1) **Survey the chapter** - look at the headings and read the introduction, summary and objectives, so as to get an overview of what the chapter deals with.

(2) **Question** - whilst undertaking the survey, ask yourself the questions that you hope the chapter will answer for you.

(3) **Read** through the chapter thoroughly, answering the questions and making sure you can meet the objectives. Attempt the exercises and activities in the text, and work through all the examples.

(4) **Recall** - at the end of each section and at the end of the chapter, try to recall the main ideas of the section/chapter without referring to the text. This is best done after a short break of a couple of minutes after the reading stage.

(5) **Review** - check that your recall notes are correct.

You may also find it helpful to re-read the chapter to try to see the topic(s) it deals with as a whole.

Note-taking

Taking notes is a useful way of learning, but do not simply copy out the text. The notes must:

- be in your own words
- be concise
- cover the key points
- be well-organised
- be modified as you study further chapters in this text or in related ones.

Trying to summarise a chapter without referring to the text can be a useful way of determining which areas you know and which you don't.

Three ways of taking notes:

Summarise the key points of a chapter.

Make linear notes - a list of headings, divided up with subheadings listing the key points. If you use linear notes, you can use different colours to highlight key points and keep topic areas together. Use plenty of space to make your notes easy to use.

Try a diagrammatic form - the most common of which is a mind-map. To make a mind-map, put the main heading in the centre of the paper and put a circle around it. Then draw short lines radiating from this to the main sub-headings, which again have circles around them. Then continue the process from the sub-headings to sub-sub-headings, advantages, disadvantages, etc.

Highlighting and underlining

You may find it useful to underline or highlight key points in your study text - but do be selective. You may also wish to make notes in the margins.

Revision

The best approach to revision is to revise the course as you work through it. Also try to leave four to six weeks before the exam for final revision. Make sure you cover the whole syllabus and pay special attention to those areas where your knowledge is weak. Here are some recommendations:

Read through the text and your notes again and condense your notes into key phrases. It may help to put key revision points onto index cards to look at when you have a few minutes to spare.

Review any assignments you have completed and look at where you lost marks - put more work into those areas where you were weak.

Practise exam standard questions under timed conditions. If you are short of time, list the points that you would cover in your answer and then read the model answer, but do try to complete at least a few questions under exam conditions.

Also practise producing answer plans and comparing them to the model answer.

If you are stuck on a topic find somebody (a tutor) to explain it to you.

Read good newspapers and professional journals, especially ACCA's Student Accountant - this can give you an advantage in the exam.

Ensure you know the structure of the exam - how many questions and of what type you will be expected to answer. During your revision attempt all the different styles of questions you may be asked.

Further reading

You can find further reading and technical articles under the student section of ACCA's website.

FORMULAE SHEET

Learning curve

$Y = ax^b$

Where Y = cumulative average time per unit to produce x units
a = the time taken for the first unit of output
x = the cumulative number of units
b = the index of learning (log LR/log 2)
LR = the learning rate as a decimal

Regression analysis

$y = a + bx$

$$b = \frac{n\sum xy - \sum x \sum y}{n\sum x^2 - (\sum x)^2}$$

$$a = \frac{\sum y}{n} - \frac{b\sum x}{n}$$

$$r = \frac{n\sum xy - \sum x \sum y}{\sqrt{(n\sum x^2 - (\sum x)^2)(n\sum y^2 - (\sum y)^2)}}$$

Demand curve

$P = a - bQ$

$$b = \frac{\text{Change in price}}{\text{Change in quantity}}$$

a = price when Q = 0

$MR = a - 2bQ$

chapter

1

Traditional and advanced costing methods

Chapter learning objectives

Upon completion of this chapter you will be able to:

- explain what is meant by the term cost driver and identify appropriate cost drivers under activity-based costing (ABC)
- calculate costs per driver and per unit using (ABC)
- compare ABC and traditional methods of overhead absorption based on production units, labour hours or machine hours
- explain what is meant by the term 'target cost'
- derive a target cost in both manufacturing and service industries
- explain the difficulties of using target costing in service industries
- describe the target cost gap
- suggest how a target cost gap might be closed
- explain what is meant by the term 'life-cycle costing' in a manufacturing industry
- identify the costs involved at different stages of the life-cycle
- explain throughput accounting and the throughput accounting ratio (TPAR), and calculate and interpret, a TPAR
- suggest how a TPAR could be improved
- apply throughput accounting to a given multi-product decision-making problem.
- discuss the issues a business faces in the management of environmental costs
- describe the different methods a business may use to account for its environmental costs

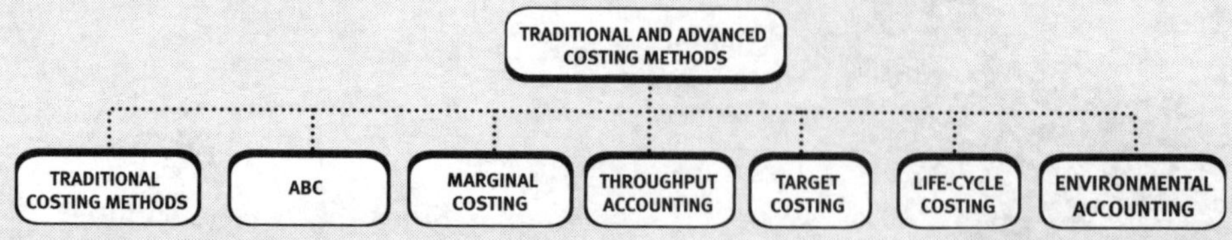

1 What is the purpose of costing?

Back to basics

In paper F2 we learnt how to determine the cost per unit for a product. We might need to know this cost in order to :

- Value inventory - the cost per unit can be used to value inventory in the statement of financial position (balance sheet).
- Record costs - the costs associated with the product need to be recorded in the income statement.
- Price products - the business will use the cost per unit to assist in pricing the product. For example, if the cost per unit is $0.30, the business may decide to price the product at $0.50 per unit in order to make the required profit of $0.20 per unit.
- Make decisions- the business will use the cost information to make important decisions regarding which products should be made and in what quantities.

How can we calculate the cost per unit?

So we know why it's so important for the business to determine the cost of its products. We now need to consider how we can calculate this cost.

There are a number of costing methods available. This chapter focuses on one of the modern costing techniques, ABC. However, in order to understand ABC and the benefits that it can bring, it is useful to start by reminding ourselves of the traditional absorption costing methods : Absorption Costing (AC) and Marginal Costing (MC).

Absorption costing

The aim of traditional absorption costing is to determine the full production cost per unit.

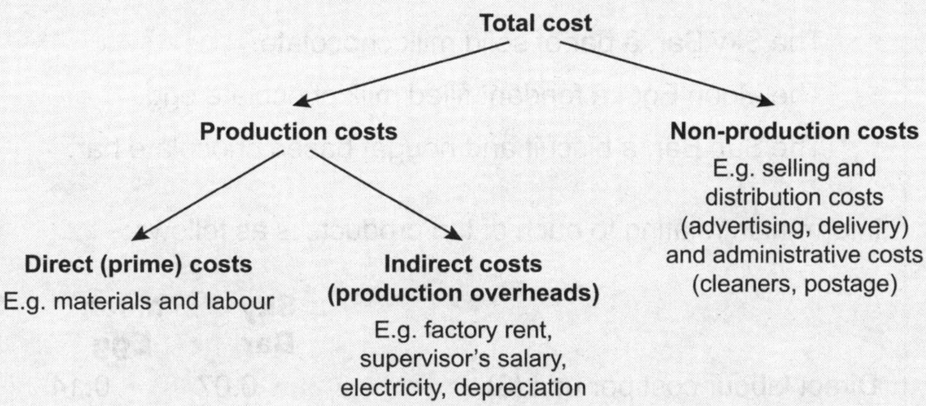

When we use absorption costing to determine the cost per unit, we focus on the production costs only. We can summarise these costs into a cost card:

	$
Direct materials per unit	X
Direct labour per unit	X
Production overhead per unit	X
Full production cost per unit	X

It is relatively easy to estimate the cost per unit for direct materials and labour. In doing so we can complete the first two lines of the cost card. However, it is much more difficult to estimate the production overhead per unit. This is an indirect cost and so, by its very nature, we do not know how much is contained in each unit. Therefore, we need a method of attributing the production overheads to each unit. All production overheads must be absorbed into units of production, using a suitable basis, e.g. units produced, labour hours or machine hours. The assumption underlying this method of absorption is that overhead expenditure is connected to the volume produced.

e.g

Illustration 1 - Absorption costing

Saturn, a chocolate manufacturer, produces three products:

- The Sky Bar, a bar of solid milk chocolate.
- The Moon Egg, a fondant filled milk chocolate egg.
- The Sun Bar, a biscuit and nougat based chocolate bar.

Information relating to each of the products is as follows:

	Sky Bar	**Moon Egg**	**Sun Bar**
Direct labour cost per unit ($)	0.07	0.14	0.12
Direct material cost per unit ($)	0.17	0.19	0.16
Actual production/ sales (units)	500,000	150,000	250,000
Direct labour hours per unit	0.001	0.01	0.005
Direct machine hours per unit	0.01	0.04	0.02
Selling price per unit ($)	0.50	0.45	0.43
Annual production overhead = $80,000			

Required:

Using traditional absorption costing, calculate the full production cost per unit and the profit per unit for each product. Comment on the implications of the figures calculated.

Illustration - Solution

Solution

As mentioned, it is relatively easy to complete the first two lines of the cost card. The difficult part is calculating the production overhead per unit, so let's start by considering this. We need to absorb the overheads into units of production. To do this, we will first need to calculate an overhead absorption rate (OAR):

$$\text{OAR} = \frac{\text{Production overhead}}{\text{Activity level}}$$

Production overhead (this is $80,000, as per the question)

Activity level (this must be chosen)

The activity level must be appropriate for the business. Saturn must choose between three activity levels:

- Units of production - This would not be appropriate since Saturn produces more than one type of product. It would not be fair to absorb the same amount of overhead into each product.
- Machine hours or labour hours – It is fair to absorb production overheads into the products based on the labour or machine hours taken to produce each unit. We must decide if the most appropriate activity level is machine or labour hours. To do this we can look at the nature of the process. Production appears to be more machine intensive than labour intensive because each unit takes more machine hours to produce than it does labour hours. Therefore, the most appropriate activity level is machine hours.

Working - OAR

$$\frac{\$80{,}000 \text{ production overhead}}{(0.01 \times 500\text{k}) + (0.04 \times 150\text{k}) + (0.02 \times 250\text{k}) \text{ hours}}$$

$$= \frac{\$80{,}000}{16{,}000 \text{ hours}}$$

= \$5 per machine hour

We can now absorb these into the units of production:

	Sky Bar	**Moon Egg**	**Sun Bar**
Production overheads (\$) = machine hours per unit x \$5	0.05	0.20	0.10

This is the difficult part done. We can now quickly complete the cost card and answer the question:

	Sky Bar	**Moon Egg**	**Sun Bar**
	\$	**\$**	**\$**
Direct labour cost per unit	0.07	0.14	0.12
Direct material cost per unit	0.17	0.19	0.16
Production overhead per unit	0.05	0.20	0.10
Full production cost per unit	**0.29**	**0.53**	**0.38**
Selling price per unit	0.50	0.45	0.43
Profit/ (loss) per unit	**0.21**	**(0.08)**	**0.05**

Outcome of absorption costing

Based on absorption costing, the Sky Bar and the Sun Bar are both profitable. However, the Moon Egg is loss making. Managers would need to consider the future of the Moon Egg. They may look at the possibility of increasing the selling price and/ or reducing costs. If this is not possible, they may make the decision to stop selling the product.

However, this may prove to be the wrong decision because absorption costing does not always result in an accurate calculation of the full production cost per unit. ABC can be a more accurate method of calculating the full production cost per unit and as a result should lead to better decisions.

2 Under- and over-absorption

A predetermined overhead absorption rate is used to smooth out seasonal fluctuations in overhead costs, and to enable unit costs to be calculated quickly throughout the year.

$$\text{Pre-determined overhead absorption rate} = \frac{\text{Budgeted overhead}}{\text{Budgeted volume}}$$

'Budgeted volume' may relate to units, direct labour hours, machine hours, etc. If either or both of the actual overhead cost or activity volume differ from budget, the use of this rate is likely to lead to what is known as under-absorption or over-absorption of overheads.

e.g

Illustration 2 - Under- and over-absorption of overheads

A company budgeted to produce 3,000 units of a single product in a period at a budgeted cost per unit as follows:

	$ per unit
Direct costs	$17
Fixed overheads	$9
Total Costs	**$26 per unit**

In the period covered by the budget, actual production was 3,200 units and actual fixed overhead expenditure was 5% above that budgeted. All other costs were as budgeted. What was the amount, if any, of over- or under-absorption of fixed overhead?

Illustration - Solution

Answer

The Budgeted fixed overhead amounts to 3,000 units × $9 = $27,000.

Over/(under)absorption = Absorbed overheads – Incurred overheads.

	$
Fixed overhead absorbed (3,200 units × $9)	28,800
Fixed overhead incurred ($27,000 × 1.05)	28,350
Over-absorbed fixed overheads	**450**

The unit cost of production will include overhead at the pre-determined rate and, generally, overhead under- or over-absorbed will be shown as a separate item in the costing income statement.

3 The modern manufacturing environment

There are two aspects of modern manufacturing that you need to be familiar with – Total Quality Management (TQM) and Just in Time (JIT).

Total Quality Management

TQM is the continuous improvement in quality, productivity and effectiveness through a management approach focusing on both the process and the product.

Fundamental features include:

- prevention of errors before they occur;
- importance of total quality in the design of systems and products;
- real participation of all employees;
- commitment of senior management to the cause;
- recognition of the vital role of customers and suppliers;
- recognition of the need for continual improvement.

Just-In-Time (JIT)

JIT is a pull-based system of production, pulling work through the system in response to customer demand. This means that goods are only produced when they are needed, eliminating large stocks of materials and finished goods.

Key characteristics for successfully operating such a system are:

High quality: possibly through deploying TQM systems.

Speed: rapid throughput to meet customers' needs.

Reliability: computer-aided manufacturing technology will assist.

Flexibility: small batch sizes and automated techniques are used.

Low costs: through all of the above.

Standard product costs are associated with traditional manufacturing systems producing large quantities of standard items. Key features of companies operating in a JIT and TQM environment are:

- high level of automation
- high levels of overheads and low levels of direct labour costs
- customised products produced in small batches
- low stocks
- emphasis on high quality and continuous improvement.

4 Reasons for the development of ABC

Absorption costing is based on the principal that production overheads are driven by the level of production. This is because the activity level in the OAR calculation can be units, labour hours or machine hours. These all increase as the level of production increases. This was true in the past, because businesses only produced one simple product or a few simple and similar products. The following points should be remembered:

- **Overheads used to be small in relation to other costs in traditional manufacturing**
  In addition, production overheads, such as machine depreciation, will have been a small proportion of overall costs. This is because production was more labour intensive and, as a result, direct costs would have been much higher than indirect costs. A rough estimate of the production overhead per unit was therefore fine.
- **Overheads are now a larger proportion of total costs in modern manufacturing**
  Manufacturing has become more machine intensive and, as a result, the proportion of production overheads, compared to direct costs, has increased. Therefore, it is important that an accurate estimate is made of the production overhead per unit.

- The nature of manufacturing has changed. Many companies must now operate in a highly competitive environment and, as a result, **the diversity and complexity of products has increased**.

e.g

Illustration 3 – Pen factories

Consider two hypothetical plants turning out a simple product: Ball-point pens. The factories are the same size and have the same capital equipment.

Every year, plant I makes 1 million units of only one product: blue pens.

Plant II, a full-line producer, also produces blue pens, but only 100,000 a year. Plant II also produces a variety of similar products: 80,000 black pens, 30,000 red pens, 5,000 green pens, 500 lavender pens, and so on. In a typical year, plant II produces up to 1,000 product variations, with volumes ranging between 100 and 100,000 units. Its aggregate annual output equals the 1 million pens of plant I.

The first plant has a simple production environment and requires limited manufacturing support facilities. With its higher **diversity** and **complexity** of operations, the second plant requires a much larger support structure. For example 1,000 different products must be scheduled through the plant, and this requires more people for :

- scheduling the machines;
- performing the set-ups;
- inspecting items;
- purchasing, receiving and handling materials;
- handling a large number of individual requests.

Expenditure on support overheads will therefore be much higher in the second plant, even though the number of units produced and sold by both plants is identical. Furthermore, since the number of units produced is identical, both plants will have approximately the same number of direct labour hours, machine hours and material purchases. The much higher expenditure on support overheads in the second plant cannot therefore be explained in terms of direct labour, machine hours operated or the amount of materials purchased.

Traditional costing systems, however, use volume bases to allocate support overheads to products. In fact, if each pen requires approximately the same number of machine hours, direct labour hours or material cost, the reported cost per pen will be identical in plant II. Thus blue and lavender pens will have identical product costs, even though the lavender pens are ordered, manufactured, packaged and despatched in much lower volumes.

The small-volume products place a much higher relative demand on the support departments than low share of volume might suggest. Intuitively, it must cost more to produce the low-volume lavender pen than the high-volume blue pen. Traditional volume-based costing systems therefore tend to overcost high-volume products and undercost low-volume products. To remedy this discrepancy ABC expands the second stage assignment bases for assigning overheads to products.

Calculating the full production cost per unit using ABC

There are five basic steps:

Step 1: Group production overheads into activities, according to how they are driven.

A cost pool is an activity which consumes resources and for which overhead costs are identified and allocated.

For each cost pool, there should be a cost driver. The terms 'activity' and 'cost pool' are often used interchangeably.

Step 2: Identify cost drivers for each activity, i.e. what causes these activity costs to be incurred.

A cost driver is a factor that influences (or drives) the level of cost.

Step 3: Calculate an OAR for each activity.

The OAR is calculated in the same way as the absorption costing OAR. However, a separate OAR will be calculated for each activity, by taking the activity cost and dividing by the cost driver information.

Step 4: Absorb the activity costs into the product.

The activity costs should be absorbed back into the individual products.

Step 5: Calculate the full production cost and/ or the profit or loss.

Some questions ask for the production cost per unit and/ or the profit or loss per unit.

Other questions ask for the total production cost and/ or the total profit or loss.

e.g

Illustration 4 - ABC

In addition to the data from illustration 1, some supplementary data is now available for Saturn company:

	$
Machining costs	5,000
Component costs	15,000
Set-up costs	30,000
Packing costs	30,000
Production overhead (as per illustration 1)	80,000

Cost driver data:

	Sky Bar	**Moon Egg**	**Sun Bar**
Labour hours per unit	0.001	0.01	0.005
Machine hours per unit	0.01	0.04	0.02
Number of production set-ups	3	1	26
Number of components	4	6	20
Number of customer orders	21	4	25

Required:

Using ABC, calculate the full production cost per unit and the profit per unit for each product. Comment on the implications of the figures calculated.

Expandable Text

Step 1: Group production overheads into activities, according to how they are driven.

This has been done above. The $80,000 production overhead has been split into four different activities (cost pools).

Step 2: Identify cost drivers for each activity, i.e. what causes these activity costs to be incurred.

Activity	**Cost driver**
Machining costs	Number of machine hours
Component costs	Number of components
Set-up costs	Number of set-ups
Packing costs	Number of customer orders

Step 3: Calculate an OAR for each activity

$$\text{OAR machining costs} = \frac{\$5{,}000 \text{ machining costs}}{16{,}000 \text{ machine hours (illustration 1)}}$$

= **$0.31 per machine hour**

$$\text{OAR component costs} = \frac{\$15{,}000 \text{ component cost}}{(4 + 6 + 20) \text{ components}}$$

= **$500 per component**

$$\text{OAR set-up costs} = \frac{\$30{,}000 \text{ set-up costs}}{(3 + 1 + 26) \text{ set-ups}}$$

= **$1,000 per set-up**

$$\text{OAR packing costs} = \frac{\$30{,}000 \text{ packing costs}}{(21 + 4 + 25) \text{ orders}}$$

= **$600 per order**

Step 5: Calculate the full production cost and the profit or loss

	Sky Bar	**Moon Egg**	**Sun Bar**
	$	**$**	**$**
Direct labour cost per unit	0.07	0.14	0.12
Direct material cost per unit	0.17	0.19	0.16
Production overhead per unit	0.04	0.06	0.21
Full production cost per unit	**0.28**	**0.39**	**0.49**
Selling price per unit	0.50	0.45	0.43
Profit/ (loss) per unit	**0.22**	**0.06**	**(0.06)**

Outcome of ABC

When comparing the results of absorption costing and ABC, the Sky Bar is slightly more profitable. The real surprise is the results for the Moon Egg and the Sun Bar. The Moon Egg is now profitable and the Sun Bar is now loss making. This is because the production overheads have been absorbed in a more accurate way.

For example:

- There are twenty components in a Sun Bar, compared with only six in a Moon Egg. It is therefore fair that the Sun Bar receives more of the component cost.
- There are only four orders for the Moon Eggs but twenty five for the Sun Bar. It is therefore fair that the Sun Bar receives more of the packing costs.

ABC absorbs overheads more accurately and should therefore result in better decision making. The managers at Saturn should be concerned about the Sun Bar and not the Moon Egg, as was previously thought. They will now have to decide if it is possible to control the Sun Bar costs and/ or increase the selling price. If not, they may decide to stop selling the product.

Test your understanding 1

Cabal makes and sells two products, Plus and Doubleplus. The direct costs of production are $12 for one unit of Plus and $24 per unit of Doubleplus.

Information relating to annual production and sales is as follows:

	Plus	**Doubleplus**
Annual production and sales	24,000 units	24,000 units
Direct labour hours per unit	1.0	1.5
Number of orders	10	140
Number of batches	12	240
Number of setups per batch	1	3
Special parts per unit	1	4

Information relating to production overhead costs is as follows:

	Cost driver	Annual cost
		$
Setup costs	Number of setups	73,200
Special parts handling	Number of special parts	60,000
Other materials handling	Number of batches	63,000
Order handling	Number of orders	19,800
Other overheads	-	216,000
		432,000

Other overhead costs do not have an identifiable cost driver, and in an ABC system, these overheads would be recovered on a direct labour hours basis.

(a) **Calculate the production cost per unit of Plus and of Doubleplus if the company uses traditional absorption costing and the overheads are recovered on a direct labour hours basis.**

(b) **Calculate the production cost per unit of Plus and of Doubleplus if the company uses ABC.**

(c) **Comment on the reasons for the differences in the production cost per unit between the two methods.**

(d) **What are the implications for management of using an ABC system instead of an absorption costing system?**

Advantages and disadvantages of ABC

ABC has a number of advantages:

- It provides a more accurate cost per unit. As a result, pricing, sales strategy, performance management and decision making should be improved.
- It provides much better insight into what drives overhead costs.
- ABC recognises that overhead costs are not all related to production and sales volume.
- In many businesses, overhead costs are a significant proportion of total costs, and management needs to understand the drivers of overhead costs in order to manage the business properly. Overhead costs can be controlled by managing cost drivers.

- It can be applied to derive realistic costs in a complex business environment.
- ABC can be applied to all overhead costs, not just production overheads.
- ABC can be used just as easily in service costing as in product costing.

Disadvantages of ABC:

- ABC will be of limited benefit if the overhead costs are primarily volume related or if the overhead is a small proportion of the overall cost.
- It is impossible to allocate all overhead costs to specific activities.
- The choice of both activities and cost drivers might be inappropriate.
- ABC can be more complex to explain to the stakeholders of the costing exercise.
- The benefits obtained from ABC might not justify the costs.

5 Marginal costing

Marginal costing is the accounting system in which variable costs are charged to cost units and fixed costs of the period are written off in full against the aggregate contribution. Its special value is in recognising cost behaviour, and hence assisting in decision making.

The **marginal cost** is the extra cost arising as a result of making and selling one more unit of a product or service, or is the saving in cost as a result of making and selling one less unit.

Contribution is the difference between sales value and the variable cost of sales. It may be expressed per unit or in total.

e.g

Illustration 5 - Marginal costing

A company manufactures only one product called XY. The following information relates to the product :

	$
Selling Price per unit	20
Direct Material Cost per unit	(6)
Direct Labour Cost per unit	(2)
Variable overhead cost per unit	(4)
Contribution per unit	**8**

Fixed costs for the period are $25,000.

Required:

Complete the following table :

Level of activity	2,500 units	5,000 units	7,500 units	10,000 units
Revenue				
Variable Costs				
Total Contribution				
Fixed costs				
Total Profit / (loss)				
Contribution per unit				
Profit / (loss) per unit				

Solution

Level of activity	2,500 units	5,000 units	7,500 units	10,000 units
Revenue	50,000	100,000	150,000	200,000
Variable Costs	30,000	60,000	90,000	120,000
Total Contribution	20,000	40,000	60,000	80,000
Fixed costs	25,000	25,000	25,000	25,000
Total Profit / (loss)	(5,000)	15,000	35,000	55,000
Contribution per unit	$8	$8	$8	$8
Profit / (loss) per unit	$(2)	$3	$4.67	$5.50

The table illustrates that contribution per unit remains constant at all levels of activity. However, profit per unit changes. Hence marginal costing is a useful method when trying to analyse and manage costs. Absorption costing does not distinguish between fixed and variable cost elements. It is not a useful method for internal reporting.

6 Throughput Accounting - Background

Throughput accounting aims to make the best use of a scare resource (bottleneck) in a JIT environment.

Throughput is a measure of profitability and is defined by the following equation:

Throughput = sales revenue - direct material cost

The aim of throughput accounting is to maximise this measure of profitability, whilst simultaneously reducing operating expenses and inventory (money is tied up in inventory).

The goal is achieved by determining what factors prevent the throughput from being higher. This constraint is called a *bottleneck*, for example there may be a limited number of machine hours or labour hours.

In the short-term the best use should be made of this bottleneck. This may result in some idle time in non-bottleneck resources, and may result in a small amount of inventory being held so as not to delay production through the bottleneck.

In the long-term, the bottleneck should be eliminated. For example a new, more efficient machine may be purchased. However, this will generally result in another bottleneck, which must then be addressed.

Main assumptions:

- The only totally variable cost in the short-term is the purchase cost of raw materials that are bought from external suppliers.
- Direct labour costs are not variable in the short-term. Many employees are salaried and even if paid at a rate per unit, are usually guaranteed a minimum weekly wage.

Throughput calculation

Hard Tiles recorded a profit of $120,000 in the accounting period just ended, using marginal costing. The contribution/sales ratio was 75%.

Material costs were 10% of sales value and there were no other variable production overhead costs. Fixed costs in the period were $300,000.

Required:

What was the value of throughput in the period?

Solution

	$
Profit	120,000
Fixed costs	300,000
Contribution	420,000
Contribution/sales ratio	75%
	$
Sales	560,000
Material costs (10% of sales)	56,000
Throughput	504,000

The Throughput Accounting Ratio

When there is a bottleneck resource, performance can be measured in terms of throughput for each unit of bottleneck resource consumed.

There are three inter-related ratios:

1. Throughput (return) per Factory Hour = $\dfrac{\text{Throughput per unit}}{\text{Product's time on the bottleneck resource}}$

2. Cost per Factory Hour = $\dfrac{\text{Total factory cost}}{\text{Total bottleneck resource time available}}$

3. Throughput Accounting Ratio (TPAR) = $\dfrac{\text{Return per factory hour}}{\text{Cost per factory hour}}$

Note: The *total factory cost* is the fixed production cost, including labour. The total factory cost may be referred to as 'operating expenses'.

Interpretation of TPAR

- TPAR>1 would suggest that throughput exceeds operating costs so the product should make a profit. Priority should be given to the products generating the best ratios.
- TPAR<1 would suggest that throughput is insufficient to cover operating costs, resulting in a loss.

Criticisms of TPAR

- It concentrates on the short-term, when a business has a fixed supply of resources (i.e. a bottleneck) and operating expenses are largely fixed. However, most businesses can't produce products based on the short term only.
- It is more difficult to apply throughput accounting concepts to the longer-term, when all costs are variable, and vary with the volume of production and sales or another cost driver. The business should consider this long-term view before rejecting products with a TPAR < 1.
- In the longer-term an ABC approach might be more appropriate for measuring and controlling performance.

Test your understanding 2

X Limited manufactures a product that requires 1.5 hours of machining. Machine time is a bottleneck resource, due to the limited number of machines available. There are 10 machines available, and each machine can be used for up to 40 hours per week.

The product is sold for $85 per unit and the direct material cost per unit is $42.50. Total factory costs are $8,000 each week.

Calculate

(a) **the return per factory hour**

(b) **the TPAR.**

Additional example on TPAR

A business manufactures a single product that it sells for $10 per unit. The materials cost for each unit of product sold is $3. Total operating expenses are $50,000 each month.

Labour hours are limited to 20,000 hours each month. Each unit of product takes 2 hours to assemble.

Required:

Calculate the throughput accounting ratio (TPAR)

Solution

- Throughput per factory (assembly) hour = $(10 – 3)/2 hours = $3.50
- Cost per factory hour = $50,000/20,000 hours = $2.50

Note: the operating expenses of $50,000 are the total factory cost.

- Throughput accounting ratio = $3.50/$2.50 = 1.40

Improving the TPAR

Options to increase the TPAR include the following:

- increase the sales price for each unit sold, to increase the throughput per unit
- reduce material costs per unit (e.g. by changing materials or switching suppliers), to increase the throughput per unit
- reduce total operating expenses, to reduce the cost per factory hour
- improve the productivity of the bottleneck, e.g. the assembly workforce or the bottleneck machine, thus reducing the time required to make each unit of product. Throughput per factory hour would increase and therefore the TPAR would increase.

Improving the TPAR

Suppose in the illustration above the following changes were made:

- the sales price were increased from $10 to $13.5
- the time taken to make each product fell from 2 hours to 1.75 hours
- the operating expenses fell from $50,000 to $45,000.

The following changes would take place:

Throughput per factory hour = $(13.5 – 3)/1.75 hours = $6.0

Cost per factory hour = $45,000/20,000 hours = $2.25

TPAR = $6.0/ $2.25= 2.67

The TPAR would nearly double, increasing from 1.4 to 2.67.

Calculation 2 - Multi-product decision making

Throughput accounting may be applied to a multi-product decision making problem in the same way as conventional key factor analysis.

The usual objective in questions is to maximise profit. Given that fixed costs are unaffected by the production decision in the short run, the approach should be to maximise the throughput earned.

Step 1: identify the bottleneck constraint.

Step 2: calculate the throughput per unit for each product.

Step 3: calculate the throughput per unit of the bottleneck resource for each product.

Step 4: rank the products in order of the throughout per unit of the bottleneck resource.

Step 5: allocate resources using this ranking and answer the question.

Test your understanding 3

Justin Thyme manufactures four products, A, B, C and D. Details of sales prices, costs and resource requirements for each of the products are as follows.

	Product A	**Product B**	**Product C**	**Product D**
	$	$	$	$
Sales price	1.40	0.80	1.20	2.80
Materials cost	0.60	0.30	0.60	1.00
Direct labour cost	0.40	0.20	0.40	1.00
	Minutes	Minutes	Minutes	Minutes
Machine time per unit	5	2	3	6
Labour time per unit	2	1	2	5
	Units	Units	Units	Units
Weekly sales demand	2,000	2,000	2,500	1,500

Machine time is a bottleneck resource and the maximum capacity is 400 machine hours each week. Operating costs, including direct labour costs, are $5,440 each week. Direct labour costs are $12 per hour, and direct labour workers are paid for a 38-hour week, with no overtime.

(a) **Determine the quantities of each product that should be manufactured and sold each week to maximise profit and calculate the weekly profit.**

(b) **Calculate the throughput accounting ratio at this profit-maximising level of output and sales.**

7 Target costing

Target costing involves setting a target cost by subtracting a desired profit from a competitive market price. Real world users include Sony, Toyota and the Swiss watchmakers, Swatch.

In effect it is the opposite of conventional 'cost plus pricing'.

e.g

Illustration 6

Music Matters manufactures and sells cds for a number of popular artists. At present, it uses a traditional cost-plus pricing system.

Cost-plus pricing system

(1) The cost of the cd is established first. This is $15 per unit.

(2) A profit of $5 per unit is added to each cd.

(3) This results in the current selling price of $20 per unit.

(2) Required profit = $5 per cd	(3) Selling price is $20 per cd
(1) Cost = $15 per cd	

However, cost-plus pricing ignores:

- The price that customers are willing to pay - pricing the cds too high could result in low sales volumes and profits.
- The price charged by competitors for similar products - if competitor's are charging less than $20 per cd for similar cds then customers may decide to buy their cds from the competitor companies.
- Cost control - the cost of the cd is established at $15 but there is little incentive to control this cost.

Target costing

Music Matters could address the problems discussed above through the implementation of target costing:

(1) The first step is to establish a competitive market price. The company would consider how much customers are willing to pay and how much competitors are charging for similar products. Let's assume this is $15 per unit.

(2) Music Matters would then deduct their required profit from the selling price. The required profit may be kept at $5 per unit.

(3) A target cost is arrived at by deducting the required profit from the selling price, i.e. $15 - $5 = $10 per unit.

(4) Steps must then be taken to close the target cost gap from the current cost per unit of $15 per unit to the target cost of $10 per unit.

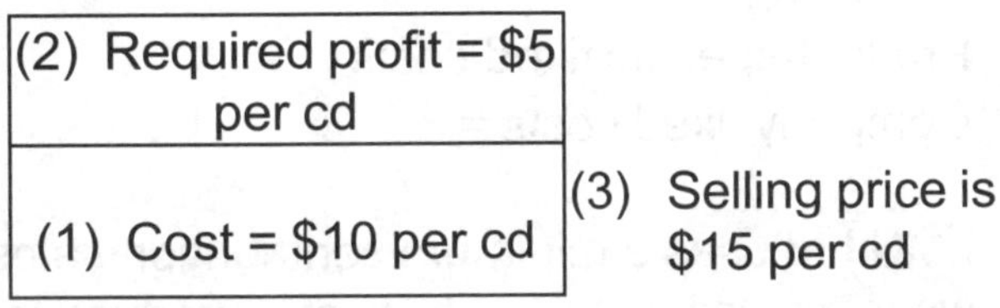

Summary of the steps used in deriving a target cost

Steps

(1) Estimate a selling price for a new product that considers how much competitors are charging and how much customers are willing to pay. This selling price will enable a firm to capture a required share of the market.

(2) Reduce this figure by the firm's required level of profit. This could take into account the return required on any new investment and on working capital requirements or could involve a target margin on sales.

(3) Produce a target cost figure for product designers to meet.

(4) Reduce costs to provide a product that meets that target cost.

Test your understanding 4

LMN Ltd makes and sells two products, X and Y. Both products are manufactured through two consecutive processes - assembly and finishing. Raw material is input at the commencement of the assembly process.

The following estimated information is available for the period ending 31 December 20X5:

	Product X	Product Y
Production/sales (units)	12,000	7,200
Selling price per unit	$75	$90
Direct material cost per unit	$20	$20
Direct labour cost per unit		
- assembly	$20	$28
- finishing	$12	$24
Product-specific fixed costs	$170,000	$90,000
Company fixed costs =	$50,000	

LMN Ltd uses a minimum contribution/sales (C/S) ratio target of 25% when assessing the viability of a product. In addition, management wish to achieve an overall net profit margin of 12% on sales in this period in order to meet return on capital targets.

Required:

Calculate the C/S ratio for each product and the overall net profit margin. Explain how target costing may be used in achieving the required returns.

Closing the target cost gap

The target cost gap is established in step 4 of the target costing process.

Target cost gap = Estimated product cost – Target cost

It is the difference between what an organisation thinks it can currently make a product for, and what it needs to make it for, in order to make a required profit.

Alternative product designs should be examined for potential areas of cost reduction that will not compromise the quality of the products.

Questions that a manufacturer may ask in order to close the gap include:

- Can any materials be eliminated, e.g. cut down on packing materials?
- Can a cheaper material be substituted without affecting quality?
- Can labour savings be made without compromising quality, for example, by using lower skilled workers?
- Can productivity be improved, for example, by improving motivation?
- Can production volume be increased to achieve economies of scale?
- Could cost savings be made by reviewing the supply chain?
- Can part-assembled components be bought in to save on assembly time?
- Can the incidence of the cost drivers be reduced?
- Is there some degree of overlap between the product-related fixed costs that could be eliminated by combining service departments or resources?

A key aspect of this is to understand which features of the product are essential to customer perceived quality and which are not. This process is known as 'value analysis'. Attention should be focused more on reducing the costs of features perceived by the customer not to add value.

Test your understanding 5

The Swiss watchmaker Swatch reportedly used target costing in order to produce relatively low-cost, similar-looking plastic watches in a country with one of the world's highest hourly labour wage rates.

Suggest ways in which Swatch may have reduced their unit costs for each watch.

Target costing in service organisations

Target costing is as relevant to the service sector as the manufacturing sector. Key issues are similar in both: the needs of the market need to be identified and understood as well as its customers and users; and financial performance at a given cost or price (which does not exceed the target cost when resources are limited) needs to be ensured.

For example, if a firm of accountants was asked to bid for a new client contract, the partners or managers would probably have an idea of what kind of price is likely to win the contract. If staff costs are billed out at twice their hourly salary cost, say, this would help to determine a staff budget for the contract. It would then be necessary to work out the hours needed and play around with the mix of juniors / senior staff to get to that target cost.

There are ways in which target costing can be applied to service-oriented businesses, and the focus of target costing shifts from the product to the service delivery system.

ILLUSTRATION : TARGET COSTING IN THE NHS

In 2005, the National Audit Office and the Audit Commission identified the need for improvements in financial skills to meet the challenges facing the health service, as first-class financial management has a vital role in delivering improvements to patients. A number of healthcare providers in the United States had recently made significant improvements to patient care and resource utilisation by adopting approaches used in manufacturing businesses, including target costing principles, which is thought to have contributed towards significant benefits in improved quality of care, decreased mortality and cost reduction.

Target costing was thought of as a better method of costing services, in order to help NHS Trusts and hospitals to meet their financial responsibility to at least break-even, by ensuring that services are delivered within budgeted costs. Therefore, a move towards a new method of funding services was initiated, with NHS Trusts being paid a pre-set **national tariff** for each service they provide, rather than a price based on their own costs.

Take the example of Mrs Smith, who suffers from a medical condition requiring hospital care. She is booked into Guy's + St Thomas's hospital NHS Foundation Trust for a procedure this month. Lambeth PCT is the responsible commissioner for Mrs Smith's care, because she is registered with a GP practice there. The national tariff for the procedure amounts to £3,236, adjusted by two daily long stay payments at £740 a day.Therefore, the reimbursement from Lambeth PCT to St Guy's hospital for the procedure would amount to a total of £3,976.

It was hoped that target costing, with targets related to the national tariff and coupled with an emphasis on value-for-money performance indicators , might provide a discipline within which Trusts could manage costs to improve efficiency. In a case like Mrs Smith's, a target cost would hopefully encourage the hospital to perform the operation within this costs and promote better scheduling, use of cheaper drugs, etc.

PROBLEMS WITH TARGET COSTING IN SERVICE INDUSTRIES

Unlike manufacturing, service industries have the following characteristics which could make target costing more difficult :

1. Bureaucracy - Davila andWouters (2004) criticised target costing for being too detailed, bureaucratic and time-consuming. Target costing does require formal procedures to assess customer needs, determine target prices and costs, break perceived value down to sub-services to come up with allowable cost per service, and apply value engineering to achieve the target cost in an iterative manner.

2. The **intangibility** of what is provided means that it is difficult to define the 'service' and attribute costs; in the NHS, it is challenging to define what a 'procedure' is. Clinical specialities cover a wide range of disparate treatments, and services include high levels of indirect cost. Consistent methods of cost attribution are needed, and this is not always straightforward. Direct charging is not always possible and there are different configurations of cost centres across providers. This may limit the consistency which can be achieved.

3. **Heterogeneity** – The quality and consistency varies, because of an absence of standards or benchmarks to assess services against. In the NHS, there is no indication of what an excellent performance in service delivery would be, or any definition of unacceptable performance.

4. The continual pressure to ensure costs are kept to a minimum can lead to **employee de-motivation**.

Value analysis

Value analysis, otherwise known as 'cost engineering' and 'value engineering', is a technique in which a firm's products, and maybe those of its competitors, are subjected to a critical and systematic examination by a small group of specialists. They can be representing various functions such as design, production, sales and finance.

Value analysis asks of a product the following questions:

- Does the use of the product contribute value?
- Is its cost proportionate to its usefulness?
- Does it need all of its features?
- Is there anything better for the intended use?
- Can a usable part be made better at lower cost?
- Can a standard product be found which will be equally usable?

- Is it made on appropriate tooling, considering the quantities used?
- Do material, labour, and overheads constitute total cost?
- Will another dependable supplier provide it for less cost?
- Is anyone buying it for less than its stated price?

The strategic implications can be measured in terms of a component's relative cost versus its relative performance. There are four different situations:

(1) If a component is both more expensive and inferior to that of a competitor, a strategic problem requiring change might be necessary. It could be, however, that the component is such a small item in terms of both cost and impact on the customer that it should be ignored.

(2) If the component is competitively superior, a value analysis, where a component's value to the customer is quantified, may suggest a price increase or promotion campaign.

(3) If a component is less expensive than but inferior to that of a competitor, a value analysis might suggest either de-emphasising that part or upgrading the relative rating.

(4) If a component is less expensive than and superior to that of a competitor, a value analysis might suggest that component is emphasised, perhaps playing a key role in promotion and positioning strategies.

A cost advantage may be obtained in many ways, e.g. economies of scale, the experience curve, product design innovations and the use of 'no-frills' product offering. Each provides a different way of competing on the basis of cost advantage.

8 Life-cycle costing

Traditional costing techniques based around annual periods may give a misleading impression of the costs and profitability of a product. This is because systems are based on the financial accounting year, and dissect the product's lifecycle into a series of annual sections. Usually, therefore, the management accounting systems would assess a product's profitability on a periodic basis, rather than over its entire life.

Lifecycle costing, however, tracks and accumulates costs and revenues attributable to each product **over its entire product lifecycle.** Hence, the **total** profitability of any given product can be determined.

A product's costs are not evenly spread through its life.

According to Berliner and Brimson (1988), companies operating in an advanced manufacturing environment are finding that about **90% of a product's lifecycle costs are determined by decisions made early in the cycle**. In many industries, a large fraction of the life-cycle costs consists of costs incurred on product design, prototyping, programming, process design and equipment acquisition.

This had created a need to ensure that the tightest controls are at the design stage, i.e. before a launch, because most costs are committed, or 'locked-in', at this point in time.

Management Accounting systems should therefore be developed that aid the planning and control of product lifecycle costs and monitor spending and commitments **at the early stages of a product's life cycle.**

The product life-cycle

The costs involved at different stages in the product life-cycle

Most products have a distinct product life-cycle:

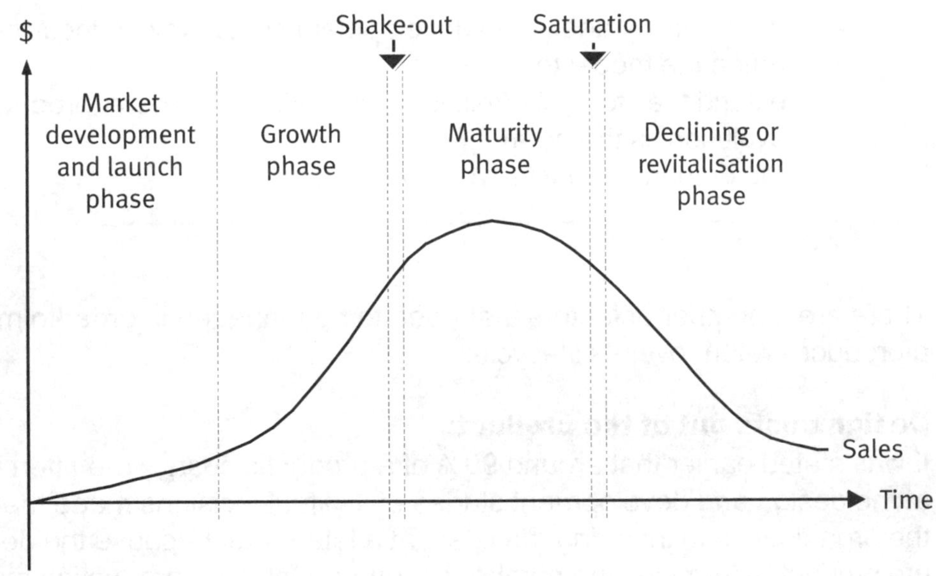

Specific costs may be associated with each stage.

(1) Pre-production/Product development stage
   – A high level of setup costs will be incurred in this stage (preproduction costs), including research and development (R&D), product design and building of production facilities.

(2) Launch/Market development stage
   – Success depends upon awareness and trial of the product by consumers, so this stage is likely to be accompanied by extensive marketing and promotion costs.

(3) Growth stage

- Marketing and promotion will continue through this stage.
- In this stage sales volume increases dramatically, and unit costs fall as fixed costs are recovered over greater volumes.

(4) Maturity stage

- Initially profits will continue to increase, as initial setup and fixed costs are recovered.
- Marketing and distribution economies are achieved.
- However, price competition and product differentiation will start to erode profitability as firms compete for the limited new customers remaining

(5) Decline stage

- Marketing costs are usually cut as the product is phased out
- Production economies may be lost as volumes fall
- Meanwhile, a replacement product will need to have been developed, incurring new levels of R&D and other product setup costs.
- Alternatively additional development costs may be incurred to refine the model to
  extend the life-cycle (this is typical with cars where 'product evolution' is the norm
  rather than 'product revolution').

There are a number of factors that need to be managed in order to maximise a product's return over its lifecycle:

Design costs out of the product:
It was stated earlier that around 90% of a product's costs were often incurred at the design and development stages of its life. Decisions made then commit the organisation to incurring the costs at a later date, because the design of the product determines the number of components, the production method, etc. It is absolutely vital therefore that design teams do not work in isolation but as part of a cross-functional team in order to minimise costs over the whole life cycle.

Value engineering helps here; for example, Russian liquid-fuel rocket motors are intentionally designed to allow leak-free welding. This reduces costs by eliminating grinding and finishing operations (these operations would not help the motor to function better anyway.)

Minimise the time to market:
In a world where competitors watch each other keenly to see what new products will be launched, it is vital to get any new product into the marketplace as quickly as possible. The competitors will monitor each other closely so that they can launch rival products as soon as possible in order to maintain profitability. It is vital, therefore, for the first organisation to launch its product as quickly as possible after the concept has been developed, so that it has as long as possible to establish the product in the market and to make a profit before competition increases. Often it is not so much costs that reduce profits as time wasted.

Maximise the length of the life cycle itself:
Generally, the longer the life cycle, the greater the profit that will be generated, assuming that production ceases once the product goes into decline and becomes unprofitable. One way to maximise the life cycle is to get the product to market as quickly as possible because this should maximise the time in which the product generates a profit.

Another way of extending a product's life is to find other uses, or markets, for the product. Other product uses may not be obvious when the product is still in its planning stage and need to be planned and managed later on. On the other hand, it may be possible to plan for a staggered entry into different markets at the planning stage.

Many organisations stagger the launch of their products in different world markets in order to reduce costs, increase revenue and prolong the overall life of the product. A current example is the way in which new films are released in the USA months before the UK launch. This is done to build up the enthusiasm for the film and to increase revenues overall. Other companies may not have the funds to launch worldwide at the same moment and may be forced to stagger it. Skimming the market is another way to prolong life and to maximise the revenue over the product's life.

e.g

Illustration 7 – Lifecycle costing

Enrono is an accounting software package which has a six-year product lifecycle. The following are the yearly costs, estimated for the entire length of the package's life :

Costs - in $,000	Year 1	Year 2	Year 3	Year 4	Year 5	Year 6
Res. & Dev.	275					
Design		120				
Production costs			120	200	200	
Marketing costs			125	170	130	60
Distribution costs			20	20	15	10
Customer Service costs			5	165	30	45

The lifecycle costs for the Enrono package can be added up as follows :

Lifecycle costs	**in $000**
Research and development	275
Design	120
Production costs	520
Marketing costs	485
Distribution costs	65
Customer Service costs	95
Total lifecycle costs	**1,560**

Lifecycle costing clearly takes into consideration the costs of the package incurred during the entire lifecycle - over $1.5 m. Accordingly, from lifecycle costing, the management can know whether the revenue earned by the product is sufficient to cover the whole costs incurred during its life cycle.

When viewed as a whole, there are opportunities for cost reduction and minimisation (and thereby scope for profit maximisation) in several categories of cost :

- For example, initiatives could be taken to reduce testing costs and therefore the 'Research and Development' category.
- Likewise, proper planning and a tight control on transportation & handling costs could minimise distribution costs.

These opportunities for cost reduction are unlikely to be found when management focuses on maximising profit in a period-by-period basis. **Only on knowing the lifecycle costs of a product can a business decide appropriately on its price.** This, coupled with planning of the different phases of the product's life, could give rise to the following tactics:

INTRODUCTION	**GROWTH**	**MATURITY**	**DECLINE**
High prices to recoup high development costs; high returns before competitors enter the market.	Competition increases; **reduce price** to remain competitive	Sales slow down and level off; the market price is maintained. Upgrades and/or new markets should be considered.	Superior products appear – our prices must be cut to maintain sales.

Customer lifecycle costing

Not all investment decisions involve large initial capital outflows or the purchase of physical assets. The decision to serve and retain customers can also be a capital budgeting decision even though the initial outlay may be small. For example a credit card company or an insurance company will have to choose which customers they take on and then register them on the company's records. The company incurs initial costs due to the paperwork, checking creditworthiness, opening policies, etc. for new customers. It takes some time before these initial costs are recouped. Research has also shown that the longer a customer stays with the company the more profitable that customer becomes to the company.

Thus it becomes important to retain customers, whether by good service, discounts, other benefits, etc. A customer's 'life' can be discounted and decisions made as to the value of, say, a 'five-year-old' customer. Eventually a point arises where profit no longer continues to grow; this plateau is reached between about five years and 20 years depending on the nature of the business. Therefore by studying the increased revenue and decreased costs generated by an 'old' customer, management can find strategies to meet their needs better and to retain them.

Many manufacturing companies only supply a small number of customers, say between six and ten, and so they can cost customers relatively easily. Other companies such as banks and supermarkets have many customers and cannot easily analyse every single customer. In this case similar customers are grouped together to form category types and these can then be analysed in terms of profitability.

For example, the UK banks analyse customers in terms of fruits, such as oranges, lemons, plums, etc. Customers tend to move from one category to another as they age and as their financial habits change. Customers with large mortgages, for example, are more valuable to the bank than customers who do not have a large income and do not borrow money. Banks are not keen on keeping the latter type of customer.

Test your understanding 6

The following details relate to a new product that has finished development and is about to be launched.

	Development	**Launch**	**Growth**	**Maturity**	**Decline**
Time period	Finished	1 year	1 year	1 year	1 year
R & D costs ($ million)	20				
Marketing costs ($ million)		5	4	3	0.9
Production cost per unit ($)		1.00	0.90	0.80	0.90
Production volume (millions)		1	5	10	4

The launch price is proving a contentious issue between managers. The marketing manager is keen to start with a low price of around $8 to gain new buyers and achieve target market share. The accountant is concerned that this does not cover costs during the launch phase and has produced the following schedule to support this:

Launch phase:		**$ million**
Amortised R&D costs	(20 ÷ 4)	5.0
Marketing costs		5.0
Production costs	(1 million × $1 per unit)	1.0
Total		11.0
Total production (units)		1 million
Cost per unit		$11.00

Prepare a revised cost per unit schedule looking at the whole lifecycle and comment on the implications of this cost with regards to the pricing of the product during the launch phase.

Lifecycle costing in the service industry

A service organisation will provide services that have life cycles. For example, a company leasing heavy machinery to clients could use LCC to predict the total costs, resources, utilisation and productivity for an asset over its entire life cycle : thus, LCC is an excellent tool for assessing alternatives, which has made it very common in the procurement of large assets.

All pertinent cash flows that go to form the complete service over the life of the machine are important, and consideration should be given in advance as to how to carry them out so as to minimise the whole-life cost. A simple model is shown below :

	Year 1	Year 2	Year 3	Year 4	Year 5	Total
Purchase cost of asset	$800,000					$800,000
Labour costs (operator)	$30,000	$31,000	$32,000	$33,000	$34,000	$160,000
Parts and Materials	$10,000	$15,000	$15,000	$18,000	$18,000	$76,000
Fuel	$80,000	$96,000	$115,200	$138,240	$165,888	$595,328
Lubricants	$ 8,000	$ 8,000	$ 8,000	$ 8,000	$ 8,000	$40,000
Disposal					($100,000)	($100,000)
Total	**$928,000**	**$150,000**	**$170,200**	**$197,240**	**$125,888**	**$1,571,328**

The total cost of owning and operating the equipment is the sum of the individual cost elements. LCC also involves understanding the detail of the individual cost elements and building these up to the ultimate life cycle cost. Then, each cost can be broken down further. For example, the 'Parts and Materials' costs can be split as follows :

	Year 1	Year 2	Year 3	Year 4	Year 5	Total
Replacement of internal motor			$26,000			$26,000
Basic service	$5,000	$ 5,000	$ 5,000	$5,000	$ 5,000	$25,000
Direct Administration costs	$1,500	$1,500	$1,500	$1,500	$1,500	$7,500
Wiring repairs	$3,500	$3,500	$3,500	$3,500	$3,500	$17,500
Total	**$10,000**	**$10,000**	**$36,000**	**$10,000**	**$10,000**	**$76,000**

For example, the internal motor change is scheduled to occur in Year 3. This is driven by an estimated life of the motor of X hours and an expected utilisation of the equipment of Y hours per year. If X or Y were to change, the model may provide a different result.

Assuming the LCC model above could be continuously updated, and the component costs automatically uploaded every time a maintenance task is performed, this would :

(1) Provide the company with more accurate and robust pricing information;

(2) Provide a real time life cycle cost model;

(3) Enable equipment managers to see and understand the impact of their decisions on the life cycle cost of the asset;

(4) Allow the company to see the forward resource for parts, labour and materials;

(5) Allow budgeting managers to plan cash outflows for the next 5 years and beyond.

9 Environmental management accounting

The importance of environmental management

Organisations are beginning to recognise that environmental awareness and management are not optional, but are important for long-term survival and profitability. All organisations:

- are faced with increasing legal and regulatory requirements relating to environmental management
- need to meet customers' needs and concerns relating to the environment
- need to demonstrate effective environmental management to maintain a good public image
- need to manage the risk and potential impact of environmental disasters
- can make cost savings by improved use of resources such as water and fuel
- are recognising the importance of sustainable development, which is the meeting of current needs without compromising the ability of future generations to meet their needs.

The contribution of environmental management accounting (EMA)

EMA is concerned with the accounting information needs of managers in relation to corporate activities that affect the environment as well as environment-related impacts on the corporation. This includes:

- identifying and estimating the costs of environment-related activities
- identifying and separately monitoring the usage and cost of resources such as water, electricity and fuel and to enable costs to be reduced
- ensuring environmental considerations form a part of capital investment decisions
- assessing the likelihood and impact of environmental risks
- including environment-related indicators as part of routine performance monitoring
- benchmarking activities against environmental best practice.

EM and effect on financial performance

There are a number of ways in which environmental issues can have an impact on the financial performance of organisations.

Improving revenue

Producing new products or services which meet the environmental needs or concerns of customers can lead to increased sales. It may also be possible to sell such products for a premium price. Improved sales may also be a consequence of improving the reputation of the business.

It is possible that in the future, rather than good environmental management resulting in improved sales, poor management will lead to losses. All businesses will be expected to meet a minimum standard related to environmental issues.

Cost reductions

Paying close attention to the use of resources can lead to reductions in cost. Often simple improvements in processes can lead to significant costs savings.

Increases in costs

There may be increases in some costs, for example the cost of complying with legal and regulatory requirements, and additional costs to improve the environmental image of the organisation. However some of these costs may be offset by government grants and this expenditure may save money in the long-term as measures taken may prevent future losses.

Costs of failure

Poor environmental management can result in significant costs, for example the cost of clean-up and fines following an environmental disaster.

Some EMA initiatives

Rolls-Royce Aerospace says up to a quarter of emissions can be cut by changes in airframe design. It adds that changes in its Environmentally Friendly Engine (EFE) programme will deliver up to another fifth and the remainder of the 50 per cent target can be met by changing the way the aircraft are operated.

Rolls are also developing fuel cell technology and alternatives to kerosene. A biofuel blended with kerosene will be used in one of the four Rolls-Royce RB211-524s powering an Air New Zealand Boeing 747-400 in the second half of 2008.

Another example of energy saving is **McCain Foods**, which buys an eighth of the UK's potatoes to make chips. It has cut its Peterborough plant's CO2 footprint by two-thirds, says corporate affairs director Bill Bartlett. It invested £10m in three 3MW turbines to meet 60 per cent of its annual electricity demand. McCain spent another £4.5m on a lagoon to catch the methane from fermenting waste water and particulates, which generates another 10 per cent of the site's electricity usage. It also wants to refine its used cooking oil, either for its own vehicles fleet or for selling on. McCain want to become more competitive and more efficient.

The Hull factory of **Smith & Nephew Wound Management** makes single-use sterile wound dressings for injuries and operations. It saved £250,000 a year by replacing a large absorption chiller with a vapour compression chiller. It also replaced four 500kW chillers with a 'ring main' run from one 1MW chiller for the whole factory; in winter this runs at 250kW. Hull saved £50,000 by shutting down four of its eight compressors. These and other efforts have cut its energy use by 38 per cent to 48m kWh a year, saving £2m since 2003, says S&N energy and utilities manager Marc Beaumont, who adds: "And there's still more to go at." He says the main driver has been cost: "Energy prices are set to go only one way. If we can drive down costs we can increase our profits."

St Gobain are leaders in the design; production and distribution of materials for the construction; industrial and consumer markets. They used to pay contractors £75 a tonne for someone to take its cardboard away. Now it uses a baler that costs £238.33 a month to rent, maintain, operate and power. The baler crushes the cardboard into 500kg bales that it sells to a paper mill for £30 a tonne.

McLenaghan has a long list of sellable wastes, from mobile phones to scrap metal to cutting-wheels, thermocouples, cutting tools and vending machine cups. They believe waste can be reused, reallocated or put into a revenue stream.

Xerox has announced 'green software' that allows its machines to spot pages with just a URL, banner, logo or legal jargon and refuse to print them.

Canon advertising says its copiers' on-demand fixing technology saved seven million tonnes of CO_2 between 1999 and 2006. And in September 2007 Dell announced its aim to be carbon neutral.

10 Identifying and accounting for environmental costs

Internal and external environmental costs

Management are often unaware of the extent of environmental costs and cannot identify opportunities for cost savings. Environmental costs can be split into two categories:

Internal costs

These are costs that directly impact on the income statement of a company. There are many different types, for example:

- improved systems and checks in order to avoid penalties/fines
- waste disposal costs

- product take back costs (i.e. in the EU, for example, companies must provide facilities for customers to return items such as batteries, printer cartridges etc. for recycling. The seller of such items must bear the cost of these "take backs)
- regulatory costs such as taxes (e.g. companies with poor environmental management policies often have to bear a higher tax burden)
- upfront costs such as obtaining permits (e.g. for achieving certain levels of emissions)
- back-end costs such as decommissioning costs on project completion

External costs

These are costs that are imposed on society at large, but not borne by the company that generates the cost in the first instance. For example,

- carbon emissions
- usage of energy and water
- forest degradation
- health care costs
- social welfare costs

However, governments are becoming increasingly aware of these external costs and are using taxes and regulations to convert them to internal costs. For example, companies might have to have a tree replacement programme if they cause forest degradation, or they receive lower tax allowances on vehicles that cause a high degree of harm to the environment. On top of this, some companies are voluntarily converting external costs to internal costs.

11 Other classifications

Other classifications include those from :

(1) **Hansen and Mendoza** :

(i) Environmental prevention costs: the costs of activities undertaken to prevent the production of waste.

(ii) Environmental detection costs: costs incurred to ensure that the organisation complies with regulations and voluntary standards.

(iii) Environmental internal failure costs: costs incurred from performing activities that have produced contaminants and waste that have not been discharged into the environment.

(iv) Environmental external failure costs: costs incurred on activities performed after discharging waste into the environment.

(2) **The US Environmental Protection Agency** makes a distinction between four types of costs :

(i) Conventional costs : raw materials and energy costs having environmental relevance

(ii) Potentially hidden costs : costs captured by accounting systems but then losing their identity in 'general overheads'

(iii) Contingent costs : costs to be incurred at a future date, e.g. clean-up costs

(iv) Image and relationship costs : costs that, by their nature, are intangible, for example the costs of preparing environmental reports.

(3) The **United Nations Division for Sustainable Development** describes environmental costs as comprising of costs incurred to protect the environment (for example, measures taken to prevent pollution) and costs of wasted material, capital and labour, ie inefficiencies in the production process.

Further examples of environmental costs

Regulatory	**Upfront**	**Voluntary (beyond compliance)**
Notification	Site studies	Community relations /outreach
Reporting	Site preparation	Monitoring / testing
Monitoring / testing	Permitting	Training
Studies / modelling	R&D	Audits
Remediation	Engineering and procurement	Qualifying suppliers
Record keeping	Installation	Reports (e.g. annual environmental reports)
Plans	Conventional costs	Insurance
Training	Capital equipment	Planning
Inspections	Materials	Feasibility studies
Manifesting	Labour	Remediation
Labelling	Supplies	Recycling
Preparedness	Utilities	Environmental studies
Protective equipment	Structures	R&D
Medical surveillance	Salvage value	Habitat and wetland protection
Environmental insurance		Landscaping
Financial assurance	**Back-End**	Other environmental projects
Pollution control	Closure / decommissioning	Financial support to environmental groups and / or researchers
Spill response	Disposal of inventory	
Storm water management Waste management	Post-closure care	
Taxes / fees	Site survey	

12 EMA techniques

The most appropriate management accounting techniques for the identification and allocation of environmental costs are those identified by the United Nations Division for Sustainable Development. These include (Source : *Student Accountant,* Issue 15):

1. Input / outflow analysis

This technique records material inflows and balances this with outflowson the basis that what comes in, must go out.

For example, if 100kg of materials have been bought and only 80kg of materials have been produced, then the 20kg difference must be accounted for in some way. It may be, for example, that 10% of it has been sold as scrap and 90% of it is waste. By accounting for outputs in this way, both in terms of physical quantities, and, at the end of the process, in monetary terms too, businesses are forced to focus on environmental costs.

2. **Flow cost accounting**

This technique uses not only material flows, but also the organisational structure. It makes material flows transparent by looking at the physical quantities involved, their costs and their value. It divides the material flows into three categories : material, system and delivery and disposal. The values and costs of each of these three flows are then calculated. The aim of flow cost accounting is to reduce the quantity of materials which, as well as having a positive effect on the environment, should have a positive effect on a business' total costs in the long run.

3. Activity-based costing

ABC allocates internal costs to cost centres and cost drivers on the basis of the activities that give rise to the costs. In an environmental accounting context, it distinguishes between environment-related costs, which can be attributed to joint cost centres, and environment-driven costs, which tend to be hidden on general overheads.

4. Lifecycle costing

Within the context of environmental accounting, lifecycle costing is a technique which requires the full environmental consequences, and, therefore, costs, arising from the production of a product to be taken account across its whole lifecycle, literally 'from cradle to grave'.

13 EMA : Advantages and disadvantages

Advantages of environmental costing	Disadvantages
• better/fairer product costs	• time consuming
• improved pricing - so that products that have the biggest environmental impact reflect this by having higher selling prices	• expensive to implement
• better environmental cost control	• determining accurate costs and appropriate costs drivers is difficult
• facilitates the quantification of cost savings from "environmentally-friendly" measures	• external costs not experienced by the company (e.g. carbon footprint) may still be ignored/unmeasured
• should integrate environmental costing into the strategic management process	• some internal environmental costs are intangible (e.g. impact on employee health) and these are still ignored
• reduces the potential for cross-subsidisation of environmentally damaging products	• a company that incorporates external costs voluntarily may be at a competitive disadvantage to rivals who do not do this

14 Chapter summary

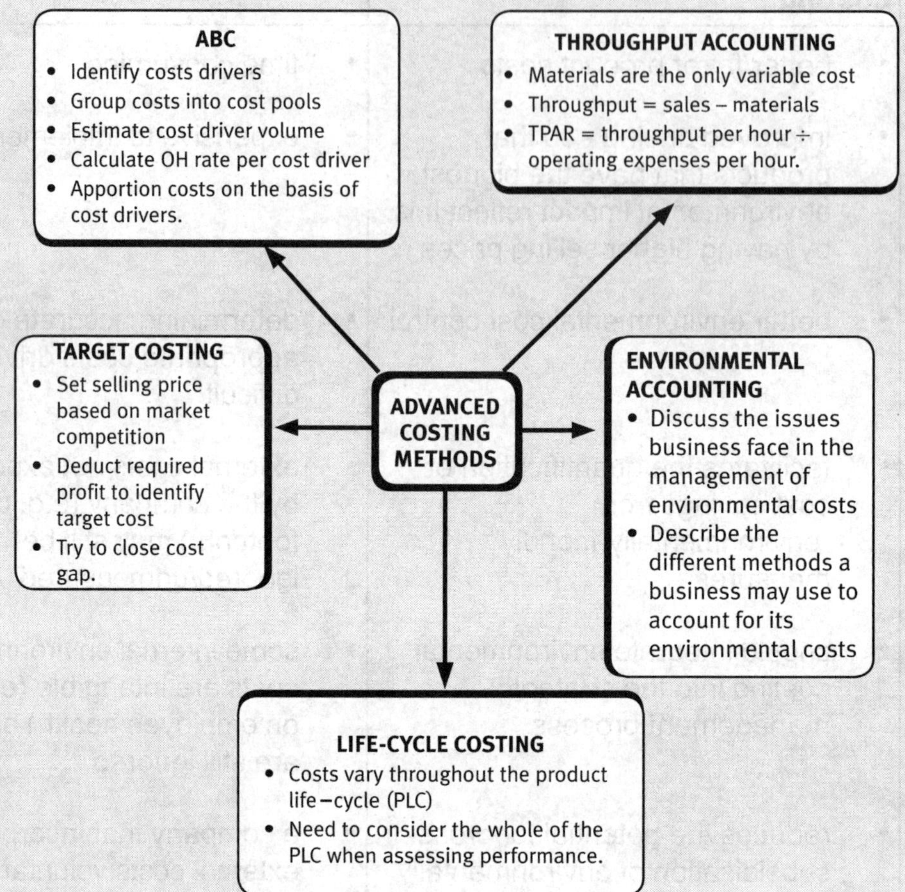

Test your understanding answers

Test your understanding 1

(a) **Traditional absorption costing**

Budgeted direct labour hours		60,000
(24,000 × 1.0) + (24,000 × 1.5)		
Budgeted overhead costs		$432,000
Recovery rate per direct labour hour		$7.20
	Plus	**Doubleplus**
	$	$
Direct costs	12.00	24.00
Production overhead	7.20	10.80
	19.20	34.80
Full production cost		

(b) **ABC**

Workings

	Plus	**Doubleplus**	**Total**
Batches	12	240	252
Setups	12	720	732
Special parts	24,000	96,000	120,000
Orders	10	140	150
Direct labour hours	24,000	36,000	60,000

Cost driver rates

Setup costs	$73,200/732	$100 per setup
Special parts handling	$60,000/120,000	$0.50 per part
Order handling	$19,800/150	$132 per order
Materials handling	$63,000/252	$250 per batch
Other overheads	$216,000/60,000	$3.60 per hour

	Plus	Doubleplus	Total
	$	$	$
Setup costs	1,200	72,000	73,200
Special parts handling costs	12,000	48,000	60,000
Order handling costs	1,320	18,480	19,800
Materials handling costs	3,000	60,000	63,000
Other overheads	86,400	129,600	216,000
	103,920	328,080	432,000
Number of units	24,000	24,000	
	$	$	
Direct cost	12.00	24.00	
Overhead cost per unit	4.33	13.67	
Full cost	16.33	37.67	

Note: In the example above the full production costs were:

	Plus	Doubleplus
Using traditional absoprtion costing	$19.20	$34.80
Using ABC	$16.33	$37.67
Assume the selling prices are	$25.00	$40.00
Using absorption costing sales margins are	23.2%	13.0%
ABC sales margins are	34.7%	5.8%

(c) **The reasons for the difference in the production cost per unit between the two methods**

- The allocation of overheads under absorption costing was unfair. This method assumed that all of the overheads were driven by labour hours and, as a result, the Double Plus received 1.5 times the production overhead of the Plus.
- However, this method of absorption is not appropriate. The overheads are in fact driven by a number of different factors. There are five activity costs, each one has its own cost driver. By taking this into account we end up with a much more accurate production overhead cost per unit.
- Using ABC, the cost per unit of a Double Plus is significantly higher. This is because the Double Plus is a much more complex product than the Plus. For example, there are 140 orders for the Double Plus but only 10 for the Plus and there are 4 special parts for the Double Plus compared to only one for the Plus. As a result of this complexity, the Double Plus has received more than three times the overhead of the Plus.
- This accurate allocation is important because the production overhead is a large proportion of the overall cost.

(d) **The implications of using ABC**

- Pricing - pricing decisions will be improved because the price will be based on more accurate cost data.
- Decision making - this should also be improved. For example, research, production and sales effort can be directed towards the most profitable products.
- Performance management - should be improved. ABC can be used as the basis of budgeting and forward planning. The more realistic overhead should result in more accurate budgets and should improve the process of performance management. In addition, an improved understanding of what drives the overhead costs should result in steps being taken to reduce the overhead costs and hence an improvement in performance.
- Sales strategy - this should be more soundly based. For example, target customers with products that appeared unprofitable under absorption costing but are actually profitable, and vice versa.

Test your understanding 2

Return per factory hour = ($85 – $42.50)/1.5 hours = $28.33

Cost per factory hour = $8,000/(10 × 40 hours) = $20

TPAR = $28.33/$20 = 1.4165

Test your understanding 3

(a)

Step 1: Determine the bottleneck constraint.

The bottleneck resource is machine time. 400 machine hours available each week = 24,000 machine minutes.

Step 2: Calculate the throughput per unit for each product.

	A	**B**	**C**	**D**
	$	$	$	$
Sales price	1.40	0.80	1.20	2.80
Materials cost	0.60	0.30	0.60	1.00
Throughput/ unit	0.80	0.50	0.60	1.80

Step 3: Calculate the throughput per machine minute

Machine time per unit	5 minutes	2 minutes	3 minutes	6 minutes
Throughput per minute	$0.16	$0.25	$0.20	$0.30

Step 4: Rank

Rank	4th	2nd	3rd	1st

Step 5: Allocate resources using this ranking and answer the question.

The profit-maximising weekly output and sales volumes are as follows.

Product	**Units**	**Machine minutes**	**Throughput per unit**	**Total throughout**
			$	$
D	1,500	9,000	1.80	2,700
B	2,000	4,000	0.50	1,000
C	2,500	7,500	0.60	1,500
		20,500		
A (balance)	700	3,500	0.80	560
		24,000		5,760
Operating expenses				5,440
Profit				320

(b) Throughput per machine hour: $5,760/400 hours = $14.40

Cost (operating expenses) per machine hour: $5,440/400 hours = $13.60.

TPAR: $14.40/$13.60 = 1.059.

Test your understanding 4

The information provided will give the following estimated product and company results:

	Product X		Product Y		
Per unit	$	$	$	$	$
Selling price		75		90	
Less: variable costs					
materials	20		20		
conversion costs	32	(52)	52	(72)	
Contribution		23		18	
C/S sales ratio		30.7%		20%	
Total for period					
Sales		900,000		648,000	1,548,000
Contribution (sales × cont/unit)		276,000		129,600	
Product-specific fixed costs		(170,000)		(90,000)	
		106,000		39,600	145,600
Company fixed costs					(50,000)
Net profit					95,600
Net profit margin on sales					6.2%

The company is falling considerably short of its 12% net profit margin target. If sales quantities and prices remain unchanged, costs must be reduced if the required return is to be reached.

Test your understanding 5

Your answer may include:

- Simplification of the production process allowing cheaper unskilled labour to be used in place of more highly paid skilled labour.
- Using plastics instead of metal for components.
- Using less packaging – e.g. expensive boxes replaced with plastic sheaths.
- Sharing components between models can result in economies of scale. (This is widely used in the car industry and has helped to reduce costs dramatically.)
- Reduce stockholding costs through the introduction of a just-in-time system.
- Using cheaper overseas labour.

Test your understanding 6

Lifecycle costs		**$ million**
Total R&D costs		20.0
Total Marketing costs	(5 + 4 + 3 + 0.9)	12.9
Total Production costs	(1 × 1 + 5 × 0.9 + 10 × 0.8 + 4 × 0.9)	17.1
Total Lifecycle costs		50.0
Total production (units)	(1 + 5 + 10 + 4)	20 million
Cost per unit	(50 ÷ 20)	$2.50

Comment

- The cost was calculated at $11 per unit during the launch phase. Based on this cost, the accountant was right to be concerned about the launch price being set at $8 per unit.
- However, looking at the whole life-cycle the marketing manager's proposal seems more reasonable.
- The average cost per unit over the entire life of the product is only $2.50 per unit. Therefore, a starting price of $8 per unit would seem reasonable and would result in a profit of $5.50 per unit.

chapter

2

Cost volume profit analysis

Chapter learning objectives

Upon completion of this chapter you will be able to:

- explain the nature of CVP analysis
- calculate and interpret break even point and margin of safety
- calculate the contribution to sales ratio, in single and multi-product situations, and demonstrate an understanding of its use
- calculate target profit or revenue in single and multi-product situations, and demonstrate an understanding of its use
- prepare break even charts and profit volume charts and interpret the information contained within each, including multi-product situations
- discuss the limitations of CVP analysis for planning and decision making.

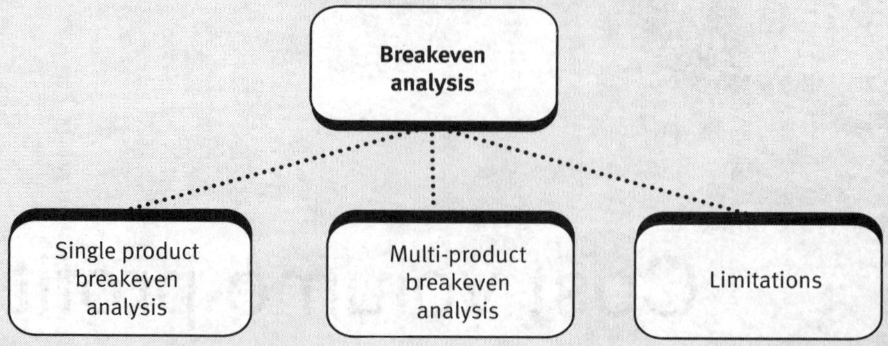

1 Break-even analysis

Also known as CVP analysis, or cost-volume-profit analysis. Break-even analysis is the study of the effects on future profit of changes in fixed cost, variable cost, sales price, quantity and mix.

CVP analysis is a particular example of *'what if?'* analysis. A business sets a budget based upon various assumptions about revenues, costs, product mixes and overall volumes. CVP analysis considers the impact on the budgeted profit of changes in these various factors.

2 Single product break-even analysis

Examples will be used to illustrate the basic formulae and calculations.

Test your understanding 1 - Break-even analysis

The following data relate to Product PQ:

Selling price	£25 per unit
Variable cost	£20 per unit

Fixed costs are £50,000.

(a) Calculate the number of units that must be made and sold in order to break even.

$$\text{Break-even point in units} = \frac{\text{Fixed cost}}{\text{Contribution per unit}}$$

(b) Calculate the level of activity that is required to generate a profit of £40,000.

$$\text{Level of activity to earn a required profit} = \frac{\text{Required Profit + Fixed Costs}}{\text{Contribution per unit}}$$

(c) The company budgets to sell 13,000 units of Product PQ.

Calculate the margin of safety.

The margin of safety is the difference between the budgeted level of activity and the break-even level of activity. It may be expressed in terms of units, sales value or as a percentage of the original budget.

(d) Calculate the Contribution/Sales ratio for Product PQ.

The C/S ratio is normally expressed as a percentage. It is constant at all levels of activity. The C/S ratio reveals the amount of contribution that is earned for every £1 worth of sales revenue.

$$\text{C/S Ratio} = \frac{\text{Contribution}}{\text{Sales}}$$

(e) Calculate the break-even point again, this time expressed in terms of sales revenue.

$$\text{Breakeven point in Sales Revenue} = \frac{\text{Fixed Costs}}{\text{C/S Ratio}}$$

(f) Calculate the sales revenue that is required to generate a profit of £40,000.

$$\text{Sales Revenue to earn a required profit} = \frac{\text{Required Profit + Fixed Costs}}{\text{C/S Ratio}}$$

3 Drawing a Basic Breakeven Chart

A basic breakeven chart records costs and revenues on the vertical axis (y) and the level of activity on the horizontal axis (x). Lines are drawn on the chart to represent costs and sales revenue. The breakeven point can be read off where the sales revenue line cuts the total cost line. We will use a basic example to demonstrate how to draw a breakeven chart. The data is:

Selling price	\$50 per unit
Variable cost	\$30 per unit
Fixed costs	\$20,000 per month
Forecast sales	1,700 units per month

The completed graph is shown below:

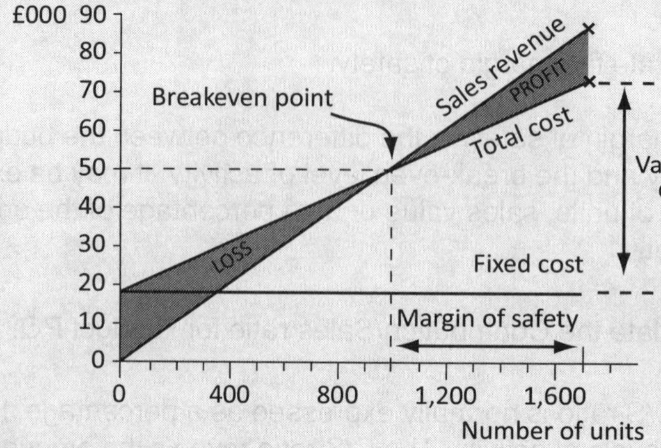

Learning to draw a chart to scale will provide a firm foundation for your understanding of breakeven charts. To give yourself some practice, it would be a good idea to follow the step-by-step guide which follows to produce your own chart on a piece of graph paper.

- *Step 1. Select appropriate scales for the axes and draw and label them.* Your graph should fill as much of the page as possible. This will make it clearer and easier to read. You can make sure that you do this by putting the extremes of the axes right at the end of the available space.

The furthest point on the vertical axis will be the monthly sales revenue, that is,

1,700 units × $50 = $ 85,000

The furthest point on the horizontal axis will be monthly sales volume of 1,700 units.

Make sure that you do not need to read data for volumes higher than 1,700 units before you set these extremes for your scales.

- *Step 2. Draw the fixed cost line and label it.* This will be a straight line parallel to the horizontal axis at the $20,000 level.

The $20,000 fixed costs are incurred in the short term even with zero activity.

- *Step 3. Draw the total cost line and label it.* The best way to do this is to calculate the total costs for the maximum sales level, which is 1,700 units in our example. Mark this point on the graph and join it to the cost incurred at zero activity, that is, $20,000.

	$
Variable costs for 1,700 units (1,700 × $30)	51,000
Fixed costs	20,000
Total cost for 1,700 units	71,000

- *Step 4. Draw the revenue line and label it.* Once again, the best way is to plot the extreme points. The revenue at maximum activity in our example is 1,700 × $50 = $85,000. This point can be joined to the origin, since at zero activity there will be no sales revenue.
- *Step 5. Mark any required information on the chart and read off solutions as required.* You can check that your chart is accurate by reading off the breakeven point and then check this against the calculation for breakeven:

$$\textbf{Breakeven point in units} = \frac{\textbf{Fixed costs}}{\textbf{Contribution per unit}}$$

= 20,000/(50 –30) = **1,000 units.**

The margin of safety can be seen as the area to the right of the breakeven point up to the forecast sales level of 1,700.

The contribution breakeven chart

One of the problems with the conventional or basic breakeven chart is that it is not possible to read contribution directly from the chart. A contribution breakeven chart is based on the same principles but it shows the variable cost line instead of the fixed cost line. The same lines for total cost and sales revenue are shown so the breakeven point and profit can be read off in the same way as with a conventional chart. However, it is also possible also to read the contribution for any level of activity.

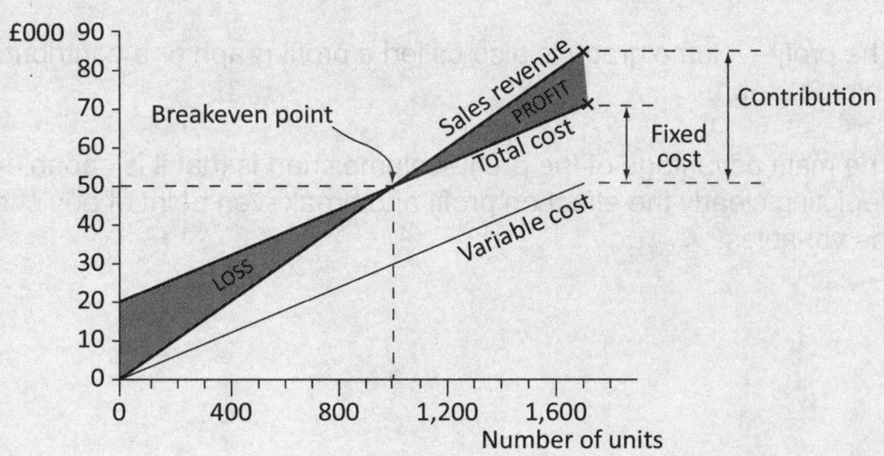

Using the same basic example as for the conventional chart, the total variable cost for an output of 1,700 units is 1,700 x $30 = $51,000. This point can be joined to the origin since the variable cost is nil at zero activity.

The contribution can be read as the difference between the sales revenue line and the variable cost line.

This form of presentation might be used when it is desirable to highlight the importance of contribution and to focus attention on the variable costs.

Ensure you are familiar with these charts and that you are able to identify all the component parts.

4 The Profit–Volume Chart

Another form of breakeven chart is the profit–volume chart. This chart plots a single line depicting the profit or loss at each level of activity. The breakeven point is where this line cuts the horizontal axis. A profit–volume graph for our example is shown below.

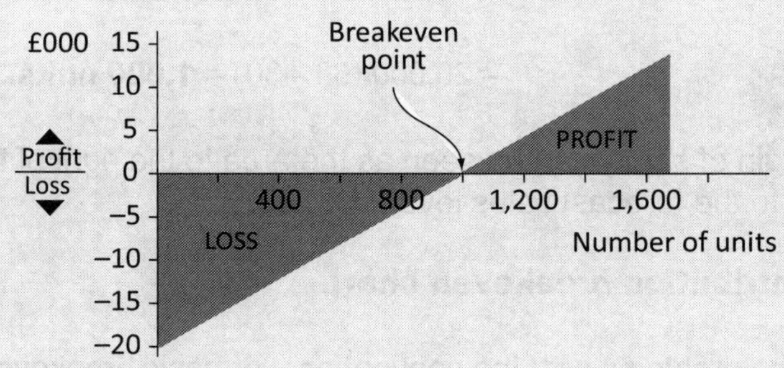

The vertical axis shows profits and losses and the horizontal axis is drawn at zero profit or loss.

At zero activity the loss is equal to $20,000, that is, the amount of fixed costs. The second point used to draw the line could be the calculated breakeven point or the calculated profit for sales of 1,700 units.

The profit–volume graph is also called a profit graph or a contribution–volume graph.

The main advantage of the profit–volume chart is that it is capable of depicting clearly the effect on profit and breakeven point of any changes in the variables.

Test your understanding 2 - RS

A company manufactures Product RS. The following data are available:

Selling price: $100 per unit
Variable cost: $60 per unit.

Fixed costs are $250,000. The company budgets to produce 12,000 units in the next period.

Required:

(a) Scenario I – Calculate:

(i) The break-even point (expressed in units and $ of revenue).

(ii) The level of activity required to generate a profit of $90,000 (expressed in units).

(iii) The margin of safety as a percentage.

(b) Using graph paper, draw a profit-volume chart for scenario I.

(c) Scenario II – Using the graph drawn in (b), illustrate and explain the impact of a change in Selling Price to $120 per unit, on:

(i) The break-even point (expressed in units and $ of revenue);

(ii) The level of activity required to generate a profit of $90,000 (expressed in units);

(iii) The margin of safety.

Test your understanding 3 - Single product

R Company provides a single service to its customers. An analysis of its budget for the year ending 31 December 20X5 shows that, in Period 3, when the budgeted activity was 6,570 service units with a sales value of $72 each, the margin of safety was 21.015%.

The budgeted contribution to sales ratio of the service is 35%.

Required:

Calculate the budgeted fixed costs in period 3.

5 Multi-Product Break-Even Analysis

The basic breakeven model can be used satisfactorily for a business operation with only one product. However, most companies sell a range of different products, and the model has to be adapted when one is considering a business operation with several products.

CVP Analysis assumes that, if a range of products is sold, sales will be in accordance with a **pre-determined sales mix**.

When a pre-determined sales mix is used, it can be depicted in the CVP Analysis by assuming average revenues and average variable costs for the given sales mix.

However, the assumption has to be made that the sales mix remains **constant**. This is defined as the relative proportion of each product's sale to total sales. It could be expressed as a ratio such as 2:3:5, or as a percentage as 20%, 30%, 50%.

The calculation of breakeven point in a multi-product firm follows the same pattern as in a single product firm. While the numerator will be the same fixed costs, the denominator now will be the **weighted average contribution margin**.

In multi-product situations, a weighted average C/S ratio is calculated by using the formula :

$$\textbf{Weighted Average C/S ratio} = \frac{\textbf{Total Contribution}}{\textbf{Total Revenue}}$$

The Weighted Average C/S ratio is useful in its own right, as it tells us what percentage each $ of sales revenue contributes towards fixed costs; it is also invaluable in helping us to quickly calculate the breakeven point in sales revenue :

$$\textbf{Breakeven revenue} = \frac{\textbf{Fixed costs}}{\textbf{Weighted Average C/S ratio}}$$

e.g

Weighted Average Contribution to Sales ratio

Company A produces Product X and Product Y. Fixed overhead costs amount to $200,000 every year. The following budgeted information is available for both products for next year :

	Product X	**Product Y**
Sales Price	$50	$60
Variable Cost	$30	$45
Contribution per unit	$20	$15
Budgeted Sales (in units)	20,000	10,000

In order to calculate the breakeven revenue for the next year, using the budgeted sales mix, we need the weighted Average C/S ratio as follows :

$$\text{Weighted Average C/S Ratio} = \frac{\text{Total Contribution}}{\text{Total Revenue}}$$

$$\text{Weighted Average C/S Ratio} = \frac{(20{,}000 \times \$20) + (\$10{,}000 \times \$15)}{(20{,}000 \times \$50) + (\$10{,}000 \times \$60)}$$

$$\text{Weighted Average C/S Ratio} = 34.375\%$$

The breakeven revenue can now be calculated this way for company A :

$$\text{Breakeven revenue} = \frac{\text{Fixed costs}}{\text{Weighted Average C/S ratio}}$$

$$\text{Breakeven revenue} = \frac{\$200{,}000}{0.34375}$$

$$\text{Breakeven revenue} = \$581{,}819$$

Calculations in the illustration above provide only estimated information because they assume that products X and Y are sold in a constant mix of 2X to 1Y. In reality, this constant mix is unlikely to exist and, at times, more Y may be sold than X. Such changes in the mix throughout a period, even if the overall mix for the period is 2:1, will lead to the actual breakeven point being different than anticipated.

6 Establishing a Target Profit For Multiple Products

The approach is the same as in single product situations, but the weighted average contribution to Sales Ratio is now used so that :

$$\textbf{Target Profit} = \frac{\textbf{Fixed costs + required profit}}{\textbf{Weighted Average C/S ratio}}$$

e.g

Target Profit in Company A

To achieve a target profit of $300,000 in Company A :

Sales revenue required for profit of $300,000 = (Fixed costs + required profit) / W.A. C/S ratio

Sales revenue required for profit of $300,000 = ($200,000 + $300,000) / 0.34375

Sales revenue required for profit of $300,000 = $1,454,545

7 Margin of Safety Calculations

The basic breakeven model for calculating the margin of safety can be adapted to multi-product environments. Three alternative approaches are considered in the example below.

e.g

Illustration

A business operation produces three products, the X, the Y and the Z. Relevant details are:

	Product X	Product Y	Product Z
Normal sales mix (units)	2	2	1
Selling price per unit	£9	£7	£5
Variable cost per unit	£6	£5	£1
Contribution per unit	£3	£2	£4
Forecast unit sales	400	400	200

Fixed costs are £2,000 per period, not attributable to individual products. A budget for the forecast is as follows:

	Product X	Product Y	Product Z	Total
Sales Revenue	£3,600	£2,800	£1,000	£7,400
Variable cost	£2,400	£2,000	£200	£4,600
Contribution	£1,200	£800	£800	£2,800
Fixed Costs				£2,000
Profit				£800

To calculate the margin of safety, three approaches are possible :

(1) Consider the products in sequence, X then Y then Z . In this case, it can be seen that breakeven occurs at 800 units of sales (400X plus 400Y) and **the margin of safety is 200 units of Z.**

(2) Consider output in terms of £ sales and assume a constant product mix (2X:2Y:1Z). Inspection of the budget (above) shows that £1 sales is associated with £0.6216 variable costs (that is, £4,600 variable costs ÷ £7,400 sales). The contribution per £1 sales is £0.3784 (i.e. £1 - £0.6216). So, if the fixed costs are £2,000 then the breakeven point is £5,285 sales and **the margin of safety is £2,115** (i.e. £7,400 forecast sales - £5,285).

(3) Consider output in terms of percentage of forecast sales and a constant product mix. Inspection of the budget shows that 1 per cent of forecast sales is associated with a contribution of £28.00 (i.e. £2,800 total contribution ÷ 100 per cent). So, if fixed costs are £2,000 it follows that the breakeven point is 71.43 per cent and **the margin of safety is 28.57 per cent.**

8 The Multi-Product Profit-Volume Graph - Step-By-Step

In a multi-product environment, two lines must be shown on the profit-volume graph: one straight line, where a constant mix between the products is assumed; and one bow shaped line, where it is assumed that the company sells its most profitable product first and then its next most profitable product and so on.

STEP 1 : Calculate the C/S ratio of each product being sold, and rank the products in order of profitability.

STEP 2 : Draw the graph, showing cumulative sales on the x-axis. For example, if we assume 3 products X, Y and Z, then the following graph could be drawn , with 'V' representing the total sales. At an output of 0, the profit earned will amount to the company's fixed costs, represented by point *k* on the chart.

STEP 3 : Draw the line *km*, that represents the profit earned by product X – the slope of the line is determined by the contribution per unit earned on sales of that product.

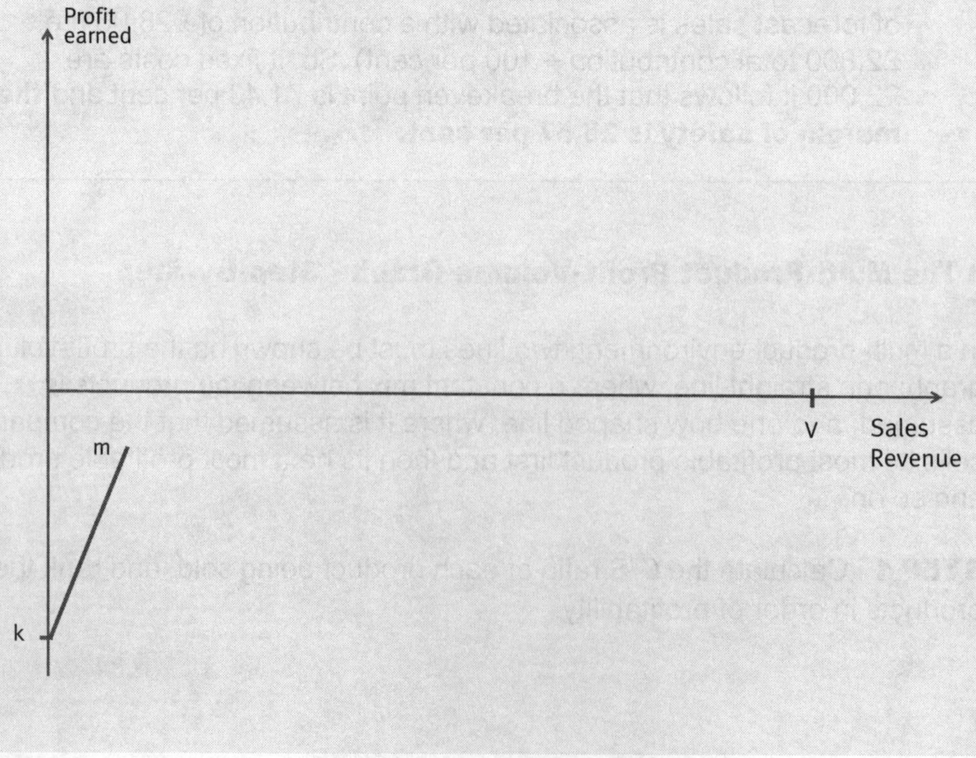

STEP 4 : Draw the line *mn*, that represents the profit earned by product y, which has a lower contribution per unit than product X. The line *nj* is the profit earned by the least profitable product, product Z.

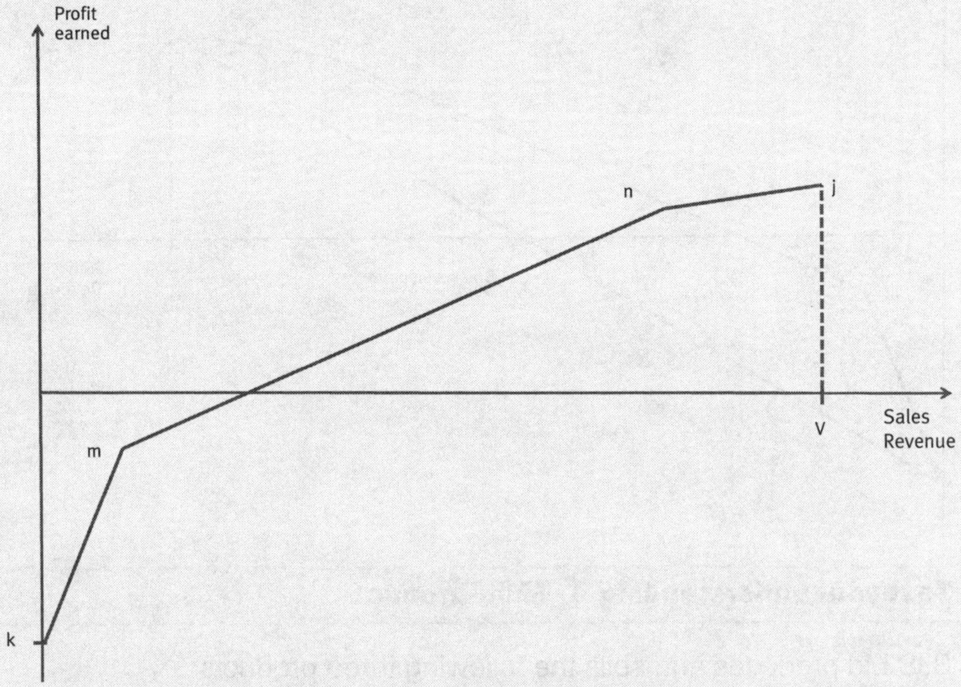

STEP 5 : Draw the line joining points *k* and *j* : it reflects the average profitability of the three products, and each point on that line represents the profit earned for the associated output, assuming that the three products are sold in the standard product mix, i.e. the mix implied in the construction of the chart. Accordingly, the indicated breakeven point only applies if the products are sold in the standard product mix.

It can also be seen that breakeven can also occur at lower levels of output, provided the proportions of the products are changed. For example, the point B where the line *kmnj* crosses the horizontal axis indicates a possible breakeven point.

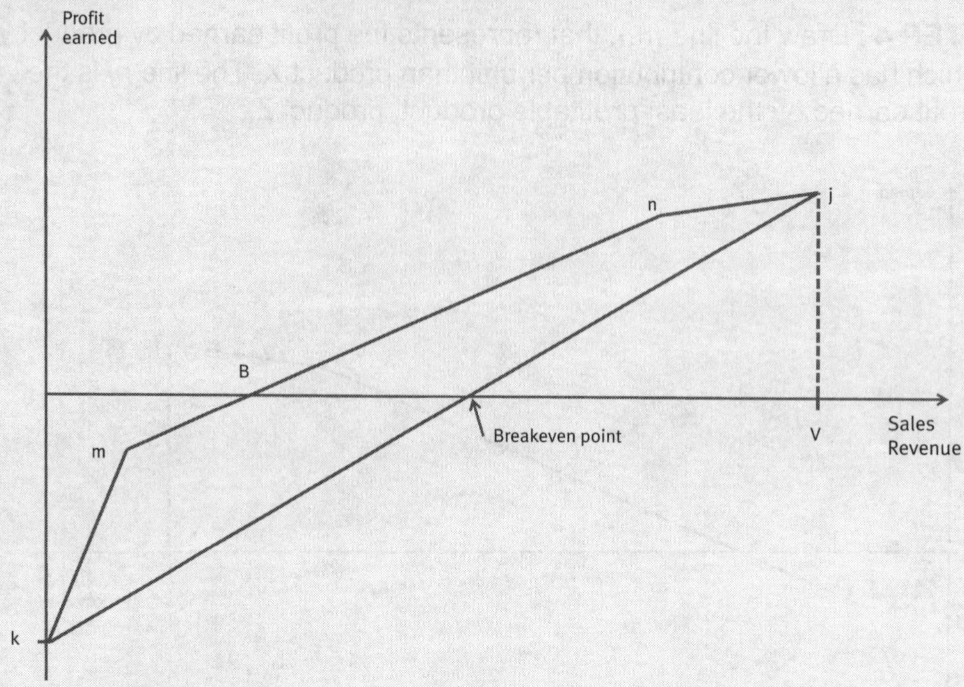

Test your understanding 4 - Multi-product

BJS Ltd produces and sells the following three products:

Product	**X**	**Y**	**Z**
Selling price per unit	£16	£20	£10
Variable cost per unit	£5	£15	£7
Contribution per unit	£11	£5	£3
Budgeted sales volume	50,000 units	10,000 units	100,000 units

The company expects the fixed costs to be £450,000 for the coming year. Assume that sales arise throughout the year in a constant mix.

Required:

(a) Calculate the weighted average C/S ratio for the products.

(b) Calculate the break-even sales revenue required.

(c) Calculate the amount of sales revenue required to generate a profit of £600,000.

(d) Draw a multi-product profit-volume chart assuming the budget is achieved.

Formula for the break-even point in a multi-product environment (expressed as sales revenue required):

$$\textbf{BREAKEVEN POINT (BEP)} = \frac{\textbf{FIXED COSTS}}{\textbf{AVERAGE C/S RATIO}}$$

Formula to achieve a specified profit in a multi-product environment (expressed as sales revenue required):

$$\textbf{REQUIRED REVENUE} = \frac{\textbf{REQUIRED PROFIT + FIXED COSTS}}{\textbf{AVERAGE C/S RATIO}}$$

9 Limitations of break-even analysis

Cost behaviour is affected by the interplay of a number of factors. Physical volume is only one of these factors; others include unit prices of input, efficiency, changes in production technology, wars, strikes, legislation, and so forth. Any CVP analysis is based on assumptions about the behaviour of revenue, costs and volume. A change in expected behaviour will alter the break-even point; in other words, profits are affected by changes in other factors besides volume. A CVP chart must be interpreted in the light of the limitations imposed by its underlying assumptions. The real benefit of preparing CVP charts is in the enrichment of understanding of the interrelationships of all factors affecting profits, especially cost behaviour patterns over ranges of volume.

The following underlying assumptions will limit the precision and reliability of a given cost-volume-profit analysis.

(1) The behaviour of total cost and total revenue has been reliably determined and is linear over the relevant range.

(2) All costs can be divided into fixed and variable elements.

(3) Total fixed costs remain constant over the relevant volume range of the CVP analysis.

(4) Total variable costs are directly proportional to volume over the relevant range.

(5) Selling prices are to be unchanged.

(6) Prices of the factors of production are to be unchanged (for example, material, prices, wage rates).

(7) Efficiency and productivity are to be unchanged.

(8) The analysis either covers a single product or assumes that a given sales mix will be maintained as total volume changes.

(9) Revenue and costs are being compared on a single activity basis (for example, units produced and sold or sales value of production).

(10) Perhaps the most basic assumption of all is that volume is the only relevant factor affecting cost. Of course, other factors also affect costs and sales. Ordinary cost-volume-profit analysis is a crude oversimplification when these factors are unjustifiably ignored.

(11) The volume of production equals the volume of sales, or changes in beginning and ending inventory levels are insignificant in amount.

Test your understanding 5

H Limited manufactures and sells two products – J and K. Annual sales are expected to be in the ratio of J:1 K:3. Total annual sales are planned to be £420,000. Product J has a contribution to sales ratio of 40% whereas that of product K is 50%. Annual fixed costs are estimated to be £120,000.

Required:

What is the budgeted break-even sales value?

Test your understanding 6

PER plc sells three products. The budgeted fixed cost for the period is £648,000. The budgeted contribution to sales ratio (C/S ratio) and sales mix are as follows:

Product	C/S ratio	Mix
P	27%	30%
E	56%	20%
R	38%	50%

Required:
What is the breakeven sales revenue?

Test your understanding 7

JK Ltd has prepared a budget for the next 12 months when it intends to make and sell four products, details of which are shown below:

Product	Sales in units (thousands)	Selling price per unit £	Variable cost per unit £
J	10	20	14.00
K	10	40	8.00
L	50	4	4.20
M	20	10	7.00

Budgeted fixed costs are £240,000 per annum and total assets employed are £570,000.

You are required:

(a) to calculate the total contribution earned by each product and their combined total contributions;

(b) to plot the data of your answer to (a) above in the form of a profit-volume graph;

(c) to explain your graph to management, to comment on the results shown and state the break-even point;

(d) to describe briefly three ways in which the overall contribution to sales ratio could be improved.

10 Chapter summary

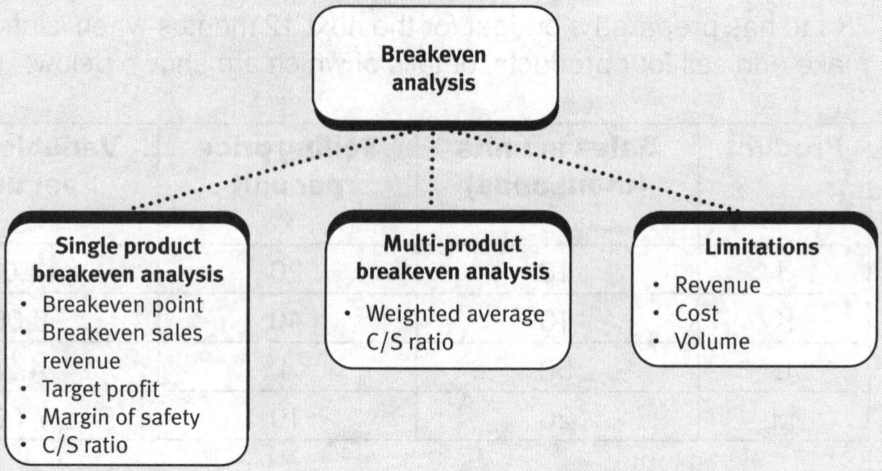

Test your understanding answers

Test your understanding 1 - Break-even analysis

(a) Contribution per unit = £25 – £20 = £5 per unit

$$\text{Break-even point in units} = \frac{\text{Fixed cost}}{\text{Contribution per unit}}$$

BEP = £50,000 ÷ £5 = 10,000 units

(b)

$$\textbf{Level of activity to earn a required profit} = \frac{\textbf{Required Profit + Fixed Costs}}{\textbf{Contribution per unit}}$$

Number of units = (£40,000 + £50,000) ÷ £5 = 18,000 units

(c)

Margin of safety = 13,000 – 10,000 = 3,000 units
In terms of sales revenue this is 3,000 × £25 = £75,000

$$\text{As a percentage of the budget} = \frac{3000}{13{,}000} \times 100\%$$
= 23.1%

(d)

$$\textbf{C/S Ratio} = \frac{\textbf{Contribution}}{\textbf{Sales}}$$

$$\text{C/S ratio} = \frac{£5}{£25}$$

C/S ratio = 20%

(e)

$$\text{Breakeven point in Sales Revenue} = \frac{\textbf{Fixed Costs}}{\textbf{C/S Ratio}}$$

BEP (in £) = £50,000 ÷ 0.20

BEP = £250,000

(f)

$$\text{Sales Revenue to earn a required profit} = \frac{\textbf{Required Profit + Fixed Costs}}{\textbf{C/S Ratio}}$$

Required sales = (£40,000 + £50,000) ÷ 0.20

i.e.**£450,000.**

Test your understanding 2 - RS

(a) **Scenario I**

(i)	Contribution per unit	= $100 – $60	= $40 per unit
	BEP (units)	= $250,000 ÷ $40	= 6,250 units
	C/S ratio	= $40/$100	= 0.40
	BEP ($ revenue)	= $250,000 ÷ 0.40	= $625,000
(ii)	Level of activity	= ($90,000 + $250,000) ÷ $40	= 8,500 units
	Level of activity	= ($90,000 + $250,000) ÷ 0.40	= $850,000
(iii)	Margin of safety	= 12,000 – 6,250	= 5,750 units
	Or expressed in $ revenue		= $575,000.

Margin of safety expressed as a % of the budget : 5,750 units / 12,000 units = 48% approx.

(b)

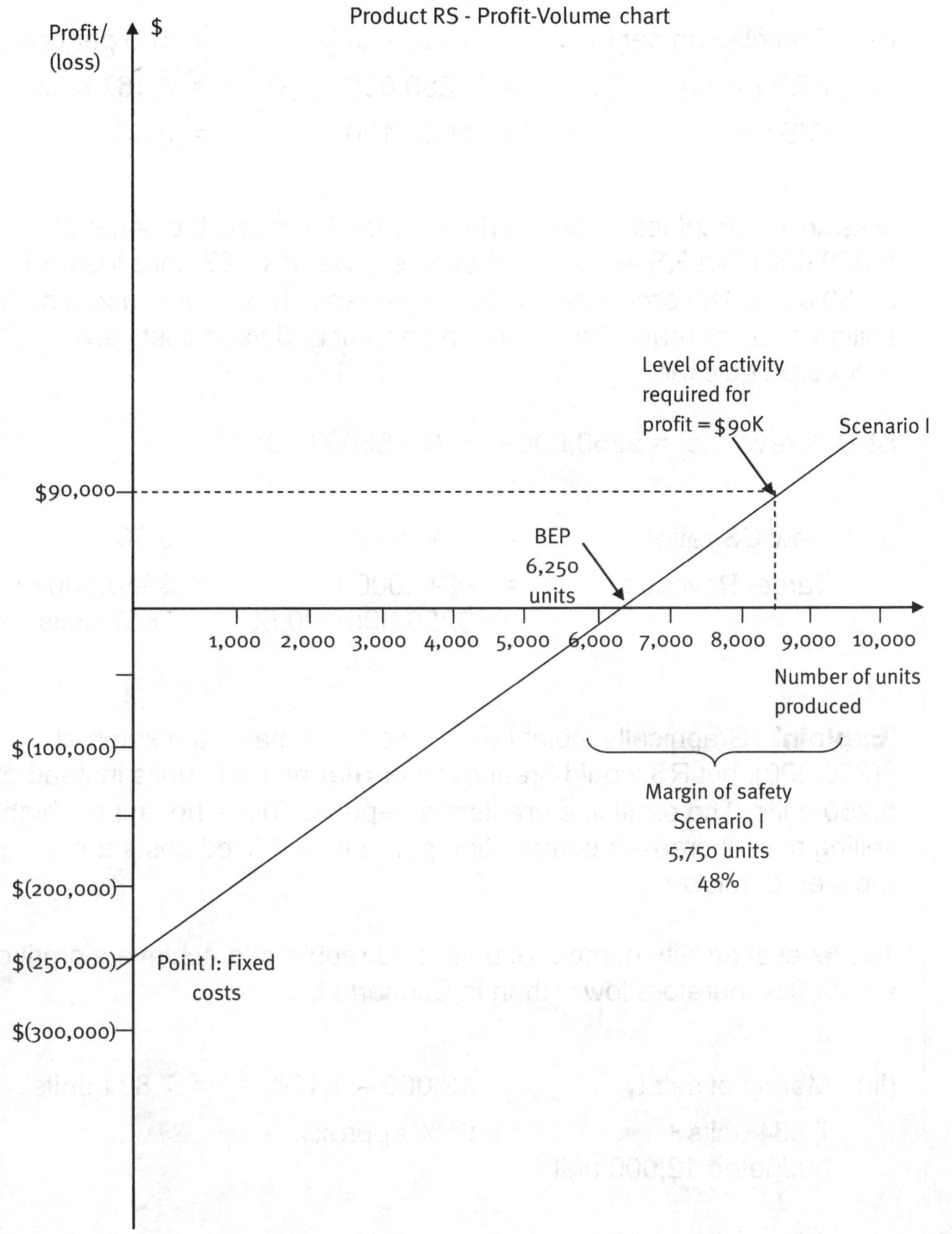
Product RS - Profit-Volume chart
Profit/ (loss)
$
$90,000
$(100,000)
$(200,000)
$(250,000)
$(300,000)
Point I: Fixed costs
BEP 6,250 units
Level of activity required for profit = $90K
Scenario I
1,000
2,000
3,000
4,000
5,000
6,000
7,000
8,000
9,000
10,000
Number of units produced
Margin of safety Scenario I 5,750 units 48%

(c) **Scenario II**

(i)	Contribution per unit	=	\$120 – \$60	= \$60 per unit
	BEP (units)	=	\$250,000 ÷\$60	= 4,167 units
	C/S ratio	=	\$60/\$120	= 0.50

'Explain' : Graphically, point I (Fixed costs) remains the same at \$(250,000), but RS would breakeven **earlier** at 4,167 units instead of 6,250 units. The profit line gradient steepens. This is because a higher selling price increased contribution per unit and fixed costs are recovered quicker.

BEP (\$ revenue) = \$250,000 ÷ 0.50 = \$500,000

(ii)	New CS ratio	=	\$60/\$120	= 0.50
	Target Revenue	=	(\$90,000 + \$250,000) ÷ 0.50	= \$680,000 or 5667 units

'Explain' : Graphically, point I (Fixed costs) remains the same at \$(250,000), but RS would breakeven **earlier** at 4,167 units instead of 6,250 units. The profit line gradient steepens. This is because a higher selling price increases contribution per unit, and fixed costs are recovered quicker.

The level of activity/number of units sold required to achieve a profit of £90,000 is therefore lower than in Scenario I.

(iii)	Margin of safety	=	12,000 – 4,166	= 7,834 units
	7,834 units ÷ budgeted 12,000 units	=	65% approx.	

'Explain' : An increased contribution impacts favourably on the margin of safety. Sales need to fall 65% short of budget before RS starts making a loss – compared with 48% in scenario I.

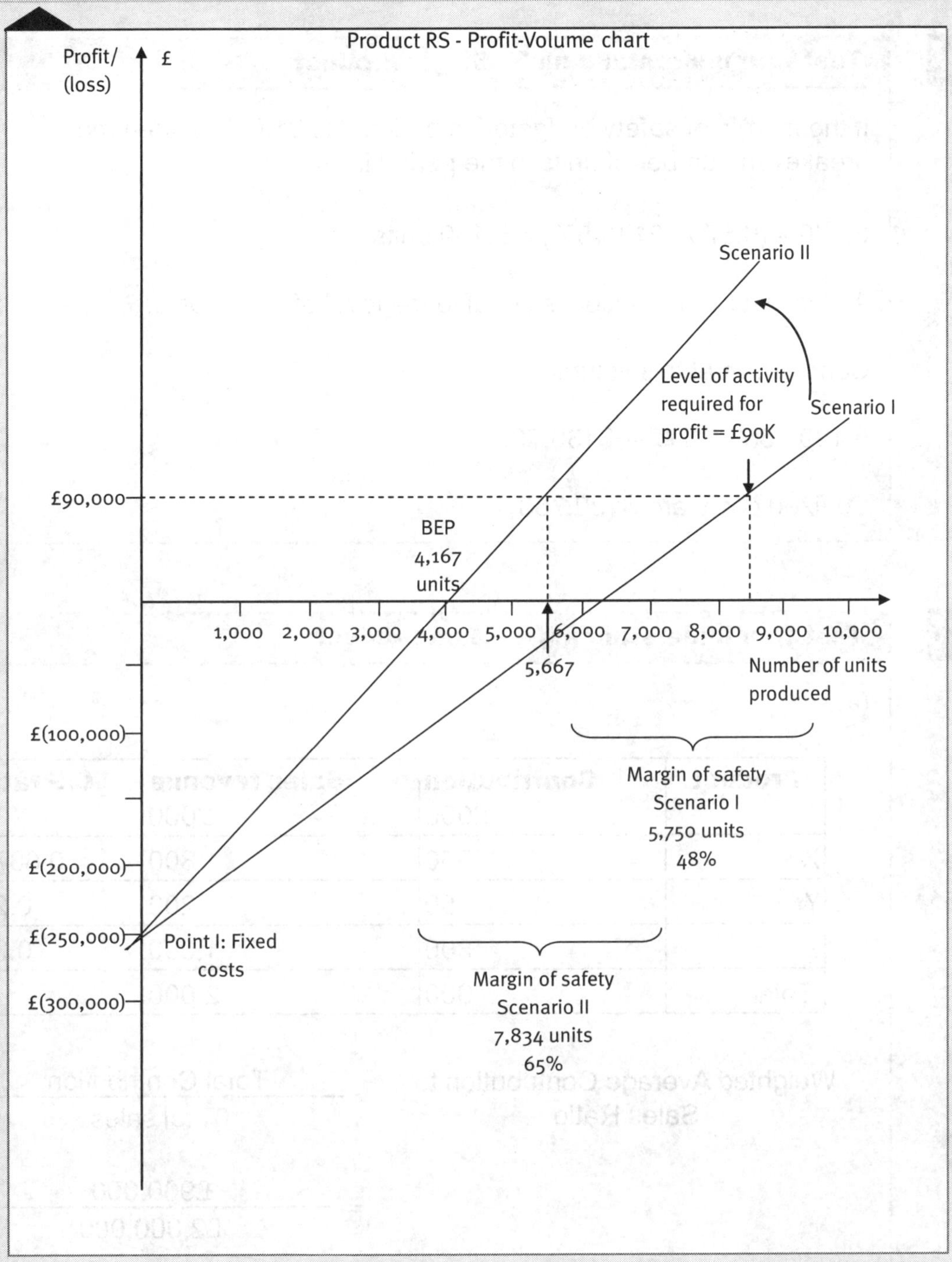
Product RS - Profit-Volume chart
Profit/ (loss)
£
Scenario II
Scenario I
Level of activity required for profit = £90K
£90,000
BEP 4,167 units
1,000
2,000
3,000
4,000
5,000
6,000
7,000
8,000
9,000
10,000
5,667
Number of units produced
£(100,000)
£(200,000)
£(250,000)
£(300,000)
Point I: Fixed costs
Margin of safety Scenario I 5,750 units 48%
Margin of safety Scenario II 7,834 units 65%

Test your understanding 3 - Single product

If the margin of safety budgeted in period 3 is 21.015%, then the breakeven number of units in the period is:

6,570 – (6,570 ´ 21.015%) = 5,189 units

At this level, contribution is equal to the level of fixed costs.

Contribution at this volume is:

5,189 ´ 35% ´ $72 = $130,763.

So fixed costs are $130,763.

Test your understanding 4 - Multi-product

(a)

Product	**Contribution** £000	**Sales revenue** £000	**C/S ratio**
X	550	800	0.6875
Y	50	200	0.25
Z	300	1,000	0.30
Total	900	2,000	

$$\text{Weighted Average Contribution to Sales Ratio} = \frac{\text{Total Contribution}}{\text{Total sales}}$$

$$= \frac{£900{,}000}{£2{,}000{,}000}$$

$$= 0.45 \text{ or } 45\%$$

(b)

$$\text{Breakeven Sales Revenue required} = \frac{\text{Fixed costs}}{\text{C/S ratio}}$$

$$= \frac{£450{,}000}{45\%}$$

$$= £1{,}000{,}000$$

(c)

$$\text{Sales Revenue Required} = \frac{\text{Fixed costs + required profit}}{\text{C/S ratio}}$$

$$= \frac{£450{,}000 + £600{,}000}{0.45}$$

$$= £2{,}333{,}333$$

Firstly, products must be ranked according to their C/S ratios. Then assume that the products are sold in the order of highest C/S ratio first. The table below provides the workings to enable the chart to be drawn.

Product	**Contribution** £000	**Cumulative Profit / (Loss)** £000	**Revenue** £000	**Cumulative Revenue** £000
		(450)		0
X	550	100	800	800
Z	300	400	1,000	1,800
Y	50	450	200	2,000

The chart is, essentially, a profit/volume chart. Cumulative profit is plotted against cumulative sales revenue. Like P/V charts for single products the line drawn starts at the fixed costs below the line.

Multi-product profit-volume chart

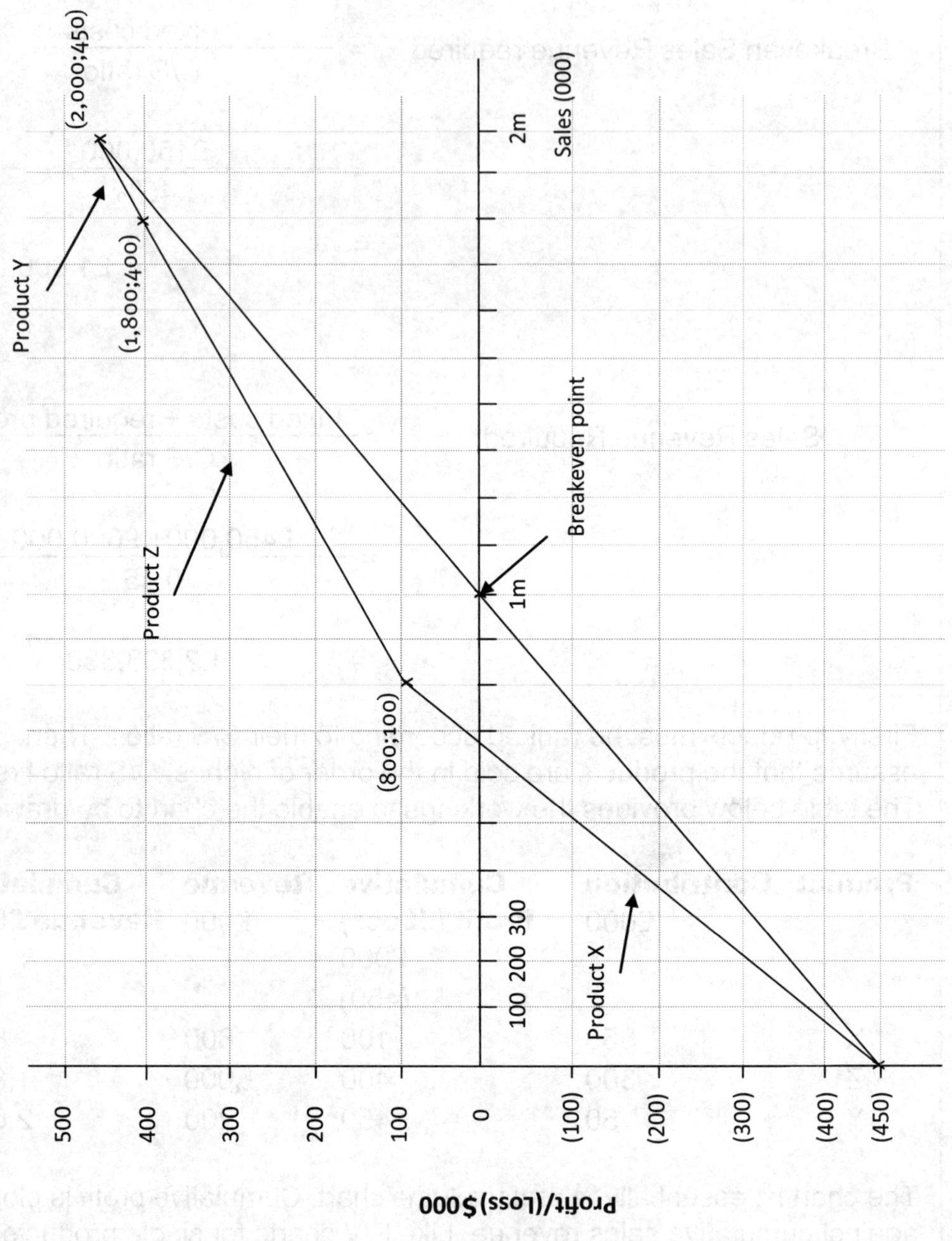

Test your understanding 5

Product	**Total Contribution**	**Total Sales Revenue**	**C/S Ratio**
	£	£	
J	42,000	105,000	40%
K	157,500	315,000	50%
	199,500	420,000	

C/S ratio of the mix = $\frac{£199,500}{£420,000}$ = 47.5%

Break-even point = $\frac{£120,000}{47.5\%}$ = £252,632

OR

C/S ratio of the mix = $\frac{(1 \text{ x } 40\%) + (3\ 8\ 50\%)}{1+3}$

= 47.5%

Breakeven point = $\frac{£120,000}{47.5\%}$

= **£252,000**

Test your understanding 6

$$\text{Breakeven point in £} = \frac{\text{Fixed Cost}}{\text{C/S ratio of the mix}}$$

C/S ratio of the mix = (0.3*27%)+(0.2*56%)+(0.5*38%) = 38.3%

$$\text{Therefore, BEP} = \frac{£648,000}{38.3\%}$$

= £1,691,906

Test your understanding 7

(a)

Product	**Revenue, in** £000	**Variable Costs** £000	**Contribution** £000	**C/S ratio**
J	200	140	60	0.30
K	400	80	320	0.80
L	200	210	(10)	(0.05)
M	200	140	60	0.30
	1,000	**570**	**430**	

(b)

Product	**Contribution, in** £000	**Cumulative Profit / (Loss)**	**Revenue** £000	**Cumulative Revenue**
		(240)		0
K	320	80	400	400
J	60	140	200	600
M	60	200	200	800
L	(10)	190	200	1,000

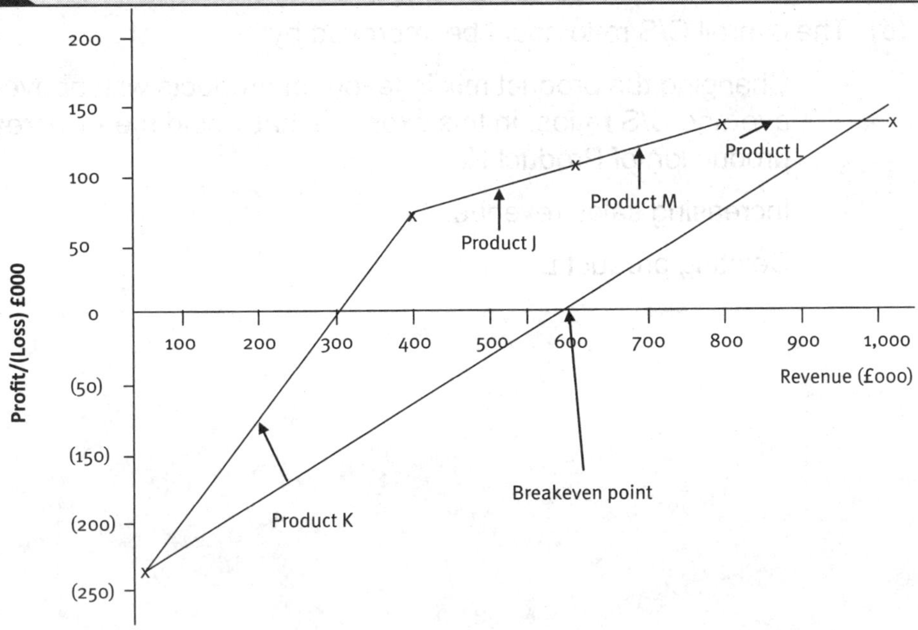

(c) The products are plotted in the order of their C/S ratios. The fixed costs of the company are £240,000. The chart reveals that if only product K is produced, the company will generate a profit of £80,000. The profit of the company is maximised at £200,000. This is achieved by producing Products K, J and M only.

If all four products are produced then JK Ltd can expect a profit of £190,000 from sales revenue of £1,000,000. If all four products are sold in the budget sales mix then the company will break even when revenue reaches £558,140. This point has been indicated on the graph. This point can also be calculated. Thus:

Average contribution/sales ratio = 430/1,000 = 43%

$$\text{Break-even point} = \frac{\text{Fixed costs}}{\text{Average C/S ratio}}$$

$$= \frac{£240,000}{0.43} = £558,140$$

(d) The overall C/S ratio could be improved by:

- Changing the product mix in favour of products with above-average C/S ratios. In this example that would mean increasing production of Product K.
- Increasing sales revenue.
- Deleting product L.

chapter

3

Planning with limiting factors

Chapter learning objectives

Upon completion of this chapter you will be able to:

- select an appropriate technique, where there is one limiting factor/key factor, to achieve desired organisational goals.
- determine the optimal production plan where an organisation is restricted by a single limiting factor, including within the context of 'make' or 'buy' decisions (covered separately in Chapter 5).
- select an appropriate technique, where there are several limiting factors/key factors, to achieve desired organisational goals.
- formulate a linear programming problem involving two products.
- determine the optimal solution to a linear programming problem using a graphical approach.
- use simultaneous equations to determine where the two lines cross to solve a multiple scarce resource problem.
- explain shadow prices (dual prices) and discuss their implications on decision making and performance management in multiple limited resource situations.
- calculate shadow prices (dual prices) and discuss their specific implications on decision making and performance management.
- explain the implications of the existence of slack, in multiple limited resource situations, for decision making and performance management.
- calculate slack and explain the specific implications of the existence of the slack for decision making and performance management.

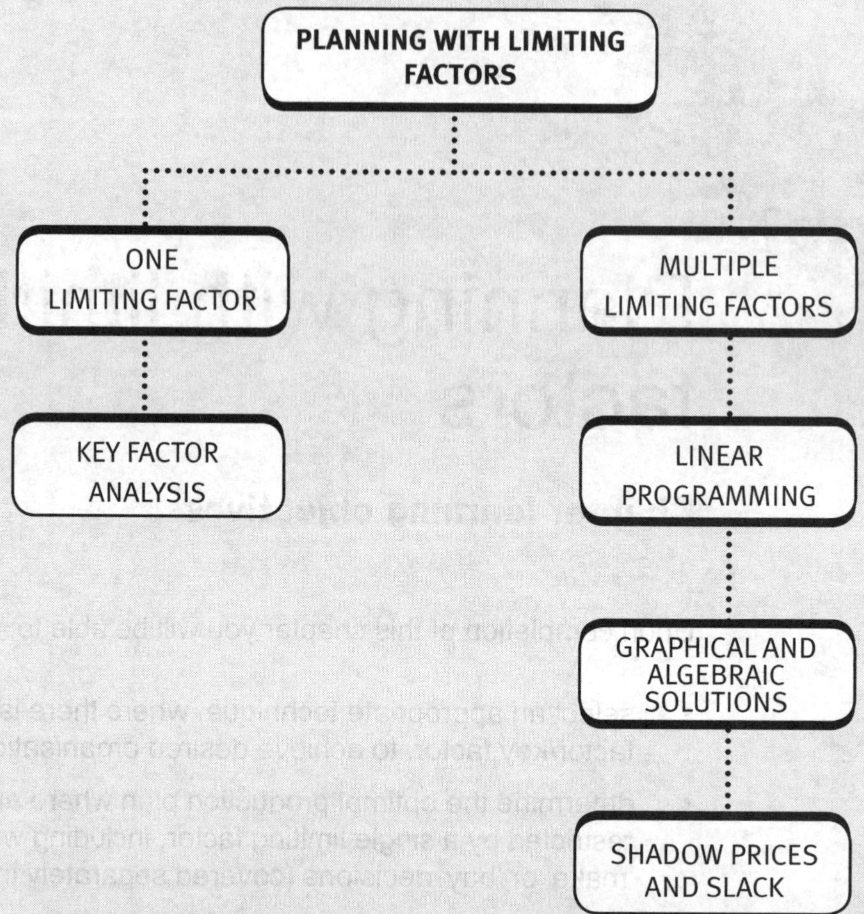

1 Introduction

Limiting factor analysis was covered in F2. In F5 the main difference is that the examination contains written questions so issues can be examined in more depth with scope for discussion. With linear programming the F5 syllabus also includes new aspects not seen before in F2.

Limiting factors

Firms face many constraints on their activity and plan accordingly:

- limited demand ;
- limited skilled labour and other production resources ;
- limited finance ('capital rationing').

Examination questions will focus on the problem of scarce resources that prevent the normal plan being achieved.

For example, a firm is facing a labour shortage this month due to sickness and, as a result, cannot produce the number of units that it would like to. How should its production plan be revised?

2 Planning with one limiting factor

Key factor analysis – calculations

The usual objective in questions is to maximise profit. Given that fixed costs are unaffected by the production decision in the short run, the approach should be to maximise the contribution earned.

If there is one limiting factor, then the problem is best solved using key factor analysis.

Step 1: identify the scarce resource.

Step 2: calculate the contribution per unit for each product.

Step 3: calculate the contribution per unit of the scarce resource for each product.

Step 4: rank the products in order of the contribution per unit of the scarce resource.

Step 5: allocate resources using this ranking and answer the question.

Test your understanding 1

X Ltd makes three products, A, B and C, of which unit costs, machine hours and selling prices are as follows:

	Product A	**Product B**	**Product C**
Machine hours	10	12	14
	$	$	$
Direct materials @ 50c per kg	7 (14 kg)	6 (12 kg)	5 (10 kg)
Direct wages @ $7.50 per hour	9 (1.2 hours)	6 (0.8 hours)	3 (0.4 hours)
Variable overheads	3	3	3
Marginal cost	19	15	11
Selling price	25	20	15
Contribution	6	5	4

Sales demand for the period is limited as follows.

Product A	4,000
Product B	6,000
Product C	6,000

Company policy is to produce a minimum of 1,000 units of Product A.

The supply of materials in the period is unlimited, but machine hours are limited to 200,000 and direct labour hours to 5,000.

Required:

Indicate the production levels that should be adopted for the three products in order to maximise profitability, and state the maximum contribution.

3 Several limiting factors – linear programming

When there is only one scarce resource the method above (key factor analysis) can be used to solve the problem. However where there are two or more resources in short supply which limit the organisation's activities then linear programming is required to find the solution.

In examination questions linear programming is used to:

- maximise contribution and/or
- minimise costs.

Formulating a linear programming problem involving two variables

The steps involved in linear programming are as follows:

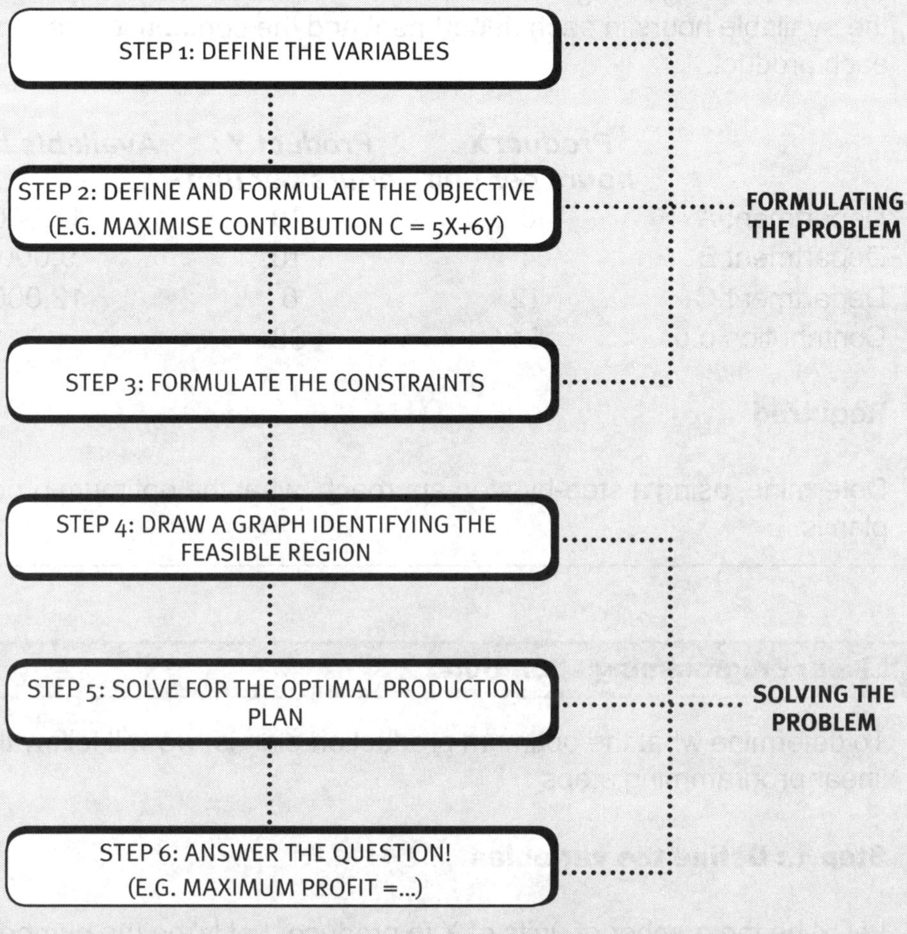

Note: Linear programming calculations will only involve two variables in exam questions.

e.g

Illustration 1 - Linear programming

A company produces two products in three departments. Details are shown below regarding the time per unit required in each department, the available hours in each department and the contribution per unit of each product:

	Product X : hours per unit	***Product Y : hours per unit***	***Available hours***
Department A	8	10	11,000
Department B	4	10	9,000
Department C	12	6	12,000
Contribution p.u.	\$4	\$8	

Required

Determine, using a step-by-step approach, what the optimum production plan is.

Linear Programming - Solution

To determine what the optimum production plan is, we will follow the linear programming steps :

Step 1 : Define the variables

Let 'x' be the number of units of X to produce; Let 'y' be the number of units of Y to produce.

Step 2 : Define and formulate the objective function

Objective function: to maximise contribution C= \$4x + \$8y

Step 3 : Formulate the constraints

Subject to:
In Department A, $8x + 10y \leq 11,000$ hours
In Department B, $4x + 10y \leq 9,000$ hours
In Department C, $12x + 6y \leq 12,000$
$0 \leq x,y$

Step 4 : Draw a graph identifying the feasible region

To draw Constraint 1 (constraint in Department A), we take the inequality '$8x + 10y \leq 11,000$ hours' and turn it into an equation : $8x + 10y = 11,000$.

To draw this constraint, we need two points. If X = 0, Y = 11,000 ÷ 10 so Y = 1,100. Likewise, if Y = 0, X = 11,000 ÷ 8 so X = 1,375.

To draw Constraint 2 (Department B) : If X =0, Y = 900 and if Y = 0, X =2,250.

To draw Constraint 3 (Department C) : If X = 0 , Y = 2,000 and if Y = 0, X = 1,000

Linear programming graph

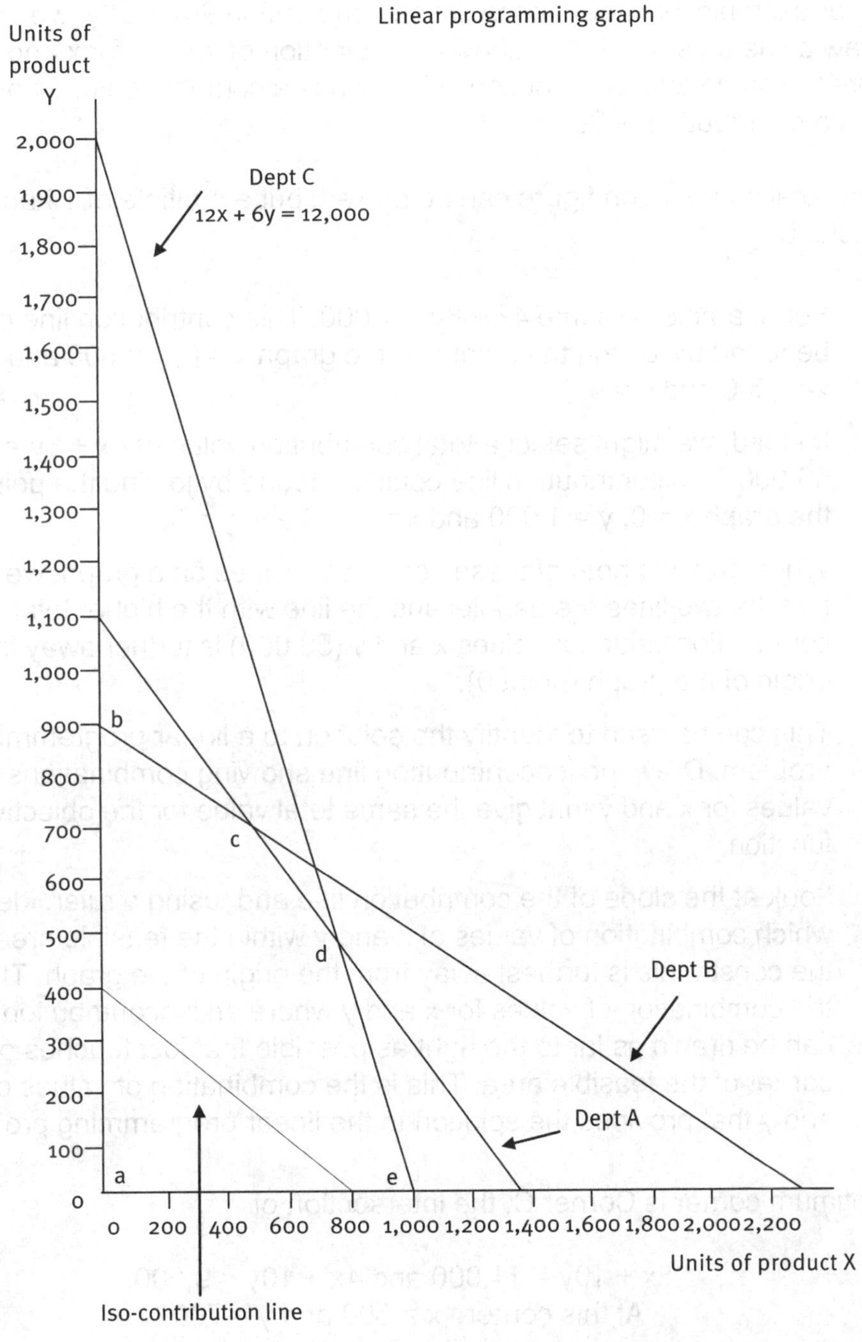

Step 5 : Finding the optimum solution - Using the isocontribution line

We do not know the maximum value of the objective function; however, we can draw an isocontribution (or 'profit') line that shows all the combinations of x and y that provide the same total value for the objective function.

If, for example, we need to maximise contribution \$4x + \$8y, we can draw a line on a graph that shows combination of values for x and y that give the same total contribution, when x has a contribution of \$4 and y has a contribution of \$8.

Any total contribution figure can be picked, but a multiple of \$4 and \$8 is easiest.

- For example, assume 4x + 8y = 4,000. This contribution line could be found by joining the points on the graph x = 0, y = 500 and x=1,000 and y = 0.
- Instead, we might select a total contribution value of 4x + 8y = \$8,000.This contribution line could be found by joining the points on the graph x = 0, y = 1,000 and x= 2,000 and y = 0.
- When drawing both of these contribution lines on a graph, we find that the two lines are parallel and the line with the higher total contribution value for values x and y (\$8,000) is further away from the origin of the graph (point 0).
- This can be used to identify the solution to a linear programming problem. Draw the isocontribution line showing combinations of values for x and y that give the same total value for the objective function.
- Look at the slope of the contribution line and, using a ruler, identify which combination of values of x and y within the feasible area for the constraints is furthest away from the origin of the graph. This is the combination of values for x and y where an isocontribution line can be drawn as far to the right as possible that just touches one corner of the feasible area. This is the combination of values of x and y that provides the solution to the linear programming problem.

Optimum corner is Corner C, the intersection of:

8x + 10y = 11,000 and 4x + 10y = 9,000
At this corner, x = 500 and y = 700.

The optimum production plan is to produce 500 units of Product X and 700 units of Product Y; The contribution at this point is maximised C = (500 x \$4) + (700 x \$8) = \$7,600.

Test your understanding 2 - Steps 1 to 3

Hebrus Inc manufactures summerhouses and garden sheds. Each product passes through a cutting process and an assembly process. One summerhouse, which makes a contribution of $50, takes six hours' cutting time and four hours' assembly time; while one shed makes a contribution of $40, and takes three hours' cutting time and eight hours' assembly time. There is a maximum of 36 cutting hours available each week and 48 assembly hours.

Cutters are paid $10 per hour and assembly workers $15 per hour.

Required:

Formulate the linear programming problem.

Step 4: Drawing the graph and identifying the feasible region

Drawing the graph

- Step 4 of the linear programming model is to represent the constraints as straight lines on a graph.
- In order to plot the constraints it is normally best to compute the intercepts of the equalities on the horizontal and vertical axes. Thus, x and y are each set equal to zero in turn and the value of y and x computed in these circumstances.

Revision of graphing a straight line

Step 4 of the linear programming model is to represent the constraints as straight lines on a graph. We do this below. In the meantime, this section contains basic revision for students who are not familiar with the process of graphing a straight line.

To begin with, we must have a linear relationship between two measurements.

Examples	y	=	3x + 1
	y	=	2x + 42 etc.

Note:

(1) To recognise a linear relationship the equation must have only 'x' not 'x' to the power of anything, e.g. x^2.

(2) A straight line has two characteristics:

(i) a slope or gradient – which measures the 'steepness' of the line

(ii) a point at which it cuts the y axis – this is called the intercept:

y = (slope × x) + intercept

e.g. y = 2x + 3

Therefore, the gradient is 2 and the point at which the line cuts the y axis is 3.

To draw a straight line graph we only need to know two points that can then be joined.

Consider the following two equations:

(i) y = 2x + 3

(ii) y = 2x - 2

In order to draw the graphs of these equations it is necessary to decide on two values for x and then to calculate the corresponding values for y. Let us use x = 0 and 3. These calculations are best displayed in tabular form.

(i) (x=0, y=3) and (x=3, y=9)

(ii) (x=0, y=-2) and (x=3, y=4)

So to draw the first line we plot the points (0, 3) and (3, 9) and simply join them up. Similarly, for the second line we plot the points (0, -2) and (3, 4) and join them up.

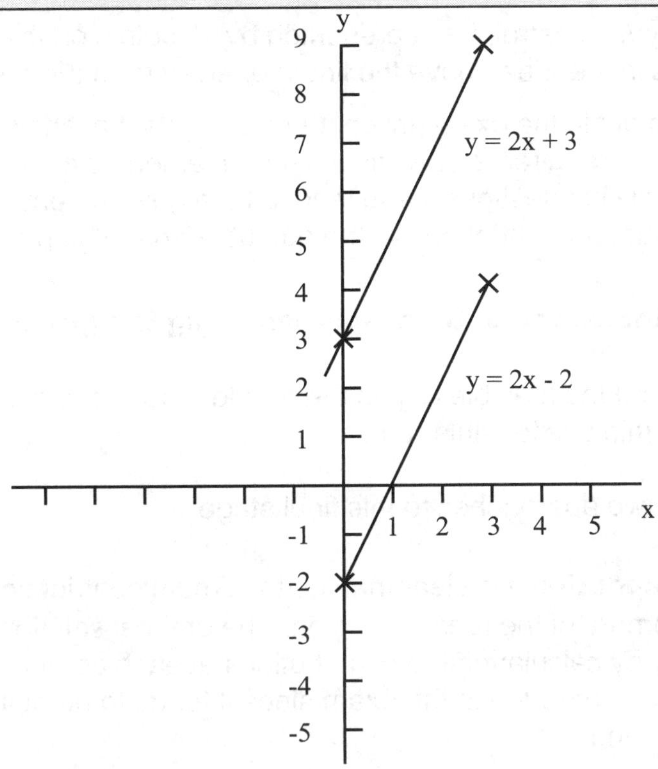

Note: The lines are parallel because the equations have the same gradient of 2.

Test your understanding 3 - Step 4

Using the information from the Hebrus example (TYU 2) you are required to plot the constraints on a graph and indicate on the graph the feasible region.

Identifying the feasible region

- Having inserted the straight lines in the graph, we are then ready to work out what is called the feasible region.
- The feasible region shows those combinations of variables which are possible given the resource constraints.
- In the TYU above the original constraints were '≤' types, so the feasible region is shown by the area bounded by the thick black line on the graph. Production can be anywhere in this area.
- The lines drawn on the graph represent equations where the LHS equals the RHS. However, the original constraint was either '≤' or '≥'.
- A '≤' type constraint is represented by all points on the line AND all points in the area below the line (i.e. nearer to the origin - the point x=0,y=0)

- A '≥' type constraint is represented by all points on the line AND all points in the area above the line (i.e. away from the origin).
- Watch out in the examination for constraints that show minimum amounts required as well as maximum amounts of constraints available. Typically in questions these tend to be a government quota that a minimum amount of one of the output needs to be produced.

Step 5: Finding the optimal solution using the graph

Having found the feasible region the problem now is to find the optimal solution within this feasible region.

There are two approaches to this final stage.

- **By inspection** it is clear that the maximum contribution will lie on one of the corners of the feasible region. The optimal solution can be reached simply by calculating the contributions at each corner. This approach is not recommended in the exam since it tends to be quite time consuming.
- **By drawing an iso-contribution line** (an objective function for a particular value of C), which is a line where all points represent an equal contribution. This is the recommended approach, particularly for more complex problems.

Test your understanding 4 - Steps 5 and 6

Using the Hebrus example again (TYU 2 and 3) you are required to find the optimal solution using the graph (Step 5).

Calculate the contribution at this point (Step 6).

Solving the problem using simultaneous equations

You may consider that the whole process would be easier by solving the constraints as sets of simultaneous equations and not bothering with a graph. This is possible and you may get the right answer, but such a technique should be used with caution and is not recommended until you have determined graphically which constraints are effective in determining the optimal solution.

Furthermore, if the question asks for a graphical solution, then a graph must be used.

The technique can, however, be used as a check, or to establish the exact quantities for the optimal solution when the graph does not give sufficient accuracy.

Test your understanding 5 - Simultaneous equations

Using the Hebrus example again (TYU 2 - 4) you are required to use simultaneous equations to verify the optimal point.

Test your understanding 6 - Additional example

Alfred Co is preparing its production plan for the coming month. It manufactures two products, the flak trap and the sap trap. Details are as follows.

	Product		**Price/wage rate**
	Flak trap	**Sap trap**	
amount/unit			
selling price ($)	125	165	
raw material (kg)	6	4	$5/kg
labour hours:			
skilled	10	10	$3/hour
semi-skilled	5	25	$3/hour

The company's fixed overhead absorption rate (OAR) is $1/labour hour (for both skilled and semi-skilled labour). The supply of skilled labour is limited to 2,000 hours/month and the supply of semi-skilled labour is limited to 2,500 hours/month. At the selling prices indicated, maximum demand for flak traps is expected to be 150 units/month and the maximum demand for sap traps is expected to be 80 units/month.

Required:

(a) Formulate the constraints for Alfred Co

(b) Plot the constraints on a graph and indicate on the graph the feasible region.

(c) Using the graph find the optimal production plan.

(d) Use simultaneous equations to accurately calculate the quantities produced at the optimal point and calculate the maximum contribution at this point.

Test your understanding 7 – Minimising costs

J Farms Ltd can buy two types of fertiliser which contain the following percentage of chemicals:

	Nitrates	Phosphates	Potash
Type X	18	5	2
Type Y	3	2	5

For a certain crop the following minimum quantities (kg) are required:

Nitrates 100 Phosphates 50 Potash 40

Type X costs £10 per kg and type Y costs £5 per kg. J Farms Ltd currently buys 1,000 kg of each type and wishes to minimise its expenditure on fertilisers.

(a) Write down the objective function and the constraints for J Farms Ltd.

(b) Draw a graph to illustrate all the constraints (equations/ inequalities), shading the feasible region.

(c) Recommend the quantity of each type of fertiliser which should be bought and the cost of these amounts.

(d) Find the saving J Farms Ltd can make by switching from its current policy to your recommendation.

Limiting factor analysis – discussion aspects

Assumptions

- There is a single quantifiable objective – e.g. maximise contribution. In reality there may be multiple objectives such as maximising return while simultaneously minimising risk.
- Each product always uses the same quantity of the scarce resource per unit. In reality this may not be the case. For example, learning effects may be enjoyed.
- The contribution per unit is constant. In reality this may not be the case:
  - the selling price may have to be lowered to sell more
  - there may be economies of scale, for example a discount for buying in bulk.

- Products are independent – in reality:
  - customers may expect to buy both products together
  - the products may be manufactured jointly together.
- The scenario is short term. This allows us to ignore fixed costs.

The assumptions apply to the analysis used when there is one limiting factor or if there are multiple limiting factors.

Shadow prices and slack

Slack

Slack is the amount by which a resource is under-utilised. It will occur when the optimum point does not fall on a given resource line.

Slack is important because unused resources can be put to another use, e.g. hired out to another manufacturer.

e.g

Illustration 2 - Slack

In the Hebrus example (TYU 2-5), the optimum point Q lies on both the cutting and assembly time lines. Therefore both resources are fully utilised and are referred to as critical constraints.

In the Alfred Co example (TYU 6), the optimum point D lies on the intersection of the skilled labour line (10x + 10y = 2,000) and the maximum demand line for flak traps (x = 150). At this point there is unutilised semi-skilled labour. This means that slack exists for semi-skilled labour. Semi-skilled labour is a non-critical constraint and this unutilised resource should be used elsewhere in the business to generate contribution.

Shadow (or dual) prices

- The shadow price of a resource can be found by calculating the increase in value (usually extra contribution) which would be created by having available one additional unit of a limiting resource at its original cost.
- It therefore represents the maximum premium that the firm should be willing to pay for one extra unit of each constraint. This aspect is discussed in more detail below.
- Non-critical constraints will have zero shadow prices as slack exists already.

Calculating shadow prices

The simplest way to calculate shadow prices for a critical constraint is as follows:

Step 1: Take the equations of the straight lines that intersect at the optimal point. Add one unit to the constraint concerned, while leaving the other critical constraint unchanged.

Step 2: Use simultaneous equations to derive a new optimal solution

Step 3: Calculate the revised optimal contribution. The increase is the shadow price for the constraint under consideration.

Test your understanding 8 - Shadow prices

In Hebrus the optimal solution was determined to be x=4 and y=4 giving an optimal contribution of $360. This solution was at the intersection of the lines:

Cutting	$6x + 3y$	=	36
Assembly	$4x + 8y$		48

Required:

Suppose one extra hour was available for the cutting process. Calculate the shadow price for this additional hour of cutting time.

Additional example on shadow prices

Using the following data, calculate the shadow price for machining time.

Maximise $C = 80x + 75y$ (contribution), subject to

(i) $20x + 25y \leq 500$ (machining time)

(ii) $40x + 25y \leq 800$ (finishing time)

The optimal solution at the intersection of the above constraints is: $x = 15$, $y = 8$.

Solution

Step 1: Machining time – the constraints become:

(i) $20x + 25y \leq 501$

(ii) $40x + 25y \leq 800$

Step 2: Subtracting (i) from (ii) gives $20x = 299$ and thus $x = 14.95$

Inserting into (i) gives

$(20 \times 14.95) + 25y = 501$

$25y = 202$

$y = 8.08$

Step 3: Original contribution = (15 × \$80) + (8 × \$75) = \$1,800.

Amended contribution = (14.95 × \$80) + (8.08 × \$75) = \$1,802.

The shadow price per machine hour is thus \$2.

Implications of shadow prices

- Management can use shadow prices as a measure of the maximum premium that they would be willing to pay for one more unit of the scarce resource.
- However, the shadow price should be considered carefully. For example, the shadow price of labour may be calculated as \$20 per hour. However, it may be possible to negotiate a lower shadow price than this.
- In addition, if more of the critical constraint is obtained, the constraint line will move outwards altering the shape of the feasible region. After a certain point there will be little point in buying more of the scarce resource since any non-critical constraints will become critical.

Additional example on linear programming

Suppose a linear programming problem gives the following results.

Constraint	Normal cost	Shadow price
Skilled labour	\$20/hour	\$12/hour
Unskilled labour	\$10/hour	zero
Materials	\$5/kg	\$3/kg

Required:

(a) Which two constraints give rise to the optimal solution?

(b) Overtime is paid at 'time-and-a-half'. Is it worth paying overtime to help relax constraints?

(c) A new product has been proposed with the following proposed costs and revenues.

	$
Selling price	80
Skilled labour – 2 hours@$20/hour	(40)
Unskilled labour – 1 hour@$10/hour	(10)
Materials – 3kg@$5/kg	(15)
Profit per unit	15

Assuming that the constraints cannot be relaxed, should the new product be manufactured?

Solution

(a) Critical constraints have non-zero dual prices, so the optimal solution will be at the intersection of skilled labour and materials.

(b) For skilled labour overtime will cost $30 per hour and the benefit will be 20+12=$32 per hour. The overtime is thus worth while and will generate a net $2 per hour benefit.

For unskilled labour there is already slack so overtime is not worthwhile.

(c) The profit statement can be revised using as follows:

	$
Selling price	80
Skilled labour – 2 hours @ (20+12)	(64)
Unskilled labour – 1 hour @ 10	(10)
Materials – 3kg @ (5+3)	(24)
Loss per unit	(18)

Incorporating the contribution lost elsewhere by reallocating scarce resources, the new product is not viable.

4 Chapter summary

PLANNING WITH LIMITING FACTORS

ONE LIMITING FACTOR

KEY FACTOR ANALYSIS

Rank options using contribution per unit of limiting factor.

MULTIPLE LIMITING FACTORS

LINEAR PROGRAMMING

1. Define variables
2. Formulate objective
3. Formulate constraints
4. Draw graph and identify feasible region
5. Solve for optimal point
6. Answer question!

ASSUMPTIONS

- Single objective
- Constant selling price
- Constant variable cost per unit
- No economies of scale or learning effects
- Products are independent
- Short term.

SHADOW PRICES AND SLACK

- Critical constraints have no slack
- Shadow price = premium a firm is willing to pay for extra resources
- Only critical constraints have non-zero shadow prices
- Relevant cost = normal cost + shadow price.

Test your understanding answers

Test your understanding 1

Step 1: Identify the scarce resource (this may be done for you in examination questions).

At potential sales level:

	Sales potential units	Total machine hours	Total labour hours
Product A	4,000	40,000	4,800
Product B	6,000	72,000	4,800
Product C	6,000	84,000	2,400
		196,000	**12,000**

Thus, labour hours are the limiting factor.

Step 2: calculate the contribution per unit for each product.

This has been done for us in the question

Step 3: calculate the contribution per unit of the scarce resource for each product, i.e. per labour hour

Product A $6/ 1.2= $5.00

Product B $5/0.8= $6.25

Product C $4/0.4= $10.00

Step 4: rank the products in order of the contribution per unit of the scarce resource.

Thus, production should be concentrated first on C, up to the maximum available sales, then B, and finally A.

However, a minimum of 1,000 units of A must be produced.

Step 5: allocate resources using this ranking and answer the question, i.e. state the maximum contribution.

Taking these factors into account, the production schedule becomes:

	Units produced	**Labour hours**	**Cumulative labour hours**	**Limiting factor**
Product A	1,000	1,200	1,200	Policy to produce 1,000 units
Product C	6,000	2,400	3,600	Sales
Product B	1,750	1,400	5,000	Labour hours

The maximum contribution is therefore as follows.

	$
A (1,000 × $6)	6,000
B (1,750 × $5)	8,750
C (6,000 × $4)	24,000
	38,750

Test your understanding 2 - Steps 1 to 3

Step 1 – define the variables
Let x = the number of summerhouses produced each week

y = the number of garden sheds produced each week.

(**Note:** Be careful to specify the time periods involved.)

Step 2 – define and formulate the objective function.

The objective here is to maximise contribution C, given by:
Maximise Contribution = 50x + 40y

Step 3 – formulate the constraints.

The constraints (limitations) here are the amounts of cutting and assembly time available.

If 1 summerhouse requires 6 hours' cutting time,

x summerhouses require 6x hours' cutting time.

If 1 shed requires 3 hours' cutting time,

y sheds require 3y hours' cutting time.

Hence total cutting time required = 6x + 3y hours.

Similarly, if one summerhouse and one shed require 4 and 8 hours' assembly time respectively, the total assembly time for x summerhouses and y sheds will be 4x + 8y.

The conventional way of setting out the constraints is to place the units **utilised** on the left, and those **available** on the right; the inequality sign is the link.

Constraint		**Utilised**		**Available**
Cutting time	(i)	6x + 3y	≤	36
Assembly time	(ii)	4x + 8y	≤	48

In addition, two other logical constraints must be stated, i.e. $x \geq 0$ and $y \geq 0$

These simply state that negative amounts of garden sheds or summerhouses cannot be made.

Test your understanding 3 - Step 4

The cutting time constraint is an inequality 6x + 3y ≤ 36 which represents a region on the graph. To identify this region we draw the line 6x + 3y = 36 (equality) and then determine which side of the line is feasible. This process is repeated for each constraint.

For the equation 6x + 3y = 36 – cutting time constraint

when x = 0, y = 36/3 = 12

when y = 0, x =36/6 = 6

To graph this constraint, we draw a straight line between the points (0, 12) and (6, 0).

For the equation 4x + 8y = 48 – assembly time constraint

when x = 0, y = 48/8 = 6

when y = 0, x =48/4 = 12

To graph this constraint, we draw a straight line between the points (0, 6) and (12, 0).

The constraints can now be represented graphically:

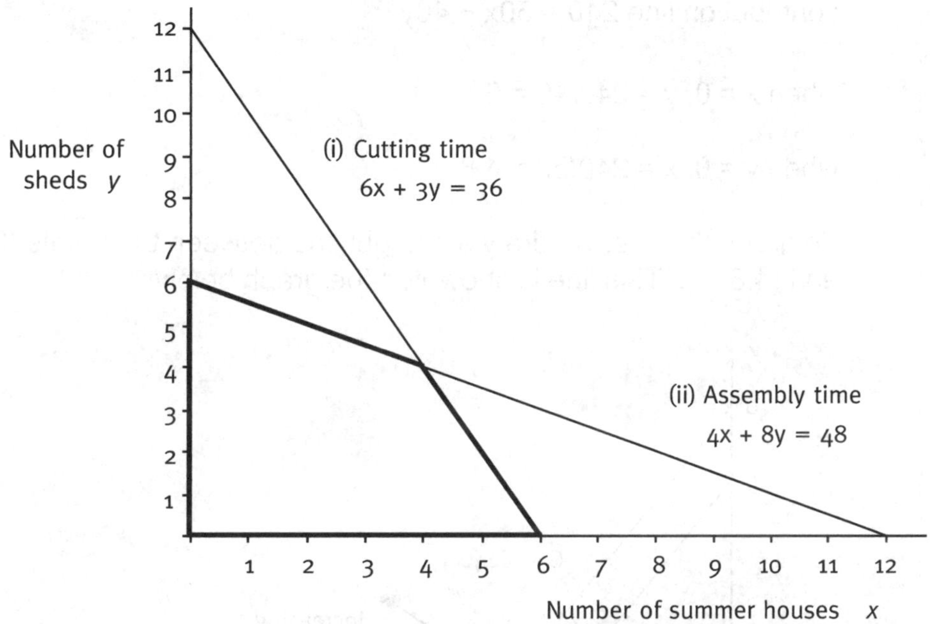

The original constraints were '≤' types, so the feasible region is shown by the area bounded by the thick black line on the graph. Production can be anywhere in this area.

Test your understanding 4 - Steps 5 and 6

Step 5: Finding the optimal solution using the graph.

Let's first consider what we mean by an iso-contribution line.

An iso-contribution line is a line where all the points represent an equal contribution.

The contribution for Hebrus is given by the equation, C = 50x + 40y (from Step 2).

- If we choose a contribution of, say, \$200 we can draw an iso-contribution line 200 = 50x + 40y

  when x = 0, y = 200/40 = 5

  when y = 0, x = 200/50 = 4

  To graph the line, we draw a straight line between the points (0, 5) and (4, 0). This line is shown on the graph below.

- If we choose another contribution of, say, \$240 we can draw an iso-contribution line 240 = 50x + 40y

  when x = 0, y = 240/40 = 6

  when y = 0, x = 240/50 = 4.8

  To graph the line, we draw a straight line between the points (0, 6) and (4.8, 0). This line is shown on the graph below.

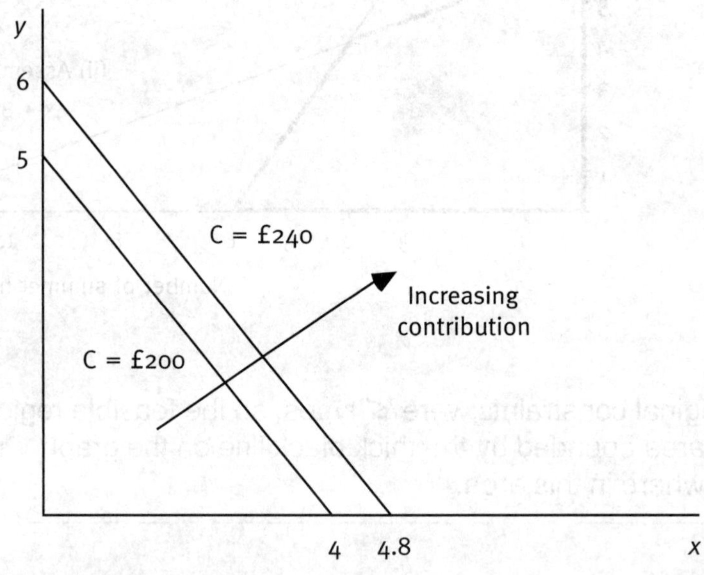

The iso-contribution lines move to and from the origin in parallel; the arrow indicates increasing contribution. The object is to get on the highest contribution line within (just touching) the binding constraints.

The optimum point is found by drawing an example of an iso-contribution line on the diagram (any convenient value of C will do), and then placing a ruler against it. Then, by moving the ruler away from the origin (in the case of a maximisation problem) or towards the origin (in the case of a minimisation problem) but keeping it parallel to the iso-contribution line, the last corner of the feasible solution space which is met represents the optimum solution.

To find the optimal point for Hebrus we have used an iso-contribution line for a contribution of $165. However, either of the iso-contribution lines discussed above, or another iso-contribution line, could have been used instead.

$165 = 50x + 40y$

when $x = 0$, $y = 165/40 = 4.125$

when $y = 0$, $x = 165/50 = 3.3$

To graph the line, we draw a straight line between the points (0, 4.125) and (3.3, 0). This line is shown on the graph below.

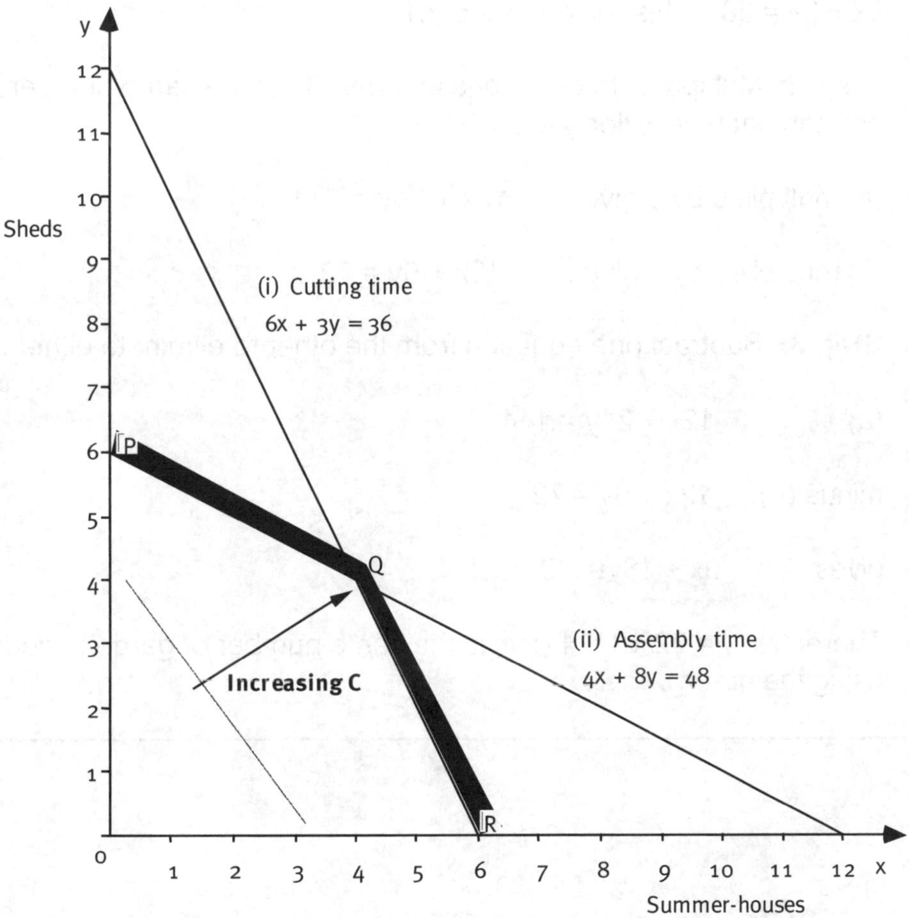

Optimal point: The highest available iso-contribution line occurs at point Q.

Step 6: Answer the question, i.e. calculate the contribution at the optimal point.

Reading from the graph, at point Q x = 4 and y = 4. This gives a maximum contribution of C = (50 × 4) + (40 × 4) = $360.

Test your understanding 5 - Simultaneous equations

Step 1: Take the equations of the two constraints that cross at the optimal point.

The optimal point is point Q. This is at the intersection of the two constraint lines:

4x + 8y = 48 this will be called (a)

6x + 3y = 36 this will be called (b)

Step 2: Multiply both equations in order to get the same number of x's or y's in each equation

(a) multiplied by 3 gives 12x + 24y = 144

(b) multiplied by 2 gives 12x + 6y = 72

Step 3: Subtract one equation from the other to eliminate either x or y

(a) 12x + 24y = 144

minus (b) 12x + 6y = 72

gives 0x + 18y = 72

Therefore, y = 72/18 = 4 (this is the same number of garden sheds found using the graph).

Step 4: Use any equation to find the missing value, i.e. either x or y

Using the value y=4 we can find the value of x. Any of the equations above can be used. For example:

4x + 8y = 48

4x + (8 × 4) = 48

4x = 16

x = 16/ 4 = 4 (this is the same number of summerhouses found using the graph.

Step 5: Answer the question

The optimal point is at x=4 and y=4. This gives a maximum contribution of C = (50 × 4) + (40 × 4) = $360 (as per TYU4).

Test your understanding 6 - Additional example

(a) **Step 1: define variables**

Let x = the number of units of flak traps produced per month.

y = the number of units of sap traps produced per month.

Step 2: objective function

The objective is to maximise contribution, C, given by C = 50x+ 40y (Working)

Working:

Contribution per flak trap = 125 — (6 × 5) — (10 × 3) — (5 × 3) = 50

Contribution per sap trap = 165 — (4 × 5) — (10 × 3) — (25 × 3) = 40

Step 3: constraints

Skilled labour	10x + 10y	≤	2,000
Semi-skilled labour	5x + 25y	≤	2,500
Max demand	x	≤	150
	y	≤	80
Non-negativity	x,y	≥	0

(b) **Step 4: draw a graph and identify the feasible region**

Skilled labour: x = 0, y = 2,000/10 = 200

y = 0, x = 2,000/10 = 200

We simply join up the points (0, 200) and (200, 0).

Semi-skilled labour: x = 0, y = 2,500/25 = 100

y = 0, x = 2,500/5 = 500

We join up the points (0, 100) and (500, 0)

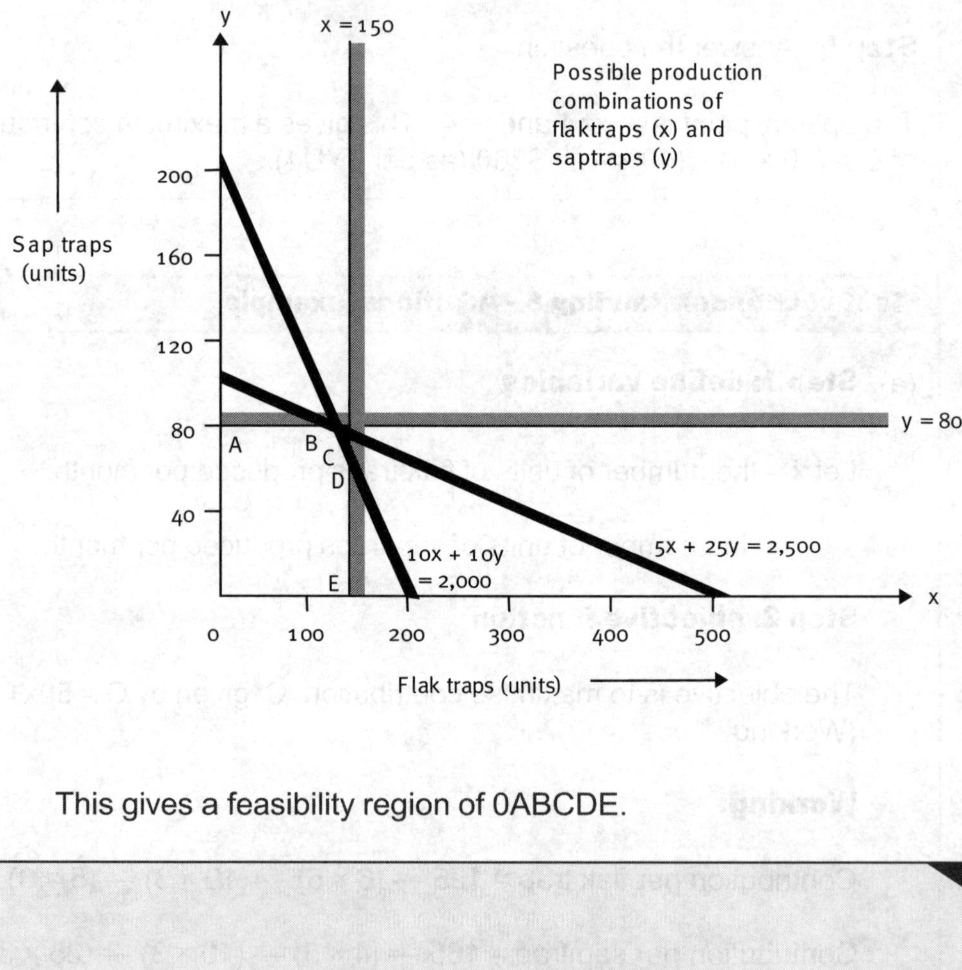

This gives a feasibility region of 0ABCDE.

(c) **Step 5: use the graph to solve the optimal production plan**

Objective is to maximise contribution C = 50x + 40y.

The iso-contribution line C=2,000 has been drawn to establish the gradient and identify the optimal solution at point D:

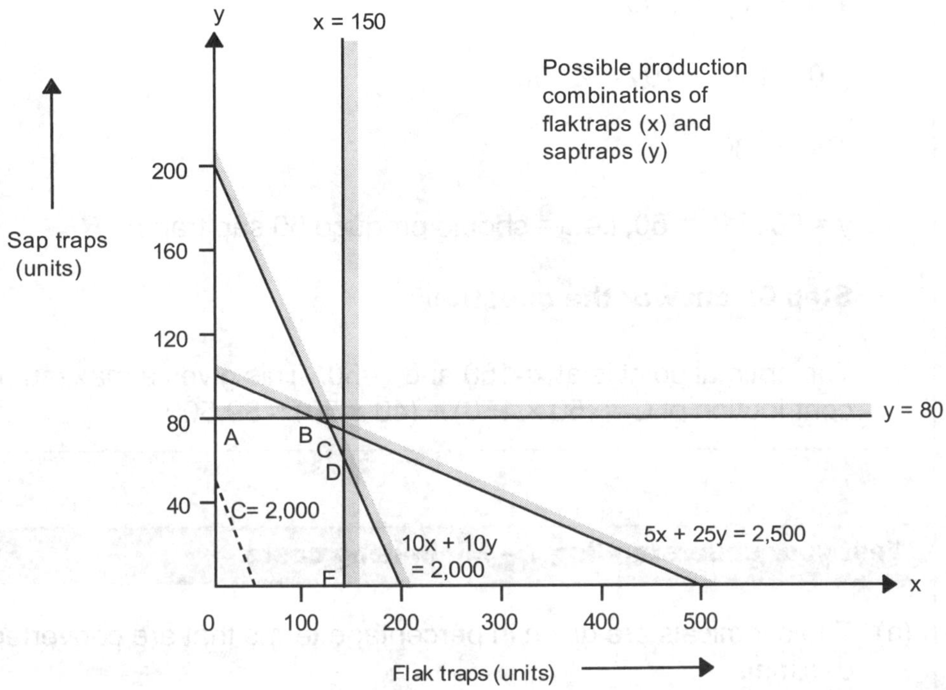

It is difficult to read the precise co-ordinates for point D but it is at the intersection of the two lines x = 150 and 10x + 10y = 2,000. This corresponds to 150 units of x (flak traps) and approximately 50-60 units of y (sap traps). The exact amounts can be found using simultaneous equations (see below).

(d) **Use simultaneous equations to accurately calculate the quantities produced at the optimal point and calculate the maximum contribution at this point.**

Take the equations of the two constraints that cross at the optimal point.

The optimal point is point D. This is at the intersection of the two constraint lines:

x = 150 this will be called (a)

10x + 10y = 2,000 this will be called (b)

Find the value of x

The solution is slightly easier here since we already know that x = 150, i.e. we should produce 150 flak traps.

Use any equation to find the missing value, i.e y

Using the value x=150 we can find the value of y.

$10x + 10y = 2,000$

$(10 \times 150) + 10y = 2,000$

$10y = 500$

$y = 500/ 10 = 50$, i.e we should produce 50 sap traps

Step 6: answer the question

The optimal point is at x=150 and y=50. This gives a maximum contribution of $C = (50 \times 150) + (40 \times 50) = \$9,500$

Test your understanding 7 – Minimising costs

(a) The chemicals are given in percentage terms that are converted to decimals.

Step 1: define the variables

Let x = number of kg of X purchased

Let y = number of kg of Y purchased

Step 2: define and formulate the objective function

Total cost: $z = 10x + 5y$, the objective function which has to be minimised.

Step 3: formulate the constraints

The constraints exist on the chemical composition of the fertilisers:

Nitrates:	$0.18x + 0.03y$	≥	100
Phosphates:	$0.05x + 0.02y$	≥	50
Potash:	$0.02x + 0.05y$	≥	40
Non-negativity:	$x \geq 0, y \geq 0$		

(b) **Step 4: draw the graph and identify the feasible region**

In this example, all the points where the lines cut the axes are required, so that the easiest way to draw the constraints is to calculate these points.

Constraint	End points	
0.18x + 0.03y = 100	x = 0, y = 100/0.03 = 3,333.3	y = 0, x = 100/0.18 = 555.5
0.05x + 0.02y = 50	x = 0, y = 50/0.02 = 2,500	y = 0, x = 50/0.05 = 1,000
0.02x + 0.05y = 40	x = 0, y = 40/0.05 = 800	y = 0, x = 40/0.02 = 2,000

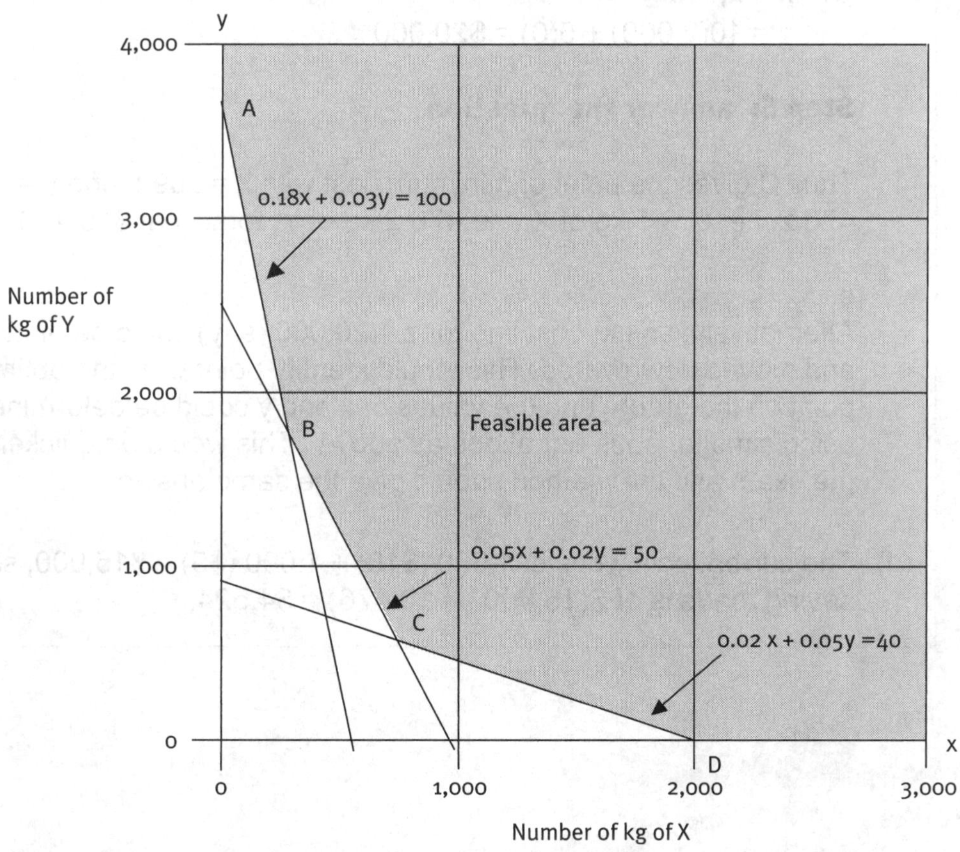

(c) **Step 5: find the optimal solution using the graph**

The inspection method has been used here, for illustration purposes only.

Considering the vertices (i.e. corners) of the feasible area.

A: x = 0 y = 3,333.3
z = 10x + 5y = 10(0) + 5(3,333.3) = $16,666.50

B: Solving 0.18x + 0.03y = 100 and 0.05x + 0.02y = 50
gives x = 238.1 and y = 1,904.8
z = 10(238.1) + 5(1,904.8) = $11,905

C: Solving 0.05x + 0.02y = 50 and 0.02x + 0.05y = 40
gives x = 809.5 and y = 476.2
z = 10(809.5) = 5(476.2) = $10,476

D: x = 2,000 y = 0
z = 10(2,000) + 5(0) = $20,000

Step 6: answer the question

Thus C gives the point of minimum cost with x = 809.5 and y = 476.2, i.e. 809.5 kg of X and 476.2 kg of Y, total cost $10,476.

or:
Alternatively, an iso-cost line for z = 20,000 (say) could be plotted and moved downwards. This would identify point C as the optimum point on the graph, and the values of x and y could be determined using simultaneous equations as above. This would be quicker in the exam and the method should give the same answer.

(d) The current policy costs: 1,000 ($10) + 1,000 ($5) = $15,000, so the saving made is of $(15,000 — 10,476) = $4,524.

Test your understanding 8 - Shadow prices

Step 1: Take the equations of the straight lines that intersect at the optimal point. Add one unit to the constraint concerned, while leaving the other critical constraint unchanged.

We would then need to solve:

Cutting	6x + 3y	=	37
Assembly	4x + 8y	=	48

Step 2: Use simultaneous equations to derive a new optimal solution

The simultaneous equations above can be solved in the same way as was seen in the previous TYU's. This gives and optimum vale of y = 3.888… and x = 4.222…

Step 3: Calculate the revised optimal contribution. The increase is the shadow price for the constraint under consideration.

The contribution. C = 50x + 40y.

At the revised optimal point this gives a revised contribution of C = (50 × 4.222…) + (40 × 3.888…) = $366.67 .

The increase of $6.67 ($366.67 - $360) is the shadow price for cutting time per hour. This represents the premium that the firm would be willing to pay for each extra hour of cutting time. The current cost is $10 per hour and therefore the maximum price that would be paid for an extra hour of cutting time is $16.67.

Note: A similar calculation can be done for assembly time giving a shadow price of $2.50 per hour.

The shadow price [illegible]

Step 1: Take the equations of the straight lines that intersect at the optimal point. Add one unit to the constraint concerned, while leaving the other constraint unchanged.

We would then need to solve:

Cutting	[illegible] + 4y	=	8[illegible]
Assembly	4x + 3y	=	48

Step 2: Use simultaneous equations to derive a new optimal solution.

The simultaneous equations above can be solved in the same way as seen in the previous example. The values of x and y [illegible] 4.688 [illegible]

Step 3: Calculate the revised optimal contribution. The increase is the shadow price for the constraint under consideration.

The contribution C = 50x + 40y

At the revised optimal point this gives a revised contribution of C = [illegible] = $38[illegible]

The increase of [illegible] is the shadow price for cutting time per hour. This represents the maximum the firm would be willing to pay for each extra hour of cutting time. [illegible] therefore the maximum price that would be paid for an extra hour of cutting time is [illegible]

Note: A similar calculation can be done for assembly time giving a shadow price of $2.50 per hour.

chapter

4

Pricing

Chapter learning objectives

Upon completion of this chapter you will be able to:

- explain the factors that influence the pricing of a product or service, e.g. costs, demand and competition
- define and explain the price elasticity of demand
- from supplied data, derive and manipulate a straight-line demand equation
- from supplied data, derive an equation for the total cost function excluding or including volume-based discounts
- using data supplied or equations derived, advise on whether or not to increase production and sales levels considering incremental costs, incremental revenues and other factors
- explain, using a simple example, all forms of cost-plus pricing strategy
- calculate, for given data, a price using a cost-plus strategy
- explain different pricing strategies
- identify suitable pricing strategies for given situations from skimming, penetration, complementary product, product-line, volume discounting
- explain, using a simple example, a price-discrimination pricing strategy
- explain, using a simple example, a relevant-cost pricing strategy
- calculate, for given data, a price using a relevant cost strategy.

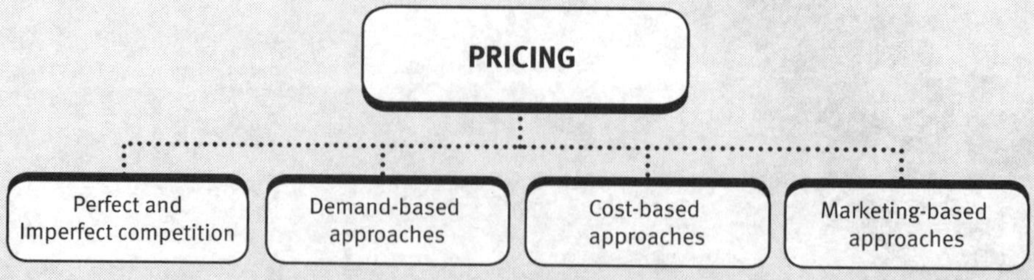

1 Introduction

Pricing is important because:

- It makes a pivotal contribution to profit maximisation – the overriding aim of most businesses.
- Businesses make profits by selling goods and services at a price higher than their cost.
- The amount that they are able to sell will often be determined by the price charged for the goods and services.

2 Different types of market structures

The price that a business can charge for its products or services will be determined by the market in which it operates.

In a **perfectly competitive** market, every buyer or seller is a 'price taker', and no participant influences the price of the product it buys or sells. Other characteristics of a perfectly competitive market include:

- **Zero Entry/Exit Barriers** – It is relatively easy to enter or exit as a business in a perfectly competitive market.
- **Perfect Information** - Prices and quality of products are assumed to be known to all consumers and producers.
- **Companies aim to maximise profits** - Firms aim to sell where marginal costs meet marginal revenue, where they generate the most profit.
- **Homogeneous Products** – The characteristics of any given market good or service do not vary across suppliers.

Imperfect competition refers to the market structure that does not meet the conditions of perfect competition. Its forms include :

- **Monopoly**, in which there is only one seller of a good. The seller dominates many buyers and can use its market power to set a profit-maximising price. Microsoft is usually considered a monopoly.

- **Oligopoly**, in which a few companies dominate the market and are inter-dependent : firms must take into account likely reactions of their rivals to any change in price, output or forms of non-price competition. For example, in the UK, four companies (Tesco, Asda, Sainsbury's and Morrisons) share 74.4% of the grocery market.
- **Monopolistic competition**, in which products are similar, but not identical. There are many producers ('price setters') and many consumers in a given market, but no business has total control over the market price.

e.g

Illustration 1 - Monopolistic competition

For example, there are many different brands of soap on the market today. Each brand of soap is similar because it is designed to get the user clean; however, each soap product tries to differentiate itself from the competition to attract consumers. One soap might claim that it leaves you with soft skin, while another that it has a clean, fresh scent. Each participant in this market structure has some control over pricing, which means it can alter the selling price as long as consumers are still willing to buy its product at the new price. If one product costs twice as much as similar products on the market, chances are most consumers will avoid buying the more expensive product and buy the competitors' products instead. Monopolistic products are typically found in retailing businesses. Some examples of monopolistic products and/or services are shampoo products, extermination services, oil changes, toothpaste, and fast-food restaurants.

3 Three broad approaches to pricing

Pricing decisions may be separated into three broad approaches :

(1) Demand-based approaches

(2) Cost-based approaches

(3) Marketing-based approaches

4 Demand-based approaches (The Economists' Viewpoint)

Most firms recognise that there exists a relationship between the selling price of their product or service and the demand. This relationship can often be described by an inverse, linear relationship:

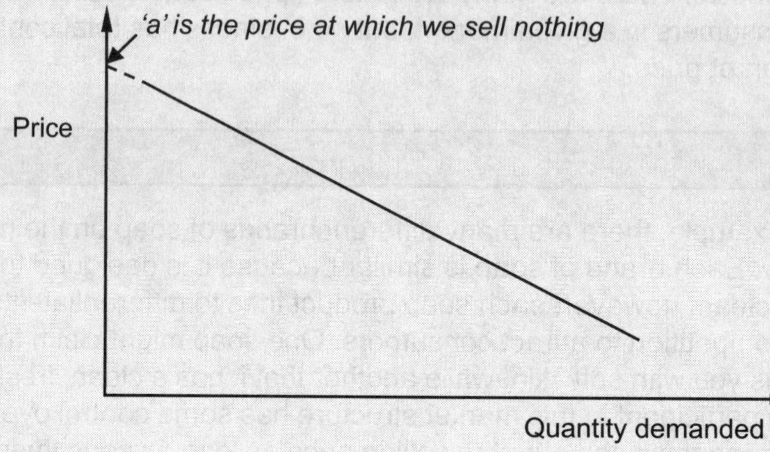

By investigating and analysing this relationship it is possible (in theory) to establish an optimum price, i.e. a price that will maximise profits. There are two methods of solution to problems investigating the relationship between price and demand: the tabular approach and the algebraic approach.

e.g

Illustration 2 - Tabular Approach

XYZ Ltd is introducing a new product. The company intends to hire machinery to manufacture the product at a cost of $200,000 per annum. However, this will only enable 60,000 units per annum to be produced, although additional machines can be hired at $80,000 per annum.

Each machine hired enables capacity to be increased by 20,000 units per annum, but it is not possible to increase production beyond 90,000 units because of shortage of space.

The minimum rental period is for one year and the variable cost is estimated to be $6 per unit produced.

There are no other fixed costs that can be specifically traced to the product. Marketing management has estimated the maximum selling prices for a range of output from 50,000 units to 90,000 units. The estimates are as follows:

Units sold	50,000	60,000	70,000	80,000	90,000	90,000 (*)
Selling Price ($)	22	20	19	18	17	15

(*) At $15 demand will be in excess of 90,000 units but production capacity will limit the sales.

What is the optimum price and quantity of units to output and sell (assume all units of production can be sold)?

Tabular Approach - Solution

Answer guide

	$	$	$	$	$	$
Price per unit	22	20	19	18	17	15
Variable cost per unit	6	6	6	6	6	6
Contribution per unit	16	14	13	12	11	9
Number of units sold	50,000	60,000	70,000	80,000	90,000	90,000
Total Contribution, in $000	800	840	910	960	990	810
Less Fixed costs, in $000	200	200	280	280	360	360
Net Profit in $000	600	640	630	680	630	450

Conclusion: To maximise profit, price should be $18, output 80,000 and one extra machine should be hired.

5 The algebraic approach

Economic theory states that the monopolist maximises profit when Marginal Cost = Marginal Revenue.

Illustration 3 - The MR= MC

Marginal Revenue is the additional revenue from selling one extra unit, for example :

Quantity	Price	Revenue	Marginal Revenue
1	$70	$70	$70
2	$60	$120	$50
3	$50	$150	$30
4	$40	$160	$10
5	$30	$150	$(10)

Marginal Cost is the cost from making one more unit. It is usually just the variable cost, e.g. MC = $30.

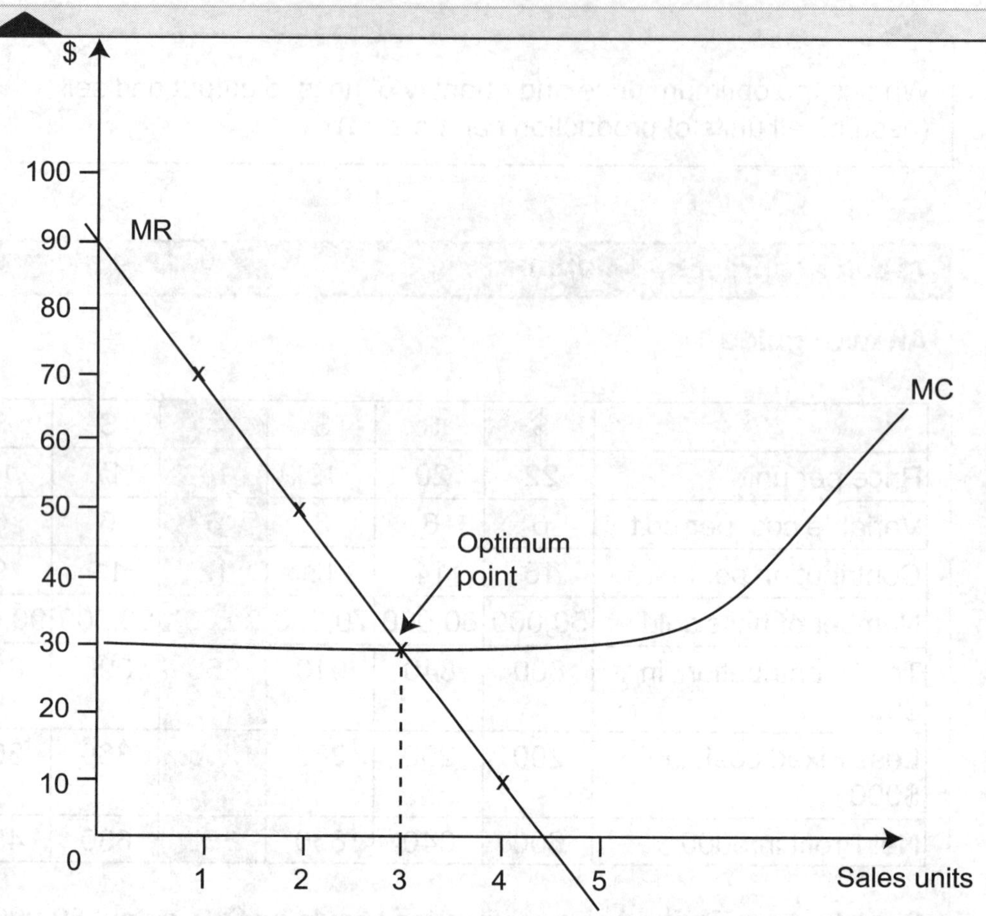

The optimum price is $50. At output less than Q = 3, the extra cost of making a unit is less than the extra revenue from selling it. At output greater than Q = 3, the extra costs of making a unit exceed the revenue from selling it.

6 Procedure for establishing the optimum price of a product

This is a general set of rules that can be applied to most questions involving algebra and pricing.

(1) Establish the linear relationship between price (P) and quantity demanded (Q). The equation will take the form:

$$P = a + bQ$$

where 'a' is the intercept and 'b' is the gradient of the line. As the price of a product increases, the quantity demanded will decrease. The equation of a straight line P= a + bQ can be used to show the demand for a product at a given price:

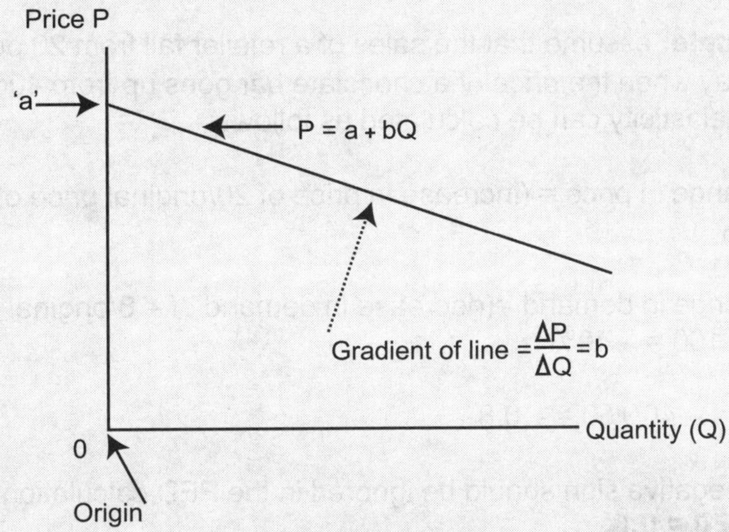

Note: 'b' is always negative because of the inverse relationship between price and quantity.

(2) Double the gradient to find the marginal revenue: **MR = a – 2bQ.**

(3) Establish the **marginal cost MC**. This will simply be the variable cost per unit.

(4) To maximise profit, **equate MC and MR** and solve to find Q.

(5) Substitute this value of Q into the price equation to find the optimum price.

(6) It may be necessary to calculate the maximum profit.

The price elasticity of demand

When a business proposes to change the price of a product or service the key question is: 'to what degree will demand be affected?'

Calculation

The price elasticity of demand measures the change in demand as a result of a change in its price.

It can be calculated as follows:

$$\text{Price elasticity of demand} = \frac{\text{Change in quantity demanded, as a percentage of demand}}{\text{Change in price, as a percentage of the price}}$$

Example: assume that the sales of a retailer fall from 20 per day to 12 per day when the price of a chocolate bar goes up from 40c to 60c. The price elasticity can be calculated as follows:

%change in price = (increase in price of 20/original price of 40) × 100 = +50%

%change in demand =(decrease in demand of – 8/original demand of 20) × 100 = – 40%

PED = – 40/+50 = – 0.8

The negative sign should be ignored in the PED calculation. Therefore the **PED = 0.8.**

Interpretation of PED

Elastic demand

If the % change in demand > the % change in price, then price elasticity > 1.

Demand is 'elastic', i.e. very responsive to changes in price.

- Total revenue increases when price is reduced.
- Total revenue decreases when price is increased.

Therefore, price increases are not recommended but price cuts are recommended.

Inelastic demand

If the % change in demand < the % change in price, then price elasticity < 1.

Demand is 'inelastic', i.e. not very responsive to changes in price.

- Total revenue decreases when price is reduced.
- Total revenue increases when price is increased.

Therefore, price increases are recommended but price cuts are not recommended.

Additional example on straight-line demand equation

(a) Find the linear relationship between price (P) and the quantity demanded (Q) in relation to the following sales and demand data:

- Selling price of \$300 = sales of 500 units per month.
- Selling price of \$330 = sales of 400 units per month.

(b) Using the price equation in (a) and assuming the variable cost per unit is \$90, calculate the optimum price and output.

(c) Calculate the maximum contribution.

Solution

a.

- P = a – bQ
- – b (gradient) = (330 – 300) ÷ (400 – 500) = – 0.3
- remembering that price (P) = 300 when 500 units are sold and substituting 0.3 for b
- 300 = a – (0.3 × 500)
- 300 = a – 150
- a = 300 + 150 = 450
- So the linear relationship (or demand function equation) is: P = 450 – 0.3Q.

(b) MR = 450 - 0.6Q
MC = VC so equating MR = MC: 90 = 450 - 0.6Q
So Q = 600
And substituting Q into Price function, P = \$270

(c) Contribution per unit = \$270 - \$90 = \$180
Total contribution = \$180 x 600 units = \$108,000

Test your understanding 1

Find the linear relationship between price (P) and the quantity demanded (Q), i.e. find the straight-line demand equation, in relation to the following sales and demand data:

- Selling price of $200 = sales of 1,000 units per month.
- Selling price of $220 = sales of 950 units per month.

Required:

(a) Use this equation to predict the quantity demanded per month if the selling price is $300.

(b) Using the price equation in (a) and assuming the variable cost per unit is $100, calculate the optimum price and output.

(c) Calculate the maximum contribution.

Test your understanding 2

The total fixed costs per annum for a company that makes one product are $100,000, and a variable cost of $64 is incurred for each additional unit produced and sold over a very large range of outputs.

The current selling price for the product is $160. At this price, 2,000 units are demanded per annum.

It is estimated that for each successive increase in price of $5 annual demand will be reduced by 50 units. Alternatively, for each $5 reduction in price, demand will increase by $50 units.

Required:

(a) Calculate the optimum output and price, assuming that if prices are set within each $5 range there will be a proportionate change in demand.

(b) Calculate the maximum profit.

7 Equation for the total cost function

Cost equations are derived from historical cost data. Once a cost equation has been established (using methods such as the high/low method which will be revised later in the course) it can be used to estimate future costs. In the exam, cost functions will be linear:

y = a + bx

- 'a' is the fixed cost per period (the intercept)
- 'b' is the variable cost per unit (the gradient)
- 'x' is the activity level (the independent variable)
- 'y' is the total cost = fixed cost + variable cost (the dependent variable).

Suppose a cost has a cost equation of y = $5,000 + 10x, this can be shown graphically as follows:

Graph of cost equation y = 5,000 + 10x

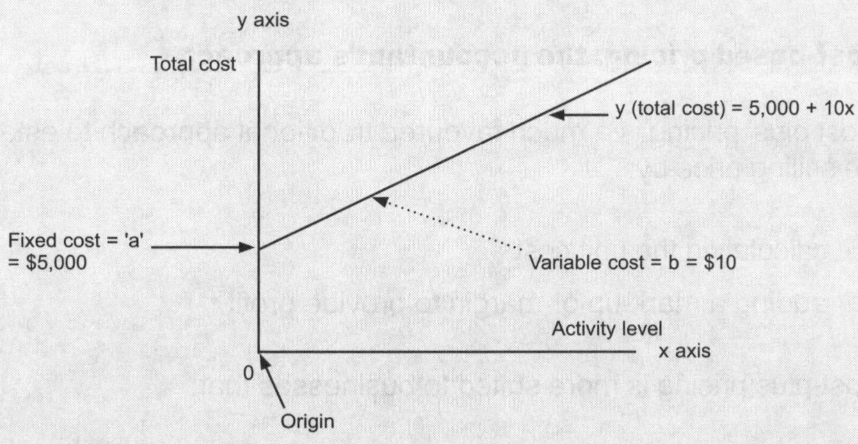

Test your understanding 3

- Fixed costs $100,000.
- Variable costs per unit $5 for volumes up to 1,000 units.
- Volumes above 1,000 units receive 5% discount on all units.

Required:

Derive the two equations for the total cost function.

Additional example on the total cost function

Consider the linear function y = 1,488 + 20x and answer the following questions.

(a) The line would cross the y axis at the point

(b) The gradient of the line is

(c) The independent variable is

(d) The dependent variable is

Solution

(a) The line would cross the y axis at the point	1,488
(b) The gradient of the line is	20
(c) The independent variable is	x
(d) The dependent variable is	y

Cost-based pricing: the accountant's approach

'Cost plus' pricing is a much favoured traditional approach to establishing the selling price by:

- calculating the unit cost
- adding a mark-up or margin to provide profit.

Cost-plus pricing is more suited to businesses that:

- sell the product in large volumes
- operate in markets dominated by price.

The unit cost may reflect:

- full cost
- production costs only
- variable costs only.

The profit is equally subjective and often reflects:

- the risk involved in the product
- competitors' mark-ups
- desired profit and/or ROCE (return on capital employed)
- type of cost used
- type of product.

It is important to understand the difference between:

- Profit mark-up: the profit is quoted as a percentage of the cost.
- Profit margin: the profit is quoted as a percentage of the selling price.

Test your understanding 4

If the full cost of an item is \$540, calculate the selling price using a 25% mark up and a 25% profit margin.

8 Cost equations including volume-based discounts

Suppliers often offer discounts to encourage the purchase of increased volumes.

Where volume-based discounts are offered a total cost equation can be derived for each volume range.

Additional example on volume-based discounts

You are given the following cost data:

Fixed costs	\$250,000.
Variable costs	\$6 per unit up to 5000 units. 10% discount on all units purchased over 5000 units.

Required:

Derive equations for the total cost function.

Solution

$y = 250,000 + 6x$ for $x \leq 5000$.

$y = 250,000 + 5.4x$ for $x > 5000$.

9 Increasing sales and production levels

When an opportunity to increase sales and production levels arises in a business the key question to answer is:

- will the increased contribution (sales less variable costs) generated by the increased sales exceed any additional fixed costs that will be incurred as a result of the increased sales level?

If the answer is 'yes' the opportunity should normally be pursued.

Test your understanding 5

An opportunity arises to increase sales by 10,000 units:

- Selling price of additional units = $10
- Variable cost of additional units = $6
- Fixed costs will increase by = $50,000

Required:

Should the opportunity be accepted?

Additional example on increasing volumes

A company produces and sells one product and its forecast for the next financial year is as follows:

	$000	$000
Sales 100,000 units @ $8		800
Variable costs:		
material	300	
labour	200	
		500
Contribution ($3 per unit)		300
Fixed costs		150
Net profit		150

In an attempt to increase net profit, two proposals have been put forward:

(a) To launch an advertising campaign costing $14,000. This will increase the sales to 150,000 units, although the price will have to be reduced to $7.

(b) To produce some components at present purchased from suppliers. This will reduce material costs by 20% but will increase fixed costs by $72,000.

Required:

Decide whether these proposals should be pursued.

Solution

Proposal (a) will increase the sales revenue but the increase in costs will be greater:

	$000
Sales (150,000 @ $7)	1,050
Variable costs (150,000 @ $5)	750
	300
Fixed costs plus advertising	164
Net profit	136

This is lower than the current forecast.

Proposal (b)

- reduces variable costs by $60,000 ($300,000 x 20%)
- but increases fixed costs by $72,000 and is therefore not to be recommended unless the total volume increases as a result of the policy (e.g. if the supply of the components were previously a limiting factor).

Conclusion

Neither proposal should be accepted.

Additional example of cost-plus pricing

When using a cost-plus pricing strategy a business should work through a step by step approach. For example:

Step 1: Establish the cost per unit. For example, if full cost is used this may be:

• raw materials	$40 per unit
• variable production costs	$40 per unit
• fixed costs based on planned volumes	$20 per unit
• total cost	$100 per unit

Step 2: Add the target profit to arrive at the selling price. For example:

- 20% mark-up = selling price of $120 per unit
- 20% sales margin = selling price of $125 per unit

Step 3: Consider how realistic the target profit is. This will depend upon:

- accurate knowledge of costs
- the selling price arrived at being one which customers are prepared to pay
- selling the planned volume of goods.

Advantages and disadvantages of cost-plus pricing

Advantages of cost-plus pricing	Disadvantages of cost-plus pricing
• Widely used and accepted. • Simple to calculate if costs are known. • Selling price decision may be delegated to junior management. • Justification for price increases. • May encourage price stability – if all competitors have similar cost structures and use similar mark-up.	• Ignores the economic relationship between price and demand. • No attempt to establish optimum price. • Different absorption methods give rise to different costs and hence different selling prices. • Does not guarantee profit – if sales volumes are low fixed costs may not be recovered. • Must decide whether to use full cost, manufacturing cost or marginal cost. • This structured method fails to recognise the manager's need for flexibility in pricing. • Circular reasoning – for example, a price increase will reduce volume, thus increasing unit costs, resulting in pressure to increase the price further.

Customer based pricing – the marketer's approach

Customer-based pricing reflects customers' perceptions of the benefits they will enjoy from purchasing the product, e.g. convenience, status. The product is priced to reflect these benefits.

This approach has regard to costs but reflects a belief that the greater understanding you have of your customer the better placed you are to price the product.

Illustration 4 – Customer-based pricing

On a remote beach in a hot country, the offer of food and drink to tourists on the beach will be perceived by them as being of significant benefit and they are likely to be prepared to pay a significant amount in excess of cost.

Test your understanding 6

Of the three approaches to pricing discussed above:

- cost-based
- customer-based
- competition-based,

which is the least likely to maximise profits and why?

Competition-based pricing

Competition-based pricing means setting a price based upon the prices of competing products.

Competing products can be classified as:

- The same type of product which is not easily distinguished from one's own products. For example, petrol sold at two competing petrol stations.
  - price changes by competitors will have a material impact.
- Substitute products which are different products but fulfil the same need, e.g. you may buy ice cream instead of soft drinks on a hot day.
  - impact of price changes will depend on relative price/performance of substitute.

10 Different pricing strategies

There are a number of different pricing strategies available to a business:

- Cost-plus pricing
- Market-skimming
- Penetration pricing
- Complementary product pricing
- Product-line pricing
- Volume discounting
- Price discrimination
- Relevant cost pricing

Each strategy will be reviewed in turn.

11 Market-skimming pricing strategy

What is market skimming?

Market skimming involves charging high prices when a product is first launched in order to maximise short-term profitability. Initially high prices may be charged to take advantage of the novelty appeal of a new product when demand is initially inelastic.

Once the market becomes saturated the price can be reduced to attract that part of the market that has not been exploited.

Conditions suitable for a market-skimming strategy

- Where the product is new and different and has little direct competition. This is the most common reason for using a market-skimming strategy.
- Where products have a short life cycle, and there is a need to recover their development costs quickly and make a profit.
- Where the strength of demand and the sensitivity of demand to price are unknown. From a psychological point of view it is far better to begin with a high price, which can then be lowered if the demand for the product appears to be more price sensitive than at first thought.
- A firm with liquidity problems may use market-skimming in order to generate high cash flows early on.

With high prices being charged potential competitors will be tempted to enter the market. For skimming to be sustained one or more significant barriers to entry must be present to deter these potential competitors. For example, patent protection, strong brand loyalty.

Test your understanding 7

What products may be priced using a market-skimming strategy?

12 Penetration pricing strategy

What is penetration pricing?

- Penetration pricing is the charging of low prices when a new product is initially launched in order to gain rapid acceptance of the product.
- Once market share is achieved, prices are increased.
- It is an alternative to market skimming when launching a new product.

Circumstances which favour a penetration policy

- If the firm wishes to increase market share.
- A firm wishes to discourage new entrants from entering the market.
- If there are significant economies of scale to be achieved from high-volume output, and so a quick penetration into the market is desirable.
- If demand is highly elastic and so would respond well to low prices.

e.g

Illustration 5 – Penetration pricing strategy

The 2006 launch of Microsoft's anti-virus product, Windows Live OneCare, was described by commentators as an example of penetration pricing. Microsoft's competitors in this market (e.g. Symantec and McAfee) reportedly lost material market share within a few months of its launch.

13 Complementary-product pricing

What is a complementary product?

A complementary product is one that is normally used with another product. An example is razors and razor blades – if sales of razors increase more razor blades will also be bought.

Other examples of complementary products are:

- game consoles and associated games
- printers and printer cartridges.

Complementary goods provide suppliers with additional power over the consumer.

e.g

Illustration 6 – What is complementary-product pricing?

A complementary-product pricing strategy can take two forms:

- The major product (e.g. a printer or a camera) is priced at a relatively low figure – to encourage the purchase and lock the consumer into subsequent purchases of relatively high price consumables (e.g. printer cartridges or memory cards). This is the most common form.
- The major product (e.g. membership of a fashionable sports or golf club) is priced at a relatively high figure – to create a barrier to entry and exit and the consumer is locked into subsequent purchases of relatively low-price facilities (e.g. court fees or green fees).

14 Product-line pricing strategy

What is a product line?

A product line is a range of products that are related to one another. All products within the product line are related but may vary in terms of style, colour, quality, price etc.

What is product-line pricing?

Product-line pricing works by:

- capitalising on consumer interest in a number of products within a range.
- making the price entry point for the basic product relatively cheap.
- pricing other items in the range more highly – in order to 'complete the set' the consumer has to pay substantially more for the additional matching items.

e.g

Illustration 7 – Product-line pricing strategy

A dinner service is being promoted. The entry point (serving plates) will be relatively cheap. Other, less essential matching items in the same range (e.g. gravy boats) will have a higher price.

15 Volume-discounting pricing strategy

What is volume-discounting pricing?

Volume discounting means offering customers a lower price per unit if they purchase a particular quantity of a product.

It takes two main forms:

- Quantity discounts – for customers that order large quantities.
- Cumulative quantity discounts – the discount increases as the cumulative total ordered increases. This may appeal to those who do not wish to place large individual orders but who purchase large quantities over time.

Benefits to the business of using a volume discounting strategy

- Increased customer loyalty – cumulative quantity discounts 'lock in' the customer since further purchases can be made at a lower cost per unit.
- Attracting new customers – an exceptional level of discount can be offered to new customers on a one-off basis, enabling the supplier to 'get his foot in the door'.
- Lower sales processing costs – an increased proportion of his sales take the form of bulk orders.
- Lower purchasing costs – high sales volumes enable the business to enjoy discounts from their suppliers, creating a virtuous circle.
- Discounts help to sell items that are bought primarily on price.
- Clearance of surplus stock or unpopular item through the use of discounts.
- Discounts can be geared to particular off-peak periods.

Conditions suitable for a volume-discounting pricing strategy

- Sales margin is substantial allowing profits to be made even after discounting.
- The product is bought on price and it is difficult to distinguish it from competing products.
- Products with a limited shelf life (for example, fashion items) may be discounted to shift them.

Recap of pricing strategies for a given situation

Situation	Pricing Strategy
• Product is new and different (e.g. new electronic product). • 'Early adopters' are prepared to pay high prices to achieve ownership. • Significant barriers to entry exist (e.g. patent protection, high capital investment, or unusually strong brand loyalty) to deter competition – in order that skimming can be sustained. • The product has a short life cycle so there is a need to recover development costs and make a profit quickly. • The business has a liquidity problem and may be attracted by the high initial cash flows available in the early stages of a product's life.	Skimming

• Strength of demand and the sensitivity of demand to price are unknown. It is much easier to lower prices than to increase them. • The business wishes to discourage newcomers from entering the market. • The business wishes to shorten the initial period of the product's life cycle in order to enter the growth and maturity stages as quickly as possible. • There are significant economies of scale to be achieved from high-volume output, and so a quick penetration into the market is desirable in order to gain those unit cost reductions. • Demand is highly elastic and so would respond well to low prices.	Penetration
• A range of products is being marketed – the products within a product line are related but may vary in terms of style, colour, quality, etc. (e.g. dinner services, cutlery sets). • Consumers will tend to buy a number of items within the range and be prepared to pay a relatively high price for the less essential items in order to build up a matching set.	Product-line
• The sales margin is substantial, allowing good profits to be made even after significant discounting (e.g. consumer software products). • The product is traditionally bought on price – it is difficult to distinguish from competing products (e.g. car tyres). • Products with a limited shelf life (e.g. fashion items).	Volume discounting

16 Price-discrimination pricing strategy

What is price-discrimination?

A price-discrimination strategy is where a company sells the same product at different prices in different markets.

Conditions required for a price-discrimination strategy

- The seller must have some degree of monopoly power, or the price will be driven down.
- Customers can be segregated into different markets
- Customers cannot buy at the lower price in one market and sell at the higher price in the other market.
- There must be different price elasticities of demand in each market so that prices can be raised in one and lowered in the other to increase revenue.

Dangers of price-discrimination as a strategy

- A black market may develop allowing those in a lower priced segment to resell to those in a higher priced segment.
- Competitors join the market and undercut the firm's prices.
- Customers in the higher priced brackets look for alternatives and demand becomes more elastic over time.

Test your understanding 8

Which products or services lend themselves to a price-discrimination strategy?

Test your understanding 9 - Recap of pricing strategies

(1) Which pricing strategies are aimed at the start of the product life cycle?

(2) Which pricing strategies seek to attract sales by offering a product at a relatively low price?

(3) Which pricing strategies lure the customer in with a relatively low-priced product in order to lock the customer in to subsequent additional purchases of similar items that are relatively highly priced?

(4) Which pricing strategy is appropriate to items that are bought primarily on price.

17 Using relevant costs to arrive at a price

What is relevant cost pricing?

The principles of relevant costing were met in paper F2 and will be reviewed in more detail in a later chapter.

Relevant costs can be used to arrive at a minimum tender price for a one-off tender or contract. The minimum price should be equal to the total of all of the relevant cash flows.

Suitability of relevant cost pricing

The use of relevant costs is only suitable for a one-off decision since:

- fixed costs may become relevant in the long run
- there are problems estimating incremental cash flows
- there is a conflict between accounting measures such as profit and this approach.

Calculations involving relevant cost pricing will be reviewed in a later chapter.

18 Chapter summary

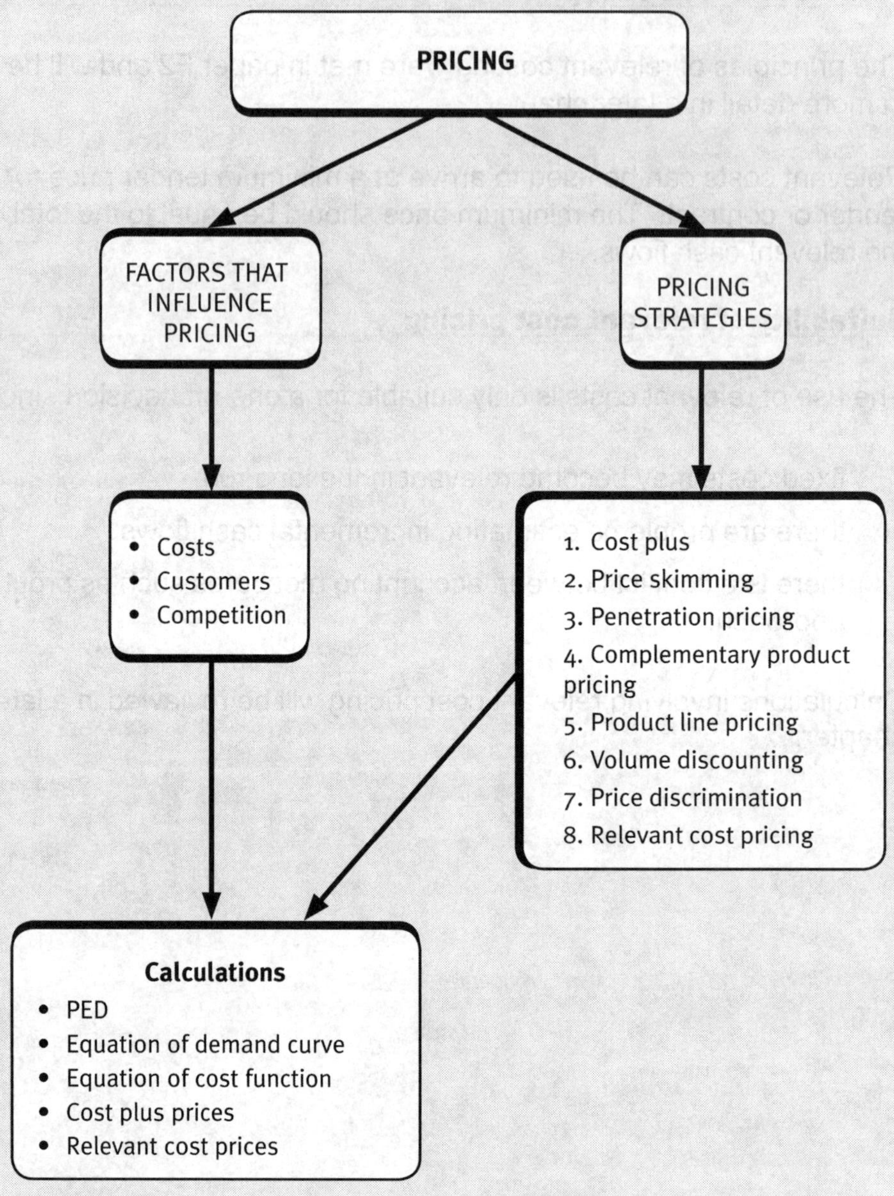

Test your understanding answers

Test your understanding 1

(a) **Step 1: Find the gradient, b**

The question provides us with two selling prices and the respective level of demand at these selling prices. Therefore, we can begin by calculating the gradient of the straight line, b.

b (gradient) = change in price/ change in quantity
= (220 – 200)/(950 – 1000) = – 0.4

Step 2: Calculate the intersect, a

Once the gradient is known the intersect can be found using either of the selling prices and demand levels given in the question.

For example, price (P) = 200 when 1000 units (Q) are sold and substituting – 0.4 for b

200 = a – (0.4 × 1,000)

200 = a – 400

a = 200 + 400 = 600

Step 3: Straight-line demand equation

So the equation is: P = 600 – 0.4Q.

Step 4: Forecast the demand at a given selling price

At a price of $300

300 = 600 – 0.4Q

0.4Q = 300

Q = 300/0.4

Quantity demanded (Q) = 750 units per month

(b) MR = 600 - 0.8Q
MC = VC so equating MR = MC: 100 = 600 - 0.8Q
So Q = 625
And substituting Q into Price function, P = $350

(c) Contribution per unit = $350 - $100 = $250
Total contribution = $250 x 625 units = $156,250

Test your understanding 2

(a) Let Q = quantity produced/sold

Gradient 'b'=

$$b = \frac{\text{Change in price}}{\text{Change in quantity}} = \frac{\$5}{\$50}$$

b = – 0.1

Price = a - 0.1Q; $160 = a – 0.1 (2,000) therefore **a = $360**

P = $360 - 0.1Q
MR = $360 - 0.2Q
MC = $64

(b) To maximise profit, MR = MC. Therefore, $360 - 0.2Q = $64

Q	= (360 - 64) ÷ 0.2	= 1,480	units
P	= 360 * 0.1 (1,480)	= $212	
Revenue	= $212 x 1,480	= $313,760	
Less Costs	= ($64 x 1,480) + $100,000	= ($194,720)	
Maximum Profit	=	$119,040	

Test your understanding 3

- Y = 100,000 + 5x for x≤1000
- Y = 100,000 + 4.75x for x>1000.

Test your understanding 4

- A 25% mark-up would produce a selling price of $675 ($540 × 125/100).
- A 25% profit margin would produce a selling price of $720 [$540 × (100/75)].

Test your understanding 5

The effect of the increased sales would be to reduce net profits by $10,000.

- $100,000 increased sales ($10 × 10,000 units)
- $60,000 increased variable costs ($6 × 10,000 units) = $40,000 additional contribution
- less additional fixed costs of $50,000 = $10,000 reduction in net profit.

Based on this analysis, the opportunity should be rejected. However, other factors need to be considered such as:

- the impact on future sales beyond the current period
- the impact of rejection on customer goodwill
- whether the extra sales would help build the firm's brand.

Test your understanding 6

Customer-based and competition-based pricing are most likely to maximise profits since they take into account the behaviour of customers and competitors, as well as the need to recover costs or obtain a particular margin on sales. Cost-based pricing, in contrast, simply reflects the objective of cost recovery or achieving a margin on sales and ignores the potential to exploit the level of customers' interest in the product or the strength of the product in the marketplace relative to competitors.

Test your understanding 7

Market skimming is often used in relation to electronic products when a new range (e.g. DVD players, plasma TV screens) are first released onto the market at a high price.

The target is the 'early adopters' of such products; their price sensitivity is relatively low because their interest in the product is substantial or they have a stronger appreciation of the qualities offered by the product.

Test your understanding 8

Examples of price discrimination include:

- lower admission prices for children at certain sporting and entertainment events
- discounts for Senior Citizens in some pubs and restaurants
- concessionary rail fares for students
- lower admission prices for females at some nightclubs.

Test your understanding 9 - Recap of pricing strategies

(1) Skimming and the penetration-pricing strategies.

(2) Penetration and volume discounting rely substantially on relatively low-price offers; this is also true to a lesser extent of complementary and product line pricing strategies.

(3) Complementary and product-line pricing strategies.

(4) Volume discounting.

chapter

5

Make or buy and other short-term decisions

Chapter learning objectives

Upon completion of this chapter you will be able to:

- explain the practical issues surrounding make versus buy and outsourcing decisions
- for given data, calculate and compare 'make' costs with 'buy-in' costs
- for given data, compare in-house costs and outsource costs of completing tasks and consider other issues surrounding this decision
- for given data, apply relevant costing principles in situations involving make or buy, shut down, one-off contracts and joint product further processing decisions.

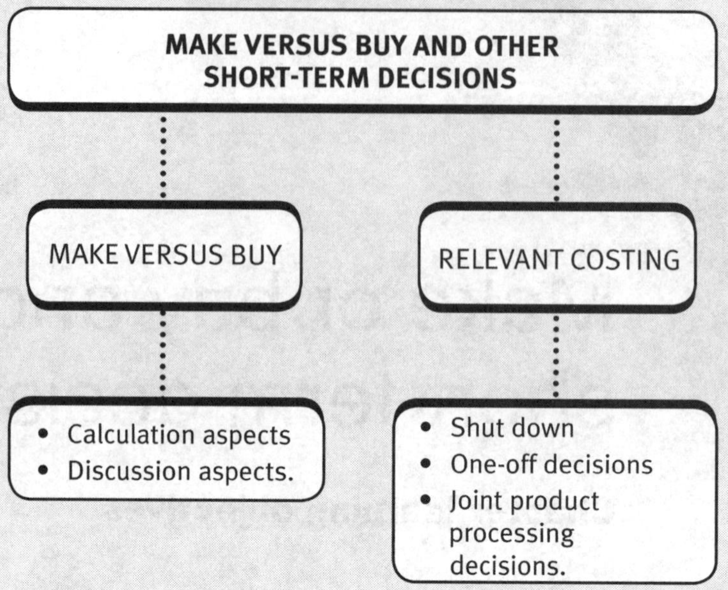

1 Introduction

This chapter will focus on a number of short-term decisions that are typically made by a business:

- Make versus buy decisions
- Shut-down decisions
- One-off contract decisions
- Further processing decisions

Each of these decisions is based on relevant costing principles. Therefore, a recap of relevant costing will be useful before looking at each of the decisions in turn.

2 Relevant costs and revenues

Decision making involves making a choice between two or more alternatives. The decision will be 'rational'; profit maximising. All decisions will be made using relevant costs and revenues.

'Relevant costs are future cash flows arising as a direct consequence of the decision under consideration.'

There are three elements here:

Cash flows. To evaluate a decision, actual cash flows should be considered. Noncash items such as depreciation and interdivisional charges should be ignored.

Future costs and revenues. This means that past costs and revenues are only useful insofar as they provide a guide to the future. Costs already spent, known as sunk costs, are irrelevant for decision making.

Differential costs and revenues. Only those costs and revenues that alter as a result of a decision are relevant. Where factors are common to all the alternatives being considered they can be ignored; only the differences are relevant.

In many short-term situations, the fixed costs remain constant for each of the alternatives being considered and thus the marginal costing approach showing sales, marginal cost and contribution is particularly appropriate.

In the long run (and sometimes in the short run) fixed costs do change and accordingly the differential costs must include any changes in the amount of fixed costs.

Relevant costs

Test your understanding of relevant and non-relevant costs by seeing if you can identify which of the following costs are relevant :

(a) The salary to be paid to a market researcher who will oversee the development of a new product. This is a new post to be created specially for the new product but the £12,000 salary will be a fixed cost. Is this cost relevant to the decision to proceed with the development of the product?

(b) The £2,500 additional monthly running costs of a new machine to be purchased to manufacture an established product. Since the new machine will save on labour time, the fixed overhead to be absorbed by the product will reduce by £100 per month. Are these costs relevant to the decision to purchase the new machine?

(c) Office cleaning expenses of £125 for next month. The office is cleaned by contractors and the contract can be cancelled by giving one month's notice. Is this cost relevant to a decision to close the office?

(d) Expenses of £75 paid to the marketing manager. This was to reimburse the manager for the cost of travelling to meet a client with whom the company is currently negotiating a major contract. Is this cost relevant to the decision to continue negotiations?

3 Opportunity cost

Opportunity cost is an important concept for decision-making purposes. It is the value of the best alternative that is foregone when a particular course of action is undertaken. It emphasises that decisions are concerned with choices and that by choosing one plan, there may well be sacrifices elsewhere in the business.

Test your understanding 1 - Opportunity cost

A company which manufactures and sells one single product is currently operating at 85% of full capacity, producing 102,000 units per month. The current total monthly costs of production amount to £330,000, of which £75,000 are fixed and are expected to remain unchanged for all levels of activity up to full capacity.

A new potential customer has expressed interest in taking regular monthly delivery of 12,000 units at a price of £2.80 per unit.

All existing production is sold each month at a price of £3.25 per unit. If the new business is accepted, existing sales are expected to fall by 2 units for every 15 units sold to the new customer.

What is the overall increase in monthly profit which would result from accepting the new business?

4 The relevant cost of materials

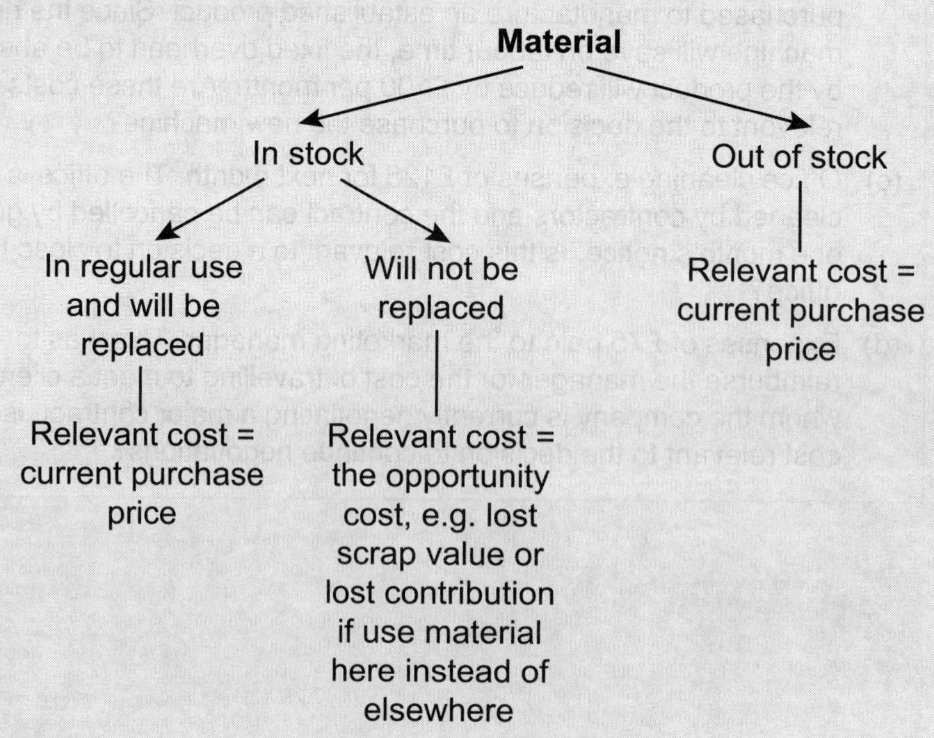

Any historic cost given for materials is **always a sunk cost** and **never relevant** unless it happens to be the same as the current purchase price.

5 The relevant cost of labour

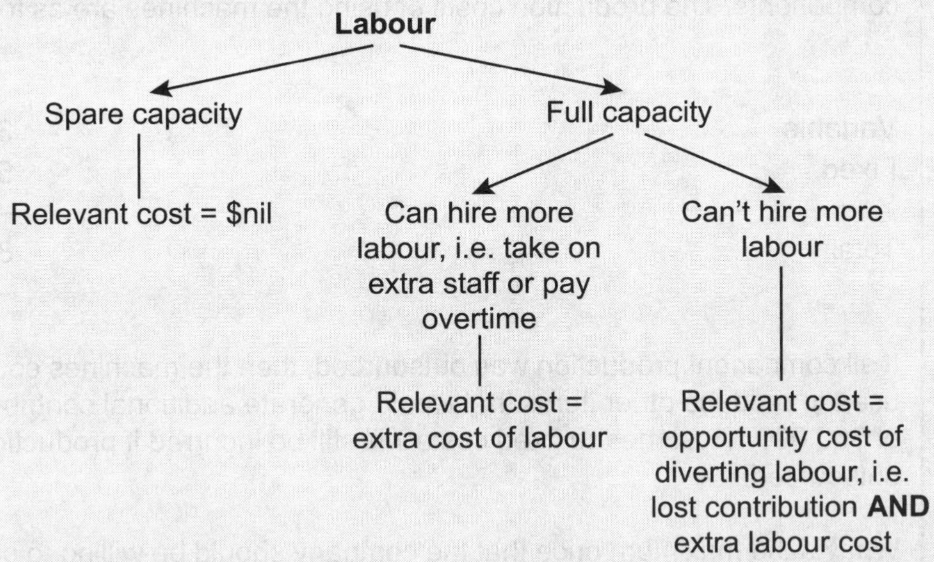

6 Make versus buy

Making the decision on financial grounds

A product should be made in-house if the relevant cost of making the product in-house is less than the cost of buying the product externally.

Spare capacity exists

Unless stated otherwise in the question, it should be assumed that there is spare capacity.

> The relevant cost of making the product in-house = the variable cost of internal manufacture plus any fixed costs directly related to that product.

No spare capacity exists

> The relevant cost of making the product in-house = the variable cost of internal manufacture plus any fixed costs directly related to that product plus the opportunity cost of internal manufacture (e.g. lost contribution from another product).

e.g

Illustration 1 - Make or buy

A factory's entire machine capacity is used to produce essential components. The production costs of using the machines are as follows.

	$
Variable	30,000
Fixed	50,000
Total	80,000

If all component production was outsourced, then the machines could be used to produce other items that would generate additional contribution of $50,000. Assume the fixed costs will still be incurred if production is outsourced.

What is the maximum price that the company should be willing to pay to the outside supplier for the components?

Solution

	$
Variable costs saved	30,000
Contribution earned (= opportunity cost)	50,000
	80,000

Test your understanding 2

Robust Ltd makes four components A, B, C and D and the associated annual costs are as follows:

	A	**B**	**C**	**D**
Production volume (units)	1,500	3,000	5,000	7,000
Unit variable costs	$	$	$	$
Direct materials	4	4	5	5
Direct labour	8	8	6	6
Variable production overheads	2	1	4	5
Total	14	13	15	16
Fixed costs directly attributable are:	3,000	6,000	10,000	7,000
The unit prices of an external supplier are:	12	16	20	24

Determine whether any of the components should be bought in from the external supplier.

Other issues to consider

In addition to the relative cost of buying externally compared to making in-house, management must consider a number of other issues before a final decision is made.

- **Reliability of external supplier:** can the outside company be relied upon to meet the requirements in terms of:
  - quantity required
  - quality required
  - delivering on time
  - price stability
- **Specialist skills:** the external supplier may possess some specialist skills that are not available in-house.
- **Alternative use of resource:** outsourcing will free up resources which may be used in another part of the business.
- **Social:** will outsourcing result in a reduction of the workforce? Redundancy costs should be considered.
- **Legal:** will outsourcing affect contractual obligations with suppliers or employees?
- **Confidentiality:** is there a risk of loss of confidentiality, especially if the external supplier performs similar work for rival companies.
- **Customer reaction:** do customers attach importance to the products being made in-house?

Test your understanding 3 - Additional question on make vs buy

KRS Ltd is considering whether to administer its own purchase ledger or to use an external accounting service. It has obtained the following cost estimates for each option:

Internal service department

	Cost	**Volume**
Purchase hardware/software	$320 pa	
Hardware/software maintenance	$750 pa	
Accounting stationery	$500 pa	
Part-time account clerk	$6,000 pa	

External services

Processing of invoices/credit notes	$0.50 per document	5,000 pa
Processing of cheque payments	$0.50 per cheque	4,000 pa
Reconciling supplier accounts	$2.00 per supplier per month	150 suppliers

Determine the cost effectiveness of outsourcing the accounting activities and identify the qualitative factors involved.

7 Shut-down decisions

Part of a business, for example a department or a product, may appear to be unprofitable. The business may have to make a decision as to whether or not this area should be shut down.

The quantifiable cost or benefit of closure

The relevant cash flows associated with closure should be considered. For example:

- the lost contribution from the area that is being closed (= relevant cost of closure)
- savings in specific fixed costs from closure (=relevant benefit of closure)
- known penalties and other costs resulting from the closure, e.g. redundancy, compensation to customers (=relevant cost of closure)
- any known reorganisation costs (= relevant cost of closure)
- any known additional contribution from the alternative use for resources released (= relevant benefit of closure).

If the relevant benefits are greater than the relevant costs of closure then closure may occur. However, before a final decision is made the business should also consider the non-quantifiable factors discussed below.

Non-quantifiable costs and benefits of closure

- Some of the costs and benefits discussed above may be non-quantifiable at the point of making the shut-down decision:
  - penalties and other costs resulting from the closure (e.g. redundancy, compensation to customers) may not be known with certainty.
  - reorganisation costs may not be known with certainty.
  - additional contribution from the alternative use for resources released may not be known with certainty

- Knock-on impact of the shut-down decision. For example, supermarkets often stock some goods which they sell at a loss. This is to get customers through the door, who they then hope will purchase other products which have higher profit margins for them. If the decision is taken to stop selling these products, then the customers may no longer come to the store.

Test your understanding 4

The management of Fiona Co is considering the closure of one of its operations, department 3, and the financial accountant has submitted the following report.

Department	**1**	**2**	**3**	**Total**
Sales (units)	5,000	6,000	2,000	13,000
Sales ($)	150,000	240,000	24,000	414,000
Cost of sales ($)				
Direct material	75,000	150,000	10,000	235,000
Direct labour	25,000	30,000	8,000	63,000
Production overhead	5,769	6,923	2,308	15,000
Gross profit ($)	44,231	53,077	3,692	101,000
Expenses ($)	15,384	18,461	6,155	40,000
Net profit ($)	28,847	34,616	(2,463)	61,000

Additional information:

- production overheads of $15,000 have been apportioned to the three departments on the basis of unit sales volume
- expenses are head office overheads, again apportioned to departments on sales volume.

As management accountant, you further ascertain that, on a cost driver basis:

- 50% of the production overheads can be directly traced to departments and so could be allocated on the basis 2:2:1.
- Similarly 60% of the expenses can be allocated 3:3:2, with the remainder not being possible to allocate.
- 80% of the so-called direct labour is fixed and cannot be readily allocated. The remaining 20% is variable and can be better allocated on the basis of sales volume.

(a) Restate the financial position in terms of the contribution made by each department and, based on these figures, make a clear recommendation.

(b) Discuss any other factors that should be considered before a final decision is made.

Additional example on shut-down decisions

Harolds fashion store comprises three departments – Men's Wear, Ladies' Wear and Unisex. The store budget is as follows:

	Men's	**Ladies'**	**Unisex**	**Total**
	$	$	$	$
Sales	40,000	60,000	20,000	120,000
Direct cost of sales	20,000	36,000	15,000	71,000
Department costs	5,000	10,000	3,000	18,000
Apportioned store costs	5,000	5,000	5,000	15,000
Profit/(loss)	10,000	9,000	(3,000)	16,000

It is suggested that Unisex be closed to increase the size of Men's and Ladies' Wear.

Required:

Determine what information is relevant or required.

Solution

Possible answers are as follows:

(a) Unisex earns $2,000 net contribution (apportioned costs will still be incurred and thus reapportioned to other departments).

(b) Possible increase in Men's/Ladies' sales volume.

(c) Will Unisex staff be dismissed or transferred to Men's/Ladies'?

(d) Reorganisation costs, e.g. repartitioning, stock disposal.

(e) Loss of custom because Unisex attracts certain types of customer who will not buy in Men's/Ladies'.

8 One-off contracts

When a business is presented with a one-off contract, it should apply relevant costing principles to establish the cash flows associated with the project.

The minimum contract price = the total of the relevant cash flows associated with the contract.

If the contract price does not cover these cash flows then it should be rejected.

Test your understanding 5

Mr Smith has been asked to quote a price for a special contract. He has already prepared his tender but has asked you to review it for him.

He has pointed out to you that he wants to quote the minimum price as he believes this will lead to more lucrative work in the future.

Mr Smith's tender

		$
Material:	A 2,000 kgs @ $10 per kg	20,000
	B 1,000 kgs @ $15 per kg	15,000
	C 500 kgs @ $40 per kg	20,000
	D 50 litres @ $12 per litre	600
Labour:	Skilled 1,000 hrs @ $25 per hr	25,000
	Semi-skilled 2,000 hrs @ $15 per hr	30,000
	Unskilled, 500 hrs @ $10 per hr	5,000
Fixed overheads 3,500 hrs @ $12 per hr		42,000
Costs of preparing the tender:		
Mr Smith's time		1,000
other expenses		500
Minimum profit (5% of total costs)		7,725
Minimum tender price		166,825

Other information

Material A

- 1,000 kgs of this material is in stock at a cost of $5 per kg.

- Mr Smith has no alternative use for his material and intends selling it for $2 per kg.
- However, if he sold any he would have to pay a fixed sum of $300 to cover delivery costs.
- The current purchase price is $10 per kg.

Material B

- There is plenty of Material B in stock and it cost $18 per kg.
- The current purchase price is $15 per kg.
- The material is constantly used by Mr Smith in his business.

Material C

- The total amount in stock of 500 kgs was bought for $10,000 some time ago for another one-off contract that never happened.
- Mr Smith is considering selling it for $6,000 in total or using it as a substitute for another material, constantly used in normal production.
- If used in this latter manner it would save $8,000 of the other material.
- Current purchase price is $40 per kg.

Material D

- There are 100 litres of this material in stock.
- It is dangerous and if not used in this contract will have to be disposed of at a cost to Mr Smith of $50 per litre.
- The current purchase price is $12 per litre.

Skilled labour

- Mr Smith only hires skilled labour when he needs it.
- $25 per hour is the current hourly rate.

Semi-skilled labour

- Mr Smith has a workforce of 50 semi-skilled labourers who are currently not fully utilised.
- They are on annual contracts and the number of spare hours currently available for this project are 1,500. Any hours in excess of this will have to be paid for at time-and-a-half.
- The normal hourly rate is $15 per hour.

Unskilled labour

- These are currently fully employed by Mr Smith on jobs where they produce a contribution of $2 per unskilled labour hour.
- Their current rate is $10 per hour, although extra could be hired at $20 an hour if necessary.

Fixed overheads

- This is considered by Mr Smith to be an accurate estimate of the hourly rate based on his existing production.

Costs of preparing the tender

- Mr Smith has spent 10 hours working on this project at $100 per hour, which he believes is his charge-out rate.
- Other expenses include the cost of travel and research spent by Mr Smith on the project.

Profit

- This is Mr Smith's minimum profit margin which he believes is necessary to cover 'general day-to-day expenses of running a business'.

Required:

Calculate and explain for Mr Smith what you believe the minimum tender price should be.

Additional example on one-off contracts

A research contract, which to date has cost the company $150,000, is under review.

If the contract is allowed to proceed:

- it will be completed in approximately one year
- the results would then be sold to a government agency for $300,000.

Shown below are the additional expenses which the managing director estimates will be necessary to complete the work.

Materials

- This material for the contract has just been purchased at a cost of $60,000.
- It is toxic; if not used in this contract it must be disposed of at a cost of $5,000.

Labour

- Skilled labour is hard to recruit.
- The workers concerned were transferred to the contract from a production department, and at a recent meeting, the production manager claimed that if the men were returned to him they could generate sales of $150,000 in the next year.
  - The prime cost of these sales would be $100,000, including $40,000 for the labour cost itself.
  - The overhead absorbed into this production would amount to $20,000.

Research staff

- It has been decided that when work on this contract ceases, the research department will be closed.
- Research wages for the year are $60,000, and redundancy and severance pay has been estimated at $15,000 now, or $35,000 in one year's time.

Equipment

- The contract utilises a special microscope which cost $18,000 three years ago.
- It has a residual value of $3,000 in another two years, and a current disposal value of $8,000.
- If used in the contract it is estimated that the disposal value in a year's time will be $6,000.

Share of general building services

- The contract is charged with $35,000 pa to cover general building expenses.
- Immediately after the contract is discontinued, the space occupied could be sub-let for an annual rental of $7,000.

Required:

Advise the managing director as to whether the contract should be allowed to proceed, explaining the reasons for the treatment of each item.

(**Note:** Ignore the time value of money.)

Solution	$
Relevant costs and revenues of proceeding with the contract	
(1) Costs to date of $150,000 sunk – ignore.	–
(2) Materials - in stock and will not be replaced There is an opportunity benefit of the disposal costs saved.	5,000
(3) Labour cost - no spare capacity and additional labour can't be hired. Opportunity cost is lost contribution of $50,000 ($150k - $100k) plus the direct cost of labour of $40,000. The overhead will be incurred anyway and so should be ignored.	(90,000)
(4) Research staff costs: Wages for the year (cost would be saved if contract did not go ahead) Increase in redundancy pay due to the delay in closure of the department ($35,000 – $15,000)	(60,000) (20,000)
(5) Equipment: Deprival value if used in the project = disposal value Disposal proceeds in one year (All book values and depreciation figures are irrelevant)	(8,000) 6,000
(6) General building services Apportioned costs - irrelevant Opportunity costs of rental foregone	 (7,000)
Total relevant cash flows associated with the contract	(174,000)
Sales value of contact	300,000
Increased contribution from contract	126,000

Advice. Proceed with the contract.

9 Further processing decisions

A further processing decision will be tested in the context of joint products in the exam.

Revision of joint product costing

Joint product costing was introduced in paper F2:

- Joint products arise where the manufacture of one product inevitably results in the manufacture of other products.
- The specific point at which individual products become identifiable is known as the split-off point.
- Costs incurred before the split-off point are called joint costs and must be shared between joint products produced.
- After separation products may be sold immediately or may be processed further. Any further processing costs are allocated directly to the product on which they are incurred.

The basis of apportionment of joint costs to products is usually one of the following:

(i) Sales value of production (also known as 'market value')

(ii) Production units

(iii) Net realisable value.

e.g

Illustration 2 - Valuation of joint products

Products A and B are two joint products with information as follows:

	Kgs produced	Kgs sold	Selling Price per kg	Joint cost
Product A	100	80	$5	
				$750
Product B	200	150	$2	

(a) **Apportionment by production units**

$$\frac{\text{Joint cost}}{\text{Kgs produced}} = \frac{\$750}{300} = \$2.50 \text{ per kg for A and B}$$

Trading results are as follows:

		Product A		***Product B***	***Total***
Sales	80 x $5.00	$400	150 x $2.00	$300	$700
Cost of Sales	80 x $2.50	($200)	150 x $2.50	($375)	($575)
Profit / (loss)		$200		($75)	$125
Value of closing stock	20 x $2.50	$50	50 x $2.50	$125	

The production ratio is 100 : 200 which means that in order to obtain 1 kg of A , it is necessary to produce 2 kgs of B. For exam purposes, you should assume that the ratio of output is fixed.

(b) **Apportionment by market value at point of separation**

	Sales Value of production	Proportion	Joint cost apportionment	Per kg
A : 100 x $5	$500	5/9	$417	$4.17
B : 200 x $2	$400	4/9	$333	$1.67
			750	

Trading results:

	A	***B***	***Total***
Sales	400	300	700
Cost of sales	333.6	250.5	585.1
Profit	66.4	49.5	114.9
Profit / Sales ratio	16.6%	16.5%	
Closing inventory	(20 x 4.17) = $83	(50 x $1.67) = $83	

Note that the apportionment is on the basis of proportionate sales value of production; Profit per unit will be the same (with a small rounding difference.)

(c) **Apportionment by Net Realisable Value**

This approach should be used in situations where the sales value at the split-off point is not known - either because the product is not saleable, or if the examiner does not tell us.

Further information is needed:

	Further processing costs	Selling price after further processing
Product A	$280 + $ 2.00 per kg	$8.40
Product B	$160 + $1.40 per kg	$4.50

Apportionment of joint costs:

	Product A	Product B	
Final Sales Value of Production (100 x $8.40; 200 x $4.50)	$840	$900	
Further Processing Cost (280 + 100 x $2; 160 + 200 x$1.40)	$480	$440	
Net Realisable value	$360	$460	
Joint cost apportionment (360;460)	329	421	
Joint cost per kg	$3.29	$2.10	
Trading results (for common process only)			
Sales			$700
Joint Costs		$750	
less closing inventory			
A : 20 x $3.29	$66		
B : 50 x $2.10	$105		
	171		
Cost of sales			$579
Profit			$121

Test your understanding 6

The following is relevant for a production process for Period 1:

Direct material Cost	$10,000
Direct Labour Cost	$5,000
Overheads	$3,000
Total costs	$18,000

The process produces joint products A and B, which are then sold at the prices given below. The output figure represents all of the output from the process:

	Product A	Product B
Units of Output	2,000	8,000
Price per Unit	$5	$2.50

Required:

Calculate the cost of sales, and gross profit for products A and B assuming:

(i) joint costs are apportioned by market value;

(ii) joint costs are apportioned by production units.

Further processing decision

When deciding whether to process a product further or to sell after split-off only future incremental cash flows should be considered:

- Any difference in revenue and any extra costs.
- Joint costs are sunk at this stage and thus not relevant to the decision.

Test your understanding 7

A firm makes three joint products, X, Y and Z, at a joint cost of $400,000. Joint costs are apportioned on the basis of weight. Products X and Z are currently processed further.

Product	Weight at split-off (tonnes)	Further processing costs (variable) $000	Sales $000
X	600	800	980
Y	200	-	120
Z	200	400	600

An opportunity has arisen to sell all three products at the split-off point for the following prices.

X	$200,000
Y	$120,000
Z	$160,000

Which of the products, if any, should the firm process further?

10 Chapter summary

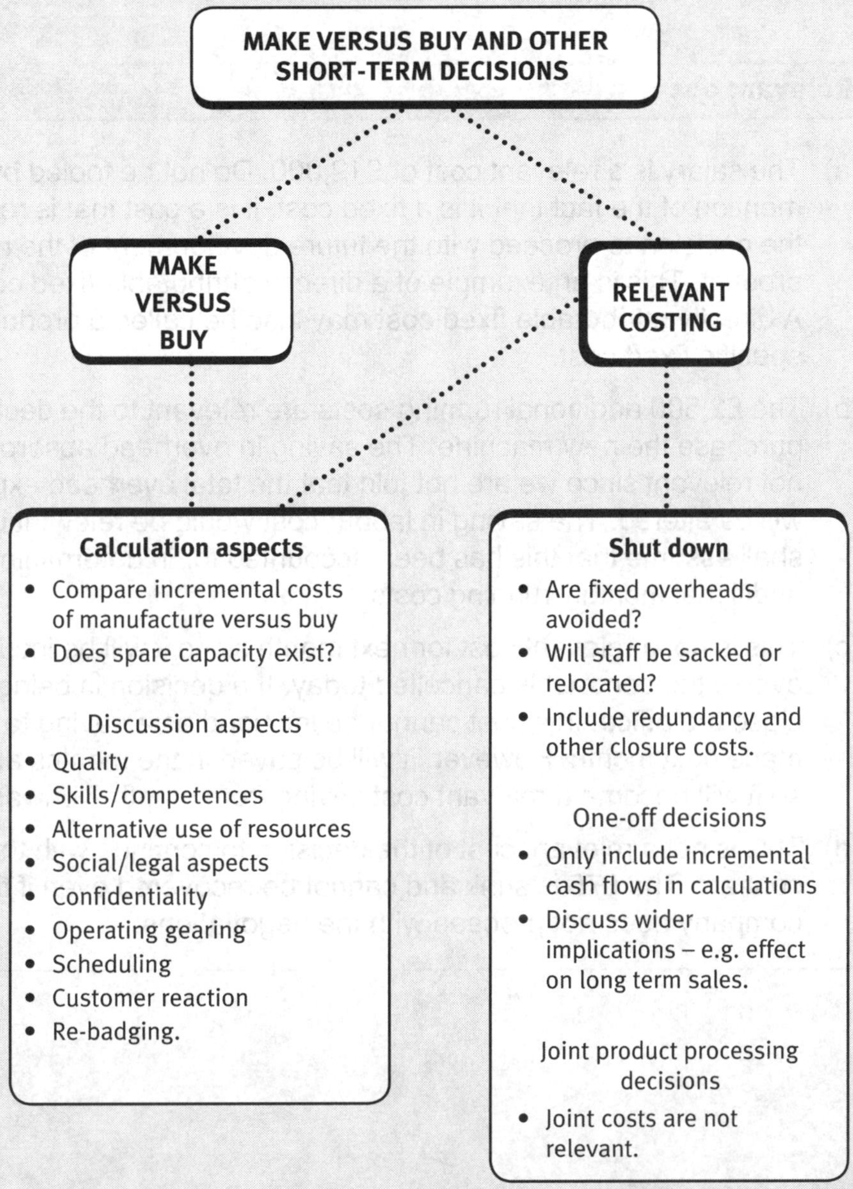

Test your understanding answers

Relevant costs

(a) The salary is a relevant cost of £12,000. Do not be fooled by the mention of the fact that it is a fixed cost, it is a cost that is relevant to the decision to proceed with the future development of the new product. This is an example of a directly attributable fixed cost. A directly attributable fixed cost may also be called a product-specific fixed cost.

(b) The £2,500 additional running costs are relevant to the decision to purchase the new machine. The saving in overhead absorption is not relevant since we are not told that the total overhead expenditure will be altered. The saving in labour cost would be relevant but we shall assume that this has been accounted for in determining the additional monthly running costs.

(c) This is not a relevant cost for next month since it will be incurred even if the contract is cancelled today. If a decision is being made to close the office, this cost cannot be included as a saving to be made next month. However, it will be saved in the months after that so it will become a relevant cost saving from month 2 onwards.

(d) This is not a relevant cost of the decision to continue with the contract. The £75 is sunk and cannot be recovered even if the company does not proceed with the negotiations.

Test your understanding 1 - Opportunity cost

100% capacity	= 102,000 ÷ 0.85	= 120,000 units

Spare capacity amounts to 18,000 units. So there is sufficient slack to meet the new order.

Variable costs	= £330,000 less £75,000	= £255,000
Variable cost per unit	= £255,000 ÷ 102,000	= £2.50
Contribution per unit from existing product		= £3.25 – £2.50 = £0.75
Contribution per unit from new product		= £2.80 – £2.50 = £0.30

	£
Increase in contribution from new product:	
£0.30 × 12,000 units	3,600
Fall in contribution from existing product:	
£0.75 × (12,000 ÷ 15) × 2	
£0.75 × 1,600	(1,200)
Net Gain in contribution	**2,400**

Test your understanding 2

	A	B	C	D
	$	$	$	$
Buy externally - unit price	12	16	20	24
Make in-house - unit variable cost	14	13	15	16
- unit fixed cost	2	2	2	1
- total	16	15	17	17
Saving/ (loss) through making in-house	-4	1	3	7

Robust Ltd should buy in component A since it would achieve savings of $4 per unit or $6,000 pa. Buying in any of the other components would increase its costs.

Test your understanding 3 - Additional question on make vs buy

Annual internal processing costs

Hardware and software	$320	
Hardware/software annual maintenance	$750	
Accounting stationery	$500	
Part time accounts clerk	$6,000	
Total	$7,570	
Annual outsourcing costs		
Processing of invoices/credit notes	$2,500	5,000 × $0.50
Processing of cheque payments	$2,000	4,000 × $0.50
Reconciling supplier accounts	$3,600	150 × $2 × 12
Total	$8,100	

It would not be cost effective to outsource the accounting activities. The present costs of $7,570 would rise to $8,100 pa

Qualitative factors include:

- predicted volumes - higher volumes will make outsourcing more expensive
- the quality of supply - will the external supplier make more errors?
- security of information.

Test your understanding 4

(a) First of all we must restate the figures so that they present the situation in its true light. Only relevant cash flows should be considered. This will enable each department to be readily evaluated on its locally controllable performance.

Department	**1**	**2**	**3**	**Total**
Sales volume (units)	5,000	6,000	2,000	13,000
Sales value ($)	150,000	240,000	24,000	414,000
Cost of sales: ($)				
Direct material	75,000	150,000	10,000	235,000
Direct labour (note 1)	4,846	5,815	1,939	12,600
Prodn overhead (note 2)	3,000	3,000	1,500	7,500
Expenses (note 3)	9,000	9,000	6,000	24,000
Contribution ($)	58,154	72,185	4,561	134,900
Other costs ($):				
Labour (note 4)				(50,400)
Overhead (note 5)				(7,500)
Expenses (note 6)				(16,000)
Net profit				61,000

Notes

(1) 80% of the labour cost is fixed and is therefore excluded from the contribution calculation. The remaining 20% has been allocated on the basis of sales volume.

(2) Only 50% of the production overheads can be directly allocated to the departments. This has been allocated in the ratio 2:2:1.

(3) Only 60% of the expenses can be directly traced to the departments. This has been allocated in the ratio 3:3:2.

(4) Fixed cost of labour is 80%.

(5) This is the remaining 50% of overheads that can't be allocated to departments.

(6) This is the remaining 40% of expenses that can't be allocated to departments.

Conclusion

From the restated figures department 3 should be kept open since:

- The department is making a contribution of $4,561 to the overall profit of the business.
- The apparent loss arises purely from inappropriate apportionment of overheads and expenses.
- If the department were closed:
  - there would be a loss of $4,561 contribution to the business and
  - on the assumption there would be no further saving on fixed costs, the profit would be reduced to $56,439.

(b) Consideration must be given to the following factors which may be non-quantifiable at present:

- Redundancy costs or costs relating to the disposal of equipment if department 3 is closed.
- The possible loss of business due to products from department 3 being unavailable to customers who buy from other departments at the same time.
- The reorganisation costs that may arise from the closure of department 3.
- Additional benefits of closure of department 3 such as labour and machinery being used to generate contribution elsewhere in the business.

Test your understanding 5

		$	$
Material A	1,000 kgs @ $2 – $300	1,700	
(note 1)	1,000 kgs @ $10	10,000	
			11,700
Material B (note 2)	1,000 kgs @$15		15,000
Material C (note 3)	500 kgs – opportunity cost		8,000
Material D (note 4)	50 litres @ $50		(2,500)
Skilled labour (note 5)	1,000 hrs @ $25		25,000
Semi-skilled labour (note 6)	500 hrs @ $22.50		11,250
Unskilled labour (note 7)	500 hrs @ $12 (opportunity cost)		6,000
Minimum tender price = total of relevant cash flows			74,450

Notes

(1) There are 1,000 kgs in stock and these will not be replaced. These would otherwise be sold at a net gain of $1,700. This gain is therefore foregone as a result of using this material in the contract. The other 1,000 kgs are out of stock and therefore the relevant cost is the current purchase price of $10 per kg.

(2) The material is in stock but will be replaced and therefore the relevant cost is the current purchase price of $15 per kg.

(3) The material is in stock and there are two options if this material is not used for the contract:

Option 1 – Sell it for $6,000.

Option 2 – Use it as a substitute and save $8,000.

Option 2 is preferable. This is therefore the opportunity cost of using it in the contract.

(4) The material is in stock and will not be replaced. The cost of disposing of 50 litres will be saved (@ $50/litre, i.e. $2,500). Saving this cost is a relevant benefit.

(5) The incremental cost of paying for the labour needed.

(6) 1,500 spare hours have already been paid for as the workforce are on annual contracts. The additional cash flow is therefore the extra 500 hours that are needed at time-and-a-half.

(7) For each hour diverted from their normal jobs contribution of $2 will be foregone. This together with the cost of paying the workers to do the project amounts to a relevant cost of $12 per kg. They would not be hired at $20 per hour as this is more expensive.

(8) Fixed overheads can be ignored as they are not incremental.

(9) Costs of preparing the tender are all sunk costs and hence must be ignored.

(10) Profit element should be ignored since a minimum contract price is being calculated.

Test your understanding 6

(a) Market value basis

	Product A	Product B	Total
Sales value	$10,000	$20,000	$30,000
Joint costs apportioned (W1)	$6,000	$12,000	$18,000
Gross Profit	$4,000	$8,000	$12,000

Working:

Joint costs allocated to Product A $= \frac{10,000}{30,000} \times \$18,000 = \$6,000$

Joint costs allocated to Product B $= \frac{20,000}{30,000} \times \$18,000 = \$12,000$

(b) Production units basis

	Product A	Product B	Total
Sales value	$10,000	$20,000	$30,000
Joint costs apportioned (W1)	$3,600	$14,400	$18,000
Gross Profit	$6,400	$5,600	$12,000

Working:

Total output units = 2,000 + 8,000 = 10,000

Joint costs allocated to Product A $= \frac{2,000}{10,000} \times \$18,000 = \$3,600$

Joint costs allocated to Product B $= \frac{8,000}{10,000} \times \$18,000 = \$14,400$

Test your understanding 7

The pre-separation (i.e. "joint") costs are not incremental and so can be ignored. The only incremental cash flows are as follows:

Product	**X**	**Y**	**Z**
	$000	$000	$000
Additional revenue from further processing	780	n/a	440
Additional costs from further processing	800	n/a	400
Benefit/ (cost) of further processing	(20)		40

Thus only Z should be processed further.

chapter

6

Risk and uncertainty

Chapter learning objectives

Upon completion of this chapter you will be able to:

- describe generally available research techniques to reduce uncertainty, e.g. focus groups, market research;
- suggest for a given situation, suitable research techniques for reducing uncertainty;
- explain, using a simple example, the use of simulation;
- explain, calculate and demonstrate the use of expected values and sensitivity analysis in simple decision-making situations;
- for given data, apply the techniques of maximax, maximin and minimax regret to decision making problems including the production of profit tables;
- calculate the value of perfect information;
- calculate the value of imperfect information.

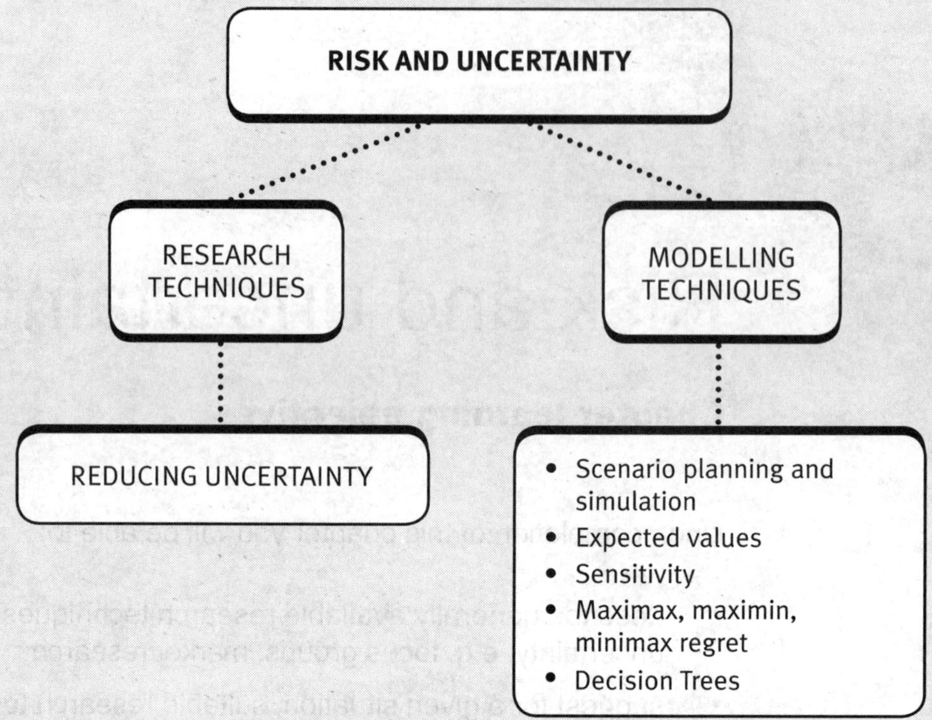

1 Introduction

Risk and uncertainty

All businesses face risk.

Risk is the variability of possible returns.

Risk management is important in a business. It is the process of understanding and managing the risks that an organisation is inevitably subject to.

Distinction between risk and uncertainty

Risk: there are a number of possible outcomes and the probability of each outcome is known.

For example, based on past experience of digging for oil in a particular area, an oil company may estimate that they have a 60% chance of finding oil and a 40% chance of not finding oil.

Uncertainty: there are a number of possible outcomes but the probability of each outcome is not known.

For example, the same oil company may dig for oil in a previously unexplored area. The company knows that it is possible for them to either find or not find oil but it does not know the probabilities of each of these outcomes.

The use of research techniques to reduce uncertainty

Market research is an important means of assessing and reducing uncertainty. For example, about the likely responses of customers to new products, new advertising campaigns and price changes.

A number of research techniques are available:

- Focus Groups
- Desk research (secondary research).
- Field research (primary research). This includes:
  - motivational and
  - measurement research.

Each method will be reviewed in turn.

Focus groups

Focus groups are a common market research tool involving small groups (typically eight to ten people) selected from the broader population. The group is interviewed through facilitator-led discussions in an informal environment in order to gather their opinions and reactions to a particular subject.

For example, a supermarket may use a focus group before a product launch decision is made in order to gather opinions on a new range of pizzas.

Problems with focus groups

- Results are qualitative.
- The small sample size means that results may not be representative.
- Individuals may feel under pressure to agree with other members or to give a 'right' answer.
- Their cost and logistical complexity is frequently cited as a barrier, especially for smaller companies. On-line focus groups are becoming more popular and help to address this issue.

Desk research

- The information is collected from secondary sources.
- It obtains existing data by studying published and other available sources of information. For example, press articles, published accounts, census information.
- It can often eliminate the need for extensive field work.

Factors to consider when using desk research

- It may not be exactly what the researcher wants and may not be totally up to date or accurate.
- However, it is quicker and cheaper than field research.

There are three main types of information that can be collected by desk research:

- Economic intelligence can be defined as information relating to the economic environment within which a company operates. It is concerned with such factors as gross national product (GNP), investment, expenditure, population, employment, productivity and trade. It provides an organisation with a picture of past and future trends in the environment and with an indication of the company's position in the economy as a whole. A great deal of information is freely available in this area from sources such as government ministries, the nationalised industries, universities and organisations such as the OECD.
- Market intelligence is information about a company's present or possible future markets. Such information will be both commercial and technical, for example, the level of sales of competitors' products recorded by the Business Monitor or Census of Production; the product range offered by existing or potential competitors; the number of outlets forming the distribution network for a company's products; the structure of that network by size, location and relation to the end user; and the best overseas markets for a company.
- Internal company data is perhaps the most neglected source of marketing information. Companies tend to record their sales information for accountancy purposes or for the management of the sales force. Conversely, many companies, especially blue-chips and public services, can often be seen to produce reams of data for no apparent reason, or because 'we always have done'. Rarely is the information collected in a form in which it can readily be used by marketing management.

Field research

- Information is collected from primary sources by direct contact with a targeted group.
- Although it is more expensive and time consuming than desk research the results should be more accurate, relevant and up to date.
- There are two types of field research:
  - motivational research
  - measurement research.

Motivational research – the objective is to understand factors that influence why consumers do or do not buy particular products.

Motivational research techniques

Some of the more common techniques in motivational research are:

- Depth interviewing – undertaken at length by a trained person who is able to appreciate conscious and unconscious associations and motivations and their significance.
- Group interviewing – where between six and ten people are asked to consider the relevant subject (object) under trained supervision.
- Word association testing – on being given a word by the interviewer, the first word that comes into the mind of the person being tested is noted.
- Triad testing – where people are asked which out of a given three items they prefer. If the three are brands of a given type of product (or three similar types), replies may show a great deal about which features of a product most influence the buying decision.

Measurement research – the objective here is to build on the motivation research by trying to quantify the issues involved.

- Sample surveys are used to find out how many people buy the product, what quantity each type of buyer purchases, and where and when the product is bought.
- This sort of information can also be collected in retail environments at the point of sale, for example, through the use of loyalty cards.

Types of measurement research

It is also possible (less accurately) to assess roughly the importance of some reasons for buying or not buying a product. The main types of measurement are:

Random sampling– where each person in the target population has an equal chance of being selected. Such samples are more likely to be representative, making predictions more reliable. However, the technique may be unfeasible in practice.

Quota sampling– where samples are designed to be representative with respect to pre-selected criteria.

- For example, if the target population is 55% women and 45% men, then a sample of 200 people could be structured so 110 women and 90 men are asked, rather than simply asking 200 people and leaving it up to chance whether or not the gender mix is typical.
- The main disadvantage of quota sampling is that samples may still be biased for non-selected criteria.

Panelling– where the sample is kept for subsequent investigations, so trends are easier to spot.

Surveying by post– the mail shot method. Unfortunately the sample becomes self-selecting and so may be biased.

Observation– e.g. through the use of cameras within supermarkets to examine how long customers spend on reading the nutritional information on food packaging.

2 Other methods of dealing with risk and uncertainty

In addition to the research techniques discussed, the following methods can be used to address risk or uncertainty.

- Sensitivity analysis
- Simulation
- Expected values
- Maximax, maximin and minimax regret
- Decision Trees

Each method will be reviewed in turn.

3 Sensitivity analysis

Sensitivity analysis takes each uncertain factor in turn, and calculates the change that would be necessary in that factor before the original decision is reversed. Typically, it involves posing 'what-if' questions.

By using this technique it is possible to establish which estimates (variables) are more critical than others in affecting a decision.

The process is as follows:

- Best estimates for variables are made and a decision arrived at.
- Each of the variables is analysed in turn to see how much the original estimate can change before the original decision is reversed. For example, it may be that the estimated selling price can fall by 5% before the original decision to accept a project is reversed.
- Estimates for each variable can then be reconsidered to assess the likelihood of the estimate being wrong. For example, what is the chance of the selling price falling by more than 5%?
- The maximum possible change is often expressed as a percentage.This formula only works for total cash flows. It cannot be used for individual units, selling prices, variable cost per unit, etc.

e.g

Illustration 1 - Sensitivity analysis

A manager is considering a make v buy decision based on the following estimates:

	If made in-house	If buy in and re-badge
	$	$
Variable production costs	10	2
External purchase costs	-	6
Ultimate selling price	15	14

You are required to assess the sensitivity of the decision to the external purchase price.

Solution

Step 1: What is the original decision?

Comparing contribution figures, the product should be bought in and re-badged:

	If made in-house	If buy in and re-badge
	$	$
Contribution	5	6

Step 2: Calculate the sensitivity (to the external purchase price)

For indifference, the contribution from outsourcing needs to fall to $5 per unit. Thus the external purchase price only needs to increase by $1 per unit (or $1/ $6 = 17%). If the external purchase price rose by more than 17% the original decision would be reversed.

Strengths of sensitivity analysis

- There is no complicated theory to understand.
- Information will be presented to management in a form which facilitates subjective judgement to decide the likelihood of the various possible outcomes considered.
- It identifies areas which are crucial to the success of the project. If the project is chosen, those areas can be carefully monitored.

4 Weaknesses of sensitivity analysis

- It assumes that changes to variables can be made independently, e.g. material prices will change independently of other variables. Simulation allows us to change more than one variable at a time.
- It only identifies how far a variable needs to change; it does not look at the probability of such a change.
- It provides information on the basis of which decisions can be made but it does not point to the correct decision directly.

5 Simulation

Simulation is a modelling technique that shows the effect of more than one variable changing at the same time.

It is often used in capital investment appraisal.

The Monte Carlo simulation method uses random numbers and probability statistics. It can include all random events that might affect the success or failure of a proposed project - for example, changes in material prices, labour rates, market size, selling price, investment costs or inflation.

The model identifies key variables in a decision : costs and revenues, say. Random numbers are then assigned to each variable in a proportion in accordance with the underlying probability distribution. For example, if the most likely outcomes are thought to have a 50% probability, optimistic outcomes a 30% probability and pessimistic outcomes a 20% probability, random numbers, representing those attributes, can be assigned to costs and revenues in those proportions.

A powerful computer is then used to repeat the decision many times and give management a view of the likely range and level of outcomes. Depending on the management's attitude to risk, a more informed decision can be taken.

This helps to model what is essentially a one-off decision using many possible repetitions. It is only of any real value, however, if the underlying probability distribution can be estimated with some degree of confidence.

e.g

Illustration 2 - The MP Organisation

The MP Organisation is an independent film production company. It has a number of potential films that it is considering producing, one of which is the subject of a management meeting next week. The film which has been code named CA45 is a thriller based on a novel by a well respected author.

The expected revenues from the film have been estimated as follows: there is a 30% chance it may generate total sales of $254,000; 50% chance sales may reach $318,000 and 20% chance they may reach $382,000.

Expected costs (advertising, promotion and marketing) have also been estimated as follows: there is a 20% chance they will reach approximately $248,000; 60% chance they may get to $260,000 and 20 % chance of totalling $272,000.

In a Monte Carlo simulation, these revenues and costs could have random numbers assigned to them:

Sales Revenue	Probability	Assign Random Numbers (assume integers)
$254,000	0.30	00-29
$318,000	0.50	30-79
$382,000	0.20	80-99
Costs		
$248,000	0.20	00-19
$260,000	0.60	20-79
$272,000	0.20	80-99

A computer could generate 20-digit random numbers such as 98125602386617556398. These would then be matched to the random numbers assigned to each probability and values assigned to 'Sales Revenues' and 'Costs' based on this. The random numbers generated give 5 possible outcomes in our example:

Random number	Sales revenue in $000	Random Number	Costs in $000	Profit
98	382	12	248	134
56	318	02	248	70
38	318	66	260	58
17	254	55	260	(6)
63	318	98	272	46

e.g

Illustration 3 - Simulation

A business is choosing between two projects, project A and project B. It uses simulation to generate a distribution of profits for each project.

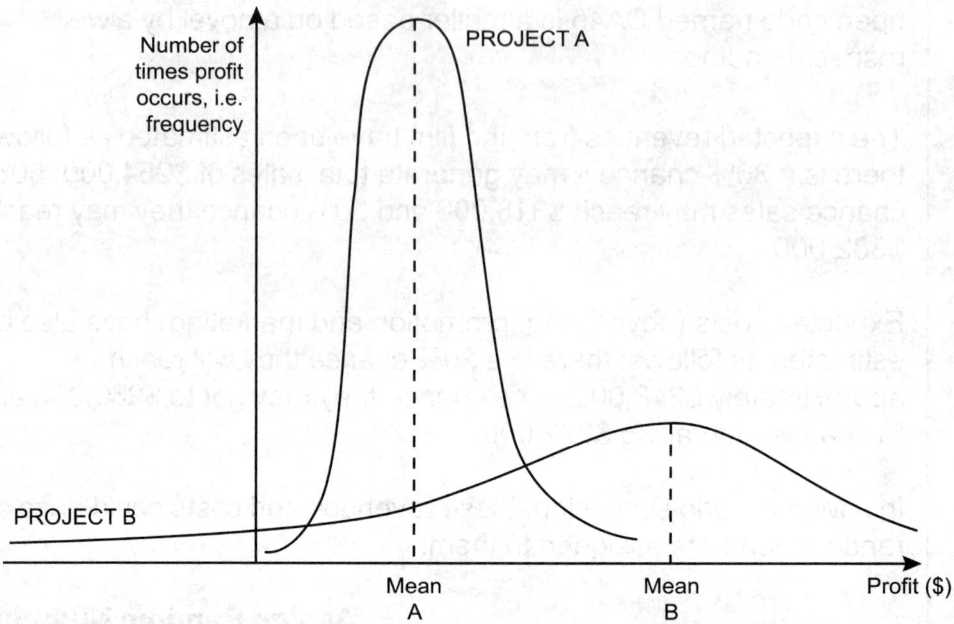

Required:

Which project should the business invest in?

Solution

Project A has a lower average profit but is also less risky (less variability of possible profits).

Project B has a higher average profit but is also more risky (more variability of possible profits).

There is no correct answer. All simulation will do is give the business the above results. It will not tell the business which is the better project.

If the business is willing to take on risk, they may prefer project B since it has the higher average return.

However, if the business would prefer to minimise its exposure to risk, it would take on project A. This has a lower risk but also a lower average return.

Drawbacks of simulation

There are major drawbacks of simulation:

- It is not a technique for making a decision, only for obtaining more information about the possible outcomes.
- Models can become extremely complex.
- The time and costs involved in their construction can be more than is gained from the improved decisions.
- Probability distributions may be difficult to formulate.

Test your understanding 1

Assess the use of simulation for a chain of betting shops.

6 Expected values (EVs)

An expected value is a weighted average of all possible outcomes. It calculates the average return that will be made if a decision is repeated again and again. In other words, it is obtained by multiplying the value of each possible outcome (x), by the probability of that outcome (p), and summing the results.

The formula for the expected value is **EV = Σpx**

Illustration 4 – Calculating EVs

Returns from a new restaurant venture depend on whether a competitor decides to open up in the same area. The following estimates are made:

Competitor opens up	Probability (p)	Project NPV (x)	px
		$	$
Yes	0.3	(10,000)	(3,000)
No	0.7	20,000	14,000
		EV =	11,000

Since the expected value shows the long run average outcome of a decision which is repeated time and time again, it is a useful decision rule for a **risk neutral decision maker**. This is because a risk neutral investor neither seeks risk or avoids it; he is happy to accept an average outcome.

Advantages and disadvantages of EVs

Advantages:

- Takes uncertainty into account by considering the probability of each possible outcome and using this information to calculate an expected value.
- The information is reduced to a single number resulting in easier decisions.
- Calculations are relatively simple.

Disadvantages:

- The probabilities used are usually very subjective.
- The EV is merely a weighted average and therefore has little meaning for a one-off project.
- The EV gives no indication of the dispersion of possible outcomes about the EV, i.e. the risk.
- The EV may not correspond to any of the actual possible outcomes.

Pay-off tables

A profit table (pay-off table) can be a useful way to represent and analyse a scenario where there is a range of possible outcomes and a variety of possible responses. A pay-off table simply illustrates all possible profits/losses.

e.g

Illustration 5 - Geoffrey Ramsbottom

Geoffrey Ramsbottom runs a kitchen that provides food for various canteens throughout a large organisation. A particular salad is sold to the canteen for $10 and costs $8 to prepare. Therefore, the contribution per salad is $2.

Based upon past demands, it is expected that, during the 250-day working year, the canteens will require the following daily quantities:

On 25 days of the year	40 salads
On 50 days of the year	50 salads
On 100 days of the year	60 salads
On 75 days	70 salads
Total 250 days	

The kitchen must prepare the salad in batches of 10 meals. Its staff has asked you to help them decide how many salads it should supply for each day of the forthcoming year.

Solution - Geoffrey Ramsbottom

Constructing a pay-off table:

- If 40 salads will be required on 25 days of a 250-day year, the probability that demand = 40 salads is :

P(Demand of 40) = 25 days ÷ 250 days

P(Demand Of 40) = 0.1

- Likewise, P(Demand of 50) = 0 .20; P(Demand of 60 = 0.4) and P (Demand of 70 = 0.30).
- Now let's look at the different values of profit or losses depending on how many salads are supplied and sold. For example, if we supply 40 salads and all are sold, our profits amount to 40 x $2 = 80.
- If however we supply 50 salads but only 40 are sold, our profits will amount to 40 x $2 - (10 unsold salads x $8 unit cost) = 0.

We can now construct a pay-off table as follows:

			Daily Supply			
		Probability	**40 salads**	**50 salads**	**60 salads**	**70 salads**
Daily demand	40 salads	0.10	$80	$0	($80)	($160)
	50 salads	0.20	$80	$100	$20	($60)
	60 salads	0.40	$80	$100	$120	$40
	70 salads	0.30	$80	$100	$120	$140

7 Maximax, maximin and minimax regret

When probabilities are not available, there are still tools available for incorporating uncertainty into decision making.

Maximax

The maximax rule involves selecting the alternative that maximises the maximum pay-off achievable.

This approach would be suitable for an optimist, or 'risk-seeking' investor, who seeks to achieve the best results if the best happens.

Illustration 6 - The Maximax rule

Following up from the pay-off table example, Geoffrey Ramsbottom's table looks as follows:

			Daily Supply			
		Probability	**40 salads**	**50 salads**	**60 salads**	**70 salads**
Daily demand	40 salads	0.10	$80	$0	($80)	($160)
	50 salads	0.20	$80	$100	$20	($60)
	60 salads	0.40	$80	$100	$120	$40
	70 salads	0.30	$80	$100	$120	$140

The manager who employs the maximax criterion is assuming that whatever action is taken, the best will happen; he/she is a risk-taker. How many salads will he decide to supply?

Answer

Here, the highest maximum possible pay-off is $140. We should therefore decide to supply 70 salads a day.

Test your understanding 2 - Applying maximax

A company is choosing which of three new products to make (A, B or C) and has calculated likely pay-offs under three possible scenarios (I, II or III), giving the following pay-off table.

Profit (loss)	**Product chosen**		
Scenario	**A**	**B**	**C**
I	20	80	10
II	40	70	100
III	50	(10)	40

Required:

Using maximax, which product would be chosen?

Maximin

The maximin rule involves selecting the alternative that maximises the minimum pay-off achievable. The investor would look at the worst possible outcome at each supply level, then selects the highest one of these. The decision maker therefore chooses the outcome which is guaranteed to minimise his losses. In the process, he loses out on the opportunity of making big profits.

This approach would be appropriate for a pessimist who seeks to achieve the best results if the worst happens.

Test your understanding 3 - Applying maximin

Required:

Using the information from the previous TYU apply the maximin rule to decide which product should be made.

e.g

Illustration 7 - The 'Maximin' rule

Following up from the pay-off table example, Geoffrey Ramsbottom's table looks as follows:

			Daily Supply			
		Probability	**40 salads**	**50 salads**	**60 salads**	**70 salads**
Daily demand	40 salads	0.10	$80	$0	($80)	($160)
	50 salads	0.20	$80	$100	$20	($60)
	60 salads	0.40	$80	$100	$120	$40
	70 salads	0.30	$80	$100	$120	$140

How many salads should we supply, using the Maximin rule?

Answer

If we decide to supply 40 salads, the minimum pay-off is $80.

If we decide to supply 50 salads, the minimum pay-off is $0.

If we decide to supply 60 salads, the minimum pay-off is ($80).

If we decide to supply 70 salads, the minimum pay-off is ($160).

The highest minimum payoff arises from supplying **40 salads**.

The minimax regret rule

The minimax regret strategy is the one that minimises the maximum regret. It is useful for a risk-neutral decision maker. Essentially, this is the technique for a 'sore loser' who does not wish to make the wrong decision.

'Regret' in this context is defined as the opportunity loss through having made the wrong decision.

e.g

Illustration 8 - The 'Minimax Regret' rule

Following up from the pay-off table example, Geoffrey Ramsbottom's table looks as follows :

		Probability	Daily Supply 40 salads	50 salads	60 salads	70 salads
Daily demand	40 salads	0.10	$80	$0	($80)	($160)
	50 salads	0.20	$80	$100	$20	($60)
	60 salads	0.40	$80	$100	$120	$40
	70 salads	0.30	$80	$100	$120	$140

How many salads should we decide to supply if the minimax regret rule is applied?

Answer

Following up from the pay-off table example, Geoffrey Ramsbottom's table looks as follows :

		Probability	Daily Supply 40 salads	50 salads	60 salads	70 salads
Daily demand	40 salads	0.10	$80	$0	($80)	($160)
	50 salads	0.20	$80	$100	$20	($60)
	60 salads	0.40	$80	$100	$120	$40
	70 salads	0.30	$80	$100	$120	$140

If the minimax regret rule is applied to decide how many salads should be made each day, we need to calculate the 'regrets'. This means we need to find the biggest pay-off for each demand row, then subtract all other numbers in this row from the largest number.

For example, if the demand is 40 salads, we will make a maximum profit of $80 if they all sell. If we had decided to supply 50 salads, we would achieve a nil profit. The difference, or 'regret' between that nil profit and the maximum of $80 achievable for that row is $80.

Regrets can be tabulated as follows:

		Daily Supply			
		40 salads	**50 salads**	**60 salads**	**70 salads**
Daily demand	40 salads	$0	$80	$160	$240
	50 salads	$20	$0	$80	$160
	60 salads	$40	$20	$0	$80
	70 salads	$60	$40	$20	$0

Conclusion

If we decide to supply 40 salads, the maximum regret is $60. If we decide to supply 50 salads, the maximum regret is $80. For 60 salads, the maximum regret is $160, and $240 for 70 salads. A manager employing the minimax regret criterion would want to minimise that maximum regret, and therefore supply 40 salads only.

8 Decision trees

A decision tree is a diagrammatic representation of a multi-decision problem, where all possible courses of action are represented, and every possible outcome of each course of action is shown.

Decision trees should be used where a problem involves a series of decisions being made and several outcomes arise during the decision-making process. Decision trees force the decision maker to consider the logical sequence of events. A complex problem is broken down into smaller, easier to handle sections.

The financial outcomes and probabilities are shown separately, and the decision tree is 'rolled back' by calculating expected values and making decisions.

Three step method

Step 1: Draw the tree from left to right, showing appropriate decisions and events / outcomes.

Some common symbols can be used: a **square** is used to represent a decision point (i.e. where a choice between different courses of action must be taken. A **circle** is used to represent a *chance* point. The branches coming away from a circle with have probabilities attached to them. All probabilities should add up to '1'.

Label the tree and relevant cash inflows/outflows and probabilities associated with outcomes.

Step2: Evaluate the tree from right to left carrying out these two actions:

(a) Calculate an EV at each outcome point.

(b) Choose the best option at each decision point.

Step 3: Recommend a course of action to management.

e.g

Decision trees

A university is trying to decide whether or not to advertise a new post-graduate degree programme.

The number of students starting the programme is dependent on economic conditions:

- If conditions are poor it is expected that the programme will attract 40 students without advertising. There is a 60% chance that economic conditions will be poor.
- If economic conditions are good it is expected that the programme will attract only 20 students without advertising. There is a 40% chance that economic conditions will be good.

If the programme is advertised and economic conditions are poor, there is a 65% chance that the advertising will stimulate further demand and student numbers will increase to 50. If economic conditions are good there is a 25% chance the advertising will stimulate further demand and numbers will increase to 25 students.

The profit expected, before deducting the cost of advertising, at different levels of student numbers are as follows:

Number of students	Profit in $
15	(10,000)
20	15,000
25	40,000
30	65,000
35	90,000
40	115,000
45	140,000
50	165,000

Required:

Demonstrate, using a decision tree, whether the programme should be advertised.

Answer - University advertising decision tree

Step 1: Draw the tree from left to right. A **square** is used to represent a decision point (i.e. whether to advertise the programme, or not advertise.).

For both options, a **circle** is used to represent a *chance* point - a poor economic environment, or a good economic environment.

Label the tree and relevant cash inflows/outflows and probabilities associated with outcomes :

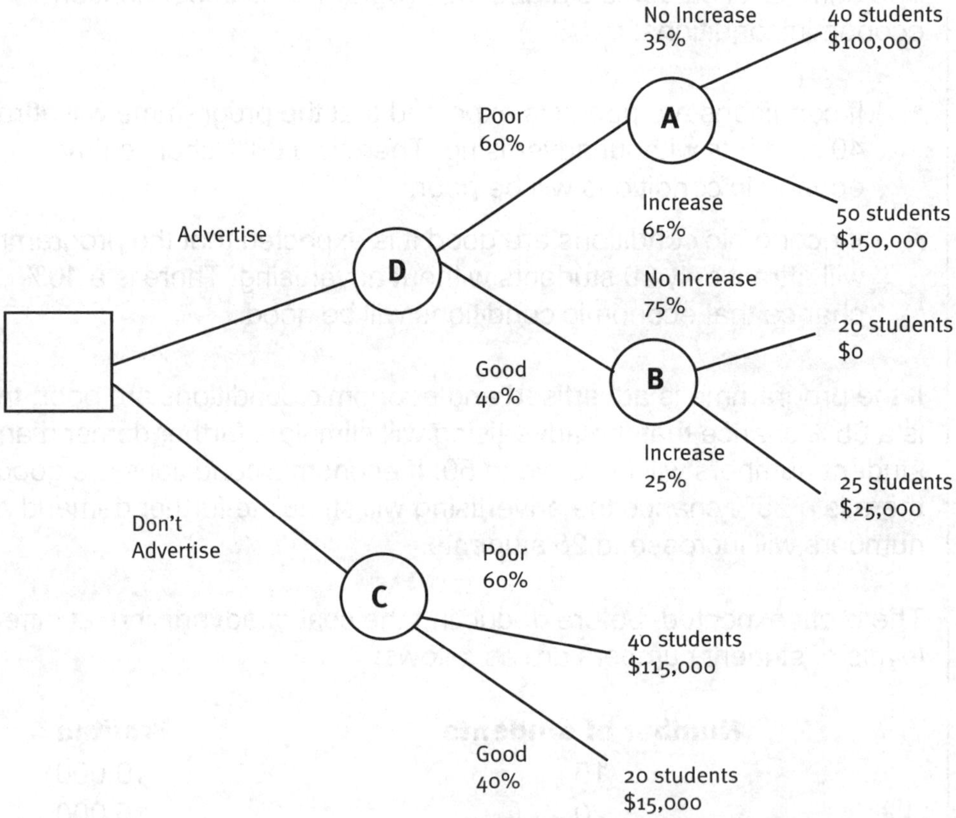

Step2: Evaluate the tree from right to left carrying out these two actions:

(a) Calculate an Expected Value at each outcome point. Working from top to bottom, we can calculate the EVs as follows:

EV (Outcome Point A) = (35% x $100,000) + (65% x $150,000) = $132,500

EV (Outcome Point B) = (0% x $0) + (25% x $25,000) = $6,250

EV (Outcome Point C) = (60% x $115,000) + (40% x $15,000) = $75,000

EV (Outcome Point D) = (60% x $132,500) + (40% x $6,250) = $82,000

(b) Choose the best option at each decision point and **recommend** a course of action to management.

At the first (and only) decision point in our tree, we should choose the option to advertise as EV ('D') is $82,000 and EV ('C) is $75,000.

9 The value of perfect information

In many questions the decision makers receive a forecast of a future outcome (for example a market research group may predict the forthcoming demand for a product). This forecast may turn out to be correct or incorrect. The question often requires the candidate to calculate the value of the forecast.

Perfect information The forecast of the future outcome is always a correct prediction. If a firm can obtain a 100% accurate prediction they will always be able to undertake the most beneficial course of action for that prediction.

Imperfect information The forecast is usually correct, but can be incorrect. Imperfect information is not as valuable as perfect information.

The value of information (either perfect or imperfect) may be calculated as follows:

Expected Profit (Outcome) WITH the information LESS Expected Profit (Outcome) WITHOUT the information

Test your understanding 4 - Geoffrey Ramsbottom

A new ordering system is being considered, whereby customers must order their salad online the day before. With this new system Mr Ramsbottom will know for certain the daily demand 24 hours in advance. He can adjust production levels on a daily basis.

How much is this new system worth to Mr Ramsbottom?

10 The value of imperfect information

Perfect information is only rarely accessible. In fact, information sources such as market research or industry experts are usually subject to error. Market research findings, for example, are likely to be reasonably accurate - but they can still be wrong.

Therefore, our analysis must extend to deal with imperfect information. The question is as follows : **how much would it be worth paying for such imperfect information**, given that we are aware of how right or wrong it is likely to be?

e.g

The Value of Imperfect Information

(a) You have the mineral rights to a piece of land that you believe may have oil underground. There is only a 10% chance that you will strike oil if you drill, but the profit is $200,000.

It costs $10,000 to drill. The alternative is not to drill at all, in which case your profit is zero.

Should you drill? Draw a decision tree to represent your problem.

(b) Before you drill, you may consult a geologist who can assess the promise of the piece of land. She can tell you whether the prospects are good or poor, but she is not a perfect predictor. If there is oil, the probability that she will say there are good prospects is 95%. If there is no oil, the probability that she will say prospects are poor is 85%.

Draw a decision tree and calculate the value of imperfect information for this geologist. If the geologist charges $7,000, would you use her services?

Solution

(a)

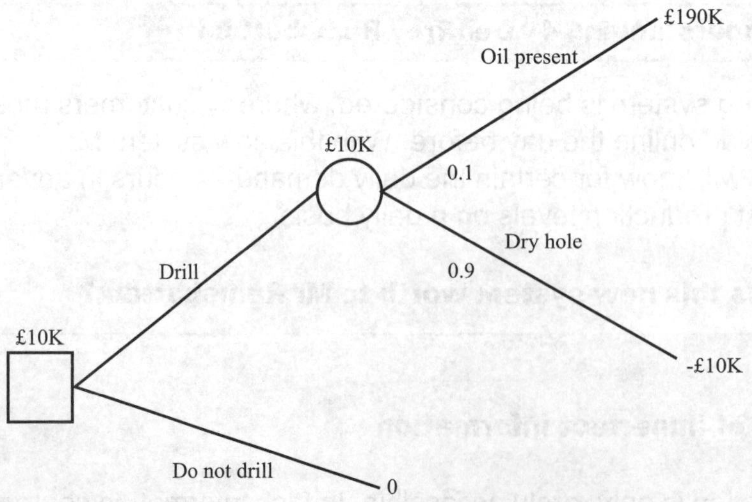

EV ('Drill') = ($190K x 0.1) + (-$10K x 0.9) so EV ('Drill') = $10K.

We should drill, because the expected value from drilling is $10K, versus nothing for not drilling.

(b) We will calculate the Expected Value of profits if we employ the geologist.

If this exceeds $10,000, the geologist would be worth employing **as long as the benefit of employing her exceeds her charge of $7,000.**

If we employ the geologist, the probabilities of her possible assessments can be tabulated as follows (assume 1,000 drills in total):

	Oil present	**No oil**	**Total**
Geologist says 'Prospects are good'	95% x 100 = 95 drills	15% x 900= 135 drills	230 drills
Geologist says 'Prospects are poor'	5% x 100 = 5 drills	85% x 900= 765 drills	770 drills
	100 drills	**900 drills**	**1,000 drills**

A decision tree can be drawn to calculate the expected value of profits if a geologist is employed:

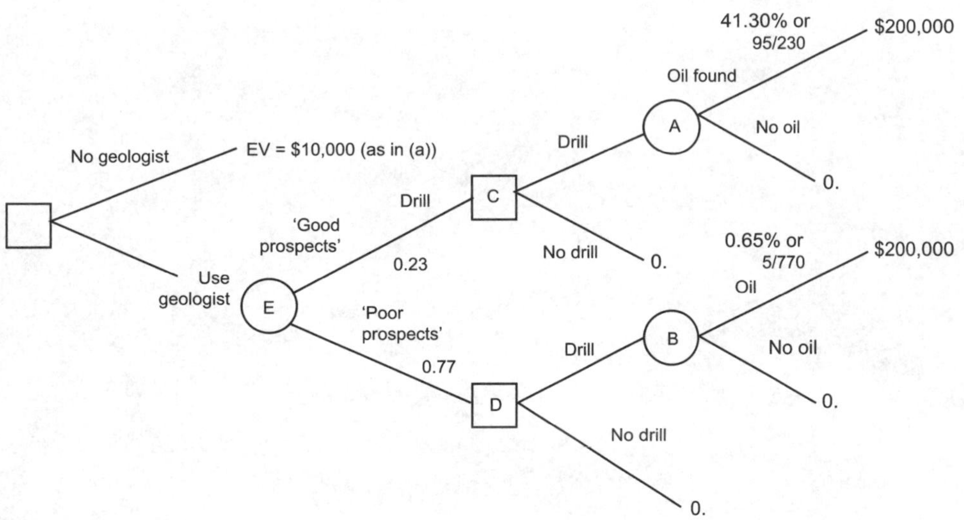

Working from right to left:

EV(A) = (41.30% x $200,000) - $10,000 drilling costs = $72,600. The decision at 'C' should be to drill, as this generates higher benefits than not drilling.

EV(B) = (0.65% x $200,000) - $10,000 drilling costs = -$8,700. The decision at 'D' should be not to drill.

EV(E) = 0.23 x $72,600 = $16,698. This is the expected value of profits if a geologist is employed and exceeds the EV of profits if she is not employed.

Expected Value of Imperfect Information = $16,698 - $10,000 = $6,698. Since this is less than the cost of buying the information ($7,000), we should not employ the geologist.

11 Chapter summary

Risk and uncertainty

- Variability in returns
- Risk aversion
- Upside v downside
- Risk v uncertainty

Research techniques

- Desk research
- Field research
- Focus groups

MODELLING TECHNIQUES

- Scenario planning and simulation
- Expected values – long-term average
- Sensitivity of decision to key estimates
- Maximax – optimist
- Maximin – pessimist
- Minimax – sore loser.

Test your understanding answers

Test your understanding 1

Simulation would be particularly useful on an operational level for analysing the possible implications of a single event, such as a major horse race or football match:

- Possible outcomes are easy to identify (e.g. win, lose, draw, 2-1,3-0, etc)
- Quoted odds can help estimate probabilities
- The outcomes of the simulation could be used to assess impact on cash flow, whether bets should be laid off with other betting agents to reduces risk, etc

Simulation could also be used for wider strategic analysis such as for assessing the possibility and implications of stricter anti-gambling legislation.

Test your understanding 2 - Applying maximax

Using maximax, an optimist would consider the best possible outcome for each product and pick the product with the greatest potential.

Here C would be chosen with a maximum possible gain of 100.

Test your understanding 3 - Applying maximin

- Using maximin, a pessimist would consider the poorest possible outcome for each product and would ensure that the maximum pay-off is achieved if the worst result were to happen.
- Therefore, product A would be chosen resulting in a minimum pay-off of 20 compared to a minimum pay-off of 10 for products B and C.

Test your understanding 4 - Geoffrey Ramsbottom

	X	P	
Supply = demand	Pay off	Probability	px
40	$80	0.1	8
50	$100	0.2	20
60	$120	0.4	48
70	$140	0.3	42
			118

E.V. with perfect information	= $118
E.V. without perfect information (Working 1)	= $90
Value of perfect information	$28 per day

Working 1 :

According to the pay-off table from Illustration 5, the Expected Value of Profits if **40 salads** are supplied can be calculated as (0.10 x $80) + (0.20 x $80) + (0.40 x $80) + (0.30 x $80) = **$80.**

Likewise :

EV ('**50 salads** daily supply') =	($0 x 10%) =	$0
	+($100 x 20%) =	$20
	+($100 x 40%) =	$40
	+($100 x 30%) =	$30
		$90
EV ('**60 salads** daily supply') =	(- $80 x 10%) =	($8)
	+($20 x 20%) =	$4
	+($120 x 40%) =	$48
	+($120 x 30%) =	$36
		$80
EV ('**70 salads** daily supply') =	(- $160 x 10%) =	($16)
	+(- $60 x 20%) =	($12)
	+($40 x 40%) =	$16
	+($140 x 30%) =	$42
		$30

Profits are therefore maximised at 50 salads and amount to $90.

chapter

7

Budgeting

Chapter learning objectives

Upon completion of this chapter you will be able to:

- explain why organisations use budgeting
- explain how budgetary systems fit within the performance hierarchy
- describe the factors which influence behaviour at work
- discuss the issues surrounding setting the difficulty level for a budget
- explain the benefits and difficulties of the participation of employees in the negotiation of targets
- explain how corporate and divisional objectives may differ and can be reconciled
- identify and resolve conflicting objectives, explaining the implications of the conflict and method of resolution.
- explain and evaluate 'top down' and 'bottom up' budgetary systems; 'rolling', 'activity-based', 'incremental' and 'zero-based' budgetary systems.
- explain and evaluate 'feed-forward' budgetary control
- select and justify an appropriate budgetary system for a given organisation
- describe the information used in various budgetary systems and the sources of the information needed
- explain the difficulties of changing a budgetary system and type of budget used
- explain how budget systems can deal with uncertainty in the environment
- explain the major benefits and dangers in using spreadsheets in budgeting.

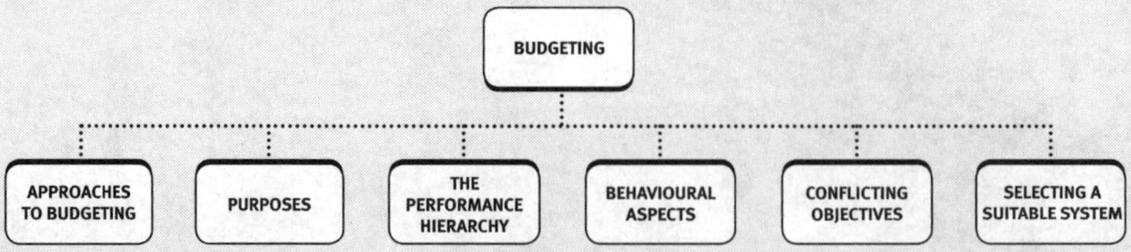

1 Purpose of budgets

A budget is a quantitative plan prepared for a specific time period. It is normally expressed in financial terms and prepared for one year.

Budgeting serves a number of purposes:

- **Planning**

  A budgeting process forces a business to look to the future. This is essential for survival since it stops management from relying on ad hoc or poorly co-ordinated planning.

- **Control**

  Actual results are compared against the budget and action is taken as appropriate.

- **Communication**

  The budget is a formal communication channel that allows junior and senior managers to converse.

- **Co-ordination**

  The budget allows co-ordination of all parts of the business towards a common corporate goal.

- **Evaluation**

  Responsibility accounting divides the organisation into budget centres, each of which has a manager who is responsible for its performance. The budget may be used to evaluate the actions of a manager within the business in terms of the costs and revenues over which they have control.

- **Motivation**

  The budget may be used as a target for managers to aim for. Reward should be given for operating within or under budgeted levels of expenditure. This acts as a motivator for managers.

- **Authorisation**

  The budget acts as a formal method of authorisation to a manager for expenditure, hiring staff and the pursuit of plans contained within the budget.

- **Delegation**

  Managers may be involved in setting the budget. Extra responsibility may motivate the managers. Management involvement may also result in more realistic targets.

2 Budgets and performance management

Budgets contribute to performance management by providing benchmarks against which to compare actual results (through variance analysis), and develop corrective measures. They take many forms and serve many functions, but most provide the basis for :

- detailed sales targets
- staffing plans
- production
- cash investment and borrowing
- capital expenditure

Budgets give managers "preapproval" for execution of spending plans, and allow them to provide forward looking guidance to investors and creditors. For example, budgets are necessary to convince banks and other lenders to extend credit.

Even in a small business, an robust business plan/budget can often result in anticipating and avoiding disastrous outcomes.
Medium and larger organisations invariably rely on budgets. This is equally true in businesses, government, and not-for-profit organizations. The budget provides a formal quantitative expression of expectations. It is an essential facet of the planning and control process. Without a budget, an organisation will be highly inefficient and ineffective.

Test your understanding 1 - Evaluation of managers

A wage award for production staff is agreed which exceeds the allowance incorporated in the budget. Discuss whether the performance of the production manager should be linked to the wage cost.

3 The performance hierarchy

As you may recall from paper F1, firms have a planning hierarchy:

- Strategic planning is long term, looks at the whole organisation and defines resource requirements. For example, to develop new products in response to changing customer needs.
- Tactical planning is medium term, looks at the department / divisional level and specifies how to use resources. For example, to train staff to deal with the challenges that this new product presents.
- Operational planning is very short term, very detailed and is mainly concerned with control. Most budgeting activities fall within operational planning and control. For example, a budget is set for the new product to include advertising expenditure, sales forecasts, labour and material expenditure etc.

The aim is that if a manager achieves short-term budgetary targets (operational plans) then there is more chance of meeting tactical goals and ultimately success for strategic plans.

The achievement of budgetary plans will impact on the eventual achievement of the tactical and strategic plans. However, budgets should also be flexible in order to meet the changing needs of the business.

4 Behavioural aspects of budgeting

Individuals react to the demands of budgeting and budgetary control in different ways and their behaviour can damage the budgeting process.

Behavioural problems are often linked to management styles, and include dysfunctional behaviour and budget slack.

Management styles (Hopwood)

Research was carried out by Hopwood (1973) into the manufacturing division of a US steelworks, involving a sample of more than 200 managers with cost centre responsibility. Hopwood identified three distinct styles of using budgetary information to evaluate management performance.

Management style	Performance evaluation	Behavioural aspects
(1) Budget constrained style	• Manager evaluated on ability to achieve budget in the short term.	• Job related pressure • May result in short-term decision making at the expense of long term goals.
	• Manager will be criticised for poor results. For example, if spending exceeds the limit set.	• Can result in poor working relations with colleagues • Can result in manipulation of data
(2) Profit conscious style	• Manager evaluated on ability to reduce costs and increase profit in the long term.	• Less job related pressure
	• For example, a manager will be prepared to exceed the budgetary limit in the short term if this will result in an increase in long term profit.	• Better working relations with colleagues • Less manipulation of data
(3) Non-accounting style	• Manager evaluated mainly on non-accounting performance indicators such as quality and customer satisfaction.	• Similar to profit conscious style but there is less concern for accounting information. • Requires significant and stringent monitoring of performance against budget

5 Setting the difficulty level of a budget

Budgetary targets will assist motivation and appraisal if they are at the right level.

An **expectations** budget is a budget set at current achievable levels. This is unlikely to motivate managers to improve but may give more accurate forecasts for resource planning, control and performance evaluation.

An **aspirations** budget is a budget set at a level which exceeds the level currently achieved. This may motivate managers to improve if it is seen as attainable but may also result in an adverse variance if it is too difficult to achieve. This must be managed carefully.

Test your understanding 2

A manager is awarded a bonus for achieving monthly budgetary targets. State three possible behavioural implications of this policy. What should be done to try to improve the process?

Test your understanding 3

A sales manager has achieved $550,000 of sales in the current year. Business is expected to grow by 10% and price inflation is expected to be 3%.

Suggest a suitable budget target for the forthcoming year.

6 Conflicting objectives

There are many examples of conflicting objectives that occur in budgeting. The illustration below identifies some common conflicts and explains how they can be resolved.

e.g

Illustration 1 – Conflicting objects

Type of conflict	Examples	Resolution
Company versus division.	• The company wishes to increase shareholder wealth. This should involve the use of NPV but divisions are assessed on accounting targets such as profit. • Similarly shareholder wealth is determined by the long term but divisions are set short term targets (see below). • Managers reject projects that dilute divisional performance, even though they beat company targets.	• Some companies try to insist that projects are assessed using NPV but then still impose accounting targets. • Give managers share options so they focus on shareholder wealth. • Use performance measures that encourage the division to accept projects which meet or exceed company target. For example, residual income (reviewed in chapter 12)
Division versus division.	• Divisions may compete for limited financial resources when setting budgets.	1 Prioritisation (e.g. using zero based budgeting – covered in chapter 7). 2 Negotiation and compromise.
Short-termism.	• Managers cut R&D to hit short term targets but erode long term competences. • Managers reject projects that are "slow starters" even though they have positive NPV.	1 Use more non-financial indicators that focus on key long term issues such as quality, productivity, etc. (These are discussed in more detail in chapter 11). 2 Link bonuses to longer time periods.

Individualism.	• The risk of budgetary slack. This is when managers participate in target setting and, as a result, make the budget too easy to achieve.	• Greater scrutiny of budgets. • Better training of managers.

Test your understanding 4

A manager is planning to retire at the end of the current period. His final bonus is based on the performance of his division for the period.

Required:

Suggest some performance management issues this raises and how they can be resolved.

7 Approaches to budgeting

Introduction

There are a number of different budgetary systems:

- Top down vs bottom up budgeting
- Incremental budgeting
- Zero-based budgeting (ZBB)
- Rolling budgets
- Activity-based budgeting
- Feed-forward control

Each system will be reviewed in turn.

Top down and bottom up budgeting

A top down budget is a budget that is set without allowing the ultimate budget holder to have the opportunity to participate in the budgeting process.

A bottom up budget is a system of budgeting in which budget holders have the opportunity to participate in setting their own budgets. Also called participative budgeting.

Advantages of bottom up budgets	Disadvantages of bottom up budgets
(1) Increased motivation due to ownership of the budget	(1) Senior managers may resent loss of control
(2) Should contain better information since employees most familiar with the department set the budget	(2) Dysfunctional behaviour: budgets may not be in line with corporate objectives as managers lack a strategic perspective and will focus on divisional concerns
(3) Increases manager's understanding and commitment	(3) Bad decisions from inexperienced managers
(4) Better communication between departments	(4) Budget preparation is slow and disputes can arise
(5) Senior managers can concentrate on strategy	(5) Budgetary slack: managers set targets that are too easy to achieve.

Test your understanding 5

Bottom up budgeting is generally seen as preferable because it leads to improved managerial motivation and performance. However, there are situations for which top down budgeting is preferable.

Describe three situations where top down budgeting would be more applicable.

Incremental budgets

An incremental budget starts with the previous period's budget or actual results and adds (or subtracts) an incremental amount to cover inflation and other known changes.

It is suitable for stable businesses, where costs are not expected to change significantly. There should be good cost control and limited discretionary costs.

Advantages of incremental budgets	Disadvantages of incremental budgets
(1) Quickest and easiest method	(1) Builds in previous problems and inefficiencies
(2) Suitable if the organisation is stable and historic figures are acceptable since only the increment needs to be justified	(2) Uneconomic activities may be continued. E.g. the firm may continue to make a component in-house when it might be cheaper to outsource.
	(3) Managers may spend unnecessarily to use up their budgeted expenditure allowance this year, thus ensuring they get the same (or a larger) budget next year.

Test your understanding 6

AW Inc produces two products, A and C. In the last year (20X4) it produced 640 units of A and 350 units of C incurring costs of $672,000. Analysis of the costs has shown that 75% of the total costs are variable. 60% of these variable costs vary in line with the number of A produced and the remainder with the number of C.

The budget for the year 20X5 is now being prepared using an incremental budgeting approach. The following additional information is available for 20X5:

- All costs will be 4% higher than the average paid in 20X4.
- Efficiency levels will remain unchanged.
- Expected output of A is 750 units and of C is 340 units.

What is the budgeted total variable cost of products A and C for the full year 20X5?

Zero-based budgeting

A 'method of budgeting that requires each cost element to be specifically justified, as though the activities to which the budget relates were being undertaken for the first time. Without approval, the budget allowance is zero'

It is suitable for:

- allocating resources in areas were spend is discretionary, i.e. non-essential. For example, research and development, advertising and training.
- public sector organisations such as local authorities.

There are four distinct stages in the implementation of ZBB:

(1) Managers should specify, for their responsibility centres, those activities that can be individually evaluated.

(2) Each of the individual activities is then described in a decision package. The decision package should state the costs and revenues expected from the given activity. It should be drawn up in such a way that the package can be evaluated and ranked against other packages.

(3) Each decision package is evaluated and ranked usually using cost/benefit analysis.

(4) The resources are then allocated to the various packages.

Advantages of ZBB	Disadvantages of ZBB
(1) Inefficient or obsolete operations can be identified and discontinued	(1) It emphasises short-term benefits to the detriment of long-term goals.
(2) ZBB leads to increased staff involvement at all levels since a lot more information and work is required to complete the budget	(2) The budgeting process may become too rigid and the organisation may not be able to react to unforeseen opportunities or threats
(3) It responds to changes in the business environment	(3) The management skills required may not be present
(4) Knowledge and understanding of the cost behaviour patterns of the organisation will be enhanced	(4) Managers may feel demotivated due to the large amount of time spent on the budgeting process
(5) Resources should be allocated efficiently and economically	(5) Ranking can be difficult for different types of activities or where the benefits are qualitative in nature

Additional information on decision packages

A decision package was defined by **Peter Pyhrr** (who first formulated the ZBB approach at Texas Instruments) as:

A document that identifies and describes a specific activity in such a manner that senior management can:

(a) evaluate and rank it against other activities competing for limited resources, and

(b) decide whether to approve or disapprove it.'

A decision package is a document that:

- analyses the cost of the activity (costs may be built up from a zero base, but costing information can be obtained from historical records or last year's budget)
- states the purpose of the activity
- identifies alternative methods of achieving the same purpose
- assesses the consequence of not doing the activity at all, or performing the activity at a different level
- establishes measures of performance for the activity.

Pyhrr identifies two types of package.

(i) Mutually exclusive packages: these contain different methods of obtaining the same objective.

(ii) Incremental packages: these divide the activity into a number of different levels of activity. The base package describes the minimum effort and cost needed to carry out the activity. The other packages describe the incremental costs and benefits when added to the base.

For example, a company is conducting a ZBB exercise, and a decision package is being prepared for its materials handling operations.

- The manager responsible has identified a base package for the minimum resources needed to perform the materials handling function. This is to have a team of five workers and a supervisor, operating without any labour-saving machinery. The estimated annual cost of wages and salaries, with overtime, would be $375,000.

- In addition to the base package, the manager has identified an incremental package. The company could lease two fork lift trucks at a cost of $20,000 each year. This would provide a better system because materials could be stacked higher and moved more quickly. Health and safety risks for the workers would be reduced, and there would be savings of $5,000 each year in overtime payments.
- Another incremental package has been prepared, in which the company introduces new computer software to plan materials handling schedules. The cost of buying and implementing the system would be $60,000, but the benefits are expected to be improvements in efficiency that reduce production downtime and result in savings of $10,000 each year in overtime payments.

The base package would be considered essential, and so given a high priority. The two incremental packages should be evaluated and ranked. Here, the fork lift trucks option might be ranked more highly than the computer software.

In the budget that is eventually decided by senior management, the fork lift truck package might be approved, but the computer software package rejected on the grounds that there are other demands for resources with a higher priority.

Test your understanding 7

For a number of years, the research division of Z Inc has produced its annual budget (for new and continuing projects) using incremental budgeting techniques. The company is now under new management and the annual budget for 20X4 is to be prepared using ZBB techniques.

Explain how Z Inc could operate a ZBB system for its research projects.

Rolling budgets

A budget (usually annual) kept continuously up to date by adding another accounting period (e.g. month or quarter) when the earliest accounting period has expired.

Suitable if:

- accurate forecasts cannot be made. For example, in a fast moving environment.
- or for any area of business that needs tight control.

Test your understanding 8

For a number of years, the research division of Z Inc has produced its annual budget (for new and continuing projects) using incremental budgeting techniques. The company is now under new management and the annual budget for 20X4 is to be prepared using ZBB techniques.

Explain how Z Inc could operate a ZBB system for its research projects.

Rolling budgets

A budget (usually annual) kept continuously up to date by adding another accounting period (e.g. month or quarter) when the earliest accounting period has expired.

Suitable if:

- accurate forecasts cannot be made. For example, in a fast moving environment.
- or for any area of business that needs tight control.

Illustration 2 – Rolling budgets

A typical rolling budget might be prepared as follows:

(1) A budget is prepared for the coming year (say January – December) broken down into suitable, say quarterly, control periods.

(2) At the end of the first control period (31 March) a comparison is made of that period's results against the budget. The conclusions drawn from this analysis are used to update the budgets for the remaining control periods and to add a budget for a further three months, so that the company once again has budgets available for the coming year (this time April – March).

(3) The planning process is repeated at the end of each three-month control period.

Advantages of rolling budgets	Disadvantages of rolling budgets
(1) Planning and control will be based on a more accurate budget.	(1) Rolling budgets are more costly and time consuming than incremental budgets
(2) Rolling budgets reduce the element of uncertainty in budgeting since they concentrate on the short-term when the degree of uncertainty is much smaller.	(2) May demotivate employees if they feel that they spend a large proportion of their time budgeting or if they feel that the budgetary targets are constantly changing
(3) There is always a budget that extends into the future (normally 12 months)	(3) There is a danger that the budget may become the last budget 'plus or minus a bit'
(4) It forces management to reassess the budget regularly and to produce budgets which are more up to date.	(4) An increase in budgeting work may lead to less control of the actual results
	(5) Issues with version control, as each month the full year numbers will change
	(6) Confusion in meetings as to each numbers the business is working towards; this can distract from the key issues. as managers discuss which numbers to achieve

Test your understanding 9

A company uses rolling budgeting and has a sales budget as follows;

	Quarter 1	Quarter 2	Quarter 3	Quarter 4	Total
	$	$	$	$	$
Sales	125,750	132,038	138,640	145,572	542,000

Actual sales for Quarter 1 were $123,450. The adverse variance is fully explained by competition being more intense than expected and growth being lower than anticipated. The budget committee has proposed that the revised assumption for sales growth should be 3% per quarter.

Update the budget as appropriate.

Activity Based Budgeting

ABB is defined as: 'a method of budgeting based on an activity framework and utilising cost driver data in the budget-setting and variance feedback processes'.

Or, put more simply, preparing budgets using overhead costs from activity based costing methodology.

Test your understanding 10 - Preparing an ABB

The operating divisions of Z plc have in the past always used a traditional approach to analysing costs into their fixed and variable components. A single measure of activity was used which, for simplicity, was the number of units produced. The new management does not accept that such a simplistic approach is appropriate for budgeting in the modern environment and has requested that the managers adopt an activity-based approach in future.

Required:

Explain how ABB would be implemented by the operating divisions of Z plc.

The advantages of ABB are similar to those provided by activity-based costing (ABC).

- It draws attention to the costs of 'overhead activities' which can be a large proportion of total operating costs.
- It recognises that it is activities which drive costs. If we can control the causes (drivers) of costs, then costs should be better managed and understood.
- ABB can provide useful information in a total quality management (TQM) environment, by relating the cost of an activity to the level of service provided.

Disadvantages of ABB

- A considerable amount of time and effort might be needed to establish the key activities and their cost drivers.
- It may be difficult to identify clear individual responsibilities for activities.
- It could be argued that in the short-term many overhead costs are not controllable and do not vary directly with changes in the volume of activity for the cost driver. The only cost variances to report would be fixed overhead expenditure variances for each activity.

Activity matrix

An activity-based budget can be constructed by preparing an activity matrix. This identifies the activities in each column, and the resources required to carry out the activities in each row.

The following 'activity matrix' shows the resources used (rows) and major functions/activities (columns) of a stores department. In this example, all the identified activities occur within a single department.

- The total current annual costs of each resource consumed by the department are shown in the final column; they have then been spread back over the various activities to establish the cost pools. The allocation of resource costs between activities will, to some extent, be subjective.
- Each of the first four activities has an identifiable cost driver, and the total resource cost driver rates can be determined (cost per unit of activity).
- The last two activities that occur within the department are non-volume related, and are sometimes referred to as 'sustaining costs'. They are necessary functions and should not be ignored in the budgeting process; however, they should not be attributed to particular cost drivers, as this would not reflect their true cost behaviour and would result in inappropriate budgets being set.

Activity cost matrix for stores department

Activity:	**Receiving deliveries**	**Issuing from store**	**Stock ordering**	**Stock counting**	**Keeping records**	**Supervision**	**Total**
Cost driver:	Deliveries	Store requisitions	Number of orders	Number of counts	–	–	
Number:	400	800	400	12			
	$000	$000	$000	$000	$000	$000	$000
Management salary	–	–	–	1	4	25	30
Basic wages	20	25	6	4	11	–	66
Overtime payments	5	–	–	5	5	–	15
Stationery, etc	1	2	2	1	3	–	9
Other	6	5	2	1	1	5	20
Total	**32**	**32**	**10**	**12**	**24**	**30**	**140**
Cost per activity unit	$80	$40	$25	$1,000			

Sustaining costs will effectively be treated as fixed costs. However, for control purposes, activity-based costs can be assumed to be variable, and actual costs can be compared with the expected costs for the given level of activity.

Test your understanding 11

Which statement is correct regarding the benefits to be gained from using ABB?

A If there is much inefficiency within the operations of a business then ABB will identify and remove these areas of inefficiency.

B In a highly direct labour intensive manufacturing process, an ABB approach will assist management in budgeting for the majority of the production costs.

C In an organisation currently operating efficiently, where the next period will be relatively unchanged from the current one, then ABB will make the budgeting process simpler and quicker.

D If an organisation produces many different types of output using different combinations of activities then ABB can provide more meaningful information for budgetary control.

Feed-forward control

A feed-forward control system operates by comparing budgeted results against a forecast. Control action is triggered by differences between budgeted and forecasted results.

In contrast, a feedback system would simply compare the actual historical results with the budgeted results.

For example, the graph below shows the feedback and feed-forward system for sales:

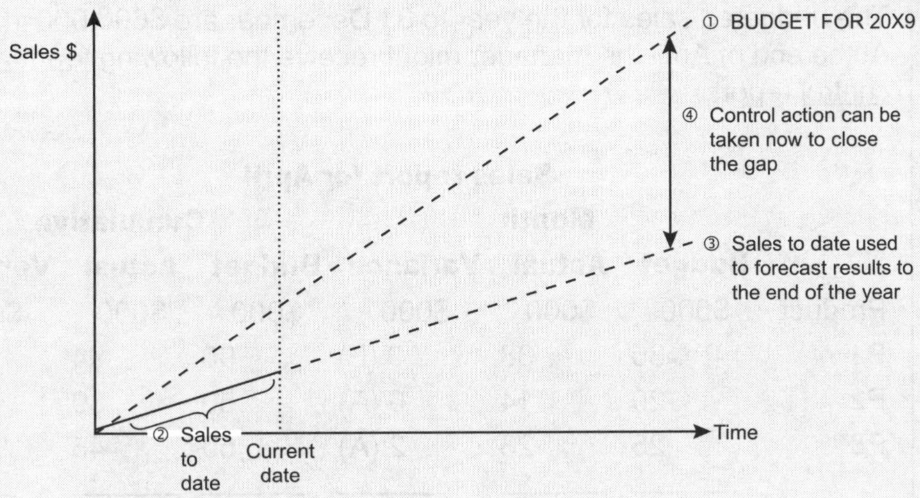

Advantages of feed-forward control	Disadvantages of feed-forward control
(1) It encourages managers to be proactive and deal with problems before they occur	(1) It may be time consuming as control reports must be produced regularly; and labour- and time-intensive
(2) Reforecasting on a monthly or continuous basis can save time when it comes to completing a quarterly or annual budget	(2) It may require a sophisticated forecasting system, which could be expensive.
	(3) Takes the focus off the day-to-day organisation

e.g

Illustration 3 – Feed-forward control

A sales manager receives monthly control reports about sales values. The budgeted sales for the year to 31 December are $600,000 in total. At the end of April the manager might receive the following feedback control report.

Sales report for April

	Month			**Cumulative**		
	Budget	**Actual**	**Variance**	**Budget**	**Actual**	**Variance**
Product	$000	$000	$000	$000	$000	$000
P1	35	38	3 (F)	90	94	4 (F)
P2	20	14	6 (A)	50	39	11 (A)
P3	25	23	2 (A)	50	45	5 (A)
Total	80	75	5 (A)	190	178	12 (A)

Alternatively, the sales manager might be presented with a **feed-forward control** report, as follows:

Sales report, April

	Budget	**Latest forecast for the year**	**Expected variance**
Product	$000	$000	$000
P1	240	250	10 (F)
P2	150	120	30 (A)
P3	210	194	16 (A)
Total	600	564	36 (A)

The use of a feed-forward control system means that corrective action can be taken to avoid expected adverse variances.

Test your understanding 12

Explain why feed-forward control may be particularly appropriate for the capital expenditure budget.

8 Selecting a suitable budgetary system

Introduction

As seen, there are many approaches to budgeting and an organisation will wish to select a system which is most appropriate.

Factors, which will determine suitability include:

- type and size of organisation
- type of industry
- type of product and product range
- culture of the organisation.

e.g

Illustration 4 – Selecting a suitable budgetary system

A hospital operates in a relatively stable financial environment, has a very high proportion of fixed costs and a diverse range of activities. Factors to consider when selecting a suitable budgetary system may be:

- An incremental approach may be suitable for all routine activities. New ventures may use a zero-based approach.
- The fixed costs may need close control and therefore some form of ABB may be appropriate.
- The culture of the organisation may dictate whether a participative or imposed budgeting style is more effective. If there are managers who are trained in budgeting and costs are mainly controllable then it may be preferable to adopt a participative approach to empower and motivate staff. If costs are mainly uncontrollable it may be preferable to use a centrally controlled, imposed budget.

Test your understanding 13

Select and justify a suitable budgeting system for a company operating in the mobile phone market.

Information for budgeting

Budgeting requires a great deal of information that can be drawn from many sources.

The main sources of information for budgeting purposes are:

- previous year's actual results
- other internal sources which may include manager's knowledge concerning the state of repair of fixed assets, training needs of staff, long-term requirements of individual customers, etc.
- estimates of costs of new products using methods such as work study techniques and technical estimates.
- statistical techniques such as linear regression (chapter 8) may help to forecast sales.
- models, such as the EOQ model, may be used to forecast optimal inventory levels.
- external sources of information may include suppliers' price lists, estimates of inflation and exchange rate movements, strategic analysis of the economic environment.

Change factors impacting budgeting

The PESTEL model met in paper F1 is useful for identifying change factors:

Political change

A change in government policy, for example fiscal policy, may affect the demand for an organisation's products, and/or the costs incurred in providing them. Any such changes will affect both short-term and long-term planning. This is one reason why planning is a continuous process.

Social change

Changes in social responsibilities and people's attitude towards them affect every organisation. In recent years there has been much more concern about social responsibilities, some of which are now recognised by law. All of these factors may impinge on the plans of the organisation.

Economic change

When there is a change in the economic climate from boom through to recession, the demands upon people's income become more focused. Money tends to be spent on necessary goods with little left for 'luxury goods' and savings. The lack of savings deters investment, with the result that plans have to be modified if they are to be realistic targets.

Technological change

When plans are made, they are based upon the use of certain methods and equipment. As technology advances, the older methods are proven to be inefficient, with the result that decisions are taken to update the operation. As a consequence, the aspects of the budgets and plans which related to the old method are no longer relevant. Revised plans must now be drawn up on the basis of the new technology.

Legal change

When plans are made they are based on the current legal framework and known changes to this are also factored in over time. However, changes to the legal framework can cause information that is used when pulling budgets together to become redundant. An example of this might be the government introducing legislation that bans fast food from being advertised during the intervals between children's TV programmes.

Test your understanding 14

Describe the sources of information required for a company's cash budget.

Changing a budgetary system

A change in the budgetary system could bring about improved planning, control and decision making.

However, before a change is made the following issues should be considered:

- Are suitably trained staff available to implement the change successfully?
- Will changing the system take up management time which should be used to focus on strategy?

- All staff involved in the budgetary process will need to be trained in the new system and understand the procedure to be followed in changing to the new approach. A lack of participation and understanding builds resistance to change.
- All costs of the systems change, e.g. new system costs, training costs, should be evaluated against the perceived benefits. Benefits may be difficult to quantify and therefore a rigorous investment appraisal of the project may be difficult to prepare.

Test your understanding 15

A large holiday complex currently uses incremental budgeting but is concerned about its very high proportion of overhead costs and is considering changing to an activity based budgeting system. Demand follows a fairly predictable seasonal pattern.

Discuss the issues that should be considered before changing to a new budgetary system.

Dealing with uncertainty in budgeting

Budgets are open to uncertainty. For example, non-controllable factors such as a recession or a change in prices charged by suppliers will contribute to uncertainty in the budget setting process.

There are several techniques available to help deal with uncertainty. These have been discussed before and include:

- Flexible budgets : these are budgets which, by recognising different cost behaviour patterns, are designed to change as the volume of activity changes. Flexible budgets are prepared under marginal costing principles, and so mixed costs are split into their fixed and variable components. This is useful at the control stage : it is necessary to compare actual results to the actual level of activity achieved against the results that should have been expected at this level of activity - which are shown by the flexible budget (more on next chapter).
- Rolling budgets: the budget is updated regularly and, as a result, uncertainty is reduced.
- Sensitivity analysis: variables can be changed one at a time and a large number of budgets produced. For example, what would happen if the actual sales volume was only 75% of the budgeted amount?
- Simulation: similar to sensitivity analysis but it is possible to change more than one variable at a time.

Spreadsheets

A spreadsheet is a computer package which stores data in a matrix format where the intersection of each row and column is referred to as a cell. They are commonly used to assist in the budgeting process.

Advantages of spreadsheets

- Large enough to include a large volume of information
- Formulae and look up tables can be used so that if any figure is amended, all the figures will be immediately recalculated. This is very useful for carrying out sensitivity analysis.
- The results can be printed out or distributed to other users electronically quickly and easily.
- Most programs can also represent the results graphically e.g. balances can be shown in a bar chart:
- **Closing cash balances**

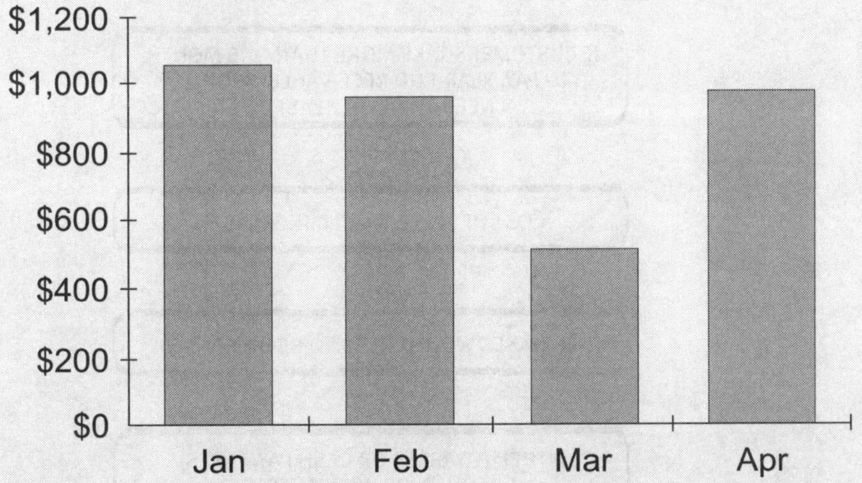

Disadvantages of spreadsheets:

- Spreadsheets for a particular budgeting application will take time to develop. The benefit of the spreadsheet must be greater than the cost of developing and maintaining it.
- Data can be accidentally changed (or deleted) without the user being aware of this occurring.
- Errors in design, particularly in the use of formulae, can produce invalid output. Due to the complexity of the model, these design errors may be difficult to locate.
- Data used will be subject to a high degree of uncertainty. This may be forgotten and the data used to produce, what is considered to be, an 'accurate' report.

- Security issues, such as the risk unauthorised access (e.g. hacking) or a loss of data (e.g. due to fire or theft).
- Version control issues can arise.
- Educating staff to use spreadsheets / models and which areas /cells to use as inputs can be time consuming.

e.g

Illustration 5 – Using spreadsheets in budgeting

When producing a master budget manually the major problem is ensuring that any initial entry in the budget or any adjustment to a budget item is dealt with in every budget that is relevant – in effect, budgets need to comply with normal double entry principles to be consistent.

Suppose, for instance, that sales in the last month were expected to rise by $10,000, what adjustments would be necessary?

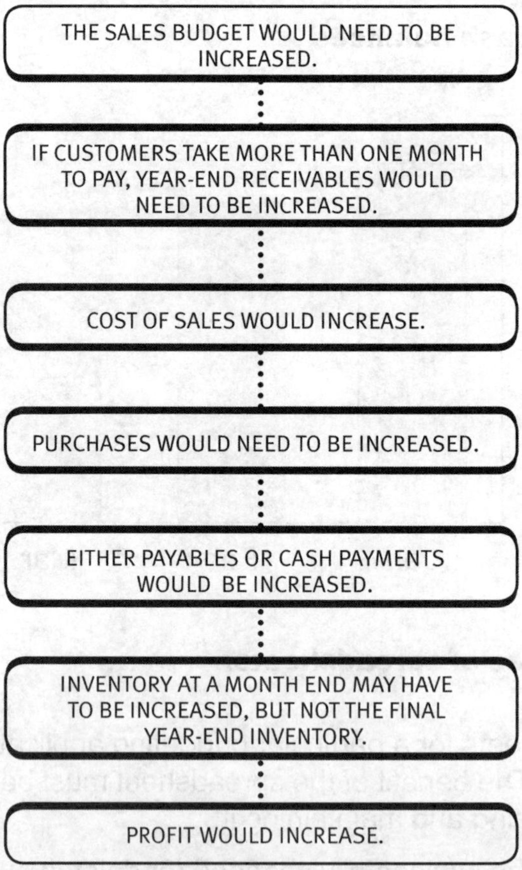

Using spreadsheets all of the above adjustments could be processed automatically if the relevant formulae were set up properly. Receivables, cost of sales, purchases, payables, cash, inventory and profit could change instantly on adjusting sales of month 12.

9 Chapter summary

BUDGETING

APPROACHES TO BUDGETING

- Top down/ bottom up budgeting
- Incremental budgets
- Zero-based budgets
- Rolling budgets
- Activity-based budgets
- Feed-forward budgets

SELECTING A SUITABLE SYSTEM

- Dealing with change
- Incorporating uncertainty
- Use of spreadsheets

Test your understanding answers

Test your understanding 1 - Evaluation of managers

The key point here is that the answer depends on who awarded the pay increase.

If this was the production manager's decision, then the cost would be controllable. Depending on the culture of the firm, the manager would then be under pressure to explain why they departed from the budget in this instance.

If awarded by, say, the board of directors, then the cost increase was not controllable by the manager and should not feature in their appraisal.

Note: The concept of controllability is important for the exam.

Test your understanding 2

The manager may try to:

- delay discretionary short-term expenditure, e.g. maintenance, at the expense of long-term performance to improve results.
- manipulate results to make sure the relevant targets are achieved.
- incorporate budgetary slack into the targets to make them easier to achieve.

The process can be improved by measuring performance against a variety of targets, including non-financial targets, and linking performance to long-term objectives.

Test your understanding 3

Sales are expected to be \$550,000 ×110% × 103% = \$623,150. The manager may accept this as a fair target for performance appraisal, planning and control purposes. To encourage the manager to improve further an aspirations target incorporating a further improvement, say to \$650,000, could be used and linked to the reward system.

Test your understanding 4

The key issue is short-termism - the manager may act to increase profit for this period (thus increasing his final bonus) without any consideration of longer term implications. These could include:

- cutting R&D
- cutting marketing expenditure
- cutting back on training
- rejecting projects that do not have high returns in year 1
- sacking non-core staff.

It will be difficult to link the bonus to a longer time scale as the manager will have retired. Instead a non-accounting style focussing on quality, productivity, brand awareness, market share, etc could be adopted, if not already in place.

Test your understanding 5

(1) Operational managers may not have the knowledge and experience to set a budget. For example, in a small business only the owner may be involved in all aspects of the business and may therefore set the budget.

(2) In times of crisis there may be insufficient time to set a participative budget and targets may have to be imposed to ensure survival.

(3) Participation has to be genuine for it to result in improved motivation. Pseudo-participation, where senior managers seek the opinions of the ultimate budget holders but do not act on these views, may lead to demotivation.

Test your understanding 6

	Total variable cost	Variable cost per unit
20X4:		
Product A	$672,000 × 75% × 60% = $302,400	$302,000 ÷ 640 units = $472.50
Product C	$672,000 × 75% × 40% = $201,600	$201,600 ÷ 350 units = $576
20X5:		
Product A	$472.50 × 1.04 × 750 units = $368,550	n/a
Product C	$576 × 1.04 × 340 units = $203,674	n/a

Test your understanding 7

Stage 1: Managers should specify the activities that can be evaluated

The managers/researchers responsible for each project should decide which projects they wish to undertake in the forthcoming period. These projects will be a mixture of continued projects and new projects.

Stage 2: Each activity is described in a decision package

For the projects which have already been started and which the managers want to continue in the next period, we should ignore any cash flows already incurred (they are sunk costs), and we should only look at future costs and benefits. Similarly, for the new projects we should only look at the future costs and benefits.

Stage 3: Each decision package is evaluated and ranked

Different ways of achieving the same research goals should also be investigated and the projects should only go ahead if the benefit exceeds the cost.

Stage 4: Resources are allocated to the various packages

Once all the potential projects have been evaluated if there are insufficient funds to undertake all the worthwhile projects, then the funds should be allocated to the best projects on the basis of a cost-benefit analysis.

ZBB is usually of a highly subjective nature. (The costs are often reasonably certain, but usually a lot of uncertainty is attached to the estimated benefits.) This can be shown by the example of a research division where the researchers may have their own pet projects, which they are unable to view in an objective light.

Test your understanding 8

Stage 1: Managers should specify the activities that can be evaluated

The managers/researchers responsible for each project should decide which projects they wish to undertake in the forthcoming period. These projects will be a mixture of continued projects and new projects.

Stage 2: Each activity is described in a decision package

For the projects which have already been started and which the managers want to continue in the next period, we should ignore any cash flows already incurred (they are sunk costs), and we should only look at future costs and benefits. Similarly, for the new projects we should only look at the future costs and benefits.

Stage 3: Each decision package is evaluated and ranked

Different ways of achieving the same research goals should also be investigated and the projects should only go ahead if the benefit exceeds the cost.

Stage 4: Resources are allocated to the various packages

Once all the potential projects have been evaluated if there are insufficient funds to undertake all the worthwhile projects, then the funds should be allocated to the best projects on the basis of a cost-benefit analysis.

ZBB is usually of a highly subjective nature. (The costs are often reasonably certain, but usually a lot of uncertainty is attached to the estimated benefits.) This can be shown by the example of a research division where the researchers may have their own pet projects, which they are unable to view in an objective light.

Test your understanding 9

The revised budget should incorporate 3% growth starting from the actual sales figure of Quarter 1 and should include a figure for Quarter 1 of the following year.

	Quarter 2	Quarter 3	Quarter 4	Quarter 1	Total
	$	$	$	$	$
Sales	127,154	130,969	134,898	138,945	531,966

Test your understanding 10 - Preparing an ABB

Step 1 Identify cost pools and cost drivers

Step 2 Calculate a budgeted cost driver rate based on budgeted cost and budgeted activity

Step 3 Produce a budget for each department or product by multiplying the budgeted cost driver rate by the expected usage.

Test your understanding 11

D is the correct answer.

Situation A would be best suited by implementing Zero Base Budgeting. Situation B does not require ABB since it has relatively low overheads. Situation C would be suitable for incremental budgeting. ABB will certainly not be quicker.

Test your understanding 12

Capital expenditure is often long-term in nature. It is more useful to compare actual costs to forecast completion costs so that action can be taken when a project is in progress rather than waiting for completion.

Test your understanding 13

The mobile phone market is intensely competitive so a company will need sophisticated systems to gather information about the market and competitors. The market is also fast changing so a rolling budget approach may be suitable to keep budget targets up to date. It will be very important to incorporate the latest information into budgets and a participative approach will be important as production managers and sales managers may have local knowledge which would improve the budgeting process.

Test your understanding 14

Internal information will be required from the:

- sales department relating to volume and estimated collection periods
- the production manager will estimate material, labour and overhead usage
- the purchasing manager will estimate material prices and payment terms
- human resources will forecast pay rates, bonus payments and overtime requirements
- the finance office may forecast payments of interest, dividends and general office costs.

External information may be required relating to forecast interest rates, tax rates, payment terms for tax, exchange rates, inflation, etc.

Test your understanding 15

An analysis of overheads should be carried out to determine the proportion that have identifiable cost drivers which differ from the normal volume related cost drivers which may be used when carrying out incremental budgeting. If a substantial volume of overhead is non-volume related then implementing ABB may lead to more accurate planning and control.

Issues, which should then be considered include:

- the development or purchase of a suitable computer system to support an ABB process;
- training of staff to operate and interpret the information produced;
- development of an implementation plan and whether this should run in tandem with the existing process for a trial period.

chapter

8

Quantitative analysis

Chapter learning objectives

Upon completion of this chapter you will be able to:

- explain and evaluate the use of high/low analysis to separate the fixed and variable elements of total cost
- explain and evaluate the use of regression analysis to separate the fixed and variable elements of total cost
- explain the use of time series analysis as a forecasting technique
- predict a future value from time series analysis data using both the additive and proportional data
- explain the use of a simple average growth model as a forecasting technique
- explain the use of judgement and experience in forecasting
- explain the learning curve effect
- estimate the learning effect and apply this to a budgetary problem
- calculate production times when the learning curve has reached a steady state
- explain the limitations of the learning curve model.

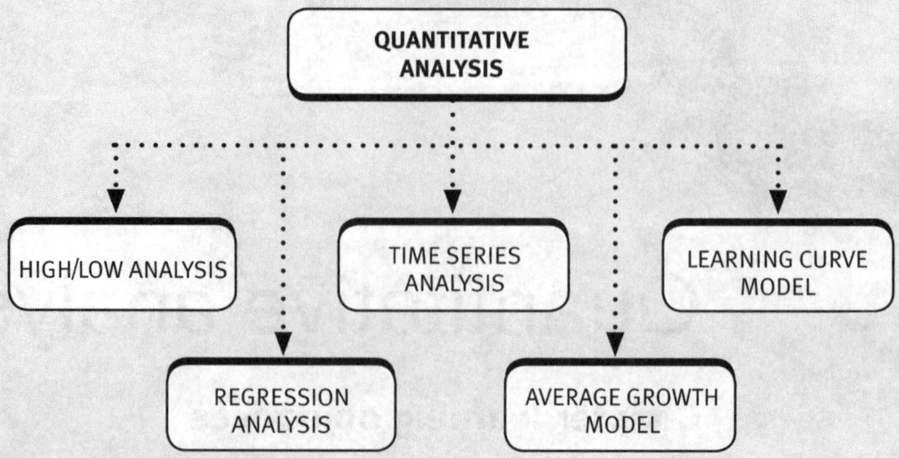

1 High/low analysis

A method of analysing a semi-variable cost into its fixed and variable elements based on an analysis of historical information about costs at different activity levels.

The fixed and variable costs can then be used to forecast the total cost at any level of activity.

The approach is as follows:

Step 1

Select the highest and lowest **activity** levels, and their costs.

Step 2

Find the variable cost/unit.

Variable cost/unit = (Cost at high level of activity – Cost at low level activity)/(High level activity – Low level activity)

Step 3

Find the fixed cost, using either the high or low activity level.

Fixed cost = Total cost at activity level — Total variable cost

Step 4

Use the variable and fixed cost to forecast the total cost for a specified level of activity.

Advantages of high/ low analysis

- The high-low method has the enormous advantage of simplicity.
- It is easy to understand and easy to use.

Disadvantages of high/ low analysis

- It assumes that activity is the only factor affecting costs.
- It assumes that historical costs reliably predict future costs.
- It uses only two values, the highest and the lowest, so the results may be distorted due to random variations in these values.

Test your understanding 1

Cost data for the six months to 31 December 20X8 is as follows:

Month	Units	Inspection costs
		$
July	340	2,240
August	300	2,160
September	380	2,320
October	420	2,400
November	400	2,360
December	360	2,280

Required:

Use high/low analysis to find the variable cost per unit and the total fixed cost. Forecast the total cost when 500 units are produced.

Additional example on high/low

Output (Units)	Total cost ($)
200	7,000
300	8,000
400	9,000

(a) Find the variable cost per unit.

(b) Find the total fixed cost.

(c) Estimate the total cost if output is 350 units.

(d) Estimate the total cost if output is 600 units.

Solution

(a) Variable cost per unit = ($9,000 – $7,000) ÷ (400 – 200)

= $10 per unit

(b) Using high activity level:

Total cost	=		$9,000
Total variable cost	=	400 × $10	$4,000
Therefore Fixed cost	=		$5,000

(c) If output is 350 units:

Variable cost	=	350 × $10 =	$3,500
Fixed cost	=		$5,000
Total cost	=		$8,500

(d) If output is 600 units:

Variable cost	=	600 × $10	$6,000
Fixed cost	=		$5,000
Total cost	=		$11,000

2 Regression analysis

Introduction

Regression is another method of forecasting. It involves using historical data to find the line of best fit between two variables (one dependent on the other), and uses this straight line to predict future values.

A scatter diagram can be drawn:

The dependent variable is y and must always be on the vertical axis, e.g. sales.

The independent variable is x and always goes on the horizontal axis, e.g. advertising spend.

Scatter diagram

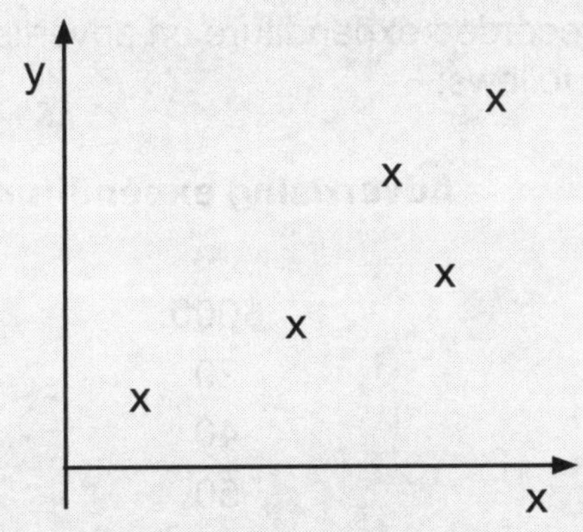

The aim is to find the best line (the 'line of best fit') through the centre of this diagram.

This straight line can then be used for forecasting, e.g. to forecast sales for any level of advertising spend.

Equation of a straight line

The equation of a straight line is $y = a + bx$

(a) is the intercept with the y axis

(b) is the gradient or slope

It can be time consuming to find the values of 'a' and 'b' by drawing the scatter diagram. Instead, the following formulae can be used to find these values.

$$b = [n\Sigma xy - \Sigma x\Sigma y]/[n\Sigma x^2 - (\Sigma x)^2]$$

$$a = (\Sigma y/n) - (b\Sigma x/n)$$

where n = sample size

Both of these formulae are given in the examination.

Test your understanding 2

A company has recorded expenditure on advertising and resulting sales for six months as follows:

Month	Advertising expenditure x $000	Sales y $000
March	20	170
April	40	240
May	50	260
June	60	300
July	30	220
August	40	250

Required:

(a) Plot the data on a scatter diagram and comment.

(b) Calculate the values of 'a' and 'b' and comment.

(c) What is the equation of the line of best fit?

(d) Forecast sales when advertising expenditure is:

(i) $50,000

(ii) $100,000

and comment on your answers.

Additional example on regression analysis

Regression analysis is being used to find the line of best fit (y = a + bx) from 11 pairs of data. The calculations have produced the following information:

$\sum x = 440$, $\sum y = 330$, $\sum x^2 = 17,986$, $\sum y^2 = 10,366$ and $\sum xy = 13,467$

Required:

(a) Find the equation of the line of best fit using regression analysis.

(b) Use your equation to forecast the value of y if x = 42.

Solution

(a) Use the formulae to find the values of a and b.

b = [11 × 13,467 — (440 × 330)]/[(11 × 17,986) — $(440)^2$]= 0.6917

a = (330 ÷ 11) — 0.6917 (440 ÷ 11) = 2.33

The equation of the line is y = 2.33 + 0.6917x

(b) If x = 42, y = 2.33 + 0.6917 × 42 = 31.38 (to 2 decimal points)

Correlation coefficient

The strength of the linear relationship between the two variables (and hence the usefulness of the regression line equation) can be assessed by calculating the correlation coefficient ("r"):

$$r = \frac{n\sum xy - \sum x \sum y}{\sqrt{\left(n\sum x^2 - (\sum x)^2\right)\left(n\sum y^2 - (\sum y)^2\right)}}$$

The correlation coefficient will be between -1 and +1.

- r is close to +1: there is a strong positive correlation between the two variables
- r is close to –1: there is a strong negative correlation between the two variables
- r is close to 0: there is little relationship between the two variables

The closer the coefficient is to +1 or –1, the better regression analysis will be as a method of forecasting.

Using the data from the previous test your understanding:

$$r = \frac{6 \times 60{,}600 - 240 \times 1{,}440}{\sqrt{\left(6 \times 10{,}600 - 240^2\right)\left(6 \times 355{,}000 - 1{,}440^2\right)}} = 0.97849\ldots$$

Coefficient of determination

The coefficient of determination = r^2

It shows the percentage change in the dependent variable, e.g. sales, that can be explained by a change in the independent variable, e.g. advertising spend.

Using the data from the previous test your understanding:

$r^2 = 0.957$

Thus 95.7% of the observed variation in sales can be explained as being due to changes in the advertising spend. This would give strong assurances that the forecasts made using the regression equation are valid.

3 Time series analysis

A time series is a series of figures relating to the changing value of a variable over time. The data often conforms to a certain pattern over time. This pattern can be extrapolated into the future and hence forecasts are possible. Time periods may be any measure of time including days, weeks, months and quarters.

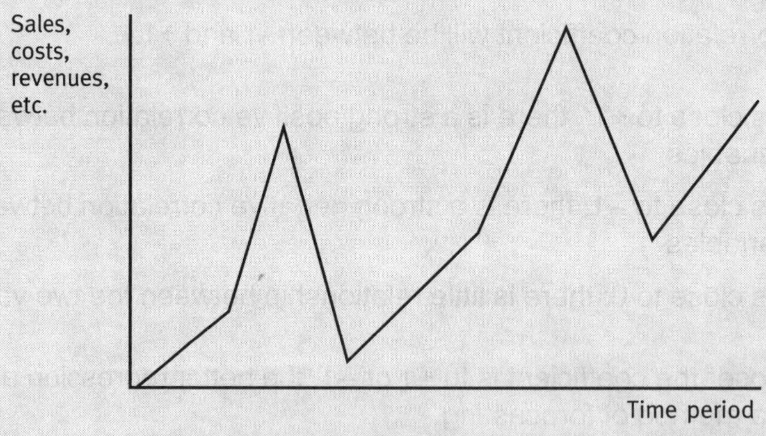

Components of a time series

- The trend – this describes the long-term general movement of the data.
- Seasonal variations – a regular variation around the trend over a fixed time period.
- Cyclical variations – economic cycle of booms and slumps.
- Residual variations – irregular, random fluctuations in the data usually caused by factors specific to the time series. They are unpredictable.

In examination problems there is generally insufficient data to evaluate the cyclical and residual variations, hence, they are ignored.

The numerical analysis

- The trend and the seasonal variation will be given in the exam.
- These can be combined, using either the additive or the multiplicative model, and used to forecast future values.

The additive model

Actual = Trend + Seasonal Variation (SV)

The SV will be expressed in absolute terms.

The multiplicative model

Actual = Trend × SV factor

The SV will be expressed as a percentage, a decimal or an index.

Test your understanding 3

A company has found that the trend in the quarterly sales of its furniture is well described by the regression equation

y =	150 + 10X
where y	equals quarterly sales ($000)
x = 1	represents the first quarter of 20X2
x = 2	represents the second quarter of 20X2
x = 5	represents the first quarter of 20X3, etc.

Based on the multiplicative model the mean seasonal quarterly index for its furniture sales is as follows:

Quarter	**1**	**2**	**3**	**4**
Seasonal index	80	110	140	70

Required:

(a) Explain the meaning of this regression equation, and set of seasonal index numbers.

(b) Using the regression equation, estimate the trend values in the company's furniture sales for each quarter of 20X7

(c) Using the seasonal index, prepare sales forecasts for the company's quarterly furniture sales in 20X7

(d) State what factors might cause your sales forecasts to be in error.

Additional example on time series

The number of customers visiting a health centre has been increasing and it is estimated that the underlying trend is for an increase of 50 customers each month. However, the numbers fluctuate depending on the month of the year.

The underlying trend value for customers in December Year 1 is 4,300.

SVs for some of the months are:

	SV factor
May	116
June	107
July	94
August	82
September	106

Required:

Prepare a forecast for the number of customers in each of the months May to September, Year 2.

Solution

	Trend	Seasonal factor	Forecast
May	4,300 + (50 × 5) = 4,550	× 1.16	5,278
June	4,300 + (50 × 6) = 4,600	× 1.07	4,922
July	4,300 + (50 × 7) = 4,650	× 0.94	4,371
August	4,300 + (50 × 8) = 4,700	× 0.82	3,854
September	4,300 + (50 × 9) = 4,750	× 1.06	5,035

4 Average growth models

Strategic plans may incorporate an objective of a target average growth of profit or sales over a number of years. There may also be requirements for a target average growth rate of productivity over a number of years.

$$1+g=\sqrt[n]{\frac{\text{Most recent figure}}{\text{Earliest figure}}}$$

g = average growth rate, as a decimal

n = number of periods of growth

Test your understanding 4

Sales are forecast to increase, on average, by 2% per quarter. Sales are currently $250,000 pa.

Required:

Calculate the budgeted sales figures for each quarter of the forthcoming year.

Calculate the average growth rate given the original and the final figure.

5 The use of judgement and experience in forecasting

Judgement and experience are important in forecasting. The quantitative models available are mainly based on past information and extrapolate these results into the future. Managers will have access to many sources of information to help them judge whether past results are likely to be good predictors of future results.

Illustration 1 – Judgement and experience in forecasting

A regression analysis has been carried out linking sales to advertising expenditure. Managers may use their judgement to modify the forecasts if they know that, for example:

- a competitor has recently launched a new product in the market
- a new advertising medium is to be used
- general forecasts of growth in the economy are less favourable
- consumers view the product as being almost out of date.

Managers may:

- forecast more than one scenario to give a most likely, a pessimistic and an optimistic scenario
- use probabilities, estimated using their own judgement and experience, to determine the expected value of a forecast.

Test your understanding 5

A manager has forecast the following sales revenues and probabilities based on a given level of advertising.

	Probability	**Sales revenue ($)**
Pessimistic	0.1	100,000
Most likely	0.6	125,000
Optimistic	0.3	140,000

Required:

Calculate the expected value of sales.

6 Learning curves

Introduction

As workers become more familiar with the production of a new product, average time (and average cost) per unit will decline.

Wrights Law: as cumulative output doubles, the cumulative average time per unit falls to a fixed percentage (referred to as the learning rate) of the previous average time.

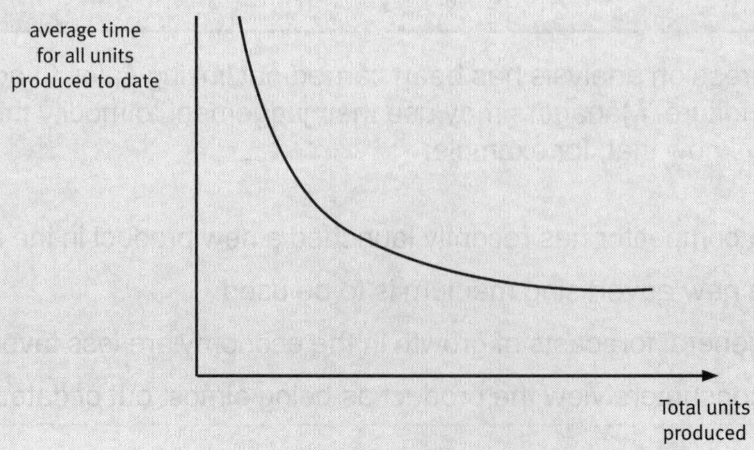

As can be seen on the graph, eventually the curve becomes almost horizontal when many units have been produced, as the learning effect is lost and production time per unit becomes a constant.

Learning curve calculations

The learning curve effect can be calculated by:

- **Method 1**: set up a table and reduce the average time by the learning rate each time the output doubles.
- **Method 2**: using the formula $y = ax^b$
  y = cumulative average time (or average cost) per unit or per batch
  a = time (or cost) for first unit or batch
  b = log r/log 2 (r = rate of learning, expressed as a decimal)
  x = cumulative output in units or in batches

Both methods will give the same answer. However, the formula is quicker and easier to use in the exam.

Test your understanding 6 - Method 1

Assume that it has taken 400 direct labour hours to manufacture the first unit of a new product. As in the past for this business it is anticipated that a 75% learning curve will occur.

Required:

Set up a table showing:

- The average time taken for the 2nd and the 4th unit.
- The total time taken for 2 units and for 4 units.

Test your understanding 7 - Method 2

Using the information from the previous test your understanding, use the formula to calculate the cumulative average time to produce four units.

Additional example on method 2

Assume that it takes 400 direct labour hours to produce the first unit of a new product and an 85% learning curve applies.

Required:

Calculate the total time to produce the third unit.

Solution

- $b = \log(0.85)/ \log 2$

  $b = -0.0706/ 0.3010 = -0.234$

- The cumulative average time to produce the first two units is

  $y = 400 \times 2^{-0.234} = 340.1.$

  The total time to produce the first two units = 340.1 × 2 = 680.2 hours.

- The cumulative average time to produce the first three units is

  $y = 400 \times 3^{-0.234} = 309.3.$

  The total time to produce the first three units = 309.3 × 3 = 927.9 hours.

- The time to produce the third unit = 927.9 — 680.2 = 247.7 direct labour hours.

Test your understanding 8

A Swiss watch making company wishes to determine the minimum price it should charge a customer for a special order of watches. The customer has requested a quotation for 10 watches (1 batch), but might subsequently place an order for a further 10. Material costs are $30 per watch. It is estimated that the first batch of 10 watches will take 100 hours to manufacture and an 80% learning curve is expected to apply. Labour plus variable overhead costs amount to $3 per hour. Setup costs are $1,000 regardless of the number of watches made.

Required:

(a) What is the minimum price the company should quote for the initial order if there is no guarantee of further orders?

(b) If the company was then to receive the follow-on order, what would the minimum price of this order be?

(c) What would be the minimum price if both orders were placed together?

(d) Having completed the initial orders for a total of 20 watches (price at the minimum levels recommended in (a) and (b)), the company thinks that there would be a ready market for this type of watch if it brought the unit selling price down to $45. At this price, what would be the profit on the first 140 'mass-production' watches (i.e. after the first 20 watches) assuming that marketing costs totalled $250?

Applications of the learning effect

- Pricing decisions: prices will be set too high if based on the costs of making the first few units.
- Work scheduling: less labour per unit will be required as more units are made. This may have management implications, e.g. workers may be laid off.
- Product viability: the viability of a product may change if a learning effect exists.
- Standard setting: if a product enjoys a learning effect but this effect is ignored, then the standard cost will be too high. The presence of a learning effect can also make standard setting difficult.
- Budgeting: the presence of a learning effect should be taken into account when setting budgets. For example, the labour budget may be reduced by a learning effect but working capital may be required sooner than expected.

The learning curve and the steady state

The learning effect will only apply for a certain range of production.

For example, machine efficiency may restrict further improvements or there may be go-slow arrangements in place.

Once the steady state is reached the direct labour hours will not reduce any further and this will become the basis on which the budget is produced.

Test your understanding 9

The first batch of a new product took 20 hours to produce. The learning rate is 90%.

Required:

If the learning effect ceases after 72 batches (i.e. all subsequent batches take the same time as the 72nd), how long will it take to make a grand total of 100 batches?

Limitations of the learning curve model

The model applies if:

- **the process is labour intensive**: modern manufacturing can be very machine intensive. The learning effect will not apply if machines limit the speed of labour.
- **there are no breaks in production**: a break in production may result in the learning effect being lost.
- **the product is new**: the introduction of a new product makes it more probable that there will be a learning effect.
- **the product is complex**: the more complex the product, the more probable that the learning effect will be significant and the longer it will take for the learning effect to reach the steady state.
- **the process is repetitive**: if the process is not repetitive, a learning effect will not be enjoyed.

It may also be difficult to identify the learning effect in practice.

The experience curve

It has been stressed that the learning curve was derived from observations of the reductions in direct labour time taken to complete successive repetitive but complex assembly tasks. However, learning rates have frequently been determined by fitting curves to total cost per unit data. For example, DePuy (1993) used this method to ascertain for the US government the learning rate achieved by defence contractors. The purpose in gathering this data was to help in price negotiations with the contractors.

The slope of the learning curves derived ranged from 0.718 to 1.021, with a mean of 0.858. These data suggest that defence contractors typically enjoy a reduction of 14 per cent of average unit cost on each doubling of output. The strict application of the learning curve phenomenon is seen in the area of direct labour, and it is arguable that, in using unit cost data, the result outlined above actually reflects the so-called 'experience curve; rather than the learning curve as strictly defined. The 'experience curve' extends the learning curve approach to areas other than direct labour. Rather than relating indirectly to cost via time, an experience curve relates directly to cost, and it is a function which shows how total cost per unit declines as output increases.

Total cost in experience curves includes all overhead types – production, marketing and distribution – and thus cost reduction arising from factors such as factory size, production technology, substitution of materials and design modifications are reflected in an experience curve.

Experience curves, like learning curves, can be regarded as statements of what will happen in practice. This could be considered to be a western approach. An alternative approach, adopted by the Japanese, is that these curves should be taken as expressions of what is desirable, and hence what should be striven for.

The improvement-oriented Japanese typically aim actively to foster a 67 per cent learning curve, as against the 80 per cent curve more usually found in the west.

7 Chapter summary

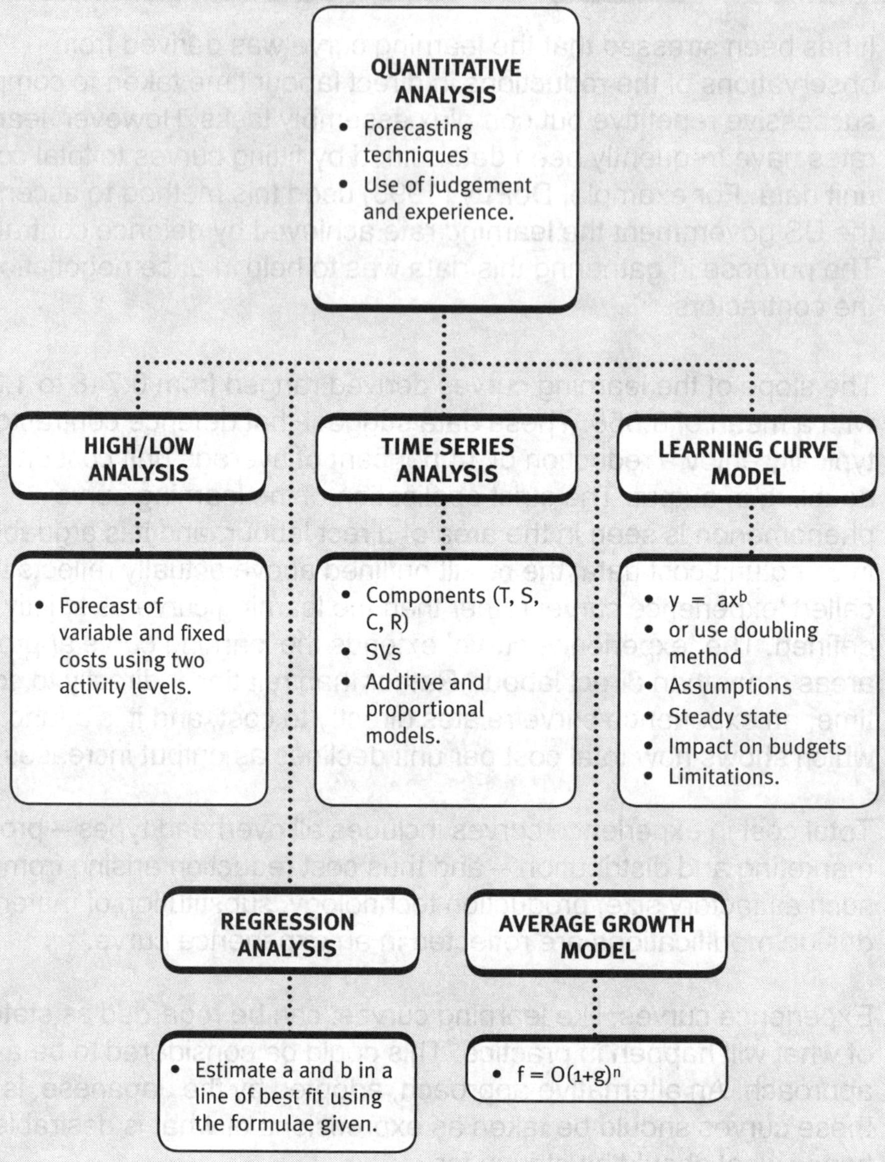

Test your understanding answers

Test your understanding 1

Step 1: Select the highest and lowest activity levels and their costs

Six months to 31/12/X8	Units produced	Inspection costs
		$
Highest month	420	2,400
Lowest month	300	2,160
Range	120	240

Step 2: Find the variable cost per unit

Variable cost per unit = $240/120 = $2 per unit

Step 3: Find the fixed cost

Fixed inspection costs are, therefore:

$2,400 — (420 units × $2) = $1,560 per month

or $2,160 — (300 units × $2) = $1,560 per month

i.e. the relationship is of the form y = $1,560 + $2x.

Step 4: Use these costs to forecast the total costs for 500 units.

Total cost = fixed cost + variable cost

Total cost = $1,560 + ($2 × 500)

Total cost = $2,560

Test your understanding 2

(a)

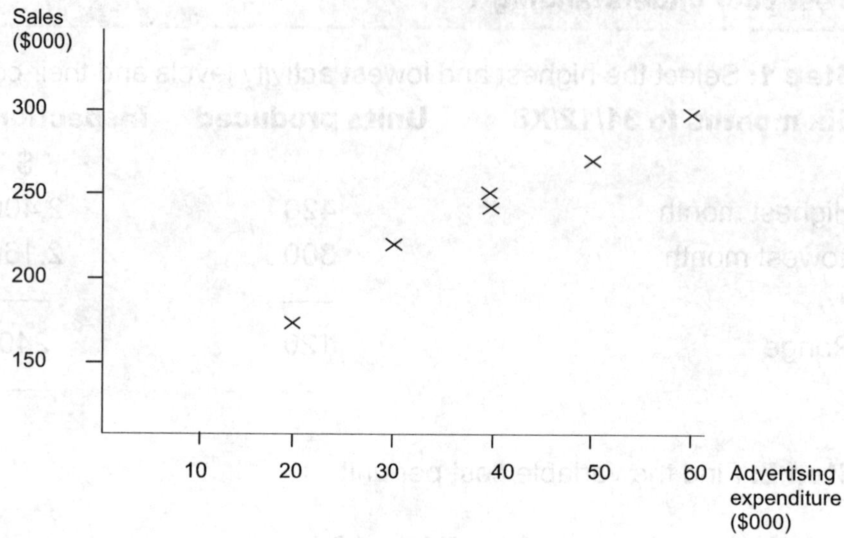

There appears to be a positive linear relationship between advertising expenditure and sales. The values of 'a' and 'b' can be found using the formulae.

(b)

x	**y**	**xy**	x^2	**y2**
20	170	3,400	400	28,900
40	240	9,600	1,600	57,600
50	260	13,000	2,500	67,600
60	300	18,000	3,600	90,000
30	220	6,600	900	48,400
40	250	10,000	1,600	62,500
240	1,440	60,600	10,600	355,000

b = ((6 × 60,600) – (240 × 1,440)) ÷ ((6 × 10,600) – 240^2) = 18,000 ÷ 6,000 = 3

a = (1,440 ÷ 6) – (3 × (240 ÷ 6)) = 120

This means that when advertising expenditure is zero, sales will be $120,000, and for every $1 spent on advertising, sales will increase by $3.

(c) Line is: y = 120 + 3x

(d) (i) Advertising is $50,000 x = 50; y = 120 + (3 × 50) = 270

Forecast sales are $270,000

This is an interpolation, i.e. the value for advertising spend is within the sample range of values and is likely to be fairly accurate.

(ii) Advertising is $100,000 x = 100; y = 120 + (3 × 100) = 420

Forecast sales are $420,000

This is an extrapolation, i.e. the value for advertising spend is outside the sample range and may be inaccurate.

Test your understanding 3

(a) y = 150 + 10x

The 150 represents the trend when x = 0, i.e. the final quarter of 20X1.

The 10 represents the increase in trend each quarter, that is we expect the trend to rise by 10 each quarter.

The seasonal indices can be interpreted as follows:

Quarter 1 = 80. This means that we expect sales to be 80% of the trend value, i.e. 20% below the trend in quarter 1.

Quarter 2 = 110. This means that we expect sales to be 10% above the trend in quarter 2.

Quarter 3 = 140. This means that we expect sales to be 40% above the trend in quarter 3.

Quarter 4 = 70. This means that we expect sales to be 30% below the trend in quarter 4.

(b) and (c)

Quarter	x	Trend (y = 150 + 10x)
1	21	150 + (10 ×21) = 360
2	22	150 + (10 × 22) = 370
3	23	150 + (10 × 23) = 380
4	24	150 + (10 × 24) = 390

Quarter	Trend	Seasonal	Sales forecast	
1	360	80	360 × 0.8 =	288
2	370	110	370 × 1.1 =	407
3	380	140	380 × 1.4 =	532
4	390	70	390 × 0.7 =	273

(d) The two main factors that may cause errors are:

(1) Extrapolation error – we may be forecasting too far beyond the original regression.

(2) We are ignoring any residual variation and cyclical variation. As a result, the forecast may be inaccurate.

Test your understanding 4

		Sales ($)
Quarter 1	($250,000/4 × 1.02)	63,750
Quarter 2	($63,750 × 1.02)	65,025
Quarter 3	($65,025 × 1.02)	66,326
Quarter 4	($66,325.5 × 1.02)	67,652
		$262,753

$$1+g=\sqrt[3]{\frac{67,652}{63,750}}$$

1 + g = 1.020

g = 0.020 = 2.0%

Test your understanding 5

- The expected value of sales revenue = (100,000 × 0.1) + (125,000 × 0.6) + (140,000 × 0.3) = $127,000
- This can be used as the sales figure in the budget.

Test your understanding 6 - Method 1

(1) Cumulative number of units	(2) Cumulative average time per unit (hours)	(1) × (2) Cumulative total hours
1	400	400
2	300 (75% of 400)	600
4	225 (75% of 300)	900

Once 2 units have been produced, and the learning process continues, the production of 2 more units will take only (900 – 600), i.e. 300 hours. This represents 150 hours per unit.

Test your understanding 7 - Method 2

- First calculate the exponent b: log r/ log 2, where r is the rate of learning (expressed as a decimal)

  b = log 0.75/log 2

  = – 0.1249/0.3010

  = – 0.4150

- Then use the formula, $y = ax^b$

  $Y = 400 \times 4^{-0.415}$ = 225 hours (as before)

Test your understanding 8

(a) **Initial order**

	$
Material (10 × $30)	300
Labour and variable overhead (100 × $3)	300
Setting-up cost (see note)	1,000
Total	$1,600
Minimum price each ($1,600 ÷ 10)	$160

Note: If there is no guarantee of a follow-up order, the setup costs must be recovered on the initial order.

(b) **Follow-on order**

– b = log 0.8/ log 2 = – 0.321928

– If production increases to 20 watches (2 batches) then the cumulative average time per batch is:

$y = ax^b$

$y = 100 \times 2^{-0.321928}$

y = 80.00 hours

– i.e. cumulative time for 20 watches (2 batches) = 160 hours

– Therefore, the time taken for the second batch of ten watches = 160 – 100 = 60 hours.

Costs are therefore:

	$
Material (10 × $30)	300
Labour and variable overhead (60 × $3)	180
Total	480
Minimum price each	48

Note: the set up costs have been recovered on the initial order and can therefore be ignored.

(c) **Both orders together**

Total costs are:

	$
Material (20 × $30)	600
Labour (160 hours x $3)	480
Set-up cost	1,000
Total	2,080
Minimum price each	104

Note: This is the mean of the two previous prices.

(d) **Mass production**

- Total production = 20 watches for the special order + 140 watches for mass production = 160 watches or 16 batches.
- $y = ax^b$

  Average time/batch for first 2 batches (i.e. first 20 watches)

  $= 100 \times 2^{-0.3219} = 80$ hours

  Total time for first 2 batches = 80 × 2 = 160 hours (as before).

- Average time per batch for first 16 batches (i.e. first 160 watches) = $100 \times 16^{-0.321928} = 40.96$ hours.

  Total time for first 16 batches = 40.96 × 16 = 655.36 hours.

  Hence total time for batches 3 to 16 (i.e. the 140 mass-produced units) = (655.36 — 160) hours = 495.36 hours.

Cost of first 140 mass-production models:

	$
Material (140 × \$30)	4,200
Labour and variable overhead (495.36 × \$3)	1,486
Marketing	250
Total cost	5,936
Revenue (140 × \$45)	6,300
Profit	364

Test your understanding 9

Step 1: Calculate the cumulative average time for the number of units/ batches at which the learning effect ceases.

$b = \log 0.9/\log 2 = -0.152003$

$y = ax^b$

Cumulative average time for 72 batches, y is:

$y = 20 \times 72^{-0.152003} = 10.44$ hrs/batch

Step 2: Calculate the cumulative average time for the number of units/ batches, at which the learning effect ceases, minus 1

x = 71 batches

$y = 20 \times 71^{-0.152003} = 10.46$ hrs/batch

Step 3: Calculate the time taken to make the unit/ batch at which the learning effect ceases.

Batches	1-71 will take 71 × 10.46 =	742.66 hrs
Batches	1-72 will take 72 × 10.44 =	751.68 hrs
Batch	72 will take	9.02 hrs

Step 4: Calculate the total time for the number of units/batches

Batches	1-72 will take	751.68 hrs
Batches	73-100 will take 28 × 9.02 =	252.56 hrs
Batches	1-100 will take	1,004.24 hrs

chapter

9

Standard costing and basic variances

Chapter learning objectives

Upon completion of this chapter you will be able to:

- explain the purpose and principles of standard costing
- describe the methods used to derive standard costs
- prepare standards that allow for idle time and waste
- explain how standard costs may be used to flex a budget
- explain and apply the principle of controllability
- calculate the following variances and explain their possible causes:
  - sales price and volume
  - materials total, price and usage
  - labour total, rate and efficiency
  - variable overhead total, expenditure and efficiency
  - fixed overhead total, expenditure, volume, capacity and efficiency
- produce an operating statement to reconcile budgeted and actual profit under standard absorption costing
- produce an operating statement to reconcile budgeted and actual profit or contribution under standard marginal costing
- explain how the learning curve will affect labour variances
- explain the major causes of idle time and waste, suggest methods for their control and calculate their effect on variances
- calculate simple activity-based costing (ABC) variances
- explain whether or not to investigate the cause of a variance.

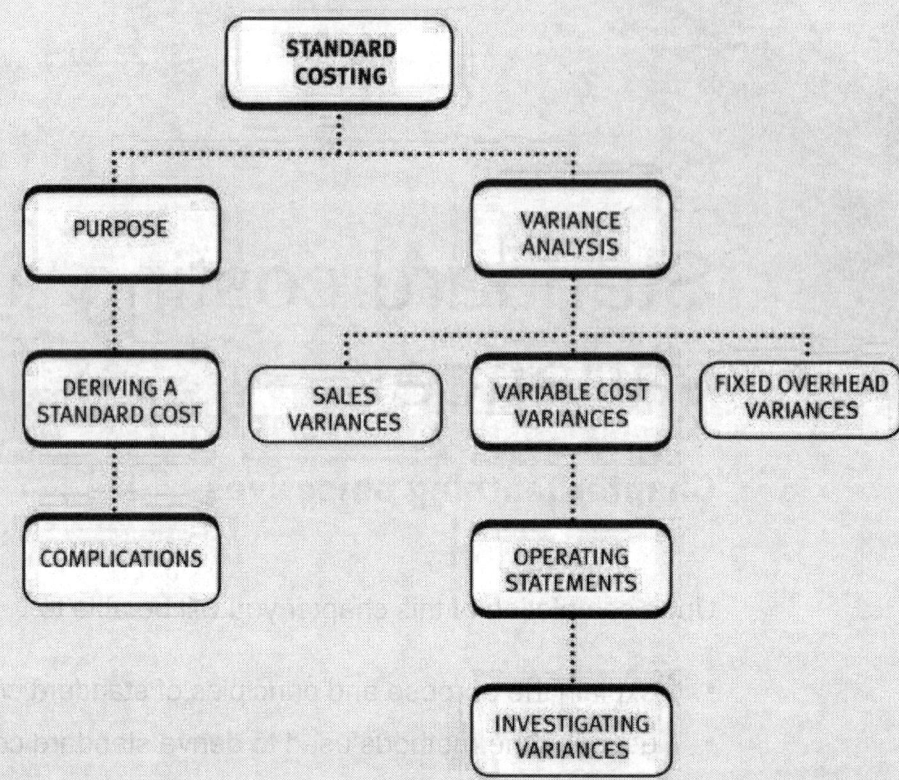

Standard costing and the basics of variance analysis were encountered in F2. In F5 you will have to cope with the following:

- new variances
- more complex calculations
- discussion of the results and implications of your calculations.

Standard costing

What is standard costing?

A standard cost for a product or service is a predetermined unit cost set under specified working conditions.

The uses of standard costs

The main purposes of standard costs are:

- **control**: the standard cost can be compared to the actual costs and any differences investigated.
- **performance measurement**: any differences between the standard and the actual cost can be used as a basis for assessing the performance of cost centre managers.

- **to value inventories**: an alternative to methods such as LIFO and FIFO.
- **to simplify accounting**: there is only one cost, the standard.

Suitability of standard costing

Standard costing is most suited to organisations with:

- mass production of homogenous products
- repetitive assembly work

The large scale repetition of production allows the average usage of resources to be determined.

Standard costing is less suited to organisations that produce non-homogenous products or where the level of human intervention is high.

McDonaldisation

Restaurants traditionally found it difficult to apply standard costing because each dish is slightly different to the last and there is a high level of human intervention.
McDonalds attempted to overcome these problems by:

- Making each type of product produced identical. For example, each Big Mac contains a pre-measured amount of sauce and two gherkins. This is the standard in all restaurants.
- Reducing the amount of human intervention. For example, staff do not pour the drinks themselves but use machines which dispense the same volume of drink each time.

Test your understanding 1

Which of the following organisations may use standard costing?

(i) **a bank**

(ii) **a kitchen designer**

(iii) **a food manufacturer**

(a) (i), (ii) and (iii)

(b) (i) and (ii) only

(c) (ii) and (iii) only

(d) (i) and (iii) only

Preparing standard costs

A standard cost is based on the expected price and usage of material, labour and overheads.

Test your understanding 2

K Ltd makes two products. Information regarding one of those products is given below:

Budgeted output/ sales for the year: 900 units

Standard details for one unit

Direct materials	40 square metres at $5.30 per square metre
Direct wages	Bonding department: 24 hours at $5.00 per hour
	Finishing department: 15 hours at $4.80 per hour
Variable overhead	$1.50 per bonding labour hour
	$1 per finishing labour hour
Fixed production overhead	$36,000
Fixed non-production overhead	$27,000

Note: Variable overheads are recovered (absorbed) using hours, fixed overheads are recovered on a unit basis.

Required:

(a) Prepare a standard cost card for one unit and enter on the standard cost card the following subtotals:

(i) Prime cost

(ii) Variable production cost

(iii) Total production cost

(iv) Total cost.

(b) Calculate the selling price per unit allowing for a profit of 25% of the selling price.

Types of standard

There are four main types of standard:

Attainable standards

- They are based upon efficient (but not perfect) operating conditions.
- The standard will include allowances for normal material losses, realistic allowances for fatigue, machine breakdowns, etc.
- These are the most frequently encountered type of standard.
- These standards may motivate employees to work harder since they provide a realistic but challenging target.

Basic standards

- These are long-term standards which remain unchanged over a period of years.
- Their sole use is to show trends over time for such items as material prices, labour rates and efficiency and the effect of changing methods.
- They cannot be used to highlight current efficiency.
- These standards may demotivate employees if, over time, they become too easy to achieve and, as a result, employees may feel bored and unchallenged.

Current standards

- These are standards based on current working conditions.
- They are useful when current conditions are abnormal and any other standard would provide meaningless information.
- The disadvantage is that they do not attempt to motivate employees to improve upon current working conditions and, as a result, employees may feel unchallenged.

Ideal standards

- These are based upon perfect operating conditions.
- This means that there is no wastage or scrap, no breakdowns, no stoppages or idle time; in short, no inefficiencies.
- In their search for perfect quality, Japanese companies use ideal standards for pinpointing areas where close examination may result in large cost savings.
- Ideal standards may have an adverse motivational impact since employees may feel that the standard is impossible to achieve.

Preparing standard costs which allow for idle time and waste

Attainable standards are set at levels which include an allowance for:

- Idle time, i.e. employees are paid for time when they are not working.
- Waste, i.e. of materials.

Test your understanding 3

The fastest time in which a batch of 20 'spicy meat special' sandwiches has been made was 32 minutes, with no hold-ups. However, work studies have shown that, on average, about 8% of the sandwich makers' time is non-productive and that, in addition to this, setup time (getting ingredients together etc.), is 2 minutes.

If the sandwich-makers are paid $4.50 per hour, what is the attainable standard labour cost of one sandwich?

Flexible budgeting

Before introducing the concept of flexible budgeting it is important to understand the following terms:

- **Fixed budget**: this is prepared before the beginning of a budget period for a single level of activity.
- **Flexible budget**: this is also prepared before the beginning of a budget period. It is prepared for a number of levels of activity and requires the analysis of costs between fixed and variable elements.
- **Flexed budget**: this is prepared at the end of the budget period. It provides a more meaningful estimate of costs and revenues and is based on the actual level of output.

Budgetary control compares actual results against expected results. The difference between the two is called a variance.

The actual results may be better (favourable variance) or worse (adverse variance) than expected.

It can be useful to present these figures in a flexible budget statement. (**Note:** This is not the same as a flexible budget).

Test your understanding 4

A business has prepared the following standard cost card based on producing and selling 10,000 units per month:

	$
Selling price	10
Variable production costs	3
Fixed production cost	1
Profit per unit	6

Actual production and sales for month 1 were 12,000 units and this resulted in the following:

	$000
Sales	125
Variable production costs	40
Fixed production costs	9
Total profit	76

Required:

Using a flexible budgeting approach, prepare a table showing the original fixed budget, the flexed budget, the actual results and the total meaningful variances.

Controllability and performance management

A cost is controllable if a manager is responsible for it being incurred or is able to authorise the expenditure.

A manager should only be evaluated on the costs over which they have control.

Test your understanding 5

The materials purchasing manager is assessed on:

- total material expenditure for the organisation
- the cost of introducing safety measures, regarding the standard and the quality of materials, in accordance with revised government legislation
- a notional rental cost, allocated by head office, for the material storage area.

Required:

Discuss whether these costs are controllable by the manager and if they should be used to appraise the manager.

Test your understanding 6

Explain whether a production manager should be accountable for direct labour and direct materials cost variances.

1 Revision of basic variance analysis

Variance analysis is the process by which the total difference between standard and actual results is analysed.

A number of basic variances can be calculated. If the results are better than expected, the variance is favourable (F). If the results are worse than expected, the variance is adverse (A).

It is important to be able to:

- calculate the variance
- explain the meaning of the variance calculated
- identify possible causes for each variance.

Once the variances have been calculated, an operating statement can be prepared reconciling actual profit to budgeted profit, under marginal costing or under absorption costing principles.

Basic variances can be calculated for sales, material, labour, variable overheads and fixed overheads. Each of these will be reviewed in turn.

Sales variances

Total sales variance

Sales price variance
- Did each unit sell for more or less than the budgeted selling price?

Sales volume variance
- Did the organisation sell more or less units than was budgeted?

Calculation

Actual Quantity Sold x Actual Price	(AQ AP)	Price Variance
Actual Quantity Sold x Standard Price	(AQ SP)	
Actual Quantity Sold x Standard Margin	(AQ SM)	Volume Variance
Budget Quantity x Standard Margin	(BQ SM)	

Note: 'Margin' = contribution per unit (marginal costing) or profit per unit (absorption costing).

Test your understanding 7 - Sales variances

W Ltd has budgeted sales of 6,500 units but actually sold only 6,000 units. Its standard cost card is as follows:

	$
Direct material	25
Direct wages	8
Variable overhead	4
Fixed overhead	18
Total standard cost	55
Standard gross profit	5
Standard selling price	60

The actual selling price for the period was $61.

Required:

Calculate the sales price and sales volume variance for the period:

(a) Using absorption costing

(b) Using marginal costing

Causes of sales variances

Variance	Favourable	Adverse
Sales price	Unexpected price increase due to: • higher than anticipated customer demand • lower than anticipated demand for competitor's products • an improvement in quality or performance	Unexpected price decrease due to: • lower than anticipated customer demand • higher than anticipated demand for competitor's products • a reduction in quality or performance
Sales volume	Unexpected increase in demand due to: • a lower price • improved quality or performance • a fall in quality or performance of competitor's products • a successful marketing campaign	Unexpected fall in demand due to: • a higher price • lower quality or performance of the product • an increase in quality or performance of competitor's products • an unsuccessful marketing campaign

Note: The sales price and volume variance may be linked. For example, an increase in the price of a product will result in a favourable sales price variance but may also result in an adverse sales volume variance, due to a fall in demand.

Materials variances

Total materials variance

Materials price variance
– Did each unit of material cost more or less than expected?

Materials usage variance
– Did actual production use more or less units of material than expected?

Calculation

Actual Quantity Bought x Actual Price	(AQ AP)	Price Variance
Actual Quantity Bought x Standard Price	(AQ SP)	
Actual Quantity Used x Standard Price	(AQ SP)	Usage Variance
Standard Quantity Used x Standard Price (for actual production	(SQ SP)	

Test your understanding 8 - Materials variances

James Marshall Co makes a single product with the following budgeted material costs per unit:

2 kg of material A at $10/kg

Actual details:

Output 1,000 units

Material purchased and used 2,200 kg

Material cost $20,900

Calculate material price and usage variances.

Causes of material variances

Variance	Favourable	Adverse
Material price	• Poorer quality materials • Discounts given for buying in bulk • Change to a cheaper supplier • Incorrect budgeting	• Higher quality materials • Change to a more expensive supplier • Unexpected price increase encountered • Incorrect budgeting
Material usage	• Higher quality materials • More efficient use of material • Change is product specification • Incorrect budgeting	• Poorer quality materials • Less experienced staff using more materials • Change in product specification • Incorrect budgeting

Note: The material price variance and the material usage variance may be linked. For example, the purchase of poorer quality materials may result in a favourable price variance but an adverse usage variance.

Labour variances

Total labour variance

Labour rate variance
– Did labour cost more or less per hour than expected?

Labour efficiency variance
– Did production take more or less hours than expected?

Calculation

Actual Hours x Actual Rate (AH AR)
Actual Hours x Standard Rate (AH SR)
} Rate Variance

Actual Hours x Standard Rate (AH SR)
Standard Hours x Standard Rate (SH SR)
} Efficiency Variance

Test your understanding 9 - Labour variances

Extract from the standard cost card for K Ltd

	$
Direct labour:	
(15 hours @ $4.80 per hour)	72

Actual direct wages for the period were:
15,500 hours costing $69,750 in total
Actual units produced 1,000

Calculate the labour rate and labour efficiency variances.

Causes of labour variances

Variance	Favourable	Adverse
Labour rate	• Lower skilled staff	• Higher skilled staff
	• Cut in overtime/ bonus	• Increase in overtime/ bonus
	• Incorrect budgeting	• Incorrect budgeting
		• Unforeseen wage increase
Labour efficiency	• Higher skilled staff	• Lower skilled staff
	• Improved staff motivation	• Fall in staff motivation
	• Incorrect budgeting	• Incorrect budgeting

Note: The labour rate variance and the labour efficiency variance may be linked. For example, employing more highly skilled labour may result in an adverse rate variance but a favourable efficiency variance.

Variable overhead variances

Total variable overhead variance

Variable overhead expenditure variance	Variable overhead efficiency variance
– Did the variable overhead cost more or less per hour than expected?	– Did production take more or less labour hours than expected?

Calculation

Actual Hours Worked x Actual Rate	(AH AR)	Expenditure Variance
Actual Hours Worked x Standard Rate	(AH SR)	
Actual Hours Worked x Standard Rate	(AH SR)	Efficiency Variance
Standard Hours Worked x Standard Rate (for actual production)	(SH SR)	

Test your understanding 10 - Variable overhead variances

Extract from the standard cost card for K Ltd

	$
Variable overhead:	
15 hours @ $1 per hour	15

Actual variable overheads for the period were:

15,500 hours — Total cost $14,900

Actual units produced 1,000

Calculate the variable overhead expenditure and variable overhead efficiency variances.

Causes of variable overhead variances

Variance	Favourable	Adverse
Var. o/h expenditure	• Unexpected saving in cost of services	• Unexpected increase in the cost of services
	• More economic use of services	• Less economic use of services
	• Incorrect budgeting	• Incorrect budgeting
Var. o/h efficiency	• As for labour efficiency	• As for labour efficiency

Fixed overhead variances

Total fixed overhead variance

- Fixed overhead expenditure variance
  - Did the fixed overhead cost more or less than expected?
- Fixed overhead volume variance
  - Did the organisation absorb more or less overhead than expected?
  - Can be split further into:
    - Fixed overhead capacity variance
      - Did employees work more or less hours than expected?
    - Fixed overhead efficiency variance
      - Did employees work faster or slower than expected?

Marginal costing system

With a marginal costing profit and loss, no overheads are absorbed, the amount spent is simply written off to the income statement.

So with marginal costing the only fixed overhead variance is the difference between what was budgeted to be spent and what was actually spent, i.e. the fixed overhead expenditure variance.

Absorption costing system

Under absorption costing we use an overhead absorption rate to absorb overheads. Variances will occur if this absorption rate is incorrect (just as we will get over/under-absorption).

So with absorption costing we calculate the fixed overhead expenditure variance and the fixed overhead volume variance (this can be split into a capacity and efficiency variance).

Calculation

Actual Cost	(AH AR)	Expenditure Variance	
Budgeted Hours x Standard Rate	(BH SR)		
Budgeted Hours x Standard Rate	(BH SR)	Capacity Variance	Volume Variance
Actual Hours x Standard Rate	(AH SR)	Efficiency Variance	
Standard Hours x Standard Rate (for actual production)	(SH SR)		

Test your understanding 11 - Fixed overhead variances

The following information is available for J Ltd for Period 4:

Budget	
Fixed production overheads	$22,960
Units	6,560
The standard time to produce each unit is 2 hours	
Actual	
Fixed production overheads	$24,200
Units	6,460
Labour hours	12,600 hrs

Required:

If J Ltd uses an absorption costing system, calculate the following:

(a) FOAR per labour hour

(b) Fixed overhead expenditure variance

(c) Fixed overhead capacity variance

(d) Fixed overhead efficiency variance

(e) Fixed overhead volume variance

Causes of fixed overhead variances

Variance	Favourable	Adverse
Fixed o/h expenditure	• Decrease in price • Seasonal effects	• Increase in price • Seasonal effects
Fixed o/h volume	• Increase in production volume • Increase in demand • Change is productivity of labour	• Decrease in production volume • Decrease in demand • Production lost through strikes
Fixed o/h capacity	• Hours worked higher than budget	• Hours worked lower than budget
Fixed o/h efficiency	• As for labour efficiency	• As for labour efficiency

Operating statement under absorption costing

The purpose of calculating variances is to identify the different effects of each item of cost/income on profit compared to the expected profit. These variances are summarised in a reconciliation statement or operating statement.

e.g

Illustration 1 – Operating statement under absorption costing

Proforma operating statement under absorption costing (AC)

			$
Budgeted profit			X
Sales volume profit variance			X/ (X)
Standard profit on actual sales (= flexed budget profit)			X
Selling price variance			X/ (X)
			X
Cost variances:	**F**	**A**	
	$	**$**	
Material price	X	(X)	
Material usage	X	(X)	
Labour rate	X	(X)	
Labour efficiency	X	(X)	
Variable overhead expenditure	X	(X)	
Variable overhead efficiency	X	(X)	
Fixed production overhead expenditure variance	X	(X)	
Fixed production overhead capacity variance	X	(X)	
Fixed production overhead efficiency variance	X	(X)	
Total			X/ (X)
Actual profit			X

Test your understanding 12 - AC operating statement

Riki Ltd, produces and sells one product only. The standard cost and price for one unit being as follows:

	$
Direct material A – 10 kilograms at $12 per kg	120
Direct material B – 6 kilograms at $5 per kg	30
Direct wages – 5 hours at $8 per hour	40
Fixed production overhead	60
Total standard cost	250
Standard gross profit	50
Standard selling price	300

The fixed production overhead included in the standard cost is based on an expected monthly output of 750 units. Riki Ltd use an absorption costing system.

During April the actual results were as follows:

	$
Sales 700 units @ $320	224,000
Direct materials:	
A: 7,500 Kg	91,500
B: 3,500 Kg	20,300
Direct wages 3,400 hours	27,880
Fixed production overhead	37,000
	176,680
Gross profit	47,320

Note: Riki Ltd does not hold any inventories.

Required:

You are required to reconcile budgeted profit with actual profit for the period, calculating the following variances:

Selling price, sales volume, material price, material usage, labour rate, labour efficiency, fixed overhead expenditure and fixed overhead volume.

Operating statement under marginal costing

The operating statement under marginal costing is the same as that under absorption costing except;

- a sales volume contribution variance is included instead of a sales volume profit variance
- the only fixed overhead variance is the expenditure variances
- the reconciliation is from budgeted to actual contribution then fixed overheads are deducted to arrive at a profit.

e.g

Illustration 2 – Operating statement under marginal costing

Proforma operating statement under marginal costing (MC)

	F	A	
			$
Budgeted contribution			
(budgeted production × budgeted contn/unit)			X
Sales volume contribution variance			X/ (X)
Standard contribution on actual sales			
(= flexed budget contribution)			X
Selling price variance			X/ (X)
			X
Variable cost variances:			
	F	**A**	
	$	$	$
Material price	X	(X)	
Material usage	X	(X)	
Labour rate	X	(X)	
Labour efficiency	X	(X)	
Variable overhead expenditure	X	(X)	
Variable overhead efficiency	X	(X)	
Total	X	(X)	X/ (X)
Actual contribution			X
Budgeted fixed production overhead			X
Fixed overhead expenditure variance			X/ (X)
Actual profit			X

Test your understanding 13 - MC operating statement

Chapel Ltd manufactures a chemical protective called Rustnot. The following standard costs apply for the production of 100 cylinders:

		$
Materials	500 kgs @ $0.80 per kg	400
Labour	20 hours @ $1.50 per hour	30
Fixed overheads	20 hours @ $1.00 per hour	20
		450

The monthly production/sales budget is 10,000 cylinders.

Selling price = $6 per cylinder.

For the month of November the following production and sales information is available:

Produced/sold	10,600 cylinders
Sales value	$63,000
Materials purchased and used 53,200 kgs	$42,500
Labour 2,040 hours	$3,100
Fixed overheads	$2,200

Required:

You are required to prepare an operating statement in a marginal costing format for November detailing all the variances.

2 Further aspects of variances

The learning curve effect and labour variances

Recap of the learning curve

When production is complex and labour intensive it may be the case that unit labour times reduce as the workforce become more familiar with the task. The learning curve effect is a mathematical model which quantifies this reduction in time taken.

The learning curve model states that each time the number of units produced doubles, the cumulative average time per unit is reduced by a constant percentage.

The learning curve model will affect labour variances since:

- The initial standard time taken to produce the item will become rapidly out of date.
- Variances calculated using out of date standards will quickly become meaningless for planning and control.

Test your understanding 14

A company has introduced a new product which is complex and labour intensive and it is expected that an 80% learning curve applies. The standard cost card for the product, based on estimates for the time required to produce the first unit, includes standard labour time of 100 hours at a cost of $8 per hour.

The first 4 units took 270 hours to produce at a cost of $2,187.

Required:

Calculate the labour rate and efficiency variances based on

(a) the initial labour standard

(b) a labour standard for 4 units which takes into account an 80% learning curve effect.

Additional example on learning curve effect

A company has introduced a new product and it is anticipated that a 90% learning curve applies. The standard cost card for the product, based on estimates for the time required to produce the first unit, includes standard labour time of 200 hours at a cost of $8 per hour.

The first 8 units took 1,150 hours to produce at a cost of $9,430.

Required:

Calculate the labour rate and efficiency variances based on a labour standard which takes into account the learning curve effect.

Solution

Standard average time per unit for the first 4 units:

$y = ax^b$

where b is the learning coefficient

b= log r/ log 2

b = log 0.9/ log 2

b = – 0.15200

$y = 200 \times 8^{-0.15200}$

= 145.80 hours

Standard time for the first 8 units:

145.80 hours × 8 units = 1,166.40 hours

Labour variances:	$	$
AH AR =	9,430	
Rate variance	}	230 (A)
AH SR = 1,150 hours × $8 =	9,200	
Efficiency variance	}	131.2 (F)
SH SR = 1,166.40 hours × $8 =	9,331.2	

Labour idle time and material waste

Idle time

Idle time occurs when employees are paid for time when they are not working e.g. due to machine breakdown, low demand or stockouts.

If idle time exists an idle time labour variance should be calculated.

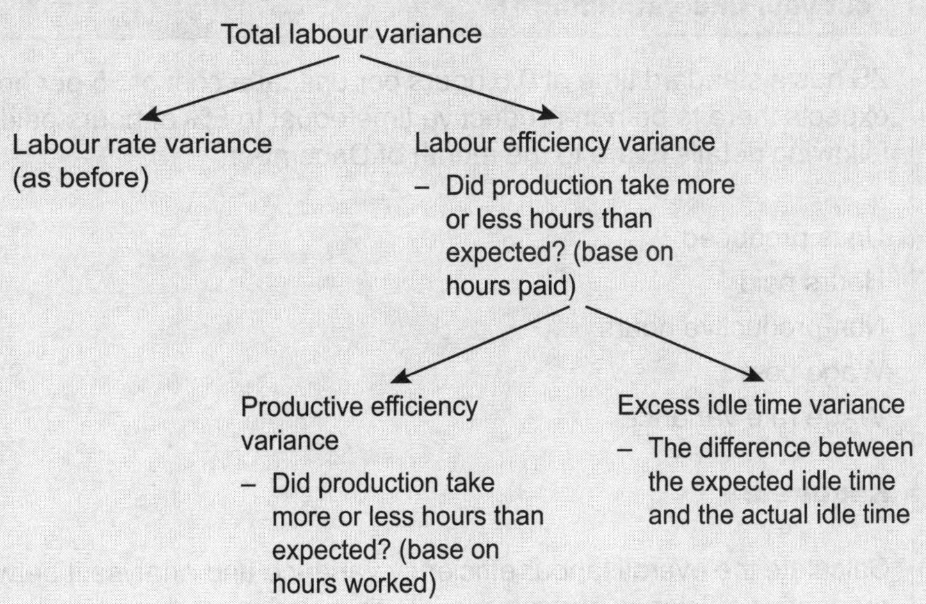

Actual Hours Paid x Actual Rate	(AH AR)	Rate Variance
Actual Hours Paid x Standard Rate	(AH SR)	
Actual Idle Time x Standard Grossed Up Rate	(AIT SGR)	Excess Idle Time Variance
Standard Idle Time x Standard Grossed Up Rate	(SIT SGR)	
Actual Hours Worked x Standard Grossed Up Rate	(AH SGR)	Productive Efficiency Variance
Standard Hours Worked x Standard Grossed Up Rate (for actual production)	(SH SGR)	

3 Controlling Idle time

Idle time can be prevented or reduced considerably by :

1. Proper maintenance of tools & machinery
2. Advanced production planning
3. Timely procurement of stores
4. Assurance of supply of power
5. Advance planning for machine utilisation

Test your understanding 15

ZS has a standard time of 0.5 hours per unit, at a cost of $5 per hour. It expects there to be non-productive time equal to 5% of hours paid. The following details relate to the month of December:

Units produced	5,400
Hours paid	3,000
Non-productive hours	165
Wage cost	$15,000
Wage rate variance	$Nil

Required:

Calculate the overall labour efficiency variance and analyse it between productive efficiency and excess idle time variances.

Test your understanding 16 - Additional idle time example

The following data relates to T plc for the month of January:

Standard productive time per unit 2 hours	
Standard wage rate per paid hour	$4.00
Actual production	1,200 units
Standard idle time as a percentage of hours paid	4%
Actual hours paid	2,600
Actual idle time hours	110

Required:

Calculate the labour efficiency variance and analyse it between productive efficiency and idle time.

Material waste

Material waste may also be a normal part of a process and could be caused by:

- evaporation
- scrapping
- testing

Waste would affect the material usage variance. The calculation will be reviewed in the next chapter.

Standard costing and activity-based costing (ABC)

- As seen in chapter 1, ABC is a method of allocating overhead costs to products using cost drivers.
- Standard costs can be compared to actuals and an overhead expenditure and efficiency variance calculated.

Where materials are not properly controlled, excess stock of some items are likely to occur with a result unnecessary tying up of capital and loss through deterioration and obsolescence. Shortages of other materials may arise at the time when they are urgently needed, and production will then be delayed.

The purchasing of materials is a highly specialised function, that can control waste by :

(1) Ordering the right quantity and quality of materials at the most favourable price;

(2) Ensuring the material arrives at the right time in the production process;

(3) Take active measures against theft, deterioration, breakage and additional storage costs.

Standard costing and activity-based costing (ABC)

- As seen in chapter 1, ABC is a method of allocating overhead costs to products using cost drivers.
- Standard costs can be compared to actuals and an overhead expenditure and efficiency variance calculated.

e.g

Illustration 3 – ABC variances

The following information relates to H Company's ordering activity for the period:

	Budget	**Actual**
Output	20,000 units	21,000 units
Activity level	4,000 orders	3,600 orders
Activity cost	$180,000	$168,000

Required

Calculate the overhead expenditure variance and the overhead efficiency variance for the ordering activity and comment briefly on the meaning of each variance.

Solution

Variable overhead expenditure variance

	$
Actual orders, 3,600, **should** cost $45 per order ($180,000/4,000 orders) =	162,000
Actual orders, 3,600, **did** cost	168,000
Variance	6,000 A

Variable overhead efficiency variance

	Orders
Actual production, 21,000 units, **should** use 0.2 orders per unit (4,000/ 20,000) =	4,200
Actual production, 21,000 units, **did** use	3,600
Variance	600 F

Variance = 600 F orders × **standard cost** of $45 per order = $27,000 F

Each unit used less than 0.2 orders, resulting in a favourable variance.

ABC Variances - Solution

Variable overhead expenditure variance

	$
Actual orders, 3,600, **should** cost $45 per order ($180,000/4,000 orders) =	162,000
Actual orders, 3,600, **did** cost	168,000
Variance	6,000 A

Variable overhead efficiency variance

	Orders
Actual production, 21,000 units, **should** use 0.2 orders per unit (4,000/ 20,000) =	4,200
Actual production, 21,000 units, **did** use	3,600
Variance	600 F

Variance = 600 F orders × **standard cost** of $45 per order = $27,000 F

Each unit used less than 0.2 orders, resulting in a favourable variance.

Test your understanding 17 - ABC variances

The following information is also available for H Company's delivery activity for the period:

	Budget	**Actual**
Output	20,000 units	21,000 units
Activity level	200 deliveries	220 deliveries
Activity cost	$50,000	$52,800

Required:

Calculate the overhead expenditure variance and the overhead efficiency variance for the delivery activity and comment briefly on the meaning of each variance.

When should a variance be investigated?

Factors to consider include:

Size

A standard is an average expected cost and therefore small variations between the actual and the standard are bound to occur. These are uncontrollable variances and should not be investigated.

In addition, a business may decide to only investigate variances above a certain amount. The following techniques could be used:

- Fixed size of variance, e.g. investigate all variances over $5,000
- Fixed percentage rule, e.g. investigate all variances over 10% of the budget
- Statistical decision rule, e.g. investigate all variances of which there is a likelihood of less than 5% that it could have arisen randomly.

Favourable or adverse

Firms often treat adverse variances as more important than favourable and therefore any investigation may concentrate on these adverse variances.

Cost

For investigation to be worthwhile, the cost of investigation must be less than the benefits of correcting the cause of the variance.

Past pattern

Variances should be monitored for a number of periods in order to identify any trends in the variances. A firm would focus its investigation on any steadily worsening trends.

The budget

The budget may be unreliable or unrealistic. Therefore, the variances would be uncontrollable and call for a change in the budget or an improvement in the budgeting process, not an investigation of the variance.

Reliability of figures

The system for measuring and recording the figures may be unreliable. If this is the case, the variances will be meaningless and should not be investigated.

Methods used when investigating variances

A process has a standard time of 50 minutes. Control limits may be set as a fixed amount, a fixed percentage or using a statistical model. Assume they are set at a fixed amount 30 and 70 minutes, and actual times recorded as follows:

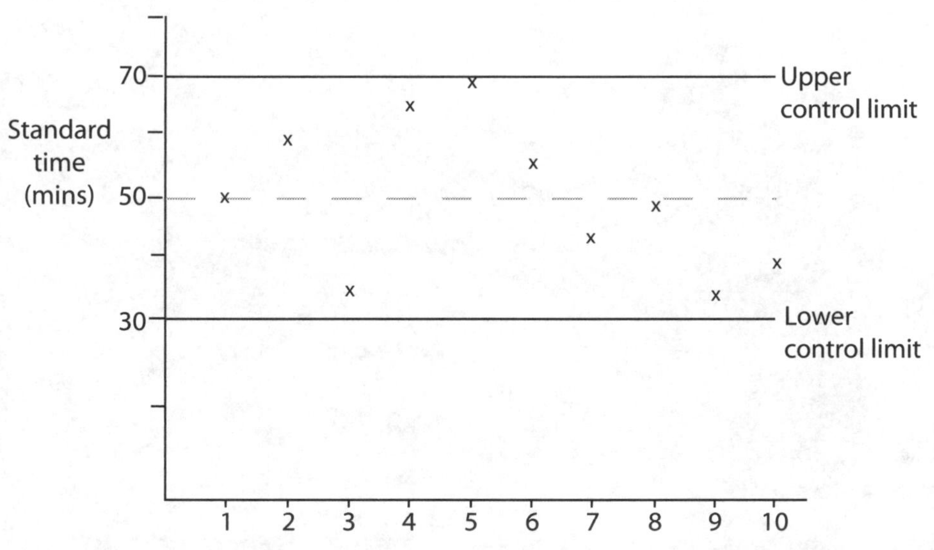

If the actual time taken falls within the bands, the variance is not significant.

Control limits should be set so that there is only a small chance of a random fluctuation falling outside them.

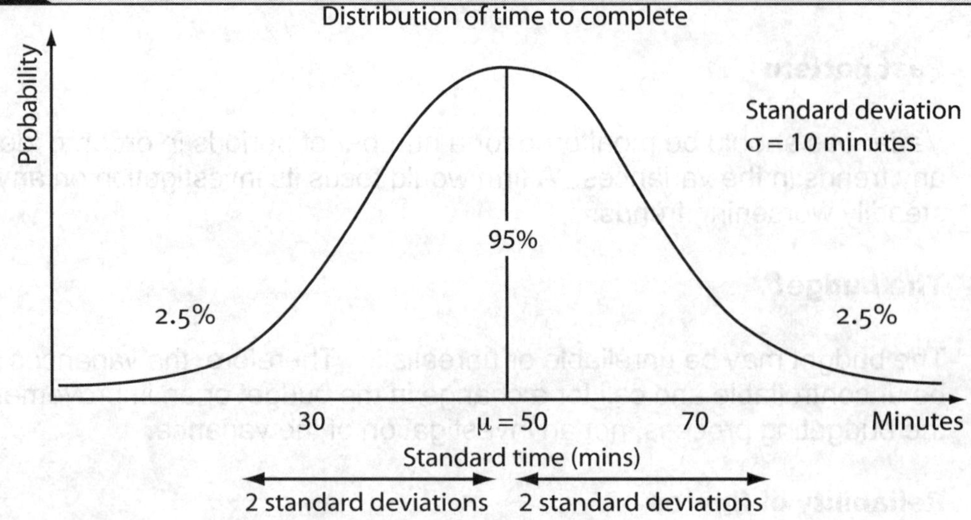

- In this example the control limits are set two standard deviations from the mean. This means that 95% of the recorded process times should lie within the control limits.
- The actual time is recorded on the chart after the completion of each process. It will soon be apparent if the mean time is shifting from 50 minutes, as the recorded times move outside the control limits.
- If more than 5% of the observed results do lie outside the control limits, then the system may be referred to as being statistically out of control. At this stage management must decide what further action to take.

4 Chapter summary

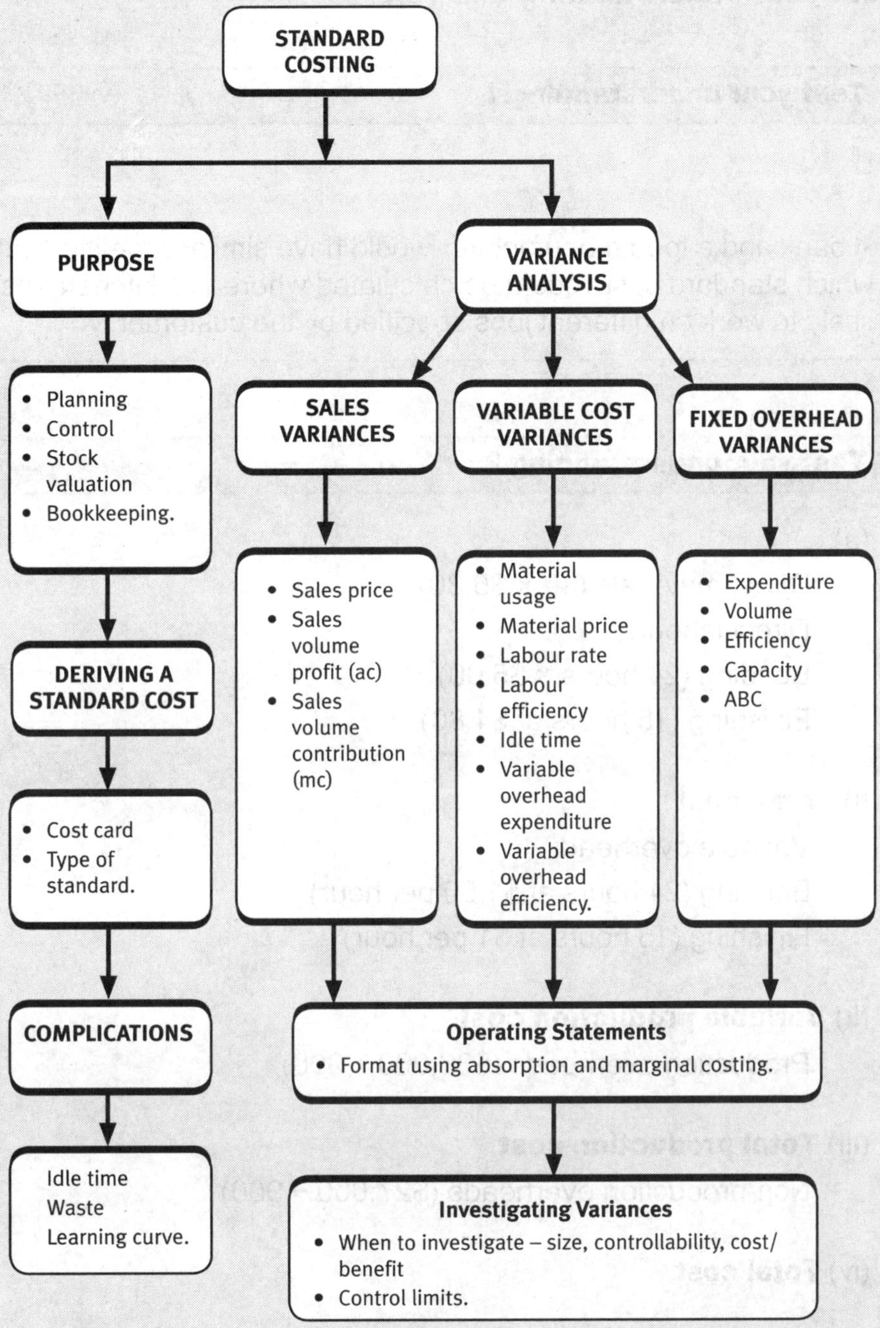

Test your understanding answers

Test your understanding 1

D

A bank and a food manufacturer would have similar repetitive output for which standard costs could be calculated whereas a kitchen designer is likely to work on different jobs specified by the customer.

Test your understanding 2

(a)	$
Direct materials (40 × $5.30)	212
Direct labour:	
Bonding (24 hours × $5.00)	120
Finishing (15 hours at $4.80)	72
(i) **Prime cost**	404
Variable overhead:	
Bonding (24 hours at $1.50 per hour)	36
Finishing (15 hours at $1 per hour)	15
(ii) **Variable production cost**	455
Production overheads ($36,000 ÷ 900)	40
(iii) **Total production cost**	495
Non-production overheads ($27,000 ÷ 900)	30
(iv) **Total cost**	525
(b)	
Profit **(**(25/75) × 525**)**	175
Price ($525 + $175)	700

Test your understanding 3

		Per batch of 20
Ideal time	(92%)	32.0 minutes
Non-productive idle time	(8%)	2.8 minutes
	(100%)	34.8 minutes
Setup time		2.0 minutes
Total time		36.8 minutes
Total cost @ $4.50/hr		$2.76
Standard labour cost per sandwich ($2.76/20)		$0.138

Test your understanding 4

	Original fixed budget	**Flexed budget**	**Actual results**	**Meaningful variance = flexed – actual**
Based on production/ sales of:	10,000 units	12,000 units	12,000 units	-
Sales	10,000 units × $10/ unit = $100,000	12,000 units × $10/ unit = $120,000	$125,000	$5,000 Fav
Variable production cost	10,000 units × $3/ unit = $30,000	12,000 units × $3/ unit = $36,000	$40,000	$4,000 Adv
Fixed production cost	10,000 units × $1/ unit = $10,000	As per original budget = $10,000	$9,000	$1,000 Fav
Profit	$60,000	$74,000	$76,000	$2,000 Fav

Test your understanding 5

The total material expenditure for the organisation will be dependent partly on the prices negotiated by the purchasing manager and partly by the requirements and performance of the production department. If it is included as a target for performance appraisal the manager may be tempted to purchase cheaper material which may have an adverse effect elsewhere in the organisation.

The requirement to introduce safety measures may be imposed but the manager should be able to ensure that implementation meets budget targets.

A notional rental cost is outside the control of the manager and should not be included in a target for performance appraisal purposes.

Test your understanding 6

- The production manager will be responsible for managing direct labour and direct material usage.
- However, the manager may not be able to influence:
  - the cost of the material
  - the quality of the material
  - the cost of labour
  - the quality of labour
- Performance should be measured against the element of direct cost which the manager can control.

Test your understanding 7 - Sales variances

(a) Under absorption costing, the variance is calculated using the standard profit per unit. **$**

Using the three line method :

Sales price variance

AQ AP = 6,000 × $61= $366,000

Variance = **$6,000 F**

AQ SP = 6,000 × $60 = $360,000

Sales volume variance

AQ SM = 6,000 × $5= $30,000

Variance = **$2,500 A**

BQ SM = 6,500 × $5 = $32,500

Alternative calculations :

6,000 units **should** have sold for 6,000 x $60 =	$360,000
6,000 units **did** sell for for 6,000 x $61 =	$366,000
Sales price variance	**$6,000 F**
Budgeted Sales	6,500 units
Actual Sales	6,000 units
Variance in units	500 units A
@ standard profit $5	**$2,500 A**

(b) The sales price variance is the same under marginal costing, but the sales volume variance is calculated using the standard contribution per unit. Here, standard contribution = $60 - ($25 +$8 + $4) = $23.

Sales volume variance

AQ SM = 6,000 × $23= $138,000

Variance = **$11,500 A**

BQ SM = 6,500 × $23 = $149,500

Alternative calculation :

Budgeted sales =	6,500
Actual sales =	6,000
Variance	500 A

Variance = 500 A units × **standard contribution** of $23 per unit = $11,500 A

Test your understanding 8 - Materials variances

Using the three line method :

$

Material price variance

AQ AP = $20,900

Variance = **$1,100 F**

AQ SP = 2,200 kgs × $10 = $22,000

Material usage variance

AQ SP = 2,200 kgs × $10= $22,000

Variance = **$2,000 A**

SQ SP = 1,000 units x 2kgs × $10 = $20,000

Alternative calculations :

2,200 kgs should have cost 2,200 x $10	$22,000
2,200 kgs **did** cost	$20,900
Materials price variance	**$1,100 F**

1,000 units of output should have used 1,000 x 2 kgs	2,000 kgs
1,000 units of output did use	2,200 kgs
Therefore variance is adverse by	200 kgs
@ standard cost per kg £10	**$2,000 A**

Test your understanding 9 - Labour variances

Labour rate variance	**$**
Actual hours paid, 15,500 hours, **should** cost $4.80 per hour	74,400
Actual hours paid, 15,500 hours, **did** cost	69,750
Variance	4,650 F

Labour efficiency variance	**Hours**
Actual production, 1,000 units, **should** take 15 hours per unit	15,000
Actual production, 1,000 units, **did** take	15,500
Variance	500 A

Variance = 500 A hours × **standard cost** of $4.80 per hour = $2,400 A

Labour rate variance - three line method

AH AR = $69,750

Variance = $4,650 F

AH SR = 15,500 × $4.80 = $74,400

Labour efficiency variance - three line method

AH SR = 15,500 × $4.80 = $74,400

Var. = $2,400 A

SH SR = (1,000 × 15 hours) × $4.80 = $72,000

Test your understanding 10 - Variable overhead variances

Variable overhead expenditure variance	**$**
Actual hours paid, 15,500 hours, **should** cost $1 per hour	15,500
Actual hours paid, 15,500 hours, **did** cost	14,900
Variance	600 F

Variable overhead efficiency variance	**Hours**
Actual production, 1,000 units, **should** take 15 hours per unit	15,000
Actual production, 1,000 units, **did** take	15,500
Variance	500 A

Variance = 500 A hours × **standard cost** of $1 per hour = $500 A

Variable overhead expenditure variance - three line method

AH AR = $14,900

Variance = $600 F

AH SR = 15,500 × $1 = $15,500

Variable overhead efficiency variance - three line method

AH SR = 15,500 × $1 = $15,500

Variance = $500 A

SH SR = (1,000 × 15 hours) × $1 = $15,000

Test your understanding 11 - Fixed overhead variances

(a) FOAR = $22,960 ÷ (6,560 units × 2 hours per unit) = $1.75 per hour

(b) **Fixed overhead expenditure variance**

	$
Budgeted fixed overhead	22,960
Actual fixed overhead	24,200
Variance	1,240 A

Fixed overhead expenditure variance - three line method

AH AR = $24,200

Var. = $1,240 A

BH SR = $22,960

(c) **Fixed overhead capacity variance**

	Hours
Budgeted hours worked = 2hours × 6,560 units	13,120
Actual hours worked	12,600
Variance	520 A

Variance in $ = 520A hours × **standard FOAR** $1.75/hr = $910 A

Fixed overhead capacity variance - three line method

BH SR = $22,960

Variance = $910 A

AH SR = 12,600 × $1.75 = $22,050

(d) **Fixed overhead efficiency variance**

	Hours
Actual production, 6,460 units, **should** take 2 hours per unit	12,920
Actual production, 6,460 units, did take	12,600
Variance	320 F

Variance in $ = 320F hours × **standard FOAR** per hour $1.75 = $560 F

Fixed overhead efficiency variance - alternative method

AH SR = 12,600 × $1.75 = $22,050

Variance = $560 F

SH SR = (6,460 × 2) × $1.75 = $22,610

(e) **Fixed overhead volume variance**

	Units
Budgeted production	6,560
Actual production	6,460
Variance	100 A

Variance in $ = 100 A units × **standard hours** of 2 × **standard FOAR** per hour $1.75 = $350 A

Fixed overhead volume variance - alternative method

BH SR = $22,960

Variance = $350 A

SH SR = (6,460 × 2) × $1.75 = $22,610

Note: The fixed overhead volume variance of $350A is the total of the capacity and efficiency variances ($910 A + $560 F).

Test your understanding 12 - AC operating statement

Material A variances:	$	$
AQ AP =	91,500	
Price variance	}	1,500 (A)
AQ SP = 7,500kg × $12 =	90,000	
Usage variance	}	6,000 (A)
SQ SP = (700 units × 10kg) × $12 =	84,000	
Material B variances:	$	$
AQ AP =	20,300	
Price variance	}	2,800 (A)
AQ SP = 3,500kg × $5 =	17,500	
Usage variance	}	3,500 (F)
SQ SP = (700units × 6kg) × $5 =	21,000	
Labour variances:	$	$
AH AR =	27,880	
Rate variance	}	680 (A)
AH SR = 3,400 hours × $8 =	27,200	
Efficiency variance	}	800 (F)
SH SR = (700units × 5 hours) × $8 =	28,000	
Fixed overhead variances:	$	$
AH AR =	37,000	
Expenditure variance	}	8,000 (F)
BH SR = 750units × $60 per unit	45,000	
Volume variance	}	3,000 (A)
SH SR = 700units × $60 per unit	42,000	
Sales variances:	$	$
AQ AP	224,000	
Price variance	}	14,000 (F)
AQ SP = 700 units × $300 per unit	210,000	
AQ SM = 700 units × $50 per unit	35,000	
Volume variance	}	2,500 (A)
BQ SM = 750 units × $50 per unit	37,500	

Operating statement

			$
Budgeted profit (750 × $50)			37,500
Sales volume variance			(2,500)
Standard profit on actual sales			35,000
Selling price variance			14,000
Cost variances:	**F**	**A**	
Material price (combined)		(4,300)	
Material usage (combined)		(2,500)	
Labour rate		(680)	
Labour efficiency	800		
Fixed overhead expenditure	8,000		
Fixed overhead volume		(3,000)	
Total	8,800	10,480	(1,680)
Actual profit			47,320

Test your understanding 13 - MC operating statement

Standard contribution = $6 – $4.30 = $1.70 per cylinder

Sales variances:	$	$
AQ AP	63,000	
Price variance		600 (A)
AQ SP = 10,600 units × $6 per unit	63,600	
AQ SM = 10,600 units × $1.70 per unit	18,020	
Volume variance		1,020 (F)
BQ SM = 10,000 units × $1.70 per unit	17,000	

Material variances:	$		$
AQ AP =	42,500		
Price variance		}	60 (F)
AQ SP = 53,200kg × $0.80 =	42,560		
Usage variance		}	160 (A)
SQ SP = (10,600 units × 5kg) × $0.80 =	42,400		
Labour variances:	$		$
AH AR =	3,100		
Rate variance		}	40 (A)
AH SR = 2,040 hours × $1.50 =	3,060		
Efficiency variance		}	120 (F)
SH SR = (10,600units × 0.2 hours) × $1.50 =	3,180		

Operating Statement	$
Budgeted contribution (10,000 x $1.70)	17,000
Sales volume contribution variance	1,020 F
Standard contribution on actual sales (10,600×1.70)	18,020
Sales price variance	(600 A)
	17,420

Variable cost variances:	**F**	**A**	
	$	$	$
Materials price	60		
Wages rate		40	
Materials usage		160	
Labour efficiency	120		
	180	200	(20 A)
Actual contribution			17,400
Budgeted fixed overhead			2,000
Fixed overhead expenditure variance			(200 A)
Actual profit			15,200

Test your understanding 14

(a)

Labour variances:	$	$
AH AR =	2,187	
Rate variance		} 27 (A)
AH SR = 270 hours × $8 =	2,160	
Efficiency variance		} 1,040 (F)
SH SR = (4 units × 100 hours) × $8 =	3,200	

(b) **Standard average time per unit for the first 4 units:**

$y = ax^b$

where $b = \log r / \log 2$

$= \log 0.8 / \log 2$

$= -0.32193$

$y = 100 \times 4^{-0.32193}$

$= 64$ hours

Standard time for the first 4 units:

64 hours × 4 units = 256 hours

Labour rate variance:

This will be unchanged since it is based on actual hours, i.e. 270 hours.

Labour efficiency variance:

AH SR (as before) =	2,160	
Efficiency variance		} 112 (A)
SH SR = 256 hours × $8 =	2,048	

- The labour efficiency variance is now $112 A
- Taking into account the learning curve effect has changed the labour efficiency variance from $1,040 F to $112 A
- This is because the actual learning rate was slower than expected
- In this type of scenario the firm could consider having different labour standards for different volumes of production.

Test your understanding 15

Labour efficiency variance

The expected idle time of 5% should be included in the standard time to produce 1 unit.

	Hours
Actual production, 5,400 units, **should** take (0.5 hours × 100/95 each) =	2,842
Actual production, 5,400 units, **did** take	3,000
Variance	158 A

Variance = 158 A hours × **standard cost** of $5 per hour = $790 A

Labour efficiency variance - alternative method

AH SR = 3,000 × $5 = $15,000

Variance = $790 A

SH SR = (5,400 × 0.5 hours × 100/95) × $5 = $14,210

This is the same formula that has been used previously but it is important to remember that the hours are always hours paid.

Productive efficiency variance

	Hours
Actual production, 5,400 units, **should** take 0.5 hours each =	2,700
Actual production, 5,400 units, **did** take (3,000 - 165)	2,835
Variance	135 A

For each productive hour worked there will be 5% non-productive time paid. The standard rate per hour should take this into account.

Variance = 135 A hours × (**standard cost** of $5 per hour × 100/95) = $711 A

Productive efficiency variance - alternative method

AH SGR = 2,835 × ($5 × 100/95) = $14,921

Variance = $711 A

SH SGR = 2,700 × ($5 × 100/95) = $14,210

Excess idle time variance	Hours
Expected idle time (3,000 hours × 5%) =	150
Actual idle time	165
Variance	15 A

For each productive hour worked there will be 5% non-productive time paid. The standard rate per hour should take this into account.

Variance = 15 A hours × (**standard cost** of $5 per hour × 100/95) = $79 A

Excess idle time variance - alternative method

AIH SGR = 165 × ($5 × 100/95) = $868.42

Variance = $79 A

SIH SGR = 150 × ($5 × 100/95) = $789.47

Test your understanding 16 - Additional idle time example

Labour efficiency variance

AH SR = 2,600 × $4 = $10,400

Variance = $400 A

SH SR = (1,200 × 2 hours × 100/96) × $4 = $10,000

Productive efficiency variance

AH SGR = (2,600 - 110) × ($4 × 100/96) = $10,375

Variance = $375 A

SH SGR = (1,200 × 2) × ($4 × 100/96) = $10,000

Excess idle time variance

AIH SGR = 110 × ($4 × 100/96) = $458.33

Variance = $25 A

SIH SGR = (2,600 × 4%) × ($4 × 100/96) = $433.33

Test your understanding 17 - ABC variances

Variable overhead expenditure variance	**$**
Actual deliveries, 220, **should** cost $250 per delivery ($50,000/200 orders) =	55,000
Actual deliveries, 220, **did** cost	52,800
Variance	2,200 F

Each delivery cost less than the standard cost of $250, resulting in a favourable variance.

Variable overhead efficiency variance	**Deliveries**
Actual production, 21,000 units, **should** use 0.01 deliveries per unit (50,000/200) =	210
Actual production, 21,000 units, **did** use	220
Variance	10 A

Variance = 10 A deliveries × **standard cost** of $250 per delivery = $2,500 A

Each unit used more than 0.01 deliveries, resulting in an adverse variance.

chapter

10

Advanced variances

Chapter learning objectives

Upon completion of this chapter you will be able to:

- define, for a manufacturing company, material mix and yield variances
- calculate, from information supplied, material mix and yield variances
- for given or calculated material mix and yield variances, interpret and explain possible causes, including possible interrelationships between them
- explain, using simple non-numerical examples, the wider issues involved in changing mix, e.g. cost, quality and performance measurement issues
- identify and explain the interrelationship between price, mix and yield, using a simple numerical example
- suggest and justify alternative methods of controlling production processes in manufacturing environments
- using revised standards supplied, calculate a revised budget
- calculate and explain sales mix and quantity variances
- from supplied data, calculate planning and operational variances for sales (including market size and market share)
- from supplied data, calculate planning and operational variances for materials
- from supplied data, calculate planning and operational variances for labour
- identify and explain those factors that, in general, should and should not be allowed to revise an original budget
- explain and resolve the typical manipulation issues in revising budgets.

- describe the dysfunctional nature of some variances in the modern environment of Just-in-time (JIT) and total quality management (TQM)
- describe the major behavioural problems resulting from using standard costs in rapidly changing environments
- discuss the major effects that variances have on staff motivation and action.

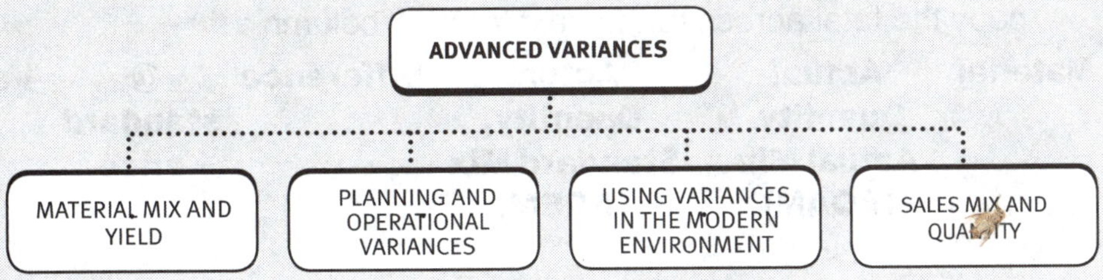

1 Material mix and yield

Introduction to material mix and yield variances

These are calculated if:

- A product contains more than one type of material.
- These materials are interchangeable.

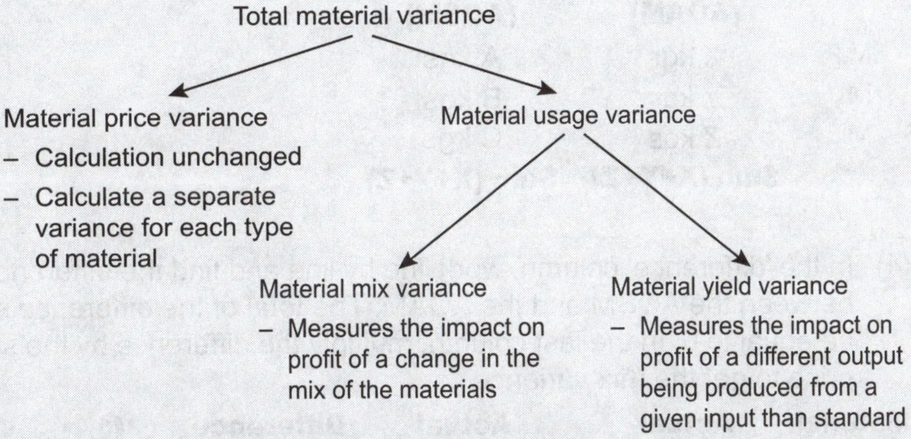

A **mix** variance is used to monitor the cost of material. For instance, if more of an expensive material has been used and less of a cheap material, then the cost will be higher - and the variance adverse.

Method :

(1) Setup the following table :

Material	**Actual Quantity, Actual Mix (AQAM)**	**Actual Quantity, Standard Mix (AQSM)**	**Difference**	**@ standard price**	**Variance in $**
M_1	X kgs				
M_2	Y kgs				
M_3	<u>Z kgs</u>				

(2) Calculate the total of the AQAM column (in kgs, litres, metres etc) and copy the total across to the next 'AQSM' column :

Material	Actual Quantity, Actual Mix (AQAM)	Actual Quantity, Standard Mix (AQSM)	Difference	@ standard price	Variance in $
M_1	X kgs				
M_2	Y kgs				
M_3	Z kgs				
	Sum (X+Y+Z)	**Sum (X+Y+Z)**			

(3) Share this total 'upwards' into the standard mix, which will be given as a proportion in the question or in the standard cost card :

Material	Actual Quantity, Actual Mix (AQAM)	Actual Quantity, Standard Mix (AQSM)	Difference	@ standard price	Variance in $
M_1	X kgs	A kgs			
M_2	Y kgs	B kgs			
M_3	Z kgs	C kgs			
	Sum (X+Y+Z)	**Sum (X+Y+Z)**			

(4) In the 'difference' column, work line by line and find the difference between the AQSM and the AQAM. The total of the difference should be equal to 0. In the last column, multiply the difference by the standard price to get the mix variance.

Material	Actual Quantity, Actual Mix (AQAM)	Actual Quantity, Standard Mix (AQSM)	Difference	@ standard price	Variance in $
M_1	X kgs	A kgs	X - A	$x	$Var.(F/A)
M_2	Y kgs	B kgs	Y - B	$x	$Var (F/A)
M_3	Z kgs	C kgs	Z - C	$x	$Var (F/A)
	Sum (X+Y+Z)	**Sum (X+Y+Z)**			**$ Total Mix**

A **yield** variance measures the efficiency of turning the inputs into outputs. If the yield variance is adverse, it suggests that actual input is lower than the expected output. This could be due to labour inefficiencies, higher waste, inferior materials, or using a cheaper mix with a lower yield.

Method 1 : The 'total' method

Actual output (given)	X
Expected outputs from actual input	X
Difference	X
Multiplied by standard material cost per unit of output	$X
Variance	$X

Method 2 : The 'individual' method

Material	Standard Quantity, Standard Mix (SQSM)	Actual Quantity, Standard Mix (AQSM)	Difference	@ standard price	Variance in $
M_1	X kgs	A kgs	X - A	$x	$Var.(F/A)
M_2	Y kgs	B kgs	Y - B	$x	$Var (F/A)
M_3	Z kgs	C kgs	Z - C	$x	$Var (F/A)
	Sum (X+Y+Z)	**Sum (X+Y+Z)**			**$ Total Yield**

'SQSM' is the standard quantity of material used for actual production, shared in the standard mix.

Test your understanding 1 - Material mix and yield

A company manufactures a chemical using two components, A and B. The standard information for one unit of the chemical are as follows:

		$
Material A	10 kg at $4 per kg	40
Material B	20 kg at $6 per kg	120
		160

In a particular period, 160 units of the chemical were produced, using 1,000 kgs of material A and 1,460 kgs of material B.

Required:

Calculate the material usage, mix and yield variances for each material.

Interpretation of material mix and yield variances

Mix - a favourable total mix variance would suggest that a higher proportion of a cheaper material is being used hence reducing the overall average cost per unit.

Yield - an adverse total yield variance would suggest that less output has been achieved for a given input, i.e. that the total input in volume is more than expected for the output achieved.

- These variances may be interrelated. A favourable material mix variance may lead to an adverse material yield variance. This is due to differences in quality between the materials used.
- Any change in mix should be judged by the impact on the overall total materials variance.
- The operating statement would include a separate line for each variance.

Test your understanding 2 - Additional mix and yield question

Hondru operates a standard costing system. The standard direct materials to produce 1,000 units of output is as follows:

Material grade	Input quantity (kgs)	Standard price per kg ($)
A	600	1.10
B	240	2.40
C	360	1.50

During April the actual output of the product was 21,000 units. The actual materials issued to production were:

Material grade	Quantity (kgs)
A	14,000
B	5,500
C	5,500

Required:

Calculate the material mix variance for each material, and in total, and calculate the total material yield variance. Comment on the figures calculated.

Test your understanding 3 - Mix and yield with material waste

Pan-Ocean Chemicals has one product, which requires inputs from three types of material to produce batches of Synthon. Standard cost details for a single batch are shown below:

Material type	Standard quantity (kgs)	Standard price per kg ($)
S1	8	0.30
S2	5	0.50
S3	3	0.40

A standard loss of 10% of input is expected. Actual output was 15,408 kgs for the previous week. Details of the material used were:

Material type	Quantity (kgs)
S1	8,284
S2	7,535
S3	3,334

Required:

Calculate the individual material mix and yield and the total usage variance.

Changing the mix – the wider issues

It has already been shown that changing the mix of material input can affect the material yield of the process. It can impact on:

- cost
- quality
- performance measurement.

e.g

Illustration 1 – Mix and yield: wider issues

A company produces pre-cast concrete sections for the construction industry. The mix of materials used to produce the concrete can be varied and different mixes are suitable for different products. Discuss the issues that management should consider when setting standard material costs.

Solution

For each product management should consider the optimum mix of input materials that will maximise profits to the business. This may involve consideration of:

- the relationship between cost, quality and price. Reducing the cost of input materials by using a greater proportion of a cheaper material may reduce the quality of the product and lead to a reduction in the price that can be charged;
- costs of reduced quality. Using a greater proportion of a cheaper input material may lead to higher quality failure costs;
- impact on other variances. Increasing the proportion of a cheaper input material may result in increased labour costs or overhead costs if this leads to more time having to be spent producing a product. Increased rejects may lead to higher overhead costs.

It may be the case that, whilst changing a material mix could lead to an overall favourable material variance this could have an adverse impact on the profitability of the business if prices have to be reduced because of reduced quality or quality failure costs exceed material cost savings. Thus it is important to set the standard mix at the level which optimises profit taking all factors into consideration.

Test your understanding 4

Discuss how the performance measurement system should be designed when the mix of input materials can be varied in a process.

The control of production processes in manufacturing environments

As well as variances, organisations can also use other performance measures and targets for controlling production processes, e.g.:

- quality measures e.g. reject rate, time spent reworking goods, % waste, % yield
- average cost of inputs
- average cost of outputs
- average prices achieved for finished products
- average margins
- % on-time deliveries
- customer satisfaction ratings.
- detailed timesheets
- % idle time

2 Sales mix and quantity variances

Sales variances can be explained as follows :

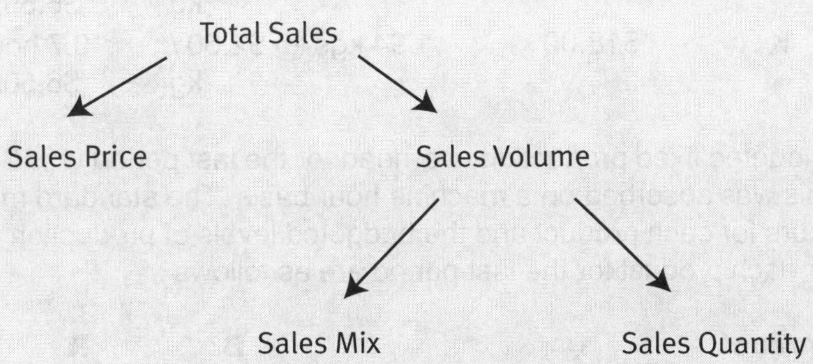

(1) **Sales price variances** are calculated by comparing the actual selling price per unit and the budgeted selling price per unit; each price variance is multiplied by the number of units for each type of product.

(2) A **sales volume variance** is the difference between the actual number of units sold, and the budgeted number. Each difference is multiplied by the budgeted profit per unit. Sales volume in turns splits into a **sales mix variance** and a **sales quantity variance**.

(3) A **sales mix variance** indicates the effect on profit of changing the mix of actual sales from the standard mix. A Sales Mix variance can be calculated in one of two ways :

(a) The difference between the actual total quantity sold in the standard mix and the actual quantities sold, valued at the standard profit per unit;

(b) The difference between the actual sales and budgeted sales, valued at the standard profit per unit less the budgeted weighted average profit per unit.

(4) A **sales quantity variance** indicates the effect on profit of selling a different total quantity from the budgeted total quantity. Like the mix variance, it can be calculated in one of two ways :

(a) The difference between actual sales volume in the standard mix and budgeted sales valued at the standard profit per unit.

(b) The difference between actual sales volume and budgeted sales valued at the weighted average profit per unit.

Test your understanding 5 - Sales mix and quantity variances

CABCo operates an absorption costing system and sells three products B, R and K which are substitutes for each other. The following standard selling price and cost data relate to these three products :

Product	Unit Selling Price	Direct Material / unit	Direct Labour / unit
B	$14.00	3 kgs @ $1.80 /kg	0.5 hours @ $6.50/ hour
R	$15.00	1.25 kgs @ $3.28 / kg	0.8 hours @ $6.50/hour
K	$18.00	1.94 kgs @ $2.50 / kg	0.7 hours @ $6.50/hour

Budgeted fixed production overhead for the last period was $81,000. This was absorbed on a machine hour basis. The standard machine hours for each product and the budgeted levels of production and sales for each product for the last period are as follows :

Product	B	R	K
Standard machine hours per unit	0.3 hours	0.6 hours	0.8 hours
Budgeted production and sales (units)	10,000	13,000	9,000

Actual volumes and selling prices for the three products in the last period were as follows :

Product	B	R	K
Actual Selling Price per unit	$14.50	$15.50	$19.00
Actual Production and sales (units)	9,500	13,500	8,500

Required:

Calculate the following variances for overall sales for the last period:

(i) sales price variance

(ii) sales volume profit variance

(iii) sales mix profit variance

(iv) sales quantity profit variance.

3 Planning and operational variances

Revised standards and budgeting

The standard is set as part of the budgeting process which occurs before the period to which it relates. This means that the difference between standard and actual may arise partly due to an unrealistic budget and not solely due to operational factors. The budget may need to be revised to enable actual performance to be compared with a standard that reflects these changed conditions.

Traditional variance

– Compares actual results with the original (flexed) budget.

Planning variance

– Compares the revised (flexed) budget and the original (flexed) budget.

– Often deemed to be uncontrollable. Management should not be held accountable.

Operational variance

– Compares actual results with the revised (flexed) budget.

– Deemed controllable. Management held responsible for operational variances.

Planning and operational variances may be calculated for:

- Sales
- Materials
- Labour

The operating statement would include a separate line for each variance calculated.

Each of the variances will be reviewed in turn.

Planning and operational variances for sales

The sales volume variance can be sub-divided into a planning and operational variance:

Original budgeted sales x standard margin	
	Market size variance (planning)
Revised budgeted sales x standard margin (to achieve target share of actual market)	
	Market share variance (operational)
Actual sales quantity x standard margin	

Test your understanding 6 - Market size and share

Hudson has a sales budget of 400,000 units for the coming year based on 20% of the total market. On each unit, Hudson makes a profit of $3. Actual sales for the year were 450,000, but industry reports showed that the total market volume had been 2.2 million.

(a) Find the traditional sales volume variance.

(b) Split this into planning and operational variances (market size and market share). Comment on your results.

Test your understanding 7 - Additional example

A company sets its sales budget based on an average price of $14 per unit and sales volume of 250,000 units. Competition was more intense than expected and the company only achieved sales of 220,000 and had to sell at a discounted price of $12.50 per unit. The company was unable to reduce costs so profit per unit fell from $4 per unit to $2.50 per unit. It was estimated that the total market volume grew by 10% from 1,000,000 units to 1,100,000 units.

Required:

(a) Calculate the sales price and volume variances.

(b) Analyse the volume variances into market share and market size.

(c) Discuss whether the price variance is a planning or operational variance.

Revising the budget

When applying planning and operating principles to cost variances (material and labour), care must be taken over flexing the budgets. The accepted approach for use in the exam is to flex both the original and revised budgets to actual production levels:

Actual results	
	Operating variance
Revised (flexed) budget	
	Planning variance
Original (flexed) budget	

Note: If pushed for time in the exam, then calculate detailed operating variances but give a single total planning variance for each category.

e.g

Illustration 2 – Revising the budget

Rhodes Co manufactures Stops which it is estimated require 2 kg of material XYZ at $10/kg In week 21 only 250 Stops were produced although budgeted production was 300. 450 kg of XYZ were purchased and used in the week at a total cost of $5,100. Later it was found that the standard had failed to allow for a 10% price increase throughout the material supplier's industry. Rhodes Ltd carries no stocks.

Planning and operational analysis

The first step in the analysis is to calculate:

(1) Actual Results

(2) Revised flexed budget(ex-post).

(3) Original flexed budget (ex-ante).

(W1)	Actual results			
	450kg for		$5,100	Operational variance
(W2)	Revised flexed budget (ex post)			
	250 units at 2kg per unit for $11/kg	=	$5,500	
(W3)	Original flexed budget (ex-ante)			Planning variance
	250 units at 2kg per unit for $10/kg	=	$5,000	

Additional example on revising the budget

A transport business makes a particular journey regularly, and has established that the standard fuel cost for each journey is 20 litres of fuel at $2 per litre. New legislation has forced a change in the vehicle used for the journey and an unexpected rise in fuel costs. It is decided retrospectively that the standard cost per journey should have been 18 litres at $2.50 per litre.

Required:

Calculate the original and revised flexed budgets if the journey is made 120 times in the period.

Solution

Original flexed budget:	
120 × 20 × $2	$4,800
Revised flexed budget:	
120 ×18 ×$2.50	$5,400

Planning and operational variances for materials

Examiner's article: visit the ACCA website, www.accaglobal.com, to review the examiner's article on this topic (March 2009).

Planning and operational variances can be calculated for materials in the same way as above.

Test your understanding 8 - Price variances

The standard cost per unit of raw material was estimated to be $5.20 per unit. However, due to subsequent improvements in technology, the general market price at the time of purchase was $5.00 per unit. The actual price paid was $5.18 per unit. 10,000 units of the raw materials were purchased during the period.

Required:

Calculate the planning and operational materials price variances. Comment on the results.

Test your understanding 9 - Price and usage variances

Holmes Ltd uses one raw material for one of their products. The standard cost per unit at the beginning of the year was $28, made up as follows:

Standard material cost per unit = 7 kg per unit at $4 per kg = $28.

In the middle of the year the supplier had changed the specification of the material slightly due to problems experienced in the country of origin, so that the standard had to be revised as follows:

Standard material cost per unit = 8 kg per unit at $3.80 per kg = $30.40.

The actual output for November was 1,400 units. 11,000 kg of material was purchased and used at a cost of $41,500.

Calculate

(a) material price and usage variances using the traditional method

(b) all planning and operational material variances.

Planning and operational variances for labour

Planning and operational variances for labour can be calculated in the same way as for materials.

Test your understanding 10

The standard hours per unit of production for a product is 5 hours. Actual production for the period was 250 units and actual hours worked were 1,450 hours. The standard rate per hour was $10. Because of a shortage of skilled labour it has been necessary to use unskilled labour and it is estimated that this will increase the time taken by 20%.

Required:

Calculate the planning and operational efficiency variances.

Test your understanding 11 - Additional example

POV Ltd uses a standard costing system to control and report upon the production of its single product. An abstract from the original standard cost card of the product is as follows:

	$	$
Selling price per unit		200
Less: 4 kgs materials @ $20 per kg	80	
6 hours labour @ $7 per hour	42	
		122
Contribution per unit		78

For period 3, 2,500 units were budgeted to be produced and sold but the actual production and sales were 2,850 units.

The following information was also available:

(1) At the commencement of period 3 the normal material became unobtainable and it was necessary to use an alternative. Unfortunately, 0.5 kg per unit extra was required and it was thought that the material would be more difficult to work with. The price of the alternative was expected to be $16.50 per kg In the event, actual usage was 12,450 kg at $18 per kg

(2) Weather conditions unexpectedly improved for the period with the result that a 50c per hour bad weather bonus, which had been allowed for in the original standard, did not have to be paid. Because of the difficulties expected with the alternative material, management agreed to pay the workers $8 per hour for period 3 only. During the period 18,800 hours were paid for.

After using conventional variances for some time, POV Ltd is contemplating extending its system to include planning and operational variances.

(a) Prepare a statement reconciling budgeted contribution for the period with actual contribution, using conventional material and labour variances.

(b) Prepare a similar reconciliation statement using planning and operational variances.

(c) Explain the meaning of the variances shown in statement (b)

When should a budget be revised?

There must be a good reason for deciding that the original standard cost is unrealistic. Deciding in retrospect that expected costs should be different from the standard should not be an arbitrary decision, aimed perhaps at shifting the blame for bad results due to poor operational management or poor cost estimation.

A good reason for a change in the standard might be:

- a change in one of the main materials used to make a product or provide a service
- an unexpected increase in the price of materials due to a rapid increase in world market prices (e.g. the price of oil or other commodities)
- a change in working methods and procedures that alters the expected direct labour time for a product or service
- an unexpected change in the rate of pay to the workforce.

These types of situations do not occur frequently. The need to report planning and operational variances should therefore be an occasional, rather than a regular, event.

If the budget is revised on a regular basis, the reasons for this should be investigated. It may be due to management attempting to shift the blame for poor results or due to a poor planning process.

Pros and cons of revising the budget

A company is operating in a fast changing environment and is considering whether analysing existing variances into a planning and operational element would help to improve performance. Discuss the advantages and disadvantages of the approach.

Solution

Advantages may include:

- Variances are more relevant , especially in a turbulent environment.
- The operational variances give a 'fair' reflection of the actual results achieved in the actual conditions that existed.
- Managers are, theoretically, more likely to accept and be motivated by the variances reported which provide a better measure of their performance.
- The analysis helps in the standard-setting learning process , which will hopefully result in more useful standards in the future.

Disadvantages:

- The establishment of ex-post budgets is very difficult . Managers whose performance is reported to be poor using such a budget are unlikely to accept them as performance measures because of the subjectivity in setting such budgets.
- There is a considerable amount of administrative work involved first to analyse the traditional variances and then to decide on which are controllable and which are uncontrollable.
- The analysis tends to exaggerate the interrelationship of variances , providing managers with a 'pre-packed' list of excuses for below standard performance. Poor performance is often excused as being the fault of a badly set budget.
- Frequent demands for budget revisions may result in bias.

Variance analysis in the modern manufacturing environment

Variance analysis may not be appropriate because:

Non-standard products

Standard product costs apply to manufacturing environments in which quantities of an identical product are output from the production process. They are not suitable for manufacturing environments where products are non-standard or are customised to customer specifications.

Standard costs become outdated quickly

Shorter product life cycles in the modern business environment mean that standard costs will need to be reviewed and updated frequently. This will increase the cost of operating a standard cost system but, if the standards are not updated regularly, they will be of limited use for planning and control purposes. The extra work involved in maintaining up-to-date standards might limit the usefulness and relevance of a standard costing system.

Production is highly automated

It is doubtful whether standard costing is of much value for performance setting and control in automated manufacturing environments. There is an underlying assumption in standard costing that control can be exercised by concentrating on the efficiency of the workforce. Direct labour efficiency standards are seen as a key to management control. However, in practice, where manufacturing systems are highly automated, the rates of production output and materials consumption, are controlled by the machinery rather than the workforce.

Ideal standard used

Variances are the difference between actual performance and standard, measured in cost terms. The significance of variances for management control purposes depends on the type of standard cost used. JIT and TQM businesses often implement an ideal standard due to the emphasis on continuous improvement and high quality. Therefore, adverse variances with an ideal standard have a different meaning from adverse variances calculated with a current standard.

Emphasis on continuous improvement

Standard costing and adherence to a preset standard is inconsistent with the concept of continuous improvement, which is applied within TQM and JIT environments.

Detailed information is required

Variance analysis is often carried out on an aggregate basis (total material usage variance, total labour efficiency variance and so on) but in a complex and constantly changing business environment more detailed information is required for effective management control.

Monitoring performance is important

Variance analysis control reports tend to be made available to managers at the end of a reporting period. In the modern business environment managers need more 'real time' information about events as they occur.

Test your understanding 12

Comment on whether standard costing applies in both manufacturing and service businesses and how it may be affected by modern initiatives of continuous performance improvement and cost reduction.

Standard costs and behavioural issues

Standard costs are set with a view to measuring actual performance against the standard, and reporting variances to the managers responsible. The aims of setting standards include:

- setting a target for performance
- motivating the managers responsible to achieve those targets
- holding these managers accountable for actual performance
- perhaps rewarding managers for good performance and criticising them for poor performance.

Managers and employees might respond in different ways to standard setting.

Factors to consider include:

The type of standard set

Individuals might respond to standards in different ways, according to the difficulty of achieving the standard level of performance.

- **Ideal standard**: When a standard level of performance is high, e.g. an ideal standard, employees and their managers will recognise that they cannot achieve it. Since the target is not achievable, they might not even try to get near it.
- **Current standard**: When the standard of performance is not challenging (e.g. a current standard), employees and their managers might be content simply to achieve the standard without trying to improve their performance.
- **Attainable standard:** An attainable standard might be set which challenges employees and their managers to improve their performance. If this attainable standard is realistic, it might provide a target that they try to achieve. Some employees will be motivated by this challenge and will work harder to achieve it. However, some employees may prefer standards to be set at a low level of performance, in order to avoid the need to work harder.
- **Basic standard**: This type of standard may motivate employees since it gives them a long-term target to aim for. However, the standard may become out of date quickly and, as result, may actually demotivate employees.

The level of participation in standard setting

Arguments in favour of participation	Arguments against participation
It could motivate employees to set higher standards for achievement.	Senior management might be reluctant to share responsibilities for budgeting.
Staff are more likely to accept standards that they have been involved in setting.	The standard-setting process could be time consuming.
Morale and actual performance levels might be improved.	Staff might want to set standards that they are likely to achieve, rather than more challenging targets. They might try to build some 'slack' into the budget
Staff will understand more clearly what is expected of them.	The standard-setting process could result in conflicts rather than co-operation and collaboration.
	Staff might feel that their suggestions have been ignored.

The use of pay as a motivator

If standards are used as a way of encouraging employees to improve their performance, motivation could be provided in the form of higher pay if targets are reached or exceeded.

However, if employees are offered a bonus for achieving standard costs, this could increase their incentive to set low standards of performance, i.e. include 'slack' in the standard cost. Lower standards will increase the probability that the standards will be achieved and a bonus will be earned.

Test your understanding 13

Which one of the following is not an advantage of participation in standard setting?

(a) The time taken to reach decisions will be quicker via assorted committee meetings.

(b) The quality of decisions should improve with collective decision making.

(c) There will be improved communication between staff.

(d) Staff are more likely to accept standards that they have helped set.

4 Chapter summary

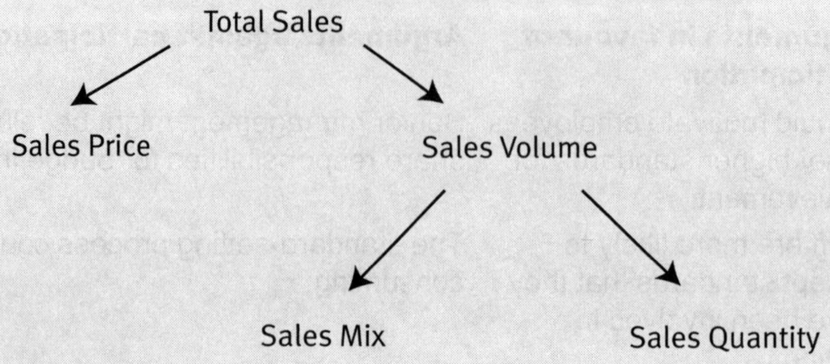

Test your understanding answers

Test your understanding 1 - Material mix and yield

Material A usage variance

AQ SP = 1,000 × $4 = $4,000

Variance = $2,400 F

SQ SP = (160 units × 10kg/unit) × $4 = $6,400

Material B usage variance

AQ SP = 1,460 × $6 = $8,760

Var. = $10,440 F

SQ SP = (160 units × 20kg/unit) × $6 = $19,200

Total usage variance = $2,400 + $10,440 = $12,840

Material mix variance

Material	Std mix	Actual material usage (kgs)	Actual usage @ std mix (kgs)	Mix variance (kgs)	Std cost per kg ($)	Mix variance ($)
A	10/30	1,000	820	180 A	4	720 A
B	20/30	1,460	1,640	180 F	6	1,080 F
		2,460	2,460	0	-	360 F

Material yield variance

Material	Std usage for actual output (kgs)	Actual usage @ std mix (kgs)	Yield variance (kgs)	Std cost per kg ($)	Yield variance ($)
A	160 × 10kg = 1,600	820	780 F	4	3,120 F
B	160 × 20kg = 3,200	1,640	1,560 F	6	9,360 F
	4,800	2,460	2,340 F	-	12,480 F

Alternatively, the material yield variance can be calculated in total using the following method:

(1)	Total input = 1,000 kgs + 1,460 kgs = 2,460 kgs.	
	This should produce (÷ 30 kgs)	82 units of output
(2)	2,460 kgs did produce	160 units of output
(3)	Difference = yield variance in units	78 units F
(4)	Value at the standard cost of	$160 per unit
(5)	Yield variance	$12,480 F

Total mix and yield variance = $12,480 F + $360 F = $12,840 F (as per the usage variance)

Test your understanding 2 - Additional mix and yield question

Material mix variance

Material	Std mix	Actual material usage (kgs)	Actual usage @ std mix (kgs)	Mix variance (kgs)	Std cost per kg ($)	Mix variance ($)
A	600/1200	14,000	12,500	1,500 A	1.10	1,650 A
B	240/1200	5,500	5,000	500 A	2.40	1,200 A
C	360/1200	5,500	7,500	2,000 F	1.50	3,000 F
		25,000	25,000	0	-	150 F

Comment

The favourable mix variance is due to more of materials A and B being used in place of material C.

Material yield variance

(1)	Total input of 25,000 kgs should produce. (÷ 1.2 kgs per unit)	20,833 units of output
(2)	25,000 kgs did produce	21,000 units of output
(3)	Difference = yield variance in units	167 units F
(4)	Value at the standard cost of (Working)	$1.78 per unit
(5)	Yield variance	$297 F

Working

Standard cost per unit = ((600 × $1.10) + (240 × $2.40) + (360 × $1.50)) ÷ 1,000 units = $1.78 per unit

Comment

The favourable variance is due to more output being achieved than was expected from the materials input.

Test your understanding 3 - Mix and yield with material waste

Material mix variance

The material mix variance is not affected by the material wastage and should be calculated in the normal way:

Material	Std mix	Actual material usage (kgs)	Actual usage @ std mix (kgs)	Mix variance (kgs)	Std cost per kg ($)	Mix variance ($)
S1	8/16	8,284	9,576.5	1,292.5 F	0.30	387.75 F
S2	5/16	7,535	5,985.3	1,549.7 A	0.50	774.85 A
S3	3/16	3,334	3,591.2	257.2 F	0.40	102.88 F
		19,153	19,153	0	-	284.22 A

Material yield variance

The yield variance will take account of the material wastage of 10%:

Material	Std usage for actual output (kgs)	Actual usage @ std mix (kgs)	Yield variance (kgs)	Std cost per kg ($)	Yield variance ($)
S1	8/16 = 8,560	9,576.5	1,016.5 A	0.30	304.95 A
S2	5/16 = 5,350	5,985.3	635.3 A	0.50	317.65 A
S3	3/16 = 3,210	3,591.2	381.2 A	0.40	152.48 A
	15,408 × 100/90 = 17,120	19,153	2,033 A	-	775. 08 A

Material usage variance

Total usage variance = $775.08 A + $284.22 A = $1,059.3 A

Test your understanding 4

In a performance measurement system managers are often rewarded for improving the performance of cost and/or revenues under their control. The production manager may be responsible for the material mix decision and, if the reward system is based on achieving cost savings, then the cheapest mix may be used. This may have a detrimental effect on company profit if quality is reduced and this leads to a lower price or quality failure costs.

It may therefore be preferable to reward managers on the basis of total company profit so that the full impact of the mix decision is taken into account.

Test your understanding 5 - Sales mix and quantity variances

Working 1 : OAR

$$\text{OAR} = \frac{\$81{,}000}{3{,}000 + 7{,}800 + 7{,}200}$$

so OAR = $4.50 per machine hour

Working 2 : Standard Profit

	B	R	K
Materials	$5.40	$4.10	$4.85
Labour	$3.25	$5.20	$4.55
Overheads	$1.35	$2.70	$3.60
Total cost	$10	$12.00	$13.00
Selling Price	$14	$15.00	$18.00
Standard Profit	$4.00	$3.00	$5.00

Working 3 : Weighted average Standard Profit

	B	R	K
Standard Profit	$4.00	$3.00	$5.00

$$\text{W.A. standard profit} = \frac{(\$4 \times 10{,}000 \text{ units}) + (\$3.00 \times 13{,}000 \text{ units}) + (\$5 \times 9{,}000 \text{ units})}{32{,}000 \text{ budgeted units}}$$

= **$3.875**

(i) **Sales price variance :**

	B	R	K
Actual Selling Price per unit	$14.50	$15.50	$19.00
Standard Selling Price per unit	$14.00	$15.00	$18.00
Variance	$1.50 F	$0.50 F	$1.00 F
	x 9,500 units	x13,500 units	x 8,500 units
Total variance	**$4,750 F**	**$6,750 F**	**$8,500 F**

Therefore, total sales price variance = $4,750 F + $6,750 F+ $8,500 F = **$20,000 F**

(ii) **Sales volume profit variance :**

	B	R	K
Expected volumes	10,000 units	13,000 units	9,000 units
Actual volumes	9,500 units	13,500 units	8,500 units
Variance	500 units A	500 units F	500 units A
x standard profit	$4.00	$3.00	$5.00
Total variance	**$2,000 A**	**$1,500F**	**$2,500 A**

Therefore, total sales volume profit variance = $2,000 A + $1,500 F+ $2,500 A = **$3,000 A**

(iii) **Sales mix profit variance :**

	Standard Mix	Standard Mix, Actual Quantity	Actual Mix, Actual Quantity	Difference	@ standard profit	Variance
B	10,000 units	9,843.75	9,500 units	343.75 F	$4	$1,375 F
R	13,000 units	12,796.875	13,500 units	703.125 A	$3	$2,109.375 A
K	9,000 units	8,859.375	8,500 units A	359.375 F	$5	$1,796.875 F
	32,000	**31,500**	**31,500**			**$1,062.5 A**

Alternative method :

	Standard Profit per unit	Weighted Average profit per unit	Difference	Difference actual sales / budgeted sales	Difference
B	$4	$3.875	$0.125	(500 units)	$62.50 A
R	$3	$3.875	$(0.875)	500 units	$437.50 A
K	$5	$3.875	$1.125	(500 units)	$562.50 A
					$1,062.5 A

(iv) **Sales quantity profit variance :**

	Standard Mix Actual Quantity	Budgeted sales	Difference	Standard profit per unit	Variance
B	9,843.75	10,000	156.25 A	$4	$62.50A
R	12,796.875	13,000	203.125 A	$3	$437.50A
K	8,859.375	9,000	140.65 A	$5	$562.50A
					$1,062.5A

Alternative method :

Budgeted Total Quantity		32,000 units
Actual Total Quantity	=	31,500 units
Variance		500 units Adverse

500 units adverse @ standard profit $3.875 = $1,937.5 Adverse

Test your understanding 6 - Market size and share

(a) Traditional sales volume variance

= (Actual units sold — Budgeted sales) × Standard profit per unit

= (450,000 — 400,000) × $3 = $150,000 F.

(b) Planning and operational variances The revised (ex-post) budget would show that Hudson Ltd should expect to sell 20% of 2.2 million units = 440,000 units.

Original sales × standard margin = 400,000 × $3= $1,200,000

Market size = $120,000 F

Revised sales × standard margin = 440,000 × $3= $1,320,000

Market share = $30,000 F

Actual sales × standard margin = 450,000 × $3= $1,350,000

-

Total sales volume variance = $120,000 F + $30,000 F = $150,000 F

Comment:

Most of the favourable variance can be attributed to the increase in overall market size. However, some can be put down to effort by the sales force which has increased its share from 20% to 20.5% (450,000/ 2,200,000).

Managers should only be appraised on the operational variance, i.e. the market share variance.

Test your understanding 7 - Additional example

(a) Sales price variance

= 220,000 × ($14 — $12.50) = $330,000 A

Sales volume variance

= (250,000 — 220,000) × $4 = $120,000 A

(b) Budgeted market share = 250,000/1,000,000 = 25%

The company would have expected to achieve sales of 25% × 1,100,000 = 275,000 in the actual market conditions.

The market size variance

= (275,000 — 250,000) × $4 = $100,000 F

The market share variance

= (275,000 — 220,000) × $4 = $220,000 A

The increased market size is favourable as the company should sell more if market share can be maintained. The market share variance was adverse as market share fell from 25% to 220,000/1,100,000 = 20%.

(c) It could be argued that the increased competition in the market was not foreseen when the budget was set and the variance is thus a planning variance. However, this line of reasoning would suggest that any unforeseen issues give rise just to planning variances. Perhaps sales managers should have identified potential threats sooner? Also, once extra competition was experienced, managers had to decide how to respond. This could have involved additional advertising rather than price cuts, e.g. it could be argued that price cuts were made to try (unsuccessfully) to protect market share, in which case managers should be held (at least partly) responsible for such a decision.

Test your understanding 8 - Price variances

AQ x AP : 10,000 X $5.18 = $51,800

> Operational variance $1,800 adverse

AQ x RSP : 10,000 X $5.00 = $50,000

> Planning Variance $2,000 favourable

AQ x SP : 10,000 × $5.20 = $52,000

Operational variance: The cost per unit was higher than the revised budgeted cost resulting in the adverse variance. This variance is controllable by management and should be linked to their performance evaluation

Planning variance: The improvement in technology resulted in a lower price per unit and hence a favourable variance. This is a planning difference and is therefore uncontrollable by management.

A traditional variance calculation would present as follows :

AQ x AP : 10,000 X $5.18 = $51,800

> Price variance $200 Favourable

AQ x SP : 10,000 X $5.20 = $52,000

Test your understanding 9 - Price and usage variances

(a) **Traditional variances**

AQAP =		$41,500	
		Price variance	$2,500 F
AQSP =	11,000 × $4 =	$44,000	
		Usage variance	$4,800 A
SQSP =	1400 × 7 × $4 =	$39,200	

(b) **Planning and Operational variances**

Price

AQ x AP		= $41,500	
		Operational Variance	**$300 F**
AQ x RSP	11,000 x $3.80	= $41,800	
		Planning Variance	**$2,200 F**
AQ × SP	11,000 x $4	= $44,000	
			$2,500 F

Usage

AQ × SP	11,000 x $4	= $44,000	
		Operational variance	**$800 F**
RSQ x SP	11,200 × $4	= $44,800	
		Planning variance	**$5,600 A**
SQ × SP	9,800 × $4	= $39,200	
			$4,800 A

Test your understanding 10

AH x SR	1,450 x $10	= $14,500	
		Operational Variance	**$500 F**
RSH x SR	1,500 x $10	= $15,000	
		Planning Variance	**$2,500 A**
SH x SR	1,250 x $10	= $12,500	
			$2,000 A

Test your understanding 11 - Additional example

(a) Reconciliation of budgeted and actual contribution using conventional variances

				$
Budgeted contribution:		2,500 × $78		195,000
Variances:		**Favourable**	**Adverse**	
		$	$	
Sales volume		27,300		
Direct material	– Price	24,900		
	– Usage		21,000	
Direct labour	– Rate		18,800	
	– Efficiency		11,900	
		52,200	51,700	
				500
Actual contribution				195,500

Assumption: No sales price variance.

Workings

Conventional variances

(i) **Materials**

Price = (Actual material purchased × standard price) — (Actual cost of material purchased)

= (12,450 × $20) — (12,450 × $18)

= $249,000 — $224,100

= $24,900 F

Usage = (Standard quantity for actual production × standard price)— (Actual material used at standard price)

= (2,850 × 4 × $20) — (12,450 × $20)

= $228,000 — $249,000

= $21,000 A

(ii) **Labour**

Rate = (Actual hours worked × standard direct labour rate) — (Actual hours worked × actual hourly rate)

= (18,800 × $7) — (18,800 × $8)

= $131,600 — $150,400

= $18,800 A

Efficiency = (Standard hours of actual production × standard rate) — (Actual hours worked × standard rate)

= (2,850 × 6 × $7) — (18,800 × $7)

= $119,700 — $131,600

= $11,900 A

Sales volume

Contribution = (Budgeted sales units × standard contribution per unit) — (Actual sales units × standard contribution per unit)

= (2,500 × $78) — (2,850 × $78)

= $195,000 — $222,300

= $27,300 F

(b) Reconciliation statement using planning and operational variances

			$
Budgeted contribution for actual sales:	2,850 × $78	222,300.00	
Planning variances:	**Favourable**	**Adverse**	
	$	$	
Material – Price	44,887.50		
– Usage		28,500	
Labour – Rate: weather	8,550.00		
– Rate: material		25,650	
	53,437.50	54,150	
			(712.50)
Revised budgeted contribution ($77.75 × 2,850)			221,587.50
Operational variances:	**Favourable**	**Adverse**	
	$	$	
Material – Price		18,675.00	
– Usage	6,187.50		
Labour – Rate	0		
– Efficiency		13,600.00	
	6,187.50	32,275.00	
			(26,087.50)
Actual contribution			195,500.00

Workings

Planning variances

(i) **Material**

= (Standard material cost) — (Revised standard material cost)

Price = (2,850 × (4 + 0.5) × $20) — (2,850 × (4 + 0.5) × $16.50)

= $256,500 — $211,612.50

= $44,887.50 F

Usage = (2,850 × 4 × $20) — (2,850 × 4.5 × $20)

= $228,000 — $256,500

= $28,500 A

(ii) **Labour rate**

(1) Weather bonus

= (2,850 × 6 × $7) — (2,850 × 6 × $6.50)

= $119,700 — $111,150

= $8,550 (F)

(2) Alternative material difficulties

= (2,850 × 6 × $6.50) — (2,850 × 6 × $8)

= $111,150 — $136,800

= $25,650 A

Therefore, revised unit contribution is as follows.

		$	$
Selling price			200.00
Direct material:	4.5 × $16.50	74.25	
Direct labour:	6 × $8	48.00	
			(122.25)
Contribution			77.75

Operational variances

(i) **Material**

Price = (12,450 × $16.50) — (12,450 × $18)

= $205,425 — $224,100

= $18,675 A

Usage = (2,850 × 4.50 × $16.50) — (12,450 × $16.50)

= $211,612.5 — $205,425

= $6,187.5 F

(ii) **Labour**

Rate = 0

Efficiency = (2,850 × 6 × $8) — (18,800 × $8)

= $136,800 — $150,400

= $13,600 A

(c) The analysis of variances in part (b) makes it possible to separate those variances which are non-controllable (the planning variances) from the variances which are controllable by the individual managers (the operational variances) .In this case the change in type of material used was unavoidable. Similarly, the change in weather conditions could not have been anticipated.

The cost implications of these changes are reflected in the planning variances. Management's attention should be focused primarily on the operational variances. In particular, why did the firm pay $18 per kg for material when this was expected to cost $16.50? The operational material usage variance indicates that less material was used than expected – this could be due to the workers spending longer working with the material (as evidenced by the adverse efficiency variance.

Test your understanding 12

Standard costing is most suited to organisations whose activities consist of a series of common or repetitive operations. Typically, mass production manufacturing operations are indicative of its area of application. It is also possible to envisage operations within the service sector to which standard costing may apply, though this may not be with the same degree of accuracy of standards which apply in manufacturing. For example, hotels and restaurants often use standard recipes for preparing food, so dealing with conference attendance can be like a mass production environment. Similarly, banks will have common processes for dealing with customer transactions, processing cheques, etc. It is possible therefore that the principles of standard costing may be extended to service industries.

In modern manufacturing and service businesses, continuous improvement and cost reduction are topical. In order to remain competitive it is essential that businesses address the cost levels of their various operations. To do this they have to deal with the costing of operations. But the drive to 'cost down' may mean in some cases that standards do not apply for long before a redesign or improvement renders them out of date. In such a setting an alternative to the use of standard costs is to compare actual costs with those of the previous operating period. We have seen above that a standard costing system has a variety of purposes. It is for management to judge their various reasons for employing standard costing and, consequently, whether their aims of continuous improvement and cost reduction render the system redundant.

Test your understanding 13

A is the correct answer.

Greater participation by staff in standard setting is likely to slow down the process of agreeing values.

chapter

11

Performance measurement and control

Chapter learning objectives

Upon completion of this chapter you will be able to:

- describe, calculate from given data, and interpret financial performance indicators (FPIs) for profitability, in both manufacturing and service businesses, and suggest methods for improving these measures
- describe, calculate from given data, and interpret FPIs for liquidity in both manufacturing and service businesses, and suggest methods for improving these measures
- describe, calculate from given data, and interpret FPIs for risk in both manufacturing and service businesses, and suggest methods for improving these measures
- describe, calculate from given data and interpret non-financial performance indicators (NFPIs) in both manufacturing and service businesses, and suggest methods for improving the performance indicated
- explain, using non-numerical examples, the causes of, and problems created by, short-termism and financial manipulation of results, and suggest methods to encourage a long-term view
- describe the main behavioural aspects of performance management
- explain the need to allow for external considerations in performance management, in general, with particular reference to:
  - stakeholders
  - market conditions
  - allowance for competitors

- describe ways in which external considerations could be allowed for in performance management, in general, and interpret performance in the light of external considerations
- using simple non-numerical examples, explain and interpret the balanced scorecard and its elements
- using simple non-numerical examples, explain and interpret the building block model proposed by Fitzgerald and Moon
- describe, using simple non-numerical examples, the difficulties of target setting in qualitative areas.

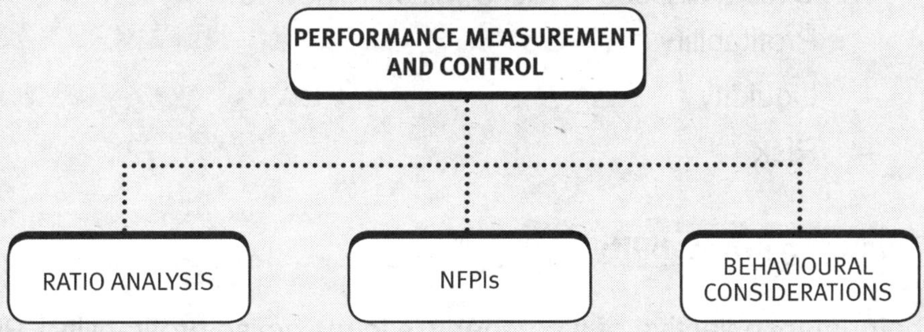

1 Introduction

The calculation of a particular indicator of performance will probably mean very little, unless it is set in some context. Establishing the value of a particular indicator will add little benefit until it is:

(1) compared with a budget;

(2) set in a trend;

(3) and/or set against a best practice benchmark.

2 Financial performance and ratio analysis

Examiner's article: visit the ACCA website, www.accaglobal.com, to review the examiner's article written on this topic (April 2008).

A key aspect of performance measurement is ratio analysis. Specific ratios are discussed below but some general considerations need to be taken into account with all ratio analysis:

- Many ratios use figures at a particular point in time and thus may not be representative of the position throughout a period. For example, seasonal trade or large one-off items may make year-end figures uncharacteristic.
- Ratios are of little use in isolation. Comparisons could be made to:
  - last year's figures to identify trends
  - competitors' results and/or industry averages to assess performance.
- Ratios can be manipulated by management. A well known example of 'window dressing' is to issue spurious invoices before the year end and then issue credit notes just after.
- As with variances, ratios indicate areas for further investigation, rather than giving a definitive answer for management.

- Three main classes of ratios will be reviewed:
  - Profitability
  - Liquidity
  - Risk

Measuring profitability

The primary objective of a company is to maximise profitability. Profitability ratios can be used to monitor the achievement of this objective.

Gross profit margin

This is the gross profit as a percentage of turnover.

$$\text{Gross profit margin} = \frac{\text{Gross profit}}{\text{Turnover}} \times 100$$

A high gross profit margin is desirable. It indicates that either sales prices are high or that production costs are being kept well under control.

Net profit margin

This is the net profit (turnover less all expenses) as a percentage of turnover.

$$\text{Net profit margin} = \frac{\text{Net profit}}{\text{Turnover}} \times 100$$

A high net profit margin is desirable. It indicates that either sales prices are high or that all costs are being kept well under control.

Return of capital employed (ROCE)

This is a key measure of profitability. It is the net profit as a percentage of the capital employed. The ROCE shows the net profit that is generated from each $1 of assets employed.

$$\text{ROCE} = \frac{\text{Net profit}}{\text{Capital employed}} \times 100$$

Where capital employed = total assets less current liabilities **or** total equity plus long term debt.

ROCE is sometimes calculated using operating profit (profit before finance charges and tax) instead of net profit. If net profit is not given in the question, use operating profit instead.

A high ROCE is desirable. An increase in ROCE could be achieved by:

- Increasing net profit, e.g. through an increase in sales price or through better control of costs.
- Reducing capital employed, e.g. through the repayment of long term debt.

The ROCE can be understood further by calculating the net profit margin and the asset turnover:

ROCE = net profit margin × asset turnover

Asset turnover

This is the turnover divided by the capital employed. The asset turnover shows the turnover that is generated from each $1 of assets employed.

$$\text{Asset turnover} = \frac{\text{Turnover}}{\text{Capital employed}}$$

A high asset turnover is desirable. An increase in the asset turnover could be achieved by:

- Increasing turnover, e.g. through the launch of new products or a successful advertising campaign.
- Reducing capital employed, e.g. through the repayment of long term debt.

Test your understanding 1 - Profitability ratios

The following figures are extracted from the accounts of Super Soups, a company selling gourmet homemade soups.

	20X9	**20X8**
	$	**$**
Total production costs	6,538,000	5,082,000
Gross profit	3,006,000	2,582,000
Net profit	590,000	574,000
Total capital employed	6,011,000	5,722,000

Required:

Using appropriate ratios, comment on the profitability of Super Soups.

Additional example on profitability ratios

Companies X and Y are both involved in retailing. Relevant information for the year ended 30 September 20X5 was as follows:

	X	Y
	$000	$000
Sales revenue	50,000	200,000
Profit before tax	10,000	10,000
Capital employed	50,000	50,000

Required:

Prepare the following ratios for both companies and comment on the results:

(a) ROCE

(b) profit margin

(c) asset turnover.

Solution

	X	Y
ROCE	$\frac{10,000}{50,000} \times 100\%$ = 20%	$\frac{10,000}{50,000} \times 100\%$ = 20%
Profit margin	$\frac{10,000}{50,000} \times 100\%$ = 20%	$\frac{10,000}{200,000} \times 100\%$ = 5%
Asset turnover	$\frac{10,000}{50,000}$ = 1	$\frac{200,000}{50,000}$ = 4

The ROCE for both companies is the same. X has a higher profit margin, whilst Y shows a more efficient use of assets. This indicates that there may be a trade-off between profit margin and asset turnover.

Measuring liquidity

A company can be profitable but at the same time encounter cash flow problems. Liquidity and working capital ratios give some indication of the company's liquidity.

Current ratio

This is the current assets divided by the current liabilities.

$$\text{Current ratio} = \frac{\text{Current assets}}{\text{Current liabilities}}$$

The ratio measures the company's ability to meet its short term liabilities as they fall due.

A ratio in excess of 1 is desirable but the expected ratio varies between the type of industry.

A decrease in the ratio year on year or a figure that is below the industry average could indicate that the company has liquidity problems. The company should take steps to improve liquidity, e.g. by paying creditors as they fall due or by better management of receivables in order to reduce the level of bad debts.

Quick ratio (acid test)

This is a similar to the current ratio but inventory is removed from the current assets due to its poor liquidity in the short term.

$$\text{Current ratio} = \frac{\text{Current assets} - \text{inventory}}{\text{Current liabilities}}$$

The comments are the same as for the current ratio.

Inventory holding period

$$\text{Inventory holding period} = \frac{\text{Inventory}}{\text{Cost of sales}} \times 365$$

This indicates the average number of days that inventory items are held for.

An increase in the inventory holding period could indicate that the company is having problems selling its products and could also indicate that there is an increased level of obsolete stock. The company should take steps to increase stock turnover, e.g. by removing any slow moving or unpopular items of stock and by getting rid of any obsolete stock.

A decrease in the inventory holding period could be desirable as the company's ability to turn over inventory has improved and the company does not have excess cash tied up in inventory. However, any reductions should be reviewed further as the company may be struggling to manage its liquidity and may not have the cash available to hold the optimum level of inventory.

Receivables (debtor) collection period

$$\text{Receivables collection period} = \frac{\text{Receivables}}{\text{Turnover}} \times 365$$

This is the average period it takes for a company's debtors to pay what they owe.

An increase in the receivables collection period could indicate that the company is struggling to manage its debts. Possible steps to reduce the ratio include:

- Credit checks on customers to ensure that they will pay on time
- Improved credit control, e.g. invoicing on time, chasing up bad debts.

A decrease in the receivables collection period may indicate that the company's has improved its management of receivables. However, a receivables collection period well below the industry average may make the company uncompetitive and profitability could be impacted as a result.

Payables (creditor) period

$$\text{Payables period} = \frac{\text{Payables}}{\text{Purchases}} \times 365$$

This is the average period it takes for a company to pay for its purchases.

An increase in the company's payables period could indicate that the company is struggling to pay its debts as they fall due. However, it could simply indicate that the company is taking better advantage of any credit period offered to them.

A decrease in the company's payables period could indicate that the company's ability to pay for its purchases on time is improving. However, the company should not pay for its purchases too early since supplier credit is a useful source of finance.

Test your understanding 2 - Liquidity ratios

Calculate the liquidity and working capital ratios for P for the year ended 31 December 20X9.

	$m
Sales revenue	1,867.5
Gross profit	489.3
Inventory	147.9
Trade receivables	393.4
Trade payables	275.1
Cash	53.8
Short-term investments	6.2
Other current liabilities	284.3

Measuring risk

In addition to managing profitability and liquidity it is also important for a company to manage its risk. The following ratios may be calculated:

Financial gearing

This is the long term debt as a percentage of equity.

$$\text{Gearing} = \frac{\text{debt}}{\text{equity}} \times 100$$

$$\textbf{or} = \frac{\text{debt}}{\text{debt} + \text{equity}} \times 100$$

A high level of gearing indicates that the company relies heavily on debt to finance its long term needs. This increases the level of risk for the business since interest and capital repayments must be made on debt, where as there is no obligation to make payments to equity.

The ratio could be improved by reducing the level of long term debt and raising long term finance using equity.

Interest cover

This is the operating profit (profit before finance charges and tax) divided by the finance cost.

$$\text{Interest cover} = \frac{\text{operating profit}}{\text{finance cost}}$$

A decrease in the interest cover indicates that the company is facing an increased risk of not being able to meet its finance payments as they fall due.

The ratio could be improved by taking steps to increase the operating profit, e.g. through better management of costs, or by reducing finance costs through reducing the level of debt.

Dividend cover

This is the net profit divided by the dividend.

$$\text{Dividend cover} = \frac{\text{net profit}}{\text{dividend}}$$

A decrease in the dividend cover indicates that the company is facing an increased risk of not being able to make its dividend payments to shareholders.

Ratio analysis

You are employed in the small business section of a medium-sized bank. Some time ago the bank provided a local manufacturing company, F, with an overdraft facility of $3,000,000. This limit was reached on 30 September 20X4 but was increased then to $5,000,000.

Your section head has just received the half-yearly financial statements of F for the period to 30 September 20X5. Having read these statements, your section head is extremely concerned as to the performance of the company over the last year and is considering recommending the termination of the overdraft facility. Before making any further decision, your section head wishes to have a second opinion. Accordingly, he leaves a file of information concerning F on your desk and requires a report recommending the best course of action.

Information contained in the file:

Item 1: Income statements:

	Six months to 30 September 20X5	Six months to 31 March 20X5
	$000	$000
Sales	10,000	11,000
Cost of sales	(5,000)	(5,500)
Gross profit	5,000	5,500
Other operating expenses	(5,000)	(4,500)
Operating profit	–	1,000
Interest payable	(1,000)	(900)
Profit/(loss) before tax	(1,000)	100
Tax estimate	–	–
Profit/(loss) after tax	(1,000)	100

Item 2: Balance sheets at 30 September

	20X5		20X4	
	$000	$000	$000	$000
Non-current assets:				
property	5,000		5,200	
plant	3,500		3,000	
		8,500		8,200
Current assets:				
inventories	3,000		2,600	
receivables	5,000		4,600	
cash in hand	80		80	
	8,080		7,280	
Current liabilities:				
trade payables	2,600		2,600	
bank overdraft	5,000		3,000	
	7,600		5,600	

NCAs	480	1,680
12% loan notes		
(secured against the property)	(4,800)	(4,800)
	4,180	5,080
Share capital ($1 shares)	4,000	4,000
Retained earnings	180	1,080
	4,180	5,080

Item 3: Estimated realisable values of the assets of F at 30 September 20X5, based on a 'forced sale' scenario:

	$000
Property	5,000
Plant	1,000
Inventories	800
Receivables	2,500
	9,300

(a) Using the items contained in the file, write a report to your section head which contains an appraisal of the performance and financial position of F and considers the implications for the bank of calling in the overdraft.

(b) Produce a short appendix to the report you have compiled in (a). This should summarise the limitations of the information available to you as a basis for making a recommendation as to the wisdom or otherwise of calling in the overdraft.

Solution

(a)

REPORT

To: Section head

From: Bank accountant

Subject: F

Date: 22 November 20X5

(a) The performance of F appears to have deteriorated in the six months to 30 September 20X5. Sales and cost of sales have both fallen by 9%, so that the gross profit percentage of 50% has been maintained. However, operating expenses have increased, so that total operating costs equal operating income. There is no longer any cover for interest payments. The interest charge has also increased, following the increase in the overdraft facility.

Despite this deterioration in performance, non-current assets and current assets have increased. The additional $2 million provided by the bank (an increase in overdraft of 66%) appears to have been used to finance the purchase of plant at a cost of approximately $500,000 (the figure represents the change shown by the balance sheet and is net of depreciation). The additional depreciation has probably contributed to the increase in operating expenses.

The retained loss for the year is $900,000 but the actual cash outflow from operating activities is much greater than this. A rough calculation is given below:

	$000
Loss	900
Less depreciation (buildings only)	(200)
Increase in inventories	400
Increase in receivables	400
	1,500

The company's financial position has deteriorated during the year. At 30 September 20X5 it had a current ratio of 1.06 :1 and a quick ratio of 0.67:1 (compared with 1.3:1 and 0.83:1 at 30 September 20X4). The company is likely to experience severe liquidity problems in the near future.

The company's gearing also gives cause for concern. The company is very dependent upon finance from outside the business. The most recent balance sheet shows a debt to equity ratio of (5,000+4,800)/4,180 =2.34. Interest on the loan notes amounts to $576,000 annually. At current activity levels, this means that there is very little profit available for distribution or investment and very little interest cover. The loan notes are barely covered by the property on which they are secured.

The combination of adverse cash flow, increase in non-current assets and working capital and fall in profits seems to suggest bad management. However, it is impossible to reach a firm conclusion without further information.

The withdrawal of the overdraft facility would result in the liquidation of the company. It is estimated that the assets would realise $9,300,000. The loan note holders would be repaid their $4,800,000 in full, leaving a balance of $4,500,000 for the other creditors. This does not cover the $7,600,000 owed to the bank and the other creditors. Assuming that all unsecured creditors would rank equally, the bank would receive 59c in the dollar or $2,950,000. The bank would make a loss of $2,050,000.

These calculations show that the bank is facing considerable risk. If the overdraft facility is to be continued, the bank should consider renegotiating the terms in order to take account of this risk.

(b) **Appendix**

Only limited information is available as a basis for making this decision.

One major shortcoming of conventional financial statements is that they are based on historical information. They give a good indication of the financial position at 30 September 20X5, but some time has already elapsed since that date. During that time the position could have changed dramatically. For example, the company could have won substantial new business, or receivables could have been realised, or inventory could have been sold. Financial statements are only of limited use in predicting the future of a company.

To make an informed decision, the bank would need information about several other factors which are not reflected in the financial statements. The velocity of circulation of working capital, the quality of the company's management and its ability to attract new business will all be crucial in determining whether or not F survives. For example, the decision to invest in additional plant and to increase inventory levels might have been taken as a result of several new orders. The bank would also need to assess the willingness of the loan note holders and other creditors to continue to support the company. For example, there is no information as to how soon the loan notes will become repayable or as to the means by which the company intends to repay the loan.

3 Issues surrounding the use of financial performance indicators to monitor performance

All of the ratios reviewed so far have concentrated on the financial performance of the business. Many of these ratios, e.g. ROCE, gross profit margin, may be used to assess the performance of a division and of the manager's in charge of that division.

Achievement of these target ratios (financial performance indicators) may be linked to a reward system in order to motivate managers to improve performance.

However, there are a number of problems associated with the use of financial performance indicators to monitor performance:

Short-termism

Linking rewards to financial performance may tempt managers to make decisions that will improve short-term financial performance but may have a negative impact on long-term profitability. E.g. they may decide to cut investment or to purchase cheaper but poorer quality materials.

Manipulation of results

In order to achieve the target financial performance and hence their reward, managers may be tempted to manipulate results. For example:

Accelerating revenue - revenue included in one year may be wrongly included in the previous year in order to improve the financial performance for the earlier year.

Delaying costs - costs incurred in one year may be wrongly recorded in the next year's accounts in order to improve performance and meet targets for the earlier year.

Understating a provision or accrual - this would improve the financial performance and may result in the targets being achieved.

Manipulation of accounting policies - for example, closing inventory values may be overstated resulting in an increase in profits for the year.

Do not convey the full picture

The use of these short-term financial performance indicators has limited benefit to the company as it does not convey the full picture regarding the factors that will drive long-term profitability, e.g. customer satisfaction, quality.

Therefore, when monitoring performance, a broader range of measures should be used. This will be reviewed in the next section.

e.g

Illustration 1 – Problems of financial performance indicators

A company may measure the performance of managers on the basis of a target ROCE. This may lead to the following undesirable behaviour:

- Managers may focus on generating short-term profit at the expense of long-term profit. For example, managers may reduce expenditure on training, research and development and maintenance.
- The ROCE will improve if the capital employed figure falls. Managers may therefore be reluctant to invest in new assets.
- Year-end results may be manipulated to improve ROCE. For example, managers may delay payments to creditors or stock purchases.
- Managers may focus their attention on financial performance and neglect non financial performance such as quality and customer service. This may improve profit in the short-term but lead to a long-term decline in profitability.

Test your understanding 3

Suggest methods of overcoming the problems of short-termism and manipulation of results and encouraging a long-term view.

4 Non-financial performance indicators (NFPIs)

Introduction

- The previous section reviewed the problems of using financial performance indicators as the sole indicator of performance.
- This section will review the use of non-financial performance indicators as an additional tool to monitor performance and maximise long-term profitability.
- As we will see, a company may choose to use a mixture of financial and non-financial performance indicators in order to achieve the optimum system for performance measurement and control.
- A firm's success usually involves focussing on a small number of critical areas that they must excel at. These factors vary from business to business but could include:
  - Having a wide range of products that people want.
  - Having a strong brand name or image.
  - Low prices.
  - Quick delivery.
  - Customer satisfaction, perhaps through high quality.
- Most of these are best assessed using non-financial performance indicators. Financial performance appraisal often reveals the ultimate effect of operational factors and decisions but non-financial indicators are needed to monitor causes.

e.g

Illustration 2 – Non-financial performance measurement

BAA (the former state-owned British Airports Authority) uses regular customer surveys for measuring customer perceptions of a wide variety of service quality attributes, including:

- the cleanliness of its facilities
- the helpfulness of its staff
- the ease of finding one's way around the airport.

Public correspondence is also analysed in detail, and comment cards are available in the terminals so that passengers can comment voluntarily on service levels received.

Duty terminal managers also sample the services and goods offered by outlets in the terminals, assessing them from a customer perspective. They check the cleanliness and condition of service facilities and complete detailed checklists, which are submitted daily to senior terminal managers.

The company has also a wealth of internal monitoring systems that record equipment faults and failures, and report equipment and staff availability.

These systems are supported by the terminal managers who circulate the terminals on a full-time basis, helping customers as necessary, reporting any equipment faults observed and making routine assessments of the level of service provided by BAA and its concessionaires.

Test your understanding 4

Better Nutrition Ltd provides advice to clients in medical, dietary and fitness matters by offering consultation with specialist staff. The budget information for the year ended 31 May 2010 is as follows :

	Budget	***Actual***
Total client enquiries		
- New Business	50,000	80,000
- Repeat business	30,000	20,000
Number of client consultations		
- New Business	15,000	20,000
- Repeat business	12,000	10,000
Mix of client consultations		
- Medical	6,000	5,500 (note)
- Dietary	12,000	10,000
- Fitness	9,000	14,500
Number of consultants employed		
- Medical	6	4 (note)
- Dietary	12	12
- Fitness	9	12
Number of client complaints	270	600

Note: Client consultations includes those carried out by outside specialists. There are now 4 full-time consultants carrying out the remainder of client consultations.

Other information:

(i) Clients are charged a fee per consultation at the rate of: medical $75; dietary $50 and fitness $50.

(ii) Health foods are recommended and provided only to dietary clients at an average cost to the company of $10 per consultation. Clients are charged for such health foods at cost plus 100% mark-up.

(iii) Each customer enquiry incurs a variable cost of $3, whether or not it is converted into a consultation.

(iv) Consultants are each paid a fixed annual salary as follows: medical $40,000; dietary $28,000; fitness $25,000.

(v) Sundry other fixed cost: $300,000.

Actual results for the year to 31 May 2010 incorporate the following additional information:

(i) A reduction of 10% in health food costs to the company per consultation was achieved through a rationalisation of the range of foods made available.

(ii) Medical salary costs were altered through dispensing with the services of two full-time consultants and sub-contracting outside specialists as required. A total of 1,900 consultations were sub-contracted to outside specialists who were paid $50 per consultation.

(iii) Fitness costs were increased by $80,000 through the hire of equipment to allow sophisticated cardio-vascular testing of clients.

(iv) New computer software has been installed to provide detailed records and scheduling of all client enquiries and consultations. This software has an annual operating cost (including depreciation) of $50,000.

Required:

(a) Prepare a statement showing the financial results for the year to 31 May 2010 in tabular format. This should show:

(i) the budget and actual gross margin for each type of consultation and for the company

(ii) the actual net profit for the company

(iii) the budget and actual margin ($) per consultation for each type of consultation
(Expenditure for each expense heading should be shown in (i) and (ii) as relevant.)

(b) Suggest ways in which each of the following performance measures could be used to supplement the financial results calculated in (a). You should include relevant quantitative analysis for each performance measure:

(1) Competitiveness

(2) Flexibility

(3) Resource utilisation

(4) Quality

(5) Innovation

The balanced scorecard

The balanced scorecard approach to performance measurement and control emphasises the need to provide management with a set of information which covers all relevant areas of performance.

It focuses on four different perspectives and uses financial and non-financial indicators.

The four perspectives are:

Customer – what is it about us that new and existing customers value?

Internal – what processes must we excel at to achieve our financial and customer objectives?

Innovation and learning – how can we continue to improve and create future value?

Financial – how do we create value for our shareholders?

Within each of these perspectives a company should seek to identify a series of goals and measures.

Test your understanding 5

Faster Pasta is an Italian fast food restaurant that specialises in high quality, moderately priced authentic Italian pasta dishes and pizzas. The restaurant has recently decided to implement a balanced scorecard approach and has established the following relevant goals for each perspective:

Perspective	**Goal**
Customer perspective	• To increase the number of new and returning customers
	• To reduce the % of customer complaints
Internal	• To reduce the time taken between taking a customer's order and delivering the meal to the customer.
	• To reduce staff turnover
Innovation and learning	• To increase the proportion of revenue from new dishes
	• To increase the % of staff time spent on training
Financial	• To increase spend per customer
	• To increase gross profit margin

The following information is also available for the year just ended and for the previous year.

	20X8	20X9
Total customers	11,600	12,000
- of which are new customers	4,400	4,750
- of which are existing customers	7,200	7,250
Customer complaints	464	840
Time between taking order and customer receiving meal	4 mins	13 mins
% staff turnover	12 %	40 %
% time staff spend training	5 %	2%
Revenue	$110,000	$132,000
- revenue from new dishes	$22,000	$39,600
- revenue from existing dishes	$88,000	$92,400
Gross profit	$22,000	$30,360

Required:

Using appropriate measures, calculate and comment on whether or not Faster Pasta has achieved its goals.

Additional example on the balanced scorecard

One example reported in management literature of how the balanced scorecard might be applied is the US case of Analog Devices (a semi conductor manufacturer) in the preparation of its five-year strategic plan for 1988-1992.

Analog Devices had as its main corporate objective:

'Achieving our goals for growth, profits, market share and quality creates the environment and economic means to satisfy the needs of our employees, stockholders, customers and others associated with the firm. Our success depends on people who understand the interdependence and congruence of their personal goals with those of the company and who are thus motivated to contribute towards the achievement of those goals.'

Three basic strategic objectives identified by the company were market leadership, sales growth and profitability.

The company adopted targets as follows:

Customer perspective

- Percentage of orders delivered on time. A target was set for the five-year period to increase the percentage of on-time deliveries from 85% to at least 99.8%.
- Outgoing defect levels. The target was to reduce the number of defects in product items delivered to customers from 500, to fewer than 10, per month.
- Order lead time. A target was set to reduce the time between receiving a customer order to delivery from 10, to less than 3, weeks.

Internal perspective

- Manufacturing cycle time. To reduce this from 15 weeks to 4-5 weeks over the five-year planning period.
- Defective items in production. To reduce defects in production from 5,000, to fewer than 10, per month.

Learning and innovation perspective

- Having products rated 'number one' by at least 50% of customers, based on their attitudes to whether the company was making the right products, performance, price, reliability, quality, delivery, lead time, customer support, responsiveness, willingness to co-operate and willingness to form partnerships.
- The number of new products introduced to the market.
- Sales revenue from new products.
- The new product sales ratio. This was the percentage of total sales achieved by products introduced to the market within the previous six quarters.
- Average annual revenues for new products in their third year.
- Reducing the average time to bring new product ideas to the market.

Financial targets were set for revenue, revenue growth, profit and return on assets. But the idea was that the financial targets would flow from achieving the other targets stated above.

Analog Devices sought to adopt financial and non-financial performance measures within a single system, in which the various targets were consistent with each other and were in no way incompatible.

Benefits of the balanced scorecard:

- It focuses on factors, including non-financial ones, which will enable a company to succeed in the long-term.
- It provides external as well as internal information.

Problems with the balanced scorecard:

- The selection of measures can be difficult. For example, how should the company measure innovation?
- Obtaining information can be difficult. For example, obtaining feedback from customers can prove difficult.
- Information overload due to the large number of measures that may be chosen.
- Conflict between measures. For example, profitability may increase in the short-term through a reduction in expenditure on staff training.

The building block model

Fitzgerald and Moon adopted a framework for the design and analysis of performance management systems. They based their analysis on three building blocks:

Dimensions

Dimensions are the goals for the business and suitable measures must be developed to measure each performance dimension. There are six dimensions in the building block model.

Standards

These are the measures used. To ensure success it is vital that employees view standards as achievable, fair and take ownership of them.

Rewards

To ensure that employees are motivated to meet standards, targets need to be clear and linked to controllable factors.

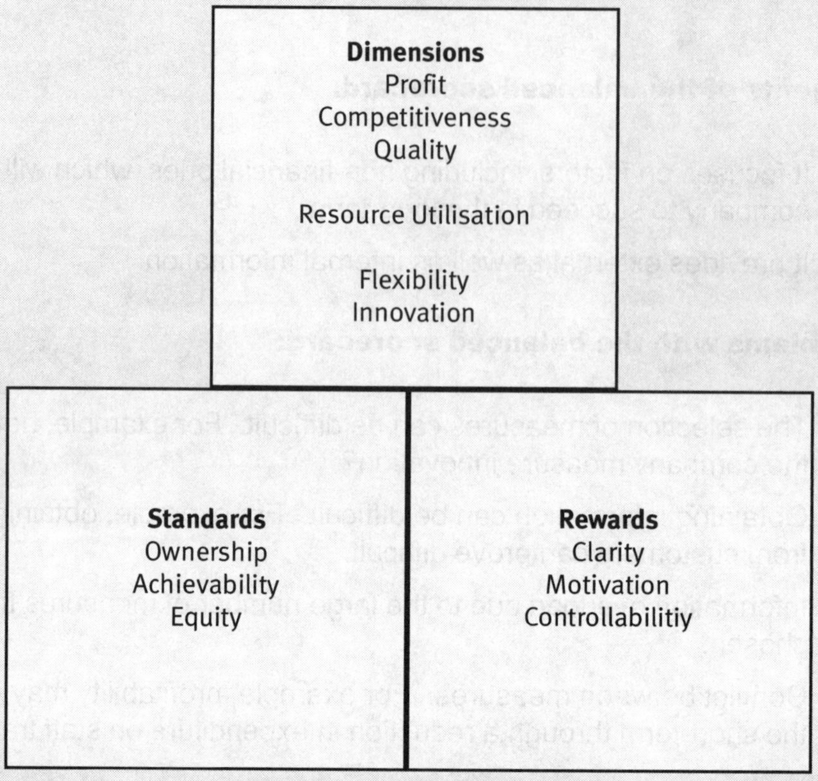

Performance Dimension (goal)	Examples of standards (measures)
Competitive performance.	Market share. Sales growth. Customer base.
Financial performance.	Profitability. Liquidity. Risk
Quality of service.	Reliability. Responsiveness. Competence.
Flexibility.	Volume flexibility. Delivery speed.
Resource utilisation.	Productivity. Efficiency.
Innovation.	Ability to innovate. Performance of the innovations.

Test your understanding 6 - Standards and rewards

Explain why it is important to:

(i) consider ownership, achievability and equity when setting standards.

(ii) consider clarity, motivation and controllability when setting rewards.

Additional example on the building block model

Required:

Using the six dimensions of Fitzgerald and Moon suggest some measures (standards) for a national car dealership network.

Solution

Dimension	Measures
Financial performance.	• Profit per dealer. • Average margins. • Average discount agreed as a % of displayed list price.
Competitive performance.	• Local market share (e.g. look at new car registrations by postcode). • National market share (e.g. from published market research data).
Quality of service.	• 'Mystery shopper data', i.e. outside consultants visit or ring dealerships posing as customers. • Post-sale satisfaction surveys of customers.
Flexibility.	• Post-sale satisfaction surveys of customers to highlight whether they felt sales staff were flexible in getting different vehicle specifications, etc.

Resource utilisation.	• Sales per employee. • Sales per square metre of available floor space. • Average length of time a second hand car (e.g. taken as part-exchange) remains unsold.
Innovation.	• Central inspection by senior staff could enable a subjective assessment of local innovation to be made.

5 External considerations

Performance measures provide useful information to management which aid in the control of the business.

However, they need to be considered in the context of the environment external to the business to gain a full understanding of how the business has performed and to develop actions which should be taken to improve performance. External considerations which are particularly important are:

- **Stakeholders** - a stakeholder is any individual or group that has an interest in the business and may include:
  - shareholders
  - employees
  - loan providers
  - government
  - community
  - customers
  - environmental groups

  Stakeholders will have different objectives and companies may deal with this by having a range of performance measures to assess the achievement of these objectives.

- **Market conditions** - these will impact business performance. For example, a downturn in the industry or in the economy as a whole could have a negative impact on performance.
- **Competitors** - the actions of competitors must also be considered. For example, company demand may decrease if a competitor reduces its prices or launches a successful advertising campaign.

Test your understanding 7 - Stakeholder considerations

NW is an electricity and gas provider for residential and business properties.

The business was nationalised in the past (State owned) but has more recently become a privatised company.

Annual data from NW's accounts are provided below relating to its first three years of operation as a private sector concern.

Also shown, for comparison, is the proforma data as included in the privatisation documents. The proforma accounts are notional accounts prepared to show the performance of the company in its last year under public ownership as if it had applied private sector accounting conventions. They also incorporate a dividend payment based on the dividend policy declared in the prospectus.

The activities of privatised utilities are scrutinised by a regulatory body, which restricts the extent to which prices can be increased.

The demand for gas and electricity in the area served by NW has risen over time at a steady 2% pa , largely reflecting demographic trends.

Key financial and operating data for year ending 31 December ($m)

	20X1 (proforma)	20X2 (actual)	20X3 (actual)	20X4 (actual)
Turnover	450	480	540	620
Met profit	26	35	55	75
Taxation	5	6	8	10
Profit after tax	21	29	47	65
Dividends	7	10	15	20
Total assets	100	119	151	191
Capital expenditure	20	30	60	75
Wage bill	100	98	90	86
Directors' emoluments	0.8	2.0	2.3	3.0
Employees (number)	12,000	11,800	10,500	10,000
Retail price index (RPI)	100	102	105	109

Required:

Using the data provided, assess the extent to which NW has met the interests of the following groups of stakeholders in its first three years as a privatised enterprise. If relevant, suggest what other data would be helpful in forming a more balanced view.

(i) Shareholders

(ii) Consumers

(iii) Workforce

(iv) Government, through NW's contribution to the achievement of the government's objectives of price stability and economic growth.

6 Chapter summary

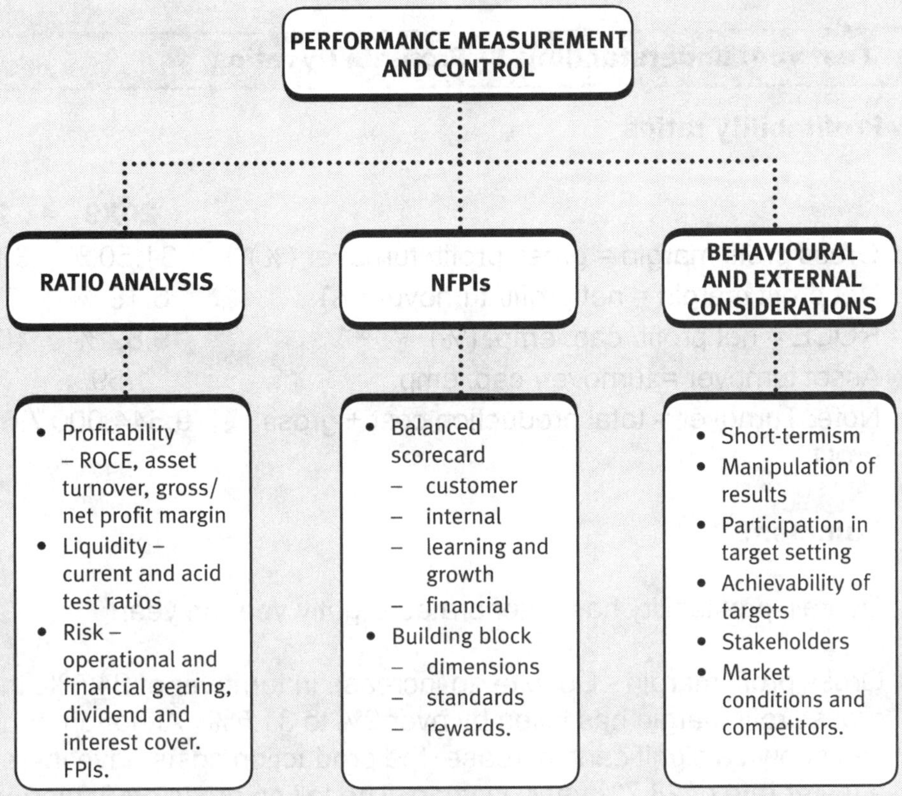

Test your understanding answers

Test your understanding 1 - Profitability ratios

Profitability ratios

	20X9	20X8
Gross profit margin = gross profit/ turnover (%)	31.50 %	33.69 %
Net profit margin = net profit/ turnover (%)	6.18 %	7.49 %
ROCE = net profit/ cap. emp. (%)	9.82 %	10.03 %
Asset turnover = turnover/ cap. emp.	1.59	1.34
Note: Turnover = total production cost + gross profit	9,544,000	7,664,000

Comment

Overall, profitability has deteriorated slightly year on year.

Gross profit margin - Despite an increase in turnover of 24.6%, the gross profit margin has fallen by over 2% to 31.5%. Although turnover has shown a significant increase, the production costs have increased at a faster rate of 28.7% year on year. The falling gross profit margin may indicate that the company is unable to achieve the same level of sales prices as it was in 20X8 or is not as efficient at controlling its production costs.

Net profit margin - Again, despite an increase in turnover of 24.6%, the net profit margin has fallen from 7.49% to 6.18%. The falling net profit margin may indicate that the company is unable to achieve the same level of sales prices as it was in 20X8 or is not as efficient at controlling all of its costs.

Asset turnover - this has actually shown a small improvement year on year from 1.34 in 20X8 to 1.59 in 20X9. This shows that the company is getting better at generating turnover from the capital employed within the business.

ROCE - Despite the improvement in asset turnover, the ROCE has actually fallen slightly from 10.03% in 20X8 to 9.83% in 20X9. This means that the company is not as good at generating net profit from its capital employed. The decrease in the ROCE is due to the fall in the net profit margin.

It would be useful to obtain a further breakdown of turnover and costs, in order to fully understand the reasons for the changes and to prevent any further decline in the ratios discussed. It would also be useful to obtain the average ratios for the industry in order to gauge Super Soups performance against that of its competitors.

Test your understanding 2 - Liquidity ratios

Current ratio	(147.9 + 393.4 + 53.8 + 6.2)/ (275.1 + 284.3) =	601.3/559.4
	=	1.07
Quick ratio	(601.3 — 147.9)/559.4 =	0.81
Receivables payment period	393.4/1,867.5 × 365 =	77 days
Inventory turnover period	147.9/(1,867.5 — 489.3) × 365 =	39 days
Payables payment period	275.1/(1,867.5 – 489.3) × 365 =	73 days

Test your understanding 3

- Rewards may be linked to a wider variety of performance measures including some non-financial measures.
- Capital investment decisions may be reviewed centrally and judged on the basis of net present value (NPV).
- Managers may be rewarded according to the overall performance of the company rather than their own responsibility centre. This may help goal congruence but may not be motivating if poorly-performing managers are rewarded in the same way as managers who are performing well.

Test your understanding 4

(a) **Operating statement for the year ended 31 May 2010**

	Medical	*Dietary*	*Fitness*	*Total*
	$000	$000	$000	$000
Budget				
Client Fees	450.0	600.0	450.0	1,500.0
Healthfood mark-up (cost x 100%)		120.0		120.0
Salaries	(240.0)	(336.0)	(225.0)	(801.0)
Budget Gross Margin	210.0	384.0	225.0	819.0
Variances				
Fee income gain / (loss)	(37.5)	(100.0)	275.0	137.5
Healthfood mark-up loss		(30.0)		(30.0)
Salaries increase	(15.0)		(75.0)	(90)
Extra fitness equipment			(80)	(80)
Actual Gross Margin				
Less Company costs				
Enquiry costs - budget				(240)
Enquiry costs -variance				(60)
General Fixed costs				(300.0)
Software systems cost				(50.0)
Actual Net Profit				106.5
Budget Margin per consultation ($)	35.00	32.00	25.00	
Actual margin per consultation ($)	28.64	25.40	23.79	

(b) Competitiveness may be measured in terms of the relative success/failure in obtaining business from enquiries from customers. The percentages are as follows.

	Budget	**Actual**
Uptake from enquiries		
New Business	30%	25%
Repeat Business	40%	50%

Repeat business suggests customer loyalty. The new business figures are disappointing, being below the budgeted level of uptake. In absolute terms, however, new business is 5,000 consultations above budget whereas repeat business is 2,000 consultations below budget.

There are variations within the types of consultation. Medical and dietary are down on budget by approximately 8% and 16% respectively. Fitness is up on budget by approximately 60%.

Flexibility may relate to the company being able to cope with flexibility of volume, delivery speed and job specification. Examples of each may be taken from the information in the management accounts. Additional fitness staff have been employed to cope with the extra volume of clients in this area of business.

Medical staff levels have been reorganised to include the use of external specialists. This provides flexibility where the type of advice required (the job specification) is wider than expected and may improve delivery speed in arranging a consultation more quickly for a client.

Dietary staff numbers are unchanged even though the number of consultations has fallen by 16% from budget. This may indicate a lack of flexibility. It may be argued that the fall in consultations would warrant a reduction in consultant numbers from 12 to 11. This could cause future flexibility problems, however, if there was an upturn in this aspect of the business.

Resource utilisation measures the ratio of output achieved from input resources. In this case the average consultations per consultant may be used as a guide:

	Average consultations per consultant		
	Budget	Actual	Rise (+) or fall (-) %
Medical (full-time only)	1,000	900	-10%
Dietary	1,000	833	-16.7%
Fitness	1,000	1,208	+20.8%

These figures show that:

(1) Medical consultants are being under-utilised. Could this be due to a lack of administrative control? Are too many cases being referred to the outside specialists? This may, however, be viewed as a consequence of flexibility - in the use of specialists as required.

(2) Dietary consultants are being under-utilised. Perhaps there should be a reduction in the number of consultants from 12 to 11 as suggested above.

(3) Fitness consultants are carrying out considerably more consultations (+20.8%) than budgeted. There are potential problems if their quality is decreasing. Overall complaints from clients are up by 120%. How many relate to fitness clients?

It may be, however, that the new cardio-vascular testing equipment is helping both throughput rates and the overall level of business from fitness clients.

Quality of service is the totality of features and characteristics of the service package that bear upon its ability to satisfy client needs. Flexibility and innovation in service provision may be key quality factors.

The high level of complaints from clients (up from 1% to 2% of all clients) indicates quality problems which should be investigated.

Quality of service may be improving. For example the new cardio-vascular testing equipment may be attracting extra clients because of the quality of information which it provides. Quality may also be aided through better management of client appointments and records following the introduction of the new software systems.

Innovation may be viewed in terms of the performance of a specific innovation. For example, whether the new computer software improved the quality of appointment scheduling and hence resource utilisation; improved competitiveness in following up enquiries and hence financial performance; improved flexibility in allowing better forward planning of consultant/client matching.

Innovation may also be viewed in terms of the effectiveness of the process itself. Are staff adequately trained in its use? Does the new software provide the data analysis which is required?

Test your understanding 5

Customer perspective

Goal: To increase the number of new and returning customers

Measure: The number of new customers has increased year on year from 4,400 to 4,750. This is an 8.0% increase. The number of returning customers has also increased slightly from 7,200 to 7,250, i.e. a 1.0% increase.

Comment: The company has achieved its goal of increasing the number of new and existing customers. It is worth noting that the proportion of customers who are returning customers has fallen slightly from 62.1% to 60.4% of the total customers. This could indicate a small drop in the level of customer satisfaction.

Goal: To decrease the % customer complaints

Measure: The percentage of customer complaints has increased from 4% (464 ÷ 11,600) to 7% (840 ÷ 12,000).

Comment: Faster Pasta should investigate the reasons for the increase in customer complaints and take the required action immediately in order to ensure that it can meet this goal in the future.

Internal perspective

Goal: To reduce the time taken between taking the customer's order and delivering the meal to the customer

Measure: The time taken has more than tripled from an average of 4 minutes in 20X8 to an average of 13 minutes in 20X9.

Comment: Customers may place a high value on the fast delivery of their food. The increase in time may be linked to the increased number of customer complaints. If this continues customer satisfaction, and therefore profitability, will suffer in the long-term. The restaurant should take steps now in order to ensure that this goal is achieved going forward.

Goal: To reduce staff turnover

Measure: This has risen significantly from 12% to 40% and hence the business has not achieved its goal.

Comment: The reasons for the high staff turnover should be investigated immediately. This may be contributing to longer waiting times and the increase in customer complaints. This will impact long-term profitability.

Innovation and learning perspective

Goal: To increase the proportion of revenue from new dishes

Measure: This has increased year on year from 20% ($22,000 ÷ $110,000) in 20X8 to 30% ($39,600 ÷ $132,000) in 20X9. Therefore, the restaurant has achieved its goal.

Comment: This is a favourable increase and may have a positive impact on long-term profitability if the new products meet the needs of the customers.

Goal: To increase the % of staff time spent on training.

Measure: This has fallen significantly from 5% to only 2% and hence the company is not achieving its goal.

Comment: Staff may be unsatisfied if they feel that their training needs are not being met. This may contribute to a high staff turnover. In addition, staff may not have the skills to do the job well and this would impact the level of customer satisfaction.

Financial perspective

Goal: to increase spend per customer

Measure: Spend per customer has increased from $9.48 ($110,000 ÷ 11,600) to $11.00 ($132,000 ÷ 12,000), i.e. a 16.0% increase.

Comment: This is a favourable increase. However, the issues discussed above must be addressed in order to ensure that this trend continues.

Goal: To increase gross profit margin.

Measure: The gross profit margin has increased year on year from 20% ($22,000 ÷ $110,000) to 23% ($30,360 ÷ $132,000).

Comment: This is a favourable increase. However, the issues discussed above must be addressed in order to ensure that this trend continues.

Test your understanding 6 - Standards and rewards

(i) Managers who participate in the setting of standards are more likely to accept and be motivated by the standards than managers on whom standards are imposed. An achievable standard is a better motivator than an unachievable one – although research has been undertaken into how much 'stretch' ought to be built into budgets. When setting standards across an organisation, care should be undertaken to ensure that all managers have equally-challenging standards. Achieving equity in this last regard may be difficult when measures used for different managers and business sectors within an organisation may be very different in character to one another.

(ii) Consideration of rewards involves use of concepts including 'clarity', 'motivation' and 'controllability'. Goal clarity contributes to motivation. For example, a standard of 'achieving 4 product innovations per year' might be a more effective motivator than 'giving a high profile to product innovation'. The actual means of motivation may involve performance-related salary bonuses, an assessment scheme point score or access to promotion channels. Managers will be better motivated if they actually control the factors contributing to achievement of the measures and standards on which their rewards are based.

Test your understanding 7 - Stakeholder considerations

Shareholders

Shareholders will want returns in the form of dividends and share price growth. By following policies to promote these requirements NW will maximise shareholder wealth.

The dividend has risen from a proforma 7c in 20X1 to 20c in 20X4. This represents growth of approximately 186% over the period. PAT has increased from 21 in 20X1 to 65 in 20X4, an increase of 210%. Since inflation is only 9% for the period, it would suggest that the needs of the shareholders have been met.

Consumers

Consumers will be interested in prices. The regulator restricts the extent by which prices can be increased.

We have information about the volume of the market (growing at 2 % pa) and can therefore measure the price rises by removing the volume growth from turnover.

	20X1	**20X2**	**20X3**	**20X4**
Turnover	\$450m	\$480m	\$540m	\$620m
	×	1/1.02 ×	$1/1.02^2$ ×	$1/1.02^3$
Turnover in 20X1 volume	450	471	519	584

We can see that after taking out the growth, prices have risen at approximately 9.1% pa, which is well above the rate of inflation for the period (1.4%).

Whether or not this is justified depends on factors such as where the money has been spent. Has it gone into capital expenditure (improving the supplies or preventing leaks) or has it been used to increase dividends?

Workforce

The workforce has fallen by 2,000 from its 12,000 level in 20X1. Whilst it is possible that NW was overstaffed, shedding over 15% of the workforce will have affected morale.

Average wages have risen from \$8,333 to \$8,600 over the period, a rise of just over 3% for the period. Had the workforce enjoyed pay rises in line with inflation they could have expected to earn \$9,083 in 20X4. This means they are actually worse off in real terms.

Without more information (e.g. skills mix of labour force, full/part-time employees) it is hard to comment, but the increased profitability of NW does not appear to have been passed on to them.

At the same time, the directors' emoluments have nearly quadrupled. We could again do with more information such as the number of directors involved. Part of the increase will be to bring fees in line with the private sector and part of it could be linked in with the share price. However, their fees as a percentage of the whole wage bill have risen from 0.8% to 3.4% over the period.

The figures probably will not include other perks such as share options.

The directors may increasingly find themselves having to justify 'fat cat' salaries.

Government

Price stability

Prices have risen by 38% in absolute, and 30% in real, terms which will not be in line with price stability.

Wages have been held down to less than the headline RPI, but at the same time directors' emoluments have risen sharply.

Economic growth

This is difficult to measure without more details, but we could calculate various ratios such as ROCE or net margin to measure the situation. Both have shown improvement over the period.

	20X1	**20X2**	**20X3**	**20X4**
Net margin	5.8%	7.2%	10.2%	12.1%

Capital expenditure has risen by 275% over the period. This would be expected to generate a knock-on growth elsewhere in the economy.

chapter

12

Divisional performance measurement and transfer pricing

Chapter learning objectives

Upon completion of this chapter you will be able to:

- explain the meaning of, and calculate from supplied data, return on investment (ROI) in the context of divisional performance appraisal
- discuss the shortcomings and benefits of using ROI for divisional performance appraisal
- explain the meaning of, and calculate from supplied data, residual income (RI) in the context of divisional performance appraisal
- discuss the shortcomings and benefits of using RI for divisional performance appraisal
- compare divisional performance using supplied data and recognise the problems that can arise from the comparison
- explain, using simple numerical examples, the basis for setting a transfer price using variable cost
- explain, using simple numerical examples, the basis for setting a transfer price using full cost
- explain, using simple numerical examples, how transfer prices can distort the performance assessment of divisions and decisions made, including dysfunctional decision making
- explain, using simple numerical examples, the principles behind allowing for intermediate markets.

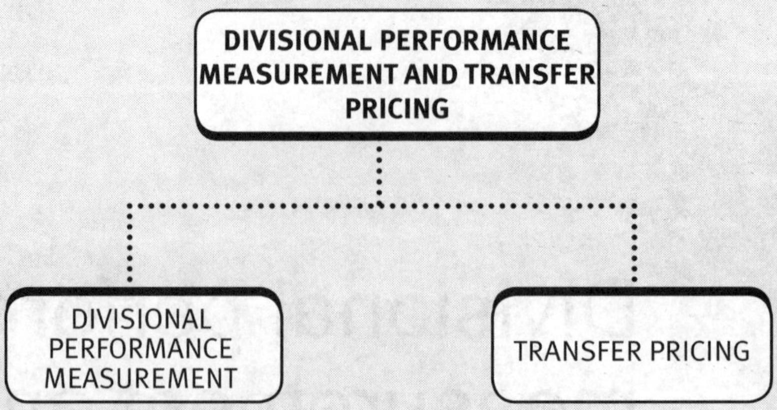

1 Divisional performance measurement

Type of division	Description	Typical measures used to assess performance
Cost centre.	• Division incurs costs but has no revenue stream, e.g. the IT support department of an organisation	• Total cost and cost per unit • Cost variances. • NFPIs related to quality, productivity & efficiency.
Profit centre.	• Division has both costs and revenue. • Manager does not have the authority to alter the level of investment in the division.	All of the above PLUS: • Total sales and market share. • Profit. • Sales variances. • Working capital ratios (depending on the division concerned). • NFPIs e.g. related to productivity, quality and customer satisfaction.
Investment centre.	• Division has both costs and revenue. • Manager does have the authority to invest in new assets or dispose of existing ones.	All of the above PLUS: • ROI. • RI. These measures are used to assess the investment decisions made by managers and are discussed in more detail below.

Important point: For each of these care must be taken to assess managers on controllable factors only. So for example, the manager of a cost centre should only be assessed on controllable costs.

Return on investment (ROI)

This is a similar measure to ROCE but is used to appraise the investment decisions of an individual department.

$$ROI = \frac{\text{Controllable profit}}{\text{Capital employed}} \times 100$$

- Controllable profit is usually taken after depreciation but before tax. However, in the exam you may not be given this profit figure and so you should use the profit figure that is closest to this. Assume the profit is controllable, unless told otherwise.
- Capital employed is total assets less long term liabilities or total equity plus long term debt. Use net assets if capital employed is not given in the question.
- Non-current assets might be valued at cost, net replacement cost or net book value (NBV). The value of assets employed could be either an average value for the period as a whole or a value as at the end of the period. An average value for the period is preferable. However, in the exam you should use whatever figure is given to you.

Test your understanding 1 - ROI calculation

An investment centre has reported a profit of $28,000. It has the following assets and liabilities:

	$	$
Non-current assets (at NBV)		100,000
Inventory	20,000	
Trade receivables	30,000	
		50,000
Trade payables	8,000	
		42,000
		142,000

Required:

Calculate the ROI for the division. State any additional information that would be useful when calculating the ROI.

Additional example on ROI

Division A of Babbage Group had investments at the year end of $56 million. These include the cost of a new equipment item costing $3 million that was acquired two weeks before the end of the year. This equipment was paid for by the central treasury department of Babbage, and is recorded in the accounts as an inter-company loan.

The profit of division A for the year was $7 million before deducting head office recharges of $800,000.

Required:

What is the most appropriate measure of ROI for Division A for the year?

Solution

Since the new equipment was bought just two weeks before the year end, the most appropriate figure for capital employed is $53 million, not $56 million.

The figure for profit should be the controllable profit of $7 million.

ROI = $7 million/$53 million = 13.2%

Evaluation of ROI as a performance measure

ROI is a popular measure for divisional performance but has some serious failings which must be considered when interpreting results.

Advantages

- It is widely used and accepted since it is line with ROCE which is frequently used to assess overall business performance.
- As a relative measure it enables comparisons to be made with divisions or companies of different sizes.
- It can be broken down into secondary ratios for more detailed analysis, i.e. profit margin and asset turnover.

Disadvantages

- It may lead to dysfunctional decision making, e.g. a division with a current ROI of 30% would not wish to accept a project offering a ROI of 25%, as this would dilute its current figure. However, the 25% ROI may meet or exceed the company's target.
- ROI increases with the age of the asset if NBVs are used, thus giving managers an incentive to hang on to possibly inefficient, obsolescent machines.
- It may encourage the manipulation of profit and capital employed figures to improve results, e.g. in order to obtain a bonus payment.
- Different accounting policies can confuse comparisons (e.g. depreciation policy).

Test your understanding 2 - Disadvantages of ROI

Nielsen Ltd has two divisions with the following information:

	Division A	Division B
	$	$
Profit	90,000	10,000
Capital employed	300,000	100,000
ROI	30%	10%

Division A has been offered a project costing $100,000 and giving annual returns of $20,000. Division B has been offered a project costing $100,000 and giving annual returns of $12,000. The company's cost of capital is 15%. Divisional performance is judged on ROI and the ROI-related bonus is sufficiently high to influence the managers' behaviour.

Required:

(a) What decisions will be made by management if they act in the best interests of their division (and in the best interests of their bonus)?

(b) What should the managers do if they act in the best interests of the company as a whole?

Residual income (RI)

RI = Controllable profit – Notional interest on capital

- Controllable profit is calculated in the same way as for ROI.
- Notional interest on capital = the capital employed in the division multiplied by a notional cost of capital or interest rate.
  - Capital employed is calculated in the same way as for ROI.
  - The selected cost of capital could be the company's average cost of funds (cost of capital). However, other interest rates might be selected, such as the current cost of borrowing, or a target ROI. (You should use whatever rate is given in the exam).

Test your understanding 3 - RI calculation

An investment centre has net assets of $800,000, and made profits before interest and tax of $160,000. The notional cost of capital is 12%.

Required:

Calculate and comment on the RI for the period.

Evaluation of RI as a performance measure

Compared to using ROI as a measure of performance, RI has several advantages and disadvantages:

Advantages

- It encourages investment centre managers to make new investments if they add to RI. A new investment might add to RI but reduce ROI. In such a situation, measuring performance by RI would not result in dysfunctional behaviour, i.e. the best decision will be made for the business as a whole.
- Making a specific charge for interest helps to make investment centre managers more aware of the cost of the assets under their control.

Disadvantages

- It does not facilitate comparisons between divisions since the RI is driven by the size of divisions and of their investments.
- It is based on accounting measures of profit and capital employed which may be subject to manipulation, e.g. in order to obtain a bonus payment.

Test your understanding 4 - ROI vs RI

An investment centre has net assets of $800,000, and made profits before interest of $160,000. The notional cost of capital is 12%. This is the company's target return.

An opportunity has arisen to invest in a new project costing $100,000. The project would have a four-year life, and would make profits of $15,000 each year.

Required:

(a) What would be the ROI with and without the investment? (Base your calculations on opening book values). Would the investment centre manager wish to undertake the investment if performance is judged on ROI?

(b) What would be the average annual RI with and without the investment? (Base your calculations on opening book values).Would the investment centre manager wish to undertake the investment if performance is judged on RI?

Additional example on ROI and RI

Two divisions of a company are considering new investments.

	Division X	Division Y
Net assets	$1,000,000	$1,000,000
Current divisional profit	$250,000	$120,000
Investment in project	$100,000	$100,000
Projected project profit	$20,000	$15,000

Company's required ROI = 18%

Required:

Assess the projects using both ROI and RI.

Solution

Consider divisional performance:

	Division X	Division Y
Without project		
Divisional ROI	25%	12%
Divisional RI ($)	+ 70,000	– 60,000
With project		
Investment ($)	1,100,000	1,100,000
Profit ($)	270,000	135,000
ROI	24.5%	12.3%
RI ($)	72,000	– 63,000
Project in isolation		
ROI	20%	15%
RI ($)	+ 2,000	– 3,000

Based on ROI, Division X will reject its project as it dilutes its existing ROI of 25%. This is the wrong decision from the company perspective as the project ROI of 20% beats the company hurdle of 18%.

Likewise Division Y will accept its project, which should be rejected as it fails to hit the company target.

In each case there is a conflict between the company and divisional viewpoints.

RI does not have this problem as we simply add the project RI to the divisional figures.

Comparing divisional performance

Divisional performance can be compared in many ways. ROI and RI are common methods but other methods could be used.

- Variance analysis – is a standard means of monitoring and controlling performance. Care must be taken in identifying the controllability of, and responsibility for, each variance.
- Ratio analysis – there are several profitability and liquidity measures that can be applied to divisional performance reports.

- Other management ratios – this could include measures such as sales per employee or square foot as well as industry specific ratios such as transport costs per mile, brewing costs per barrel, overheads per chargeable hour.
- Other information – such as staff turnover, market share, new customers gained, innovative products or services developed.

Test your understanding 5

Comment on the problems that may be involved in comparing divisional performance.

2 Transfer pricing

Introduction

A transfer price is the price at which goods or services are transferred from one division to another within the same organisation.

Objectives of a transfer pricing system

- Goal congruence

The decisions made by each profit centre manager should be consistent with the objectives of the organisation as a whole, i.e. the transfer price should assist in maximising overall company profits. A common feature of exam questions is that a transfer price is set that results in sub-optimal behaviour.

- Performance measurement

The buying and selling divisions will be treated as profit centres. The transfer price should allow the performance of each division to be assessed fairly. Divisional managers will be demotivated if this is not achieved.

- Autonomy

The system used to set transfer prices should seek to maintain the autonomy of profit centre managers. If autonomy is maintained, managers tend to be more highly motivated but sub-optimal decisions may be made.

- Recording the movement of goods and services.

In practice, an extremely important function of the transfer pricing system is simply to assist in recording the movement of goods and services.

Setting the transfer price

There are two main methods available:

Method 1: Market based approach

If an external market exists for the transferred goods then the transfer price could be set at the external market price.

Advantages of this method:

- The transfer price should be deemed to be fair by the managers of the buying and selling divisions. The selling division will receive the same amount for any internal or external sales. The buying division will pay the same for goods if they buy them internally or externally.
- The company's performance will not be impacted negatively by the transfer price because the transfer price is the same as the external market price.

Disadvantages of this method:

- There may not be an external market price.
- The external market price may not be stable. For example, discounts may be offered to certain customers or for bulk orders.
- Savings may be made from transferring the goods internally. For example, delivery costs will be saved. These savings should ideally be deducted from the external market price before a transfer price is set.

Method 2: Cost based approach

The transferring division would supply the goods at **cost plus a % profit**.

A standard cost should be used rather than the actual cost since:

- Actual costs do not encourage the selling division to control costs.
- If a standard cost is used, the buying division will know the cost in advance and can therefore put plans in place.

There are a number of different standard costs that could be used:

- Full cost
- Marginal (variable) cost
- Opportunity cost.

Each of these will be reviewed.

Test your understanding 6 - Full cost and marginal cost

A company has two profit centres, Centre A and Centre B. Centre A supplies Centre B with a part-finished product. Centre B completes the production and sells the finished units in the market at $35 per unit. There is no external market for Centre A's part-finished product.

Budgeted data for the year:

	Division A	Division B
Number of units transferred/sold	10,000	10,000
Material cost per unit	$8	$2
Other variable costs per unit	$2	$3
Annual fixed costs	$60,000	$30,000

Required:

Calculated the budgeted annual profit for each division and for the company as a whole of the transfer price for the components supplied by division A to division B is:

(a) Full cost plus 10%

(b) Marginal cost plus 10%

(c) Evaluate both transfer prices from the perspective of each individual division and from the perspective of the company as a whole.

Test your understanding 7 - Opportunity cost approach

A company operates two divisions, Able and Baker. Able manufactures two products, X and Y. Product X is sold to external customers for $42 per unit. The only outlet for product Y is Baker.

Baker supplies an external market and can obtain its semi-finished supplies (product Y) from either Able or an external source. Baker currently has the opportunity to purchase product Y from an external supplier for $38 per unit. The capacity of division Able is measured in units of output, irrespective of whether product X, Y or a combination of both are being manufactured.

The associated product costs are as follows:

	X	Y
	$	$
Variable costs per unit	32	35
Fixed overheads per unit	5	5
Total unit costs	37	40

Required:

Using the above information, advise on the determination of an appropriate transfer price for the sale of product Y from division Able to division Baker under the following conditions:

(i) when division Able has spare capacity and limited external demand for product X

(ii) when division Able is operating at full capacity with unsatisfied external demand for product X.

Additional example on transfer pricing

Archer Group has two divisions, Division X and Division Y. Division X manufactures a component X8 which is transferred to Division Y. Division Y uses component X8 to make a finished product Y14, which it sells for $20. There is no external market for component X8.

Costs are as follows:

	Division X	**Division Y**
	Component X8	Product Y14
Variable production cost	$5 per unit	$3 per unit*
Annual fixed costs	$40,000	$80,000

*Excluding the cost of transferred units of X8.

The budgeted output and sales for Product Y14 is 20,000 units. One unit of component X8 goes into the manufacture of one unit of Y14.

The profit of the company as a whole will be maximised if Divisions X and Y produce up to their capacity, or to the maximum volume of sales demand. For each extra unit sold, the marginal revenue is $20 and the marginal cost is $8 ($5 + $3); therefore the additional contribution is $12 for each extra unit of Y14 made and sold.

Since there is no external market for component X8, the transfer price will be cost-based. 'Cost' might be marginal cost or full cost. The transfer price might also include a mark-up on cost to allow a profit to Division X.

The maximum transfer price that the buying division will pay

Division Y has a marginal cost of $3 per unit, and earns revenue of $20 for each unit sold. In theory, Division Y should therefore be prepared to pay up to $17 ($20 — $3) for each unit of X8.

It could be argued, however, that Division Y would not want to sell Product Y14 at all if it made a loss. Division Y might therefore want to cover its fixed costs as well as its variable costs. Fixed costs in Division Y, given a budget of 20,000 units, are $4 per unit. The total cost in Division Y is $7 ($3 + $4). On this basis, the maximum transfer price that Division Y should be willing to pay is $13 ($20 — $7).

Transfer price = marginal cost

The short-term opportunity cost to Division X of transferring units of X8 to Division Y is the marginal cost of production, $5.

At a transfer price of $5, Division X would be expected to sell as many units of X8 to Division Y as Division Y would like to buy.

However, although marginal cost represents the opportunity cost to Division X of transferring units of X8, it is not an ideal transfer price.

- At a transfer price of $5, Division X would make $0 contribution from each unit transferred. The Division would therefore make a loss of $40,000 (its fixed costs).
- This transfer price would not motivate the manager of Division X to maximise output.
- It is unlikely that the manager of Division X would be prepared to negotiate this price with Division Y, and a decision to set the transfer price at $5 would probably have to be made by head office.
- If Division X is set up as a profit centre, a transfer price at marginal cost would not provide a fair way of measuring and assessing the division's performance.

Transfer price = marginal cost plus

If the transfer price is set at marginal cost plus a mark-up for contribution, the manager of Division X would be motivated to maximise output, because this would maximise contribution and profit (or minimise the loss).

As indicated earlier, Division Y would want to buy as much as possible from Division X provided that the transfer price is no higher than $17, or possibly $13.

If a transfer price is set at marginal cost plus a mark-up for contribution, the 'ideal' range of prices lies anywhere between $5 and $17. The size of the mark-up would be a matter for negotiation. Presumably, the transfer price that is eventually agreed would be either:

- imposed by head office, or
- agreed by negotiation between the divisional managers, with the more powerful or skilful negotiator getting the better deal on the price.

Additional requirement:

Discuss the implications of setting the transfer cost at full cost plus.

Solution

There is an argument that the opportunity cost of transfer, in the absence of an intermediate market, is full cost.

This assumes that, if the selling division decided against making any transfers at all, it would save all costs, both marginal and fixed costs, by shutting down.

In the above example, the full cost for Division X of making component X8 is $7 ($5 variable plus $2 fixed).

At this price, Division X would want to sell as many units as possible to Division Y, and Division Y would buy as many units as it could, subject to the limit on capacity or sales demand.

However, although full cost represents the long-term opportunity cost to Division X of transferring units of X8, it is not an ideal transfer price.

- At a transfer price of $7, Division X would make $0 profit from each unit transferred. If output and sales are less than the budget of 20,000, Division X would make a loss due to the under-absorbed fixed overhead. If output and sales are more than the budget of 20,000, Division X would make a profit due to the over-absorbed fixed overhead. The only ways in which Division X could make a profit are therefore:
  - to hope that sales demand exceeds the budgeted volume, and/or
  - reduce its variable costs and fixed cost expenditures.
- It is unlikely that the manager of Division X would be prepared to negotiate this price with Division Y, and a decision to set the transfer price at $7 would probably have to be made by head office.
- If Division X is set up as a profit centre, a transfer price at full cost would not provide a fair way of measuring and assessing the division's performance.

Test your understanding 8 - Additional example

Manuco company has been offered supplies of special ingredient Z at a transfer price of $15 per kg by Helpco company, which is part of the same group of companies. Helpco processes and sells special ingredient Z to customers external to the group at $15 per kg. Helpco bases its transfer price on full cost plus 25% profit mark-up. The full cost has been estimated as 75% variable and 25% fixed. Internal transfers to Manuco would enable $1.50 per kg of variable packing cost to be avoided.

Required:

Discuss the transfer prices at which Helpco should offer to transfer special ingredient Z to Manuco in order that group profit maximising decisions are taken in each of the following situations:

(i) Helpco has an external market for all its production of special ingredient Z at a selling price of $15 per kg.

(ii) Helpco has production capacity for 9,000kg of special ingredient Z. An external market is available for 6,000 kgs of material Z.

(iii) Helpco has production capacity for 3,000 kg of special material Z. An alternative use for some of its spare production capacity exists. This alternative use is equivalent to 2,000kg of special ingredient Z and would earn a contribution of $6,000. There is no external demand.

3 Chapter summary

DIVISIONAL PERFORMANCE MEASUREMENT AND TRANSFER PRICING

- **DIVISIONAL PERFORMANCE MEASUREMENT**
  - ROI = EBIT/CE x 100%
  - RI = EBIT – notional interest
  - Notional interest = CE x cost of capital
  - Dysfunctional behaviour
    - conflict with NPV in the short-term
    - manipulation of profit/CE
  - Alternative performance measures: variances, ratios, non-quantitative measures.
- **TRANSFER PRICING**
  - Objectives
  - General rule = variable cost + opportunity cost
  - Market prices
  - Cost based
    - variable cost
    - full cost
  - Dysfunctional behaviour.

Test your understanding answers

Test your understanding 1 - ROI calculation

- ROI might be measured as: $28,000/$142,000 = 19.7%.
- However, suppose that the centre manager has no responsibility for debt collection. In this situation, it could be argued that the centre manager is not responsible for trade receivables, and the centre's CE should be $112,000. If this assumption is used, ROI would be $28,000/$112,000 = 25.0%.

Test your understanding 2 - Disadvantages of ROI

(a)	**Division A**	**Division B**
	$000	$000
Old ROI	90/300	10/100
	= 30%	= 10%
New ROI	(90 + 20)/(300 + 100)	(10 + 12)/(100 + 100)
	= 27.5%	= 11%
Will manager want to accept project?	No	Yes

The manager of Division A will not want to accept the project as it lowers her ROI from 30% to 27.5%. The manager of Division B will like the new project as it will increase their ROI from 10% to 11%. Although the 11% is bad, it is better than before.

(b) Looking at the whole situation from the group point of view, we are in the ridiculous position that the group has been offered two projects, both costing $100,000. One project gives a profit of $20,000 and the other $12,000. Left to their own devices then the managers would end up accepting the project giving only $12,000. This is because ROI is a defective decision-making method and does not guarantee that the correct decision will be made.

Test your understanding 3 - RI calculation

If performance is measured by RI, the RI for the period is:

	$
Profit before interest and tax	160,000
Notional interest (12% × $800,000)	96,000
RI	64,000

(**Note:** Capital employed is not available in this question and therefore net assets should be used as a substitute value).

Investment centre managers who make investment decisions on the basis of short-term performance will want to undertake any investments that add to RI, i.e. if the RI is positive.

Test your understanding 4 - ROI vs RI

(a) ROI

	Without the investment	**With the investment**
Profit	$160,000	$175,000
Capital employed	$800,000	$900,000
ROI	20.0%	19.4%

ROI would be lower; therefore the centre manager will not want to make the investment. since his performance will be judged as having deteriorated. However, this results in dysfunctional behaviour since the company's target is only 12%.

(b) RI

		Without the investment		**With the investment**
		$		$
Profit		160,000		175,000
Notional interest	($800,000 × 12%)	(96,000)	($900,000 × 12%)	(108,000)
RI		64,000		67,000

The investment centre manager will want to undertake the investment because it will increase RI. This is the correct decision for the company since RI increases by $3,000 as a result of the investment.

Test your understanding 5

Problems may include:

- Divisions may operate in different environments. A division earning a ROI of 10% when the industry average is 7% may be considered to be performing better than a division earning a ROI of 12% when the industry average is 15%.
- The transfer pricing policy may distort divisional performance.
- Divisions may have assets of different ages. A division earning a high ROI may do so because assets are old and fully depreciated. This may give a poor indication of future potential performance.
- There may be difficulties comparing divisions with different accounting policies (e.g. depreciation).
- Evaluating performance on the basis of a few indicators may lead to manipulation of data. A wider range of indicators may be preferable which include non-financial measures. It may be difficult to find non-financial indicators which can easily be compared if divisions operate in different environments.

Test your understanding 6 - Full cost and marginal cost

(a)

	Division A ($)	**Division B ($)**	**Total ($)**
Sales:			
- internal	10,000 × $17.60 (W1) = 176,000	n/a	176,000
- external	n/a	10,000 × $35 = 350,000	350,000
Costs:			
- transfer costs	n/a	(176,000) (as above)	(176,000)
- variable costs	10,000 × $10 = (100,000)	10,000 × $5 = (50,000)	(150,000)
- fixed costs	(60,000)	(30,000)	(90,000)
Profit	16,000	94,000	110,000

(b)

	Division A ($)	**Division B ($)**	**Total ($)**
Sales:			
- internal	10,000 × $11 (W2) = 110,000	n/a	110,000
- external	n/a	10,000 × $35 = 350,000	350,000
Costs:			
- transfer costs	n/a	(110,000) (as above)	(110,000)
- variable costs	10,000 × $10 = (100,000)	10,000 × $5 = (50,000)	(150,000)
- fixed costs	(60,000)	(30,000)	(90,000)
Profit/ (loss)	(50,000)	160,000	110,000

Working 1

	$
Material cost per unit	8
Other variable costs per unit	2
Fixed cost per unit ($60,000 ÷ 10,000)	6
Full cost	16
Plus 10% profit	1.60
Transfer price = full cost + 10%	17.60

Working 2

	$
Material cost per unit	8
Other variable costs per unit	2
Total variable cost	10
Plus 10% profit	1
Transfer price = marginal cost + 10%	11

(c)

- Division A would prefer the transfer price to be set at full cost plus 10%. This would give them a budgeted profit of $16,000, compared to a loss of $50,000 when the marginal cost transfer price is used.
- Division B would prefer the transfer price to be set at variable cost + 10%. This gives them a profit of $160,000 compared with a profit of $94,000 if the full cost transfer price is used.
- There is a natural conflict between the divisions and the transfer price would have to be negotiated to ensure that each division views it as being fair.
- The company as a whole will be indifferent to the transfer price. There is no external market for Division A's goods and the profit will be $110,000 regardless of the transfer price set.

Test your understanding 7 - Opportunity cost approach

(i) The transfer price should be set between $35 and $38. Able has spare capacity, therefore the marginal costs to the group of Able making a unit is $35. If the price is set above $38, Baker will be encouraged to buy outside the group, decreasing group profit by $3 per unit.

(ii) If Able supplies Baker with a unit of Y, it will cost $35 and they (both Able and the group) will lose $10 contribution from X ($42 sales – $32 variable cost). So long as the bought-in external price of Y to Baker is less than $45, Baker should buy from that external source. The transfer price should therefore be set at $45.

Test your understanding 8 - Additional example

(i) Since Helpco has an external market, which is the opportunity foregone, the relevant transfer price would be the external selling price of $15 per kg. This will be adjusted to allow for the $1.50 per kg avoided on internal transfers due to packing costs not required.

The transfer price offered by Helpco should be $15 — $1.50 = $13.50 per kg.

(ii) In this situation Helpco has no alternative opportunity for 3,000kg of its special ingredient Z. It should, therefore, offer to transfer this quantity at marginal cost. This is variable cost less packing costs avoided = $9 (W1) — $1.50 = $7.50 per kg.

Working 1: Total cost = $15 × 80% = $12, Variable cost = $12 × 75% = $9.)

If Manuco require more than 3,000 kgs the transfer price should be set at the adjusted selling price of $13.50 per kg as in (i) above.

(iii) Helpco Ltd has an alternative use for some of its production capacity, which will yield a contribution equivalent to $3 per kg of special ingredient Z ($6,000/2,000kg). The balance of its square capacity (1,000kg) has no opportunity cost and should still be offered at marginal cost.

Helpco should offer to transfer:

2,000kg at $7.50 + $3 = $10.50 per kg; 1,000kg at $7.50per kg (= MC).

chapter

13

Performance measurement in not-for-profit organisations

Chapter learning objectives

Upon completion of this chapter you will be able to:

- comment on the problems, with particular reference to not-for-profit organisations and the public sector, of having non-quantifiable objectives in performance management
- describe how performance could be measured in not-for-profit organisations
- comment on the problems, using simple examples, of having multiple objectives in not-for-profit organisations and the public sector
- describe, in outline, value for money (VFM) as a public sector objective.

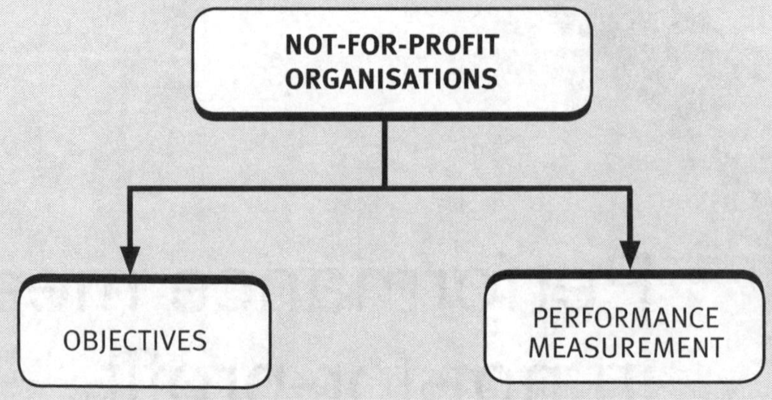

1 The problem of non-quantifiable objectives

The not-for-profit sector incorporates a diverse range of operations including national government, local government, charities, executive agencies, trusts and so on. The critical thing about such operations is that they are not motivated by a desire to maximise profit.

Many, if not all, of the benefits arising from expenditure by these bodies are non-quantifiable (certainly not in monetary terms, e.g. social welfare). The same can be true of costs. So any cost/benefit analysis is necessarily quite judgemental, i.e. social benefits versus social costs as well as financial benefits versus financial costs. The danger is that if benefits cannot be quantified, then they might be ignored.

Another problem is that these organisations often do not generate revenue but simply have a fixed budget for spending within which they have to keep (i.e. a capital rationing problem). Value for money ('VFM') is often quoted as an objective here but it does not get round the problem of measuring 'value'.

Illustration 1 – The problem of non-quantifiable objectives

A hospital might use a cheaper cleaning firm because of difficulties evaluating how well the cleaning is being done. This may create problems in many areas:

- It may indirectly lead to the spread of infection which is costly to eliminate.
- Nursing staff may become demotivated as they are unable to carry out their own work effectively.
- The general public may lose confidence in the quality of the service.

Test your understanding 1

Discuss how a hospital should determine whether to allocate limited surgical resources to expensive organ transplants or to more routine hip/knee joint replacements.

2 Performance measurement in not-for-profit organisations

Not-for-profit organisations may have some non-quantifiable objectives but that fact does not exempt them from the need to plan and control their activities.

e.g

Illustration 2 – Performance measurement in not-for-profit

A university is an example of a non-profit making organisation. The performance of this not-for-profit organisation must be assessed. Measures include:

University overall:

- overall costs compared with budget
- numbers of students
- amount of research funding received
- proportion of successful students (by grade)
- quality of teaching – as measured by student and inspector assessments
- number of publications by staff.

Individual department or faculty:

- cost per student
- cost per examination pass
- staff/student ratios
- students per class
- number of teaching hours per member of staff
- availability of learning resources, e.g. personal computer (PC) per student ratio
- number of library books per student
- average age of library books.

Test your understanding 2

St Alice's Hospice is a charity which collects funds and donations and utilises these in the care of terminally ill patients. The governing body has set the manager three performance objectives for the three months to 30 June 20X7:

- to achieve a level of donations of $150,000
- to keep administration costs to no more than 8% of donations
- to achieve 80% of respite care requested from the community.

Actual results were as follows:

	April	May	June
Donations($)	35,000	65,000	55,000
Administration costs ($)	2,450	5,850	4,400
Respite care requests (days)	560	570	600
Respite care provided (days)	392	430	510

Prepare a statement to assist the manager in evaluating performance against objectives and comment on performance.

3 The problem of multiple objectives

Multiple stakeholders in not-for-profit organisations give rise to multiple objectives. As a result, there is a need to prioritise objectives or to make compromises between objectives.

e.g

Illustration 3 –The problem of multiple objectives

A hospital will have a number of different groups of stakeholders, each with their own objectives. For example:

- Employees will seek a high level of job satisfaction. They will also aim to achieve a good work-life balance and this may result in a desire to work more regular daytime hours.
- Patients will want to be seen quickly and will demand a high level of care.

There is potential conflict between the objectives of the two stakeholder groups. For example, if hospital staff only work regular daytime hours then patients may have to wait a long time if they come to the hospital outside of these hours and the standard of patient care will fall dramatically at certain times of the day, if most staff only work regular hours.

The hospital must prioritise the needs of the different stakeholder groups. In this case, the standard of patient care would be prioritised above giving staff the regular daytime working hours that they would prefer. However, in order to maintain staff morale an element of compromise should also be used. For example, staff may have to work shifts but may be given generous holidays allowances or other rewards instead.

Test your understanding 3

Describe the different groups of stakeholders in an international famine relief charity. Explain how the charity may have conflicting objectives and the impact this may have on the effective operation of the organisation.

4 Value for money (VFM)

A common method of assessing public sector performance is to assess value for money (VFM). This comprises three elements:

Economy – an input measure. Are the resources used the cheapest possible for the quality required?

Efficiency – here we link inputs with outputs. Is the maximum output being achieved from the resources used?

Effectiveness – an output measure looking at whether objectives are being met.

Illustration 4 – Value for money

Value for money in a university would comprise the three element of:

Economy - this is about balancing the cost with the quality of the resources. Therefore, it will review areas such as the cost of books, computers and teaching compared with the quality of these resources. It recognises that the organisation must consider its expenditure but should not simply aim to minimise costs. e.g. low cost but poor quality teaching or books will hinder student performance and will damage the reputation of the university.

Efficiency - this focuses on the efficient use of any resources acquired. For example:

- How often are the library books that are bought by the university taken out on loan by students?
- What is the utilisation of IT resources?
- What % of their working time do lecturers spend teaching or researching?

Effectiveness - this measures the achievement of the organisation's objectives. For example:

- The % of students achieving a target grade.
- The % of graduates who find full time employment within 6 months of graduating.

Test your understanding 4

A local authority may have 'maintaining an acceptable quality of life for elderly residents' as one of its objectives. It has several means by which it may achieve this objective, including:

- providing 'meals on wheels' (Social Services Department)
- providing a mobile library (Libraries Department)
- maintaining access to and facilities in local parks (Parks Department)
- providing police support to the elderly at home (Police Department)
- providing nursing homes (Housing Department).

Required:

Explain how the local authority would determine whether the service was effective in providing VFM.

5 Chapter summary

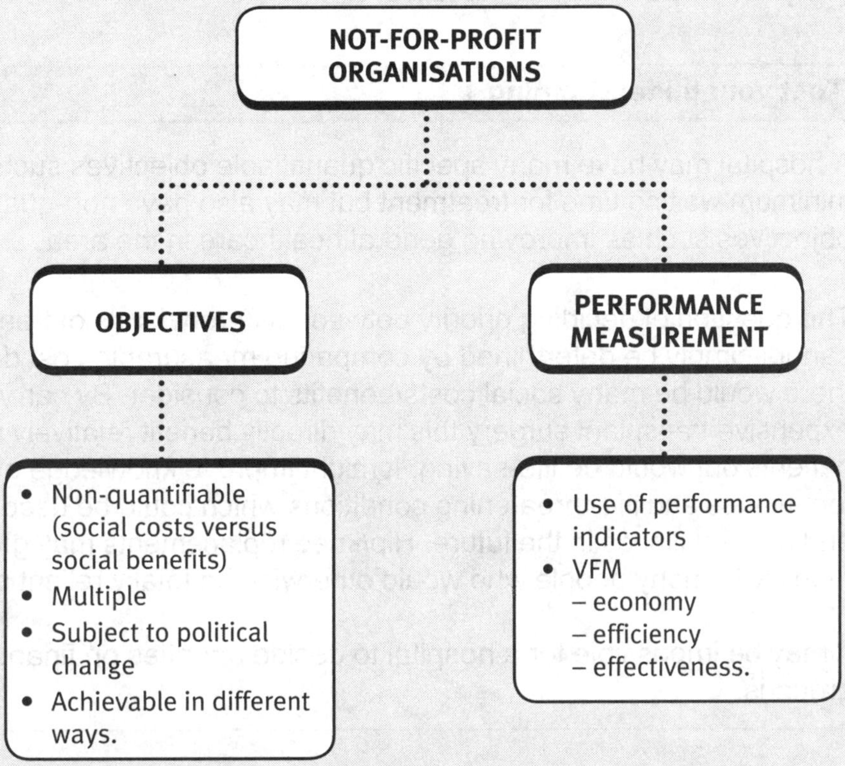

Test your understanding answers

Test your understanding 1

A hospital may have many specific quantifiable objectives such as a minimum waiting time for treatment but may also have non-quantifiable objectives such as improving general healthcare in the area.

The question of deciding priority between different kinds of treatment cannot simply be determined by comparing measurable cost data as there would be many social costs/benefits to consider. By carrying out expensive transplant surgery this may directly benefit relatively few patients but would be life-saving. It might improve knowledge of surgical techniques and life-threatening conditions which could be used to detect and prevent illness in the future. Hip/knee replacements may give mobility to many people who would otherwise be totally reliant on carers.

It may be impossible for a hospital to decide priorities on financial grounds.

Test your understanding 2

	April	**May**	**June**
Administration costs as a % of donations	7%	9%	8%
Target	8%	8%	8%
Respite care provided	70%	75.4%	85%

Total donations received have exceeded the target for the period. There is no discernable trend and it is possible that there were special fund-raising activities in May which generated greater income. Administration costs have been within the target of 8% in April and June but exceeded the target in May. More information is needed to establish why this occurred. There has been a steady improvement in the level of respite care provided and in June the target was exceeded.

Test your understanding 3

The stakeholders will include donors, people needing aid, voluntary staff, paid staff, the governments of the countries granting and receiving aid.

There may be conflicting objectives. Donors and people needing aid will want all of the funds to be spent on famine relief. Management staff may require a percentage of the funds to be spent on administration and promotion in order to safeguard the long-term future of the charity.

Donors may have their own views on how donations should be spent which conflict with management staff.

The charity may wish to distribute aid according to perceived need. Governments in receiving countries may have political reasons for distorting information relating to need.

These conflicts may make it difficult to set clear objectives on which all stakeholders agree.

Test your understanding 4

All of these departmental activities contribute to achievement of the objective. The problem is to find the optimum combination of spending for each of the departments.

- Many elderly people continue to live in their own homes, but are just on the threshold of requiring accommodation in a nursing home. A small cutback in spending in one area (e.g. the withdrawal of a mobile library) may push a lot of elderly people over that threshold. There is then an enormous demand for extra spending by the Housing Department. Nursing home accommodation is an expensive last resort in caring for the elderly.
- An occasional visit by a care worker or a police officer may enable many elderly people to stay in their own homes for much longer than would otherwise be the case.

The key to effectiveness is in finding an optimum pattern of spending to achieve a given objective.

chapter

14

Question & Answers

1 Advanced costing methods

ROCHE (ABC)

Questions

Roche has recently set up a small business, which manufactures three different types of chair to customer order. Each type is produced in a single batch per week and dispatched as individual items. The size of the batch is determined by the weekly customer orders. The three different types of chair are known as the Type A, the Type B and the Type C. The Type A is a fully leather-upholstered chair and is the most expensive of the range. The Type B is the middle-of-the-range chair, and has a comfortable leather seat. The cheapest of the range, the Type C, is purely a wooden chair, but Roche feels it has great potential and hopes it will provide at least 50% of the sales revenue.

Roche has employed Mr F, an experienced but unqualified accountant, to act as the organisation's accountant. Mr F has produced figures for the past month, July 2010, which is considered a normal month in terms of costs:

Profit statement for July 2010:

	$	$
Sales Revenue		79,800
Material costs	17,250	
Labour costs	27,600	
Overheads	34,500	
		79,350
Profit		450

	Type A	**Type B**	**Type C**
Units produced and sold during July	30	120	150
	$	$	$
Selling price per chair	395	285	225
Less: Costs per chair			
Material	85	60	50
Labour	120	100	80
Overhead absorbed on labour hours	150	125	100
	355	285	230
Profit per chair	40	0	(5)

Roche hopes to use these figures as the basis for budgets for the next three months. The managers are pleased to see that the organisation has made its first monthly profit, however small it might be. On the other hand, they are unhappy with Mr F's advice about the loss-making Type C, which is, either to reduce its production or to increase its price. Roche's managers are concerned because this advice goes against its marketing strategy. After much discussion Mr F says that he has heard of a newer type of costing system, known as activity-based costing (ABC), and that he will recalculate the position on this basis. In order to do this, Mr F has extracted the following information:

	Type A	**Type B**	**Type C**
Wood (metres) per chair	10	9	9
Leather (metres) per chair	4	2	0
Labour (hours) per chair	24	20	16

The overheads included in July's profit statement comprised:

Set-up costs	$5,600
Purchasing and checking leather hide	$4,000
Purchase of wood	$2,400
Quality inspection of leather seating	$3,200
Despatch and transport	$6,000
Administration and personnel costs	$13,300

Required:

(a) Use the ABC technique to prepare a revised product cost statement for July 2010 such as Mr F might produce.

(b) Drawing upon the information form Roche to illustrate your answer, explain why the use of ABC provides an adequate basis for Roche's managers to make decisions on the future production volume and price of the Type C.

HENSAU LTD

Questions

Hensau Ltd has a single production process for which the following costs have been estimated for the period ending 31 December 20X8:

	$
Material receipt and inspection cost	15,600
Power cost	19,500
Material handling cost	13,650

Three products - X, Y and Z are produced by workers who perform a number of operations on material blanks using hand held electrically powered drills. The workers have a wage rate of $9 per hour.

The following budgeted information has been obtained for the period ending 31 December 20X8:

	Product X	Product Y	Product Z
Production quantity (units	2,000	1,500	800
Batches of material	10	5	16
Data per product unit			
Direct material (sq. metres)	4	6	3
Direct material ($)	5	3	6
Direct labour (minutes)	24	40	60
Number of power drill operations	6	3	2

Overhead costs for material receipt and inspection, process power and material handling are presently each absorbed by product units using rates per direct labour hour.

An activity based costing investigation has revealed that the cost drivers for the overhead costs are as follows:

- Material receipt and inspection: number of batches of material.
- Process power: number of power drill operations.
- Material handling: quantity of material (sq. metres) handled.

Required:

(a) to prepare a summary which shows the budgeted product cost per unit for each of the products X, Y and Z for the period ending 31 December 20X8 detailing the unit costs for each cost element:

(i) using the existing method for the absorption of overhead costs and

(ii) using an approach which recognises the cost drivers revealed in the activity based costing investigation;

(iii) discuss the implications of Hensau making the decision to switch to ABC

(17 marks)

(b) to explain the relevance of cost drivers in activity based costing. Make use of figures from the summary statement prepared in (a) to illustrate your answer.

(8 marks)

(Total: 25 marks)

2 Planning with limiting factors

QUARKO CO

Questions

Quarko Co manufactures two products, Xerxes and Yoraths. No inventories are held. The following data relates to the budget for each unit of product.

	Xerxes	**Yorath**
Budgeted sales price	$51	$36
Direct material costs	$3	$4
Machining department time	4 hours	2 hours
Finishing department time	30 minutes	30 minutes
Variable overheads	$5	$6
Expected weekly demand (units)	100	100

Fixed costs are $13,000 per quarter. Direct materials are known to be in short supply, with only $600 worth being available to purchase each week. There are currently twelve people working in the machining department (paid $6 per hour) and two in the finishing department (paid $8 per hour). Due to the specialised nature of the work involved in each area, skills are not transferable between the departments. All employees work a 40-hour week. Assume that there are twelve weeks in the three month period.

Required:

(a) Calculate the shortfall (in hours) in each department if production were to reach the expected demand levels at the budgeted selling prices.

(3 marks)

(b) Calculate the optimum production plan per week if the company aims to maximise profits, and indicate the budgeted profit for the three month period.

(12 marks)

(c) Calculate how much Quarko would be willing to pay for more machining hours.

(5 marks)

(Total: 20 marks)

3 Pricing

CAR COMPONENTS INC

Questions

Car Components Inc ('CCI') manufactures and sells brake and suspension components used in the car industry. Some components are sold through garages and motor factors to the public but the bulk are sold direct to car manufacturers. In particular, CCI has provided components for many years to Victor Motors, its largest client, who takes 40% of CCI's output. Pricing has always been based on full production cost plus 25%.

Intense competition within the car industry has seen CCI's market share decline and last year it only operated at 70% capacity. CCI's clients have not been immune to industry pressure either and recently Victor Motors was bought out by a multinational manufacturer. The new owners have decided that the component contract would now be put out to tender each year and have made it clear that price, while not the only consideration, would be a major factor in deciding on the preferred supplier.

The management accountant of CCI has put together the following cost schedule for the CCI contract for the next year:

		$000
Materials	Note 1	5,000
Labour	Note 2	2,000
Variable overheads		1,000
Fixed overheads	Note 3	2,000
		10,000

Note 1: There is currently $500,000 of materials inventory. If not used on Victor Motor components this would be sold to a third party, but incur a net loss (after delivery charges are taken into account) of $100,000.

Note 2: Victor Motors components are highly specialised. If the contract was lost, then all of the current staff making Victor components would have to be made redundant. Redundancy costs re-estimated to be $500,000 now or $600,000 in one year's time.

Note 3: Fixed overheads consist of unavoidable company-wide costs and depreciation. If the contract is lost then machinery would be sold for $600,000 now or $450,000 in one year.

Required:

(a) Calculate the incremental cost of completing the Victor Motors contract for one more year and suggest a minimum tender price.

(8 marks)

(b) Discuss the factors that must be taken into consideration when bidding for the Victor contract.

(8 marks)

(Total: 16 marks)

4 Make or buy and other short-term decisions

ACCESS INC

Questions

Access Inc makes electrically-driven disability scooters aimed at elderly and/or disabled customers. At present wheels and tyres are bought from external suppliers but all other parts are manufactured in-house. The scooters have a strong reputation due mainly to innovative designs, special power units that can be recharged at home and seats that enable easy access for a wide range of disabilities. Access Inc also sells power units to other firms.

Current monthly costs are as follows.

	Seating Department	Power unit Department
	$	$
Costs		
Direct materials	9,300	4,140
Direct labour	12,600	9,450
Apportioned overheads	26,700	17,200
	48,600	30,790
Production level	60 units	90 units

Note: The power unit department currently produces 90 units a month – 60 being used in Access' own scooters, and 30 being sold externally at $376 each.

A new order has been won to supply an additional 10 scooters per month. However, the directors are considering how best to meet the additional demand:

- Sufficient capacity exists for the company to increase its monthly production to 70 scooters, except that making an extra 10 seating assemblies would require reallocation of labour and other resources from the power unit to the seating department. This would cut power unit output by 20 units per month.
- The alternative course would be to buy 10 seating assemblies from an outside supplier and fit the 10 power units from the present production of 90 units. The cheapest quote for seating assemblies is $610 per assembly.

Required:

(a) Based on the figures given, show whether Access should make or buy the extra seats. Discuss what other factors should be considered before a final decision is taken to make or to buy the extra seats.

(10 marks)

(b) Comment on the relevance of the apportioned overhead cost figures to your recommendation.

(2 marks)

(Total: 12 marks)

BROWN LTD

Questions

Brown Ltd is a company which has in inventory some materials of type XY which cost $150,000 but which are now obsolete and have a scrap value of only $42,000. Other than selling the material for scrap there are only two alternative uses for them.

Alternative 1

Converting the obsolete materials into a specialized product which would require the following additional work and materials

Material A	600 units
Material B	1,000 units
Direct labour:	
5,000 hours unskilled	
5,000 hours semi-skilled	
5,000 hours highly skilled	15,000 hours
Extra selling and delivery expenses	$54,000
Extra advertising	$36,000

The conversion would produce 900 units of saleable product and these could be sold for $600 per unit.

Material A is already in inventory and is widely used within the firm. Although present inventories together with orders already planned will be sufficient to facilitate normal activity, any extra material used by adopting this alternative will necessitate such materials being replaced immediately. Material B is also in inventory but it is unlikely that any additional supplies can be obtained for some considerable time because of an industrial dispute. At the present time material B is normally used in the production of product Z which sells at $780 per unit and incurs total variable cost (excluding material B) of $420 per unit. Each unit of product Z uses four units of material B.

The details of materials A and B are as follows:

	Material A	Material B
	$	$
Acquisition cost at time of purchase	200 per unit	20 per unit
Net realizable value	170 per unit	36 per unit
Replacement cost	180 per unit	

Alternative 2

Adapting the obsolete materials for use as a substitute for a sub-assembly which is regularly used within the firm. Details of the extra work and materials required are:

Material C	1,000 units
Direct labour:	
4,000 hours unskilled	
1,000 hours semi-skilled	
4,000 hours highly skilled	9,000 hours

1,200 units of the sub-assembly are regularly used per quarter at a cost of $1,800 per unit. The adaptation of material XY would reduce the quantity of the subassembly purchased from outside the firm to 900 units for the next quarter only. However, as the volume purchased would be reduced some discount would be lost, and the price of those purchased from outside would increase to $2,100 per unit for that quarter.

Material C is not available externally but is manufactured by Brown Ltd. The 1,000 units required would be available from inventories but would be produced as extra production. The standard cost per unit of material C would be as follows:

	$
Direct labour, 6 hours unskilled labour	36
Raw materials	26
Variable overhead, 6 hours at $2	12
Fixed overhead, 6 hours at $6	36
	110

The wage rates and overhead recovery rates for Brown Ltd are:

Variable overhead	$2 per direct labour hour
Fixed overhead	$6 per direct labour hour
Unskilled labour	$6 per direct labour hour
Semi-skilled labour	$8 per direct labour hour
Highly skilled labour	$10 per direct labour hour

The unskilled labour is employed on a casual basis and sufficient labour can be acquired to exactly meet the production requirements. Semi-skilled labour is part of the permanent labour force but the company has temporary excess supply of this type of labour at the present time. Highly skilled labour is in short supply and cannot be increased significantly in the short term; this labour is presently engaged in meeting the demand for product L which requires 4 hours of highly skilled labour. The contribution from the sale of one unit of product L is $48.

Required:

For each of the alternatives 1 and 2, prepare a cost-benefit analysis based on a schedule of relevant costs. Your answer should include a conclusion as to whether the inventories of material XY should be sold, converted into a specialized product (alternative 1) or adapted for use as a substitute for a sub-assembly (alternative 2).

(20 marks)

CARIBEE LTD

Question

(a) Next year's forecasted trading results for Caribee Ltd, a small company manufacturing three different types of product, are shown below:

	Product A	**Product B**	**Product C**	**Total**
Selling price /unit	$10	$12	$8	
	$000	$000	$000	$000
Sales	100	96	32	228
Variable cost of sales:				
Prime cost	40	38	13	91
Variable overhead	20	18	11	49
Share of general fixed				
Overhead	30	27	10	67
Profit/(loss)	10	13	(2)	21

Required:

Explain how the company's forecasted profits would be affected if product C were discontinued. It should be assumed that sales of the remaining products would not be affected; any other assumptions made should be included with your explanation

(4 marks)

(b) The production director of Caribee Ltd has just been informed that next year's supplies of a material used in the manufacture of each of the three products will be restricted to 92,000 kg; no substitute material is available and the estimated consumption of this restricted material, per product, is:

Product A	8 kg per unit
Product B	4 kg per unit
Product C	1 kg per unit

The sales director estimates that the maximum demand for each product is that which is shown in the original forecast in (a) above. Assume that inventories of materials, work in progress or finished goods cannot be carried.

Required:

Calculate the optimum quantities of products A, B and C which should be manufactured next year in order to maximise company profits.

(9 marks)

(Total 13 marks)

5 Risk and uncertainty

PRODUCT TOM

Questions

Product 'Tom' is a highly perishable commodity which can be sold on the retail market for $20 per case or for animal food @ $1 per case. Tom costs $10 per case from the wholesale market and is only suitable for sale at the retail market for up to 24 hours after purchase.

Orders for 'Tom' must be placed in advance each day.

Amanda, a market stall owner, has kept the following records of sales of the Tom over the past 50 days.

Daily sales	Days sold
10	15
20	25
30	10

Required:

(a) Prepare a summary that shows the forecast net margin earned by Amanda for each possible outcome.

(6 marks)

(b) On the basis of maximising expected value, advise Amanda.

(1 mark)

(c) On the basis of using the maximin and maximax criteria, advise Amanda.

(4 marks)

(d) Use minimax regret to advise Amanda.

(4 marks)

(Total: 15 marks)

SITERAZE LTD

Questions

Siteraze Ltd is a company which engages in site clearance and site preparation work. Information concerning its operations is as follows:

(i) It is company policy to hire all plant and machinery required for the implementation of all orders obtained, rather than to purchase its own plant and machinery.

(ii) Siteraze Ltd will enter into an advance hire agreement contract for the coming year at one of three levels high, medium or low, which correspond to the requirements of a high, medium or low level of orders obtained.

(iii) The level of orders obtained will not be known when the advance hire agreement contract is entered into. A set of probabilities have been estimated by management as to the likelihood of the orders being at a high, medium or low level.

(iv) Where the advance hire agreement entered into is lower than that required for the level of orders actually obtained, a premium rate must be paid to obtain the additional plant and machinery required.

(v) No refund is obtainable where the advance hire agreement for plant and machinery is at a level in excess of that required to satisfy the site clearance and preparation orders actually obtained.

A summary of the information relating to the above points is as follows:

Level of orders	Turn over	Probability	Plant and machinery hire costs	
	$000		Advance hire $000	Conversion premium $000
High	15,000	0.25	2,300	
Medium	8,500	0.45	1,500	
Low	4,000	0.30	1,000	
Low to medium				850
Medium to high				1,350
Low to high				2,150
Variable cost (as a percentage of turnover) 70				

Required:

(a) Prepare a summary which shows the forecast net margin earned by Siteraze Ltd for the coming year for each possible outcome.

(6 marks)

(b) On the basis of maximising expected value, advise Siteraze whether the advance contract for the hire of plant and machinery should be at the low, medium or high level.

(5 marks)

(c) Explain how the risk preferences of the management members responsible for the choice of advance plant and machinery hire contract may alter the decision reached in (b) above.

(6 marks)

(Total: 17 marks)

6 Budgeting 1

BUDGET BEHAVIOUR

Questions

For many organisations in both the private and public sectors the annual budget is the basis of much internal management information. When preparing and using budgets, however, management and the accountant must be aware of their behavioural implications.

Required:

(a) Briefly discuss four purposes of budgets.

(8 marks)

(b) Explain the behavioural factors which should be borne in mind and the difficulties of applying them in the process of budgeting and budgetary control.

(12 marks)

(Total: 20 marks)

7 Budgeting 2

ZERO-BASED BUDGETING

Questions

(a) Explain why Zero Based Budgeting might be a useful tool to employ to ensure that budgetary requirements are kept up to date.

(4 marks)

(b) Describe the steps needed to be undertaken in order to implement a Zero Based Budgeting system in respect of:

- the questioning of why expenditure needs to be incurred
- how a decision is made as to which activities should be provided with a budget, and
- what questions should be asked when budgeted activities need to be ranked to allocate scarce resources.

(8 marks)

(c) Critically assess the use of Zero Based Budgeting as a tool that might be used to motivate employees.

(6 marks)

(d) Explain the advantages of encouraging employee participation in budget setting.

(7 marks)

(Total: 25 marks)

8 Quantitative analysis

FASHION CO

Questions

Fashion Co, a manufacturer of fashion garments, is investigating whether or not to accept a retailer's order for 100,000 winter coats which will be codenamed Winners.

The following information is available in relation to Winners:

(1) The 100,000 garments will be manufactured in batches of 1000 garments. Fashion Co has been offered a price of $50,000 for each batch of 1000 garments supplied to the retailer.

(2) New machinery costing $250,000 will have to be purchased for this contract and it is estimated that this machinery will have a value of $25,000 at the end of the contract.

(3) A 75% learning curve will apply for the first 60 batches of Winners after which a steady state production time will apply. The labour time per batch after the first 60 batches will therefore be equal to the time for the 60th batch. The cost of the first batch was measured at $15,000. This was for 1500 hours at $10 per hour.

(4) Variable overhead will be 30% of the direct labour cost.

(5) Given the above learning effect for labour, direct material will be $10,000 per batch for the first ten batches, $7,500 per batch for the next ten and $6,000 per batch thereafter.

(6) A new warehouse will have to be rented for three months to store Winners at a cost of $5,000 per month

Fashion Co is seeking to achieve a net profit equal to 80% of the sales revenue arising from the manufacture and sale of Winners.

Required:

(a) Prepare detailed calculations to show whether the targeted 80% net profit margin will be achieved.

(12 marks)

(b) Calculate what length of time the second batch will take if the actual rate of learning is

(i) 70%

(ii) 80%

(5 marks)

(c) Suggest specific steps that Fashion Co could take to improve the net margin calculated above.

(8 marks)

(Total: 25 marks)

9 Standard costing and basic variances

MALCOLM REYNOLDS

Questions

Malcolm Reynolds makes and sells a single product, Product Q, with the following standard specification for materials:

	Quantity	Price per kg
	kg	$
Direct material X	12	40
Direct material Y	8	32

It takes 20 direct labour hours to produce one unit with a standard direct labour cost of $10 per hour.

The annual sales/production budget is 2,400 units evenly spread throughout the year. The standard selling price was $1,250 per unit.

The budgeted production overhead, all fixed, is $288,000 and expenditure is expected to occur evenly over the year, which the company divides into 12 calendar months. Absorption is based on direct labour hours.

For the month of October the following actual information is provided.

	$	$
Sales (220 units)		264,000
Cost of sales		
Direct materials used	159,000	
Direct wages	45,400	
Fixed production overhead	23,000	
		227,400
Gross profit		36,600
Administration costs		13,000
Selling and distribution costs		8,000
		21,000
Net profit		$15,600

Costs of opening inventory, for each material, were at the same price per kilogram as the purchases made during the month but there had been changes in the materials inventory levels, viz.:

	1 October	**30 October**
	kg	kg
Material X	680	1,180
Material Y	450	350

Material X purchases were 3,000 kg at $42 each.

Material Y purchases were 1,700 kg at $30 each

The number of direct labour hours worked was 4,600 and the total wages incurred $45,400.

Work-in-progress and finished goods inventories may be assumed to be the same at the beginning and end of October

Required:

(a) to present a standard product cost for one unit of product Q showing the standard selling price and standard gross profit per unit

(3 marks)

(b) to calculate appropriate variances for the materials, labour, fixed production overhead and sales, noting that it is company policy to calculate material price variances at time of issue to production (i.e. based on usage not purchases)and that the firm does not calculate mix and yield variances

(12 marks)

(c) to present a statement for management reconciling the budgeted gross profit with the actual gross profit

(5 marks)

(Total: 20 marks)

MAY LTD

Questions

May Ltd produces a single product for which the following data are given:

Standards per unit of product:

Direct material	4 kg at $3 per kg
Direct labour	2 hours at $6.40 per hour

Actual details for given financial period:

Output produced in units		38,000
Direct materials :		$
Purchased	180,000 kg for	504,000
Issued to production	154,000 kg	
Direct labour	78,000 hours worked for	546,000

There was no work in progress at the beginning or end of the period.

Required:

(a) Calculate the following variances:

(i) direct labour total;

(ii) direct labour rate;

(iii) direct labour efficiency;

(iv) direct materials total;

(v) direct materials price, based on issues to production;

(vi) direct materials usage.

(b) Discuss whether in each of the following cases, the comment given as the possible reason for the variance, is consistent with the variance you have calculated in (a) above.

(i) Direct labour rate variance: the union negotiated wage increase was $0.60 per hour lower than expected;

(ii) Direct labour efficiency variance: the efficiency of labour was commendable.

(iii) Direct materials price variance: the procurement manager has ignored the economic order quantity and, by obtaining bulk quantities, has purchased material at less than the standard price;

(iv) Direct materials usage variance: material losses in production were less than had been allowed for in the standard;

(20 marks)

SAM MENDES LTD

Questions

Sam Mendes Ltd is a manufacturing company which produces a variety of products. The following information relates to one of its products - Product W:

Standard cost data			$
Selling price			100
Direct Material X	5 kg @ $3/kg	15	
Direct Material Y	4 kg @ $5/kg	20	
Direct Labour	3 hrs @ $8/hr	24	
Variable overheads	3 hrs @ $6/hr	18	
			77
Contribution per unit			23

The budgeted production is 24,000 units per annum evenly spread throughout the year, with each calendar month assumed to be equal. March is a bad month in terms of sales revenue and it is expected that sales will only be 1,700 units during the month. Fixed overheads were expected to be $144,000 per year and are absorbed on a labour hour basis.

Actual results for the month of March were that sales were 2,200 units at a price of $90. There was no change in stock of finished goods or raw materials.

The purchases during the month were 11,300 kg of material X at $2.80 per kg and 8,300 kg of material Y at $5.30 per kg.

4,800 labour hours were worked at a rate of $8.10 per hour and 1,600 hours at $8.30.

The actual variable overheads for the period were $33,000 and the fixed overheads were $12,500.

The company uses an absorption costing system and maintains its raw materials account at standard.

Required:

Calculate appropriate variances for the month of March in as much detail as possible and present an operating statement reconciling budgeted profit with actual profit.

You are not required to calculate mix or yield variances as Sam Mendes Ltd does not sub-analyse the material usage or labour efficiency variances.

(20 marks)

10 Advanced variances

PAINT MIXERS INC

Questions

Paint Mixers Inc manufactures and sells a range of paints, including a high performance green paint that will attach to any surface without flaking or peeling.

The purchasing manager is responsible for buying the three ingredients (blue paint, yellow paint and a specialist bonding agent) that are used to make green paint whilst the production manager is responsible for mixing the paints and the volume and quality of green paint that is produced. Both the purchasing manager and the production manager joined the company on January 1st in the current year.

The standard ingredients of the green paint mix are as follows:

		$
2 litres blue paint	@ $2.5 per litre	= 5.0
7 litres yellow paint	@ $3.0 per litre	= 21.0
1 litre bonding agent	@ $10.0 per litre	= 10.0
Total cost to produce 9 litres of green paint		= 36.0
Standard cost of one litre of green paint		= 4.0

The Managing Director wishes to compare the performance of the purchasing manager and the production manager during their first three months at the company. The Sales Director has commented that sales are significantly up and appear to be on a rising trend, customers being very happy with the quality of the paint they have purchased in the first quarter of the year.

The Finance Director has produced the table below showing the variance results for the first three months of the year.

Table 1

F = Favourable A = Adverse

	$	$	$
	January	February	March
Material Price variance	3000 (A)	2000 (A)	1000 (A)
Material Mix variance	2000 (A)	750 (A)	100 (F)
Material Yield variance	4000 (A)	2000 (A)	50 (F)
Total variance	9000 (A)	4750 (A)	850 (A)

Production activity levels throughout the period varied little and the standard monthly material total cost was approximately $20,000.

Required:

(a) Using the information in Table 1:

I explain the significance of the three variances above (the price, mix and yield variances) and assess the extent to which each variance is controllable by the purchasing manager and the production manager.

(6 marks)

II Compare the performance of the purchasing manager and the production manager taking into account the cost variance results and the comments of the sales director.

(10 marks)

(b) The Finance Director has provided the following data in relation to April's production of 5000 litres of green paint.

Purchases in April

1000	litres blue paint	@ $2.6 per litre =	$2,600
4000	litres yellow paint	@ $3.1 per litre =	$12,400
500	litres bonding agent	@ $9.9 per litre =	$4,950
5500	litres		$19,950

Required:

Calculate the material price, mix and yield variances for April.

(9 marks)

(Total: 25 marks)

INSPECTION DEPARTMENT

Questions

A company has an inspection department in which operatives examine fruit in order to extract blemished input before the fruit is transferred to a processing department. The input to the inspection department comes from a preparation department where the fruit is washed and trimmed.

Inventories cannot be built up because of the perishable nature of the fruit. This means that the inspection department operations are likely to have some idle time during each working day.

A standard output rate in kilos per hour from the inspection process has been agreed as the target to be aimed for in return for wages paid at a fixed rate per hour irrespective of the actual level of idle time.

The standard data for the inspection department are as follows:

(i) standard idle time: as a percentage of total hours paid for: 20%;

(ii) standard wage rate per hour: $6.00;

(iii) standard output efficiency is 100% i.e., one standard hour of work is expected in each hour excluding idle time hours;

(iv) wages are charged to production at a rate per standard hour sufficient to absorb the standard level of idle time.

The labour variance analysis for November for the inspection department was as follows:

Variances	$	Expressed in % terms
Efficiency	1,050 (F)	2.2 (F)
Idle time	300 (A)	2.5 (A)
Wage rate	1,600 (A)	3.3 (A)

The actual data for the inspection department for the three months December to February are as follows:

	Dec.	Jan.	Feb.
Standard hours of output achieved	6,600	6,700	6,800
Labour hours paid for	8,600	8,400	8,900
Idle time hours incurred	1,700	1,200	1,400
Actual wages earned	$53,320	$54,600	$57,850

Required:

(a) to calculate the labour productive efficiency variances, excess labour idle time variances and labour rate variances for each of the three months December to February. Interpret the variances calculated.

(12 marks)

(b) in order to highlight the trend and materiality of the variances calculated in (a) above, express them as percentages of the standard

(6 marks)

(Total: 18 marks)

11 Performance measurement and control

SUCCESS SERVICES CO

Questions

The following information relates to Success Services Co, a provider of productivity-improving software to small and medium sized businesses.

The company was founded by and is wholly owned by David Speed. David Speed was MD of the business until the end of last year when he handed over control to his son, Michael Speed. Michael has an MBA and at the start of the current year introduced a number of initiatives aimed at giving greater authority and incentives to middle management.

You have been provided with financial information relating to the company in Appendix1. In Appendix 2 you have been provided with non-financial information which is based on the balanced scorecard format.

Appendix 1: Financial information	Current year	Previous year
Turnover ($'000)	4,900	3,400
Net profit	987	850
Interest cover	3x	5x
Average trade receivables days (industry average 40 days)	42	30

Appendix 2: Balanced Scorecard (Extract)

Customer perspective	Current year	Previous year
Number of customers	910	620
% of sales from new software products	24%	15%
% on time installation of software products	47%	65%
Average value of software sales	4,180	5,300
% customers who complained	4.5%	1.5%

Internal perspective	Current year	Previous year
Number of new software products launched	2	0
% of tenders for new business won	38%	24%

Learning and growth perspective	Current year	Previous year
Average annual no. of lines of code written by each programmer	4,800	4200
Average no. of bugs per 1000 lines of code	64	48
% staff who have completed software development course	10%	18%
Employee retention rate	75%	90%

Required:

(a) Using the information in Appendix 1 only, comment on the financial performance of the company (briefly consider growth, profitability, gearing and credit management)

(8 marks)

(b) Explain why non financial information such as that shown in appendix 2 is likely to give a more reliable indication of the likely future prosperity of the company than the financial information given in Appendix 1.

(5 marks)

(c) Using the data from Appendix 2 comment on the performance of the business. Include separate comments on the three perspectives, customer, internal and learning and growth, and provide a concluding comment on the overall performance of the business.

(12 marks)

(Total: 25 marks)

12 Divisional performance measurement and transfer pricing

KDS

Questions

KDS is an engineering company which is organised for management purposes in the form of several autonomous divisions. The performance of each division is currently measured by calculation of its return on investment (ROI). KDS's existing accounting policy is to calculate ROI by dividing the net assets of each division at the end of the year into the operating profit generated by the division during the year. Cash is excluded from net assets since all divisions share a bank account controlled by KDS's head office. Depreciation is on a straight-line basis.

The divisional management teams are paid a performance-related bonus conditional upon achievement of a 15% ROI target. On 20 December 20X5 the divisional managers were provided with performance forecasts for 20X5 which included the following:

Forecast	**Net assets at 31 December 20X5**	**20X5 operating profit**	**ROI**
	$	$	
Division K	4,400,000	649,000	14.75%
Division D	480,000	120,000	25.00%

Subsequently, the manager of Division K invited members of her management team to offer advice. The responses she received included the following:

- From the divisional administrator:

  'We can achieve our 20X5 target by deferring payment of a $90,000 trade debt payable on 20 December until 1 January. I should add that we will thereby immediately incur a $2,000 late payment penalty.'

- From the works manager:

  'We should replace a number of our oldest machine tools (which have nil book value) at a cost of $320,000. The new equipment will have a life of eight years and generate cost savings of $76,000 per year. The new equipment can be on site and operational by 31 December 20X5.'

- From the financial controller:

  'The existing method of performance appraisal is unfair. We should ask head office to adopt residual income (RI) as the key performance indicator, using the company's average 12% cost of money for a finance charge.'

Required:

(a) Compare and appraise the proposals of the divisional administrator and the works manager, having regard to the achievement of the ROI performance target in 20X5 and to any longer term factors you think relevant.

(12 marks)

(b) Explain the extent to which you agree or disagree with the financial controller's proposal.

(8 marks)

(c) Explain how non-financial performance measures could be used to assess the performance of divisions K and D.

(5 marks)

(Total: 25 marks)

13 Performance measurement in not-for-profit organisations

SATELLITE NAVIGATION SYSTEMS

Questions

S Inc installs complex satellite navigation systems in cars, at a very large national depot. The standard cost of an installation is shown below. The budgeted volume is 1,000 units installed each month. The operations manager is responsible for three departments, namely: purchasing, fitting and quality control. S Inc purchases navigation systems and other equipment from different suppliers, and most items are imported. The fitting of different systems takes differing lengths of time, but the differences are not more than 25% from the average, so a standard labour time is applied.

Standard cost of installation of one navigation system

	$	Quantity	Price ($)
Materials	400	1 unit	400
Labour	320	20 hours	16
Variable overheads	140	20 hours	7
Fixed overheads	300	20 hours	15
Total standard cost	1,160		

The operations department has gathered the following information over the last few months. There are significant difficulties in retaining skilled staff. Many have left for similar but better paid jobs and as a result there is a high labour turnover. Exchange rates have moved and commentators have argued that this will make exports cheaper, but S Inc has no exports and has not benefited. Some of the fitters have complained that one large batch of systems did not have the correct adapters and would not fit certain cars, but this was not apparent until fitting was attempted. Rent, rates, insurance and computing facilities have risen in price noticeably.

The financial results for September to December are shown below.

Operating statement for S Inc for September to December

	September	October	November	December	4 months
	$	$	$	$	$
Standard cost of actual output	1,276,000	1,276,000	1,102,000	1,044,000	4,698,000
Variances materials					
Price	5,505 F	3,354 F	9,520 A	10,340 A	11,0 A
Usage	400 A	7,200 A	800 A	16,000 A	24,400 A
Labour					
Rate	4,200 A	5,500 A	23,100 A	24,000 A	56,800 A
Efficiency	16,000 F	0	32,000 A	32,000 A	48,000 A
Variable overheads					
Expenditure	7,000 A	2,000 A	2,000 F	0	7,000 A
Efficiency	7,000 F	0	14,000 A	14,000 A	21,000 A
Fixed overheads					
Expenditure	5,000 A	10,000 A	20,000 A	20,000 A	55,000 A
Volume	30,000 F	30,000 F	15,000 A	30,000 A	15,000 F
Actual costs	1,234,095	1,267,346	1,214,420	1,190,340	4,906,201

A = adverse variance F = favourable variance

Required:

(a) Prepare a report to the operations manager of S Inc commenting on the performance of the company for the four months to 31 December. State probable causes for the key issues you have included in your report and state the further information that would be helpful in assessing the performance of the company.

(15 marks)

(b) Prepare a percentage variance chart for material usage and material price for the four-month period. Explain how this could be used to decide whether or not to investigate the variances.

(10 marks)

(Total: 25 marks)

Test your understanding answers

ROCHE (ABC)

Answers

(a)

	Type A	Type B	Type C	Total
Production units	30	120	150	300
Wood (metres) per chair	10	9	9	2730
Leather (metres) per chair	4	2	0	360
Labour hours per chair	24	20	16	5520

There are three single batches made per week, hence there are three set-ups per week. Assuming four weeks in one month, this becomes 12 set-ups per month.

	$	Cost driver	Cost driver rate
Set-up costs	5,600	12 set-ups	$466.67 per set-up
Purchasing and checking leather hides	4.000	360 m leather	$11.11 per metre
Purchase of wood	2,400	2,730 m wood	$0.879 per m
Quality inspection of leather seating	3,200	360 m leather	$8.889 per metre
Despatch and transport	6,000	300 chairs	$20 per chair
Administration and personnel costs	13,300	5,520 hours	$2.409 per hour

	Type A	Type B	Type C
Setup (4 setups each)	1,866.67	1,866.67	1,866.67
Purchasing leather	1,333.33	2,666.67	0
Purchasing wood	263.74	949.45	1,186.81
Quality inspection	1,066.67	2,133.33	0
Despatch	600.00	2,400.00	3,000.00
Administration	1734.78	5,782.61	5,782.61
Total overhead	**6,865.19**	**15,798.73**	**11,836.09**
Number of units	÷ 30	÷120	÷150
Overhead per unit	**228.84**	**131.66**	**78.91**
Material	85	60	50
Labour	120	100	80
Total Cost per unit	433.84	291.66	208.91
Selling price	395	285	225
Profit / Loss	**(38.84)**	**(6.66)**	**16.09**

(b) ABC is a more detailed analysis of overheads and shows a different view, i.e. that only the simple wooden chair Type C was making a profit. The more luxurious chairs are making a loss especially the top of range Type A model. This analysis may be of more use for long-term planning.

The plan for the other two leather chairs needs to be reviewed. Either the overhead costs for purchasing leather and quality control must be reduced and/or the sales prices need to be revised upwards. If these options are not viable then Roche may need to downsize the business and produce a single product, the Type C.

HENSAU LTD

Answers

(a)

(i) The existing overhead absorption rate is:

$$\frac{15{,}600+19{,}500+13{,}650}{(2{,}000\times24/60)+(1500\times40/60)+(800\times60/60)} = \frac{\$48{,}750}{2{,}600 \text{ hours}} \quad \$18.75 \text{ per hour}$$

Unit cost

	Product X	*Product Y*	*Product Z*
Direct material	5.00	3.00	6.00
Direct labour	3.60	6.00	9.00
Production overhead	7.50	12.50	18.75
	$16.10	$21.50	$33.75

(ii) Cost driver rates

Material receipt and inspection	$= \frac{\$15,600}{10+5+16} =$	\$503.23 per batch
Process power	$= \frac{\$19,500}{(2,000 \times 6)+(1,500 \times 3)+(800 \times 2)}$ = \$1.0773 per power drill operation	
Material handling	$= \frac{\$1,650}{(2,000\times4)+(1,500\times6)+(800\times3)}$	=\$0.70361 per sq. metre handled

	Product X	*Product Y*	*Product Z*
Direct material	5.00	3.00	6.00
Direct labour	3.60	6.00	9.00
Production overhead			
Material receipt/inspection (W1)	2.52	1.68	10.06
Process power (W2)	6.46	3.23	2.15
Material handling (W3)	2.81	4.22	2.11
Cost per unit	\$20.39	\$18.13	\$29.32

Workings

(W1) Material receipt/inspection

Product X 503.23/batch × 10 batches/2,000 units = \$2.52/unit
Product Y 503.23/batch × 5 batches/1,500 units = \$1.68/unit
Product Z 503.23/batch × 16 batches/800 units = \$10.06/unit

(W2) Process power

Cost/unit
Product X \$1.0773/operation × 6 operations = \$6.46
Product Y \$1.0773/operation ×3 operations = \$3.23
Product Z \$1.0773/operation × 2 operations = \$2.15

(W3) Material handling

Cost/unit
Product X \$0.70361/m^2 of material × 4m^2 = \$2.81
Product Y \$0.70361/m^2 of material × 6m^2 = \$4.22
Product Z \$0.70361/m^2 of material × 3m^2 = \$2.11

(iii) ABC will have the following implications for Hensau:

- Pricing can be based on more realistic cost data - the cost per unit under ABC has increased by 26.6% for product X whereas the cost per unit has decreased by 15.7% for product Y and 13.1% for product Z. The price of the products will be based on this more realistic cost and therefore pricing will be improved.
- Decision making will be improved - the more realistic product costs means that Hensau can focus on the products which give the highest margin and may decide to stop selling products which give a low or negative margin. Information on sales prices would be required in order to calculate these margins.
- Performance management can be improved - Hensay will focus on the most profitable products and, as a result, performance should be improved. In addition, control should be improved since the more realistic costs will form the basis of the budget.

(b) A cost driver is that factor which is most closely related to the way in which the costs of an activity are incurred. It could be said to cause the costs. Under ABC we do not restrict ourselves to just six possible OARs. We choose whatever basis we consider suitable to charge overheads to the product.

A good example of the superiority of ABC over absorption costing is that of process power in part (a) above. Under traditional absorption costing Product Z was the dearest for process power merely because it used the most labour hours per unit. - a fact completely and utterly unconnected with the way in which process power costs are incurred. Under ABC we investigate the business and actually take the time to find out what factor is most closely related to the cost and use that factor to charge overheads. Here we find that Product X should be the dearest because it uses the most power drill operations.

ABC supporters would argue that this cost/power drill operation is useful information. Costs are $1.0773 per power drill operation and thus product X costs $6.46. This cost is not insignificant and in fact is nearly as much as the direct material cost and direct labour cost combined. It would be inconceivable that the direct material costs and direct labour costs would not be very carefully controlled and yet under traditional absorption costing the process power costs would be included within the general overheads and would not be subject to such severe scrutiny. Under ABC, once we realise that power drill operations cost $1.0773 each then when designing new products, we would have better cost information and thus would be able to make better informed decisions.

QUARKO CO

Answers

(a) **Department shortfall**

	Machining	Finishing
Hours available per week	40 × 12	40 × 2
	= 480	= 80
Hours required for production		
Xerxes	100 × 4	100 × 0.5
Yorath	100 × 2	100 × 0.5
	= 600	= 100
Shortfall	120 hours	20 hours

(b) **Optimum production plan**

Let x = number of units of Xerxes produced each week

y = number of units of Yoraths produced each week

C = total contribution per week

Contribution per unit is as follows.

	Xerxes	Yorath
	$	$
Selling price	51	36
Less : Variable costs		
Direct material	(3)	(4)
Machining cost	(24)	(12)
Finishing cost	(4)	(4)
Variable overheads	(5)	(6)
Contribution per unit	15	10

The objective function is to maximise

C = 15x + 10y

subject to constraints of

(1)	Materials	3x + 4x	≤ 600
(2)	Machining time	4x + 2y	≤ 480
(3)	Finishing time	0.5x + 0.5y	≤ 80
	Non-negativity	x ≥ 0, y	≥ 0

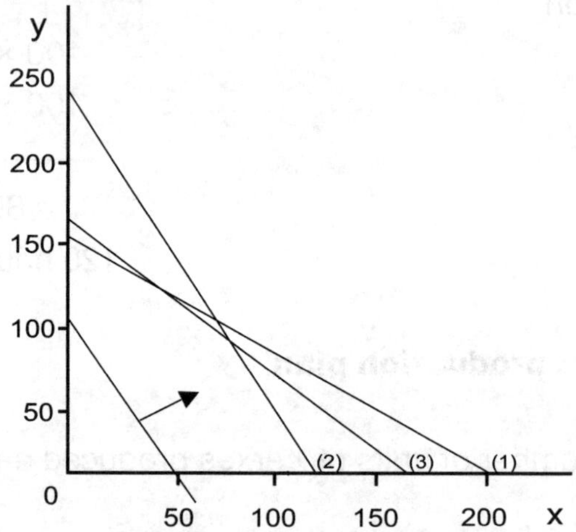

The optimum point is where (2) and (3) cross.

Thus simultaneously

Thus simultaneously		
solving	4x + 2y	= 480
and	0.5x + 0.5y	= 80
gives		
	x = 80 and	y = 80

Therefore the optimum production plan is to manufacture 80 of both.

This gives a budgeted profit as follows.

Contribution per week	= (15 × 80) + (10 × 80)
	= $2,000
Contribution for period	= $2,000 × 12
	= $24,000
Budgeted profit	= $(24,000 – 13,000)
	= $11,000

(c) **Obtaining extra machining hours**

Suppose one extra hour of machining time was available each week.

The optimal solution would now be found at the intersection of

	4x + 2y	= 481
and	0.5x + 0.5y	= 80

Solving these simultaneously gives x = 80½ and y = 79½ and a total contribution of

C = (15 x 80½) + (10 x 79½) = $2002.50

This is an increase of $2.50 over the existing optimal solution.

Quarko would thus be willing to pay a premium of $2.50 over the normal cost ($6 per hour) for extra machining hours or $8.50 an hour.

CAR COMPONENTS INC

Answers

(a) Relevant costs are as follows:

		$000
Materials	W1	4,400
Labour	W2	2,100
Variable overheads		1,000
Fixed overheads	W3	150
The minimum tender price is thus $7,650,000		**7,650**

Workings

(W1) Materials

	$000
Cost of buying extra materials (5,000-500)	(4,500)
Historic cost of items in inventory-junk	-
Opportunity saving re disposed costs	100
	(4,400)

(W2) Labour

	$000
Salary for next year	(2,000)
Incremental redundancy costs (600-500)	(100)
	(2,100)

(W3) fixed overheads

	$000
Unavoidable costs and depreciation	-
Fall in disposal proceeds	(150)
	(150)

(b) The following considerations should be taken into account when putting together a tender:

Costs

- A calculation of the extra costs involved in continuing the contract is shown in part (a) and would tend to indicate that the minimum price that could be offered is $7,650,000. At this price, however, CCI will not make any contribution to its profit.
- The calculation was based on the estimates provided but any change in these could lead to losses on the contract if this minimum price was quoted.
- The original pricing policy of cost plus 25% allowed CCI a large margin, which may have encouraged the company to ignore possible production inefficiencies.

Customers

- It is likely, however, that in order to secure this price in the past CCI will have had to reveal its costs to Victor Motors. This will have given the customer considerable power over CCI and is therefore a disadvantage of such a policy.
- However, the specialist nature of Victor Components would suggest that there may be quality issues and other teething problems if Victor awarded the contract to a new supplier.
- CCI has enjoyed a long business relationship with Victor and it is important that it continues to stay on good terms with the Victor management as they are likely to have a major impact on the awarding of the contract. They may also be able to advise on the likely price level of the successful bid
- CCI also needs to find out from Victor management how likely it is that the contract will actually be awarded to different companies each year, or whether there is a strong possibility that the initial successful bid will keep the contract for some time. The incremental costs in part (a) have been based on one year only.
- If CCI were to lose the contract, it may have an impact on its reputation in the car industry and a consequent loss of business from other sources.

Competition

- It will be important to know what other component manufacturers are likely to be involved in the tender. CCI must try to identify possible rivals and then estimate the general nature of such competitors' costs and therefore possible tender levels.
- Other firms are also likely to have spare capacity, so may bid on the basis of variable rather than full cost. However, competitors may have to commit to significant investment in new machinery and retooling to be able to make Victor's specialist components.

Other factors

- Victor currently accounts for 40% of CCI's output. Should the contract be lost CCI would result in operating at only 42% capacity (70 x 60%). It is questionable whether CCI would remain a viable operation under such circumstances.

ACCESS INC

Answers

(a) **Buy v Make**

	$
The buy alternative	
Cost of bought-in seats: 10 × $610	6,100
	6,100
The make alternative	
Sales of power units forgone: 20 × $376	7,520
Cost savings of making fewer batteries:	
(4,140 + 9,450) / 90 × 20	(3,020)
Increase in cost of making seats:	
(9,300 + 12,600) / 60 × 10	3,650
	8,150

Note: In either case, 10 external sales of power units will be lost as these are now used internally. You could have included the cost of these lost sales in both of the above calculations. It is quicker to recognise they are a common cash flow and hence not relevant to the decision.

On the basis of the information given the required seats should be bought in rather than made.

The following factors should also be considered before a final decision is made:

- The external supplier can produce seats of the same quality as Access Inc.
- Customers will not view bought-in seats as inferior.
- Dependence on an external supplier of extra seating assemblies does not lead to difficulty in maintaining sales volume in the future.
- None of the apportioned overheads are incremental – see answer to part (b) below.

- The average variable costs of production calculated above are constant over the relevant range of output, i.e. no economies of scale or learning effects result from the increased production.
- No goodwill is lost by the reduction in sales of power units to the existing external clients.
- No additional transport costs are encountered.
- Demand will be maintained at the increased level

(b) **Relevance of overhead cost figures**

In the short run apportioned overhead costs are not relevant to the decision, on the assumption that they are all fixed and not variable. Therefore the decision is not affected by their apportionment. However, in the long run all costs become relevant and, given the relatively high fixed cost/unit charge to the seating department, the decision may need further consideration.

BROWN LTD

Answers

Proceeds from sale of XY $42,000

Alternative 1

		$000	$000
Material A	Replacement value 600 x $180	108	
Material B	Benefit foregone from Z 1000/4 x $360	90	
			198
Unskilled labour 5000 x $6		30	
Semi skilled		Nil	
Skilled: Direct cost	5000 x $10	50	
Opportunity cost	5000/4 x $48	60	
			140
Variable overhead	15,000 x $2		30
Selling and delivery			54
Advertising			36
Total cost			458
Revenue 900 x $600			540
Benefit			82

Alternative 2

		$000	$000
Material C Variable cost per unit	$74 x 1000	74	
			74
Unskilled labour	4000 x $6	24	
Semi skilled		Nil	
Skilled: Direct cost	4000 x $10	40	
Opportunity cost	4000/4 x $48	48	
		—	
			112
Variable overhead	9,000 x $2		18
Total cost			204
Benefit Amount normally paid for sub-assembly 1200 x $1800		2160	
Less amount paid now	900 x $2100	(1890)	270
Net Benefit			66

In conclusion, Alternative 1 is preferable to both selling material XY and Alternative 2.

CARIBEE LTD

Answers

(a) The question asked how would the company's forecasted profits be affected if product C were discontinued. There are many ways of answering the question. The method shown below re-presents the table without Product C and using marginal costing principles, as absorption costing ideas would never help us a make a short term decision.

	Product A	*Product B*	*Total*
	$000	*$000*	*$000*
Sales	*100*	*96*	*196*
Variable cost	*60*	*56*	*116*
Contribution	*40*	*40*	*80*
Fixed cost			*67*
Profit			*13*

If Product C were discontinued, profit would fall by $8,000 to $13,000. The $8,000 represents the lost contribution from Product C.

I have assumed that the fixed costs will not change as a result of the decision. If some of the fixed costs were specific to Product C, then if Product C were discontinued then those specific fixed costs would be avoidable. I have assumed that this is not the case.

(b) This is a limiting factor decision - the limiting factor being kg of material. The decision is made on the basis of contribution per unit of limiting factor, i.e. contribution per kg of material.

	Product A	Product B	Product C
	$	$	$
Selling Price	10	12	8
Variable cost (W1)	6	7	6
Contribution per unit	4	5	2
No of kg per unit	8	4	1
Contribution per KG	0.5	1.25	2
Priority	3rd	2nd	1st

	Units	kg per Unit	Materials kg	Contribution $
Product C	4,000	1	4,000	8,000
Product B	8,000	4	32,000	40,000
Product A	7,000 Bal2	8	56,000Bal	28,000
			92,000	76,000
Fixed cost				67,000
Profit				9,000

Workings

(W1)

We are told the selling price per unit and the total sales in $000. We can therefore work out budgeted no. of units sold.

Product A	$100,000/$10	10,000 units
Product B	$96,000/$12	8,000 units
Product C	$32,000/$8	4,000 units

We can then work out the variable cost per unit:

Product A	($40,000 + $20,000)/10,000 units=	$6
Product B	($38,000 + $18,000)/8,000 units =	$7
Product C	($13,000 + $11,000)/4,000 units =	$6

PRODUCT TOM

Answers

(a)

Outcome - Demand	Probability	10 Cases	Action- Order 20 Cases	30 Cases
		$	$	$
10 cases	0.3	100	10	(80)
20 cases	0.5	100	200	110
30 cases	0.2	100	200	300
Expected net margin		100	143	91

(b) If Amanda wishes to maximise E.V. she should order 20 cases per day

(c) Maximin –

worst outcomes Amanda should order 10 cases/day	100	10	(80)
Maximin –			
best outcomes Amanda should order 30 cases/day	100	200	300

If Amanda wishes to maximise E.V. she should order 20 cases per day.

(d)

Demand	Order		
	10	20	30
	$	$	$
10	0	90	180
20	100	0	90
30	200	100	0
Maximum regret	200	100	180

Amanda should order 20 cases per day.

SITERAZE LTD

Answers

Level of advance order	Level of demand	Contribution	Fixed cost	Net margin
		$000	$000	$000
High	High	4,500	2,300	2,200
High	Medium	2,550	2,300	250
High	Low	1,200	2,300	(1,100)
Medium	High	4,500	1,500 + 1,300	1,700
Medium	Medium	2,550	1,500	1,050
Medium	Low	1,200	1,500	(300)
Low	High	4,500	1,000 + 2,150	1,350
Low	Medium	2,550	1,000 + 850	700
Low	Low	1,200	1,000	200

Workings

Variable cost is 70% of turnover, so contribution is 30% of turnover, therefore:

Demand	*Turnover* $000	*Contribution* $000
High	15,000	4,500
Medium	8,500	2,550
Low	4,000	1,200

	$000
High Level	
EV = 0.25 x 2,200 + 0.45 x 250 + 0.3 x (1,100)	=332.5
Medium Level	
EV = 0.25 x 1,700 + 0.45 x 1,050 + 0.3 x (300)	=807.5
Low Level	
EV = 0.25 x 1,350 + 0.45 x 700 + 0.3 x 200	=712.5

The advance order should be placed at the medium level. The expected net margin would be $807,500.

(c) This is a rather obscure reference to maximin and maximax. The tiny clue being that maximin is a risk-averse technique and maximax is a risk-seeking technique. (Expected values is a risk-neutral technique.)

Maximin

For each option calculate the worst possible outcome and then choose the best of those. This is a pessimist's viewpoint.

Option	*Worst Possible Outcome (Net Margin) ($000)*
High	(1,100)
Medium	(300)
Low	200

Using this criterion the advance order should be placed at the low level. Net margin would be at least $200,000. This attitude would be described as **risk-averse.**

Maximax

For each option calculate the best possible outcome and then choose the best of those. This is an optimist's point of view

Option	*Best Possible Outcome (Net Margin) ($000)*
High	2,200
Medium	1,700
Low	1,350

Using this criterion the advance order should be placed at the high level. Net margin could be as much as $2,200,000. This attitude would be described as **risk-seeking.**

Expected values

Using an expected value criterion would be described as **risk-neutral**. We have seen in part (b) that using this criterion would result in the advance order being placed at the medium level.

BUDGET BEHAVIOUR

Answers

(a) An answer should cover four purposes from the six provided below.

Planning

The budget is a major short-term planning device placing the overall direction of the company into a quarterly, monthly and, perhaps, weekly focus. It ensures that managers have thought ahead about how they will utilise resources to achieve company policy in their area.

Control

Once a budget is formulated a regular reporting system can be established so that the extent to which plans are, or are not, being met can be established. Some form of management by exception can be established so that deviations from plans are identified and reactions to the deviation developed if desirable.

Co-ordination

As organisations grow the various departments benefit from the co-ordination effect of the budget. In this role budgets ensure that no one department is out of line with the action of others. They may also hold in check anyone who is inclined to pursue his or her own desires rather than corporate objectives.

Communication

The construction of the budget can be a powerful aid to defining or clarifying the lines of horizontal or vertical communication within the enterprise. Managers should have a clearer idea of what their responsibilities are, what is expected of them, and are likely to work better with others to achieve it.

Performance evaluation

When budgets are 'tailored' to a department or manager they become useful tools for evaluating how the manager or department is performing. If sales targets are met or satisfactory service provided within reasonable spending limits then bonus or promotion prospects are enhanced.

Motivation

The value of a budget is enhanced still further if it not only states expectations but motivates managers to strive towards those expectations. This is more likely achieved if a manager has had some involvement in the budget construction, understands its implications and agrees it is fair and controllable by him/her.

(b) If budgetary control is to be successful, attention must be paid to behavioural aspects, i.e. the effect of the system on people in the organisation and vice versa. The following are some of the points which should be borne in mind:

Budget difficulty

It is generally agreed that the existence of some form of target or expected outcome is a greater motivation than no target at all. The establishment of a target, however, raises the question of the degree of difficulty or challenge of the target. If the performance standard is set too high or too low then sub-optimal performance could be the result. The degree of budget difficulty is not easy to establish. It is influenced by the nature of the task, the organisational culture and personality factors. Some people respond positively to a difficult target others, if challenged, tend to withdraw their commitment.

Budgets and performance evaluation

The emphasis on achievement of budget targets can be increased, but also the potential for dysfunctional behaviour, if the budget is subsequently used to evaluate performance. This evaluation is frequently associated with specific rewards such as remuneration increases or improved promotion prospects. In such cases it is likely that individuals will concentrate on those items which are measured and rewarded neglecting aspects on which no measurement exists. This may result in some aspects of the job receiving inadequate attention because they are not covered by goals or targets due to the complexity of the situation or the difficulty of measurement.

Managerial style

The use of budgets in evaluation and control is also influenced by the way they are used by the superior. Different management styles of budget use have been observed, for example:

Budget constrained	–	placing considerable emphasis on meeting budget targets
Profit conscious	–	where a balanced view is taken between budget targets, long-term goals and general effectiveness
Non-accounting	–	where accounting data is seen as relatively unimportant in the evaluation of subordinates.

The style is suggested to influence, in some cases, the superior/subordinate relationship, the degree of stress and tension involved and the likelihood of budget attainment. The style adopted and its implications are affected by the environment in which management is taking place. For example, the degree of interdependency between areas of responsibility, the uncertainty of the environment and the extent to which individuals feel they influence results are all factors to consider in relation to the management style adopted and its outcomes.

Participation

It is often suggested that participation in the budget process and discussion over how results are to be measured has benefits in terms of budget attitude and performance. Views on this point are varied however, and the personality of the individuals participating, the nature of the task (narrowly defined or flexible) and the organisation structure influence the success of participation. But a budget when carefully and appropriately established can extract a better performance from the budgetee than one in which these considerations are ignored.

Bias

Budgetees who are involved in the process from which the budget standards are set are more likely to accept them as legitimate. However, they may also be tempted to seize the opportunity to manipulate the desired performance standard in their favour. That is, they may make the performance easier to achieve and hence be able to satisfy personal goals rather than organisational goals. This is referred to as incorporating 'slack' into the budget. In this context there may be a relationship between the degree of emphasis placed on the budget and the tendency of the budgetee to bias the budget content or circumvent its control.

Any organisational planning and control system has multiple objectives but primary amongst these is encouraging staff to take organisationally desirable actions. It is never possible to predict with certainty the outcomes of all behavioural interaction however it is better to be aware of the various possible behavioural implications than to be ignorant of them.

ZERO-BASED BUDGETING

Answers

Note: this answer is longer than required in the exam but gives an indication of the potential scope of an answer.

Introduction

(a) Zero Based Budgeting (ZBB) is a method of budgeting that re-examines, at each budgeting exercise, whether the budgeted activity is to be funded at any level. Hence, the budgeting exercise begins at **a zero or nil cost base**. It is a device that is particularly useful when an organisation is unsure if its costs are at the most efficient levels. Most efficient costs are not the same as minimum levels, since very low costs might impinge on service or product quality. The purpose of ZBB is to overcome inefficient forms of budgeting that might lead to **slack practices**, which consume more resources than the most effective and efficient organisations face.

(b) There are a series of steps that would ordinarily be taken in order to implement an effective ZBB system.

The questioning of why expenditure needs to be incurred

The development of a questioning attitude to activities that incur costs is the first step to ensuring that costs are kept to most efficient levels. It is important to recall that ZBB, in the short term, can only change costs over which the organisation has short-term control. Longer-term, or period costs, can only be changed over a longer horizon. Taxes and other regulatory costs cannot be the focus of ZBB because they are difficult to influence.

Thus ZBB can be immediately effective where costs can be related to identifiable activities. The questions that might emerge in such situations are as follows:

Can costs associated with an activity be isolated? If costs cannot be identified to a particular activity to a degree that provides management with confidence that they can change the costs then there is little point in applying ZBB techniques to the cost.

An even more basic question is to ask how important the activity is to the business and what, if the costs can be identified, is the total cost saving that might result should the activity be stopped. In this respect, it is important to identify effects on costs elsewhere in the business. If the activity to be stopped absorbed fixed costs, then the fixed costs will have to be re-apportioned without absorption to the activity that is to be stopped.

Moreover, there may be joint costs such that stopping one activity may have an uncertain effect on joint costs incurred with another activity. Is the activity in question the cheapest way of providing the service or contribution to production? Thus, it is important not to ask simply if the costs relating to the activity are the most efficient, but are there alternatives that might reduce costs still further and still maintain a given level of service or production.

A more fundamental question about conducting ZBB processes is whether the benefits of employing ZBB outweigh the costs. It is important to appreciate that conducting a ZBB exercise is not a costless process if, as will inevitably be the case, management time is consumed.

How a decision is made as to which activities should be provided with a budget?

Budgeted activities should be capable of being monitored and controlled. If an activity is recognised as a budget centre, and is going to be subject to a ZBB process, then it is important that management undertake the task of monitoring costs in relation to activity and taking corrective action when appropriate. Thus, if an activity consumes resources and is capable of being monitored and controlled then it should be provided with a budget. This will then make the activity subject to ZBB processes.

'Decision packages' are sometimes referred to in the context of ZBB and activities. These relate to how activities can be described when thinking about how ZBB can be used to judge an activity.

There are two types of decision activity:

(1) **Mutually exclusive decisions:** When ZBB assessments are made of an activity, alternative courses of action are sometimes benchmarked against existing activities. A choice is then made over which activity might be the preferable course of action. The preferred choice will involve budgeted information, but may also involve other factors such as product quality and service level provision.

(2) **Incremental decisions:** ZBB assessments are often related to the level of activity within a budget centre. Thus, there will be a minimum level of activity that provides the essential level of product or service. This is often referred to as the **'base' activity**. Further levels of activity are then incremental and, subject to correctly identifying and isolating the variable costs related to an activity, ZBB assessments can be made separately of both the base and the incremental activities. This division might then provide management with an understanding of the degree of flexibility the organisation has.

What questions should be asked when budgeted activities need to be ranked to allocate scarce resources?

The allocation of scarce resources is a key management task. Scarce resources will have to be allocated to the activities of a business in terms of providing appropriate labour and materials, along with any other costs related to an activity. Whilst ZBB is most often applied to support activities the technique can also be applied to a production process.

Some sorting of **ranking** will have to be applied in order to determine which activities are funded by a budget against those that are not. The key question for budgeting purposes relates to:

(1) defining the appropriate decision package (as described above)

(2) the importance of the activity in relation to the organisation in terms of:

– support for the organisation's objective (for example, maximising shareholder wealth)

– support for other service or product activities

(3) how the ranking system is to be used:

– are all activities to be funded above a certain rank, or

– is there a scaling of funds allocated against funds requested as determined by the rank, or

– is there a combination of methods?

Essentially, a judgement has to be made by management of the benefit of the activity to the organisation. Theoretically, this is best achieved by determining deprival value. In practice, deprival values are difficult tools and some level of arbitrary judgement has to take place in which non-financial factors might play a significant role.

(c) **Critical assessment of the use of Zero Based Budgeting as a tool that might be used to motivate employees**

The motivation of employees is one of the most difficult tasks facing management since the problems are complex and not always referable to financial performance indicators. To the extent that employees are not responsive to financial performance indicators then ZBB is going to be less effective as a device to motivate employees.

The problem of employee motivation is one of achieving goal congruence with the organisational objectives. ZBB can be useful in this respect as a method of tackling the problem of incentivising employees to achieve targeted performance when a clear understanding of the activities and their related decision packages is essential for the management tasks of monitoring and controlling an activity.

In this respect ZBB has the following advantages

(d) (1) It ensures that only forward looking objectives are addressed. This limits the potential for historical abuses in budget-setting to be established. Employees can be set targets that are consistent with the future objectives of the organisation.

(2) Building 'budget slack' is minimised because, in principle, the entire costs of an activity are reviewed at each budget-setting stage. Employees are then set realistic targets that relate to activity levels that are the most efficient.

(3) Managers are made to understand, as part of the ZBB process, the activity itself. This reduces tension between those who decide (management) and those who have to implement manager decisions. Claims that management do not really understand the nature of an activity are thus reduced.

(4) ZBB encourages flexibility in employees since they know that, potentially, activities may be stopped. Flexibility induces goal consistency by enabling incentive schemes to reflect activity. In other words, employees are more likely to be responsive to management directives if they are aware and trust that the budget setting process encourages and supports payments that are responsive to flexibility.

(e) **The advantages of encouraging employee participation in budget-setting**

Generally, participative budget-setting will result in:

(1) An informed budget-setting process, such that management are aware of the detail of budgeted activities as provided by the people who work daily within the budgeted activity.

(2) Avoiding the criticism that budgets are unrealistic.

(3) Reducing the adverse effects of budget imposition when difficult management decisions have to be made (e.g. staff reduction).

(4) Employees become aware and more involved in the management activities of the organisations. To the extent that they become more aware, then a greater understanding of the needs of the organisation as a whole is reached.

(5) Co-ordination within an activity might be improved. If activities are jointly budgeted, or are part of the same process, then co-ordination between activities might be improved.

(6) Budgetary slack may be reduced as management become more aware of the operational activities within an activity.

(7) Achievable budgets are more likely to be set.

(8) When budgets are not met management are more likely to have a deeper knowledge of the operational issues involved.

(9) There is less risk that budgets will be undermined by subordinates.

FASHION CO

Answers

(a)

		$	$
	100 batches		
Sales	@ $50,000		5,000,000
Costs:			
Direct materials	W1	655,000	
Direct labour	W2	229,460	
Variable overhead	W3	68,838	
Rent		15,000	
Depreciation		225,000	
			(1,193,298)
Net profit			3,806,702
Net margin			76.13%

The targeted net profit margin of 80% of sales will not be achieved.

Workings

(1) Direct materials

	$
First 10 @ $10,000	100,000
Second 10 @ $7,500	75,000
Remaining 80 @ $6,000	480,000
Total	655,000

(2) Direct labour

All batches after the first 60 will take the same time as the 60th batch. To calculate the time for the 60th batch we need to take the time of 59 batches from the time of 60 batches.

In the learning curve formula b = logr / log 2 = log0.75 / log2 = –0.415

60 batches	**59 batches**
Cumulative average time per batch $y = ax^b$	Cumulative average time per batch $y = ax^b$
$y = 1{,}500 \times 60^{-0.415}$	$y = 1{,}500 \times 59^{-0.415}$
y = 274.3 hours per batch	y = 276.2 hours per batch
Total time for 60 batches	Total time for 59 batches
= 274.3 × 60	= 276.2 × 59
= 16,458.0 hours	= 16,295.8 hours

Time to make the 60th batch = 16,458.0 – 16,295.8 = 162.2hours

Total time for the 100 batches = 16,458 + (162.2 × 40) = 22,946 hours.

Total cost of the first 100 batches = 22,946 × $10 per hour = $229,460

(3) Variable overhead is 30% of direct labour = 30% × 229,460 = $68,838

(b) The learning rate measures the relationship between the average time taken between two points when production doubles. Since we:

- can work out the average rate for the two batches by X the time of the first batch by the learning factor
- can then work out the total time taken for the two batches by doubling the average rate
- know the time of **first** batch (1500 hours) we can then calculate the time of the **second** batch by simply deducting the time of the first batch from the average rate.

70%

Time for first batch	1500
Average time taken for two batches @ 70% 1500 × 0.7	1050
Therefore total time for two batches 2 × 1050	2100
Therefore time taken for second batch (2100 – 1500)	600

80%

Time for first batch	1500
Average time taken for two batches @ 80% 1500 × 0.8	1200
Therefore total time for two batches 2 × 1050	2400
Therefore time taken for second batch (2400 – 1500)	900

Note: The 70% learning rate produces a lower average time (1050 hours) than the 80% learning rate (1200 hours) and hence is the faster learning rate of the two.

(c) Steps that could be taken to improve the net profit margin include:

- Negotiate a higher price with the retailer. The ability of Fashion Co to negotiate a higher price will depend upon a number of factors including its reputation for quality and delivery and the ease with which the retailer could find alternative suppliers that can deliver garments of the required quality and quantity by the required delivery date.
- Reduce the labour cost by identifying a simpler and faster production method that does not affect the quality or appearance of the finished garment.
- Increase the learning rate. This may be possible via a review of the training procedures and the recruitment of more highly skilled staff. Both these approaches however are likely to involve additional time and costs in the short term.
- Explore the possibility of outsourcing the production to another manufacturer in a lower cost area. This is a major step that would require careful evaluation but it has the substantial attraction - in addition to the possibility of reducing production costs – of eliminating depreciation costs of $225,000 since Fashion Co would no longer have to purchase machinery to satisfy this order.
- Explore the use of substitute materials that would not prejudice the quality or appearance of the garment. Any changes would have to be discussed and agreed with the retailer.
- Investigate ways to reduce the level of variable overhead
- Seek to deliver production direct to the retailer and thereby avoid the storage costs of $15,000.

MALCOLM REYNOLDS

Answers

(a) **Standard product cost**

	$	$
Standard selling price		1,250
Material X 12 kg @ $40/kg	480	
Material Y 8 kg @ $32/kg	256	
Direct labour 20 hrs @ $10/hr	200	
Production overhead (W1)	120	
		1,056
Standard gross profit		194

(b) **Material X variances**

	$	
SQSP		
12 kg/unit × 220 units × $40/kg	= 105,600	Usage
AQSP		$5,600 F
2,500 kg (W2) × $40/kg	= 100,000	
AQAP		$5,000 A
2,500 kg x $42/kg	= 105,000	Price

Material Y variances

	$	
SQSP		
8 kg/unit × 220 units × $32/kg	= 56,320	Usage
AQSP		$1,280 A
1,800 kg (W2) × $32/kg	= 57,600	
AQAP		$3,600 F
1,800kg × $30/kg	= 54,000	Price

Direct labour variances

	$	
SHSR		
20 hrs/unit × 220 units × $10/hr	= 44,000	Efficiency
AHSR		$2,000 A
4,600 hrs × $10/hr	= 46,000	
AHAR		$600 F
	= 45,400	Rate

Fixed Overhead Expenditure variance

	$
Budgeted Cost (W3)	24,000
Actual Cost	23,000
	1,000 F

Fixed Overhead Volume variance

Units	
Budgeted output (2,400 units p.a. ÷ 12 months)	200
Actual output	220
	20 F
× Std Fixed Overhead Cost per unit	×120
	$2,400 F

Sales price variance

	$
Std selling price	1,250
Actual selling price ($264,000/220 units)	1,200
	50 A
× Actual no of units sold	× 220
	$11,000 A

Selling volume profit variance

Units	
Budgeted sales	200
Actual sales	220
	20 F
x Std profit per unit	× 194
	$3,880 F

(c) **Operating Statement**

				$
Budgeted gross profit (W4)				38,800
Sales volume profit variance				3,880 F
Standard profit on actual sales				42,680
Sales price variance				11,000 A
				31,680
		Favourable	**Adverse**	
Cost variances				
Material X	Usage	5,600		
	Price		5,000	
Material Y	Usage		1,280	
	Price	3,600		
Direct labour	Efficiency		2,000	
	Rate	600		
Fixed Prod	Expenditure	1,000		
overhead	Volume	2,400		
		13,200	8,280	4,920 F
Actual gross profit				36,600

Workings

(W1) Fixed overhead per unit = $288,000/2,400 units = $120 per unit

(W2)	Material X	Material Y
	Kg	Kg
Op inventory	680	450
+ Purchases	3,000	1,700
	3,680	2,150
- Cl inventory	1,180	350
Materials issued/used	2,500	1800

(W3) Budgeted fixed overhead per month = $288,000/12 = $24,000

(W4) Budgeted profit = 200 units × $194 = $38,800

MAY LTD

Answers

(a) **Direct labour variances**

SHSR					
2 hrs/unit × 38,000 units	×	$6.40/hr	=	486,400	Efficiency $12,800 A
AHSR					
78,000 hrs	×	$6.40/hr	=	499,200	
AHAR					$46,800 F Rate
	×		=	546,000	

(i) $59,600 A ($12,800 A + $46,800 A)

(ii) $46,800 A

(iii) $12,800 A

Direct material variances

SQSP					
4 kg/unit × 38,000 units	×	$3/kg	=	456,000	Usage
AQSP					$6,000 A
154,000 kg	×	$3/kg	=	462,000	
AQAP					$30,800 F
154,000 kg	×	$2.80/kg	=	431,200	Price

The requirement in part (v) asks for the price variance to be calculated at the time of issue, which is the same as at the time of usage, so the quantity must be the quantity issued/ used.

The actual price of the material is $504,000/180,000 kg

(iv) $24,800 F ($6,000 A + $30,000 F)

(v) $30,800 F

(vi) $6,000 A

(b)

(i) Inconsistent. In fact the wage increase was $0.60 per hour higher than expected.

(ii) Inconsistent. The workforce were inefficient.

(iii) Consistent. A bulk purchase discount should lead to cheaper materials and hence a favourable material price variance.

(iv) Inconsistent. If the losses had been less than expected then the usage variance would have been favourable.

SAM MENDES LTD

Answers

Standard product cost

			$
Standard Selling price			100
Material X	5 kg @ $3/kg	15	
Material Y	4 kg @ $5/kg	20	
Direct labour	3 hrs @ $8/hr	24	
Variable overheads	3 hrs @ $6/hr	18	
Fixed overheads (W1)	3 hrs @ $2/hr	6	
			83
Standard profit per unit			17

Material X variances

SQSP 5 kg/unit × 2,200 units	×	$3/kg	=	33,000	
					Usage $900 A
AQSP 11,300 kg	×	$3/kg	=	33,900	
					$2,260 F Price
AQAP 11,300 kg	×	$2.8/kg	=	31,640	

Material Y variances

SQSP 4 kg/unit × 2,200 units	×	$5/kg	=	44,000	
					Usage $2,500 F
AQSP 8,300 kg	×	$5/kg	=	41,500	
					$2,490 A Price
AQAP 8,300 kg	×	$5.30/kg	=	43,990	

SHSR 3 hrs/unit × 2,200 units	×	$8/hr	=	52,800	
					Efficiency $1,600 F
AHSR 6,400 hrs	×	$8/hr	=	51,200	
					$960 A Rate
AHAR (4,800 hrs × $8.10) + (1,600 hrs × $8.30)			=	52,160	

Variable overhead variances

		$	
SHSR			
3 hrs/unit x 2,200 units x $6/hr	=	39,600	Efficiency
AHSR			$1,200 F
6,400 hrs x $6/hr	=	38,400	
AHAR			$5,400 F
	=	33,000	Expenditure

Labour variances

Fixed production overhead variances

Budgeted cost	= 12,000	Expenditure $500	A
Actual cost	= 12,500		

SHSR 3 hrs/unit × 2,200 units	×	$2/hr	= 13,200	Efficiency	
AHSR 6,400 hrs	×	$2/hr	= 12,800	$400	F
BHSR 6,000 hrs	×	$2/hr	= 12,000	$800 Capacity	F

Selling volume profit variance

	Units
Budgeted sales	1,700
Actual sales	2,200
	500 F
x Std profit per unit	x 17
	$8,500 F

Selling price variance

	$
Std selling price	100
Actual selling price	90
	10 A
x Actual No of units sold	x 2,200
	$22,000 A

Operating Statement

	$
Budgeted gross profit (W2)	28,900
Sales volume profit variance	8,500 F
Standard profit on actual sales	37,400
Selling price variance	22,000 A
	15,400

		Favourable	Adverse	
Cost variances		$	$	
Material X	Usage		900	
	Price	2,260		
Material Y	Usage	2,500		
	Price		2,490	
Direct labour	Efficiency	1,600		
	Rate		960	
Variable Overhead	Efficiency	1,200		
	Expenditure	5,400		
Fixed Prod overhead	Expenditure		500	
	Efficiency	400		
	Capacity	800		
		14,160	4,850	9,310 F
Actual profit (W3)				24,710

Workings

(W1)

Budgeted fixed overheads are $144,000 per year and the budgeted output is 24,000 units for the year. Thus the budgeted/standard fixed cost per unit is $6.

The overheads are absorbed on direct labour hours and each unit takes 3 hours. Therefore the budgeted/standard fixed overhead is $2 per hour ($6 ÷ 3 hours).

(W2)

Budgeted profit = $17 per unit x Budgeted SALES of 1,700 units = $28,900.

(W3)		$	$
Sales	2,200 units x $90		198,00
Direct Material X	11,300 kg x $2.80/kg	31,640	
Direct Material Y	8,300 kg x $5.30/kg	43,990	
Direct labour	(4,800 hrs x $8.10) + (1,600 hrs x $8.30)	52,160	
Variable overheads		33,000	
Fixed overheads		12,500	
			173,290
Actual Profit			24,710

PAINT MIXERS INC

Answers

(a)

(i) **Significance and controllability of the variances**

Material price variance

This variance indicates whether Paint Mixers Inc has paid more (adverse) or less (favourable) for its materials input than the standard price set for the period. An adverse variance, for example, could be the result of an unexpected increase in raw material prices that has been passed on by their bonding agent suppliers.

Price variances are controllable to the extent that the purchasing manager can periodically review potential sources of supply to ensure that they are sourcing their materials from a competitively priced supplier. With the blue and yellow paints there is likely to be a large number of potential suppliers so purchasing managers should be able to threaten to switch suppliers to get good deals. The company is however in a weaker position in relation to the pricing of bonding agent and may be unable to prevent price rises.

Material mix variance

This variance arises when the ingredients are not mixed in standard proportions and it indicates whether the actual mix is cheaper or costlier than the standard mix. For example, adding more bonding agent (relatively very expensive) and less blue paint (relatively cheap) will increase the cost of the mix. A more expensive mix will produce an adverse variance. The recipe determines the mix and the recipe is determined by the production manager and hence is entirely under the control of the production manager.

Material yield variance

A yield variance arises when the output is less or more than the input should have produced and is a measure of the productivity of the manufacturing process. 10 litres of input produces 9 litres of green paint. If more than 9 litres of green paint is produced from the 10 litres input the variance is favourable. A favourable yield variance can be the result of operational efficiency (eg reduced wastage) or a change in the mix.

The production manager controls the production process and is therefore able to manage the yield. In particular, the production manager should be able to ensure that the appropriate quality of materials are used and that wastage is minimized.

(ii) **Performance of the purchasing manager and the production manager**

Cost efficiency

The purchasing manager was responsible for a series of significant adverse material price variances in the first three months of the year which averaged approx 10% of the standard monthly spend.

The adverse variances have steadily declined over the three months (from $3000 to $1000) and if this level of progress is maintained a favourable variance will arise in April. We do not know whether the adverse variances were the result of poor purchasing decisions or the inevitable result of, say, increased commodity prices. The steadily improving trend suggests that the purchasing manager is in control of the situation and that he may have inherited a purchasing environment of rising prices that were not fully reflected in the cost standards. The comments of the Sales Director suggest that the purchasing manager has not sacrificed quality in order to achieve this improving position.

The production manager was also responsible, in his first two months, for significant adverse variances - in relation to both the mix of materials used and the yield achieved. His performance in the first month was exceptionally poor – the adverse mix and yield variances of $6,000 equalled approximately 30% of the standard monthly spend.

The production manager controls both the mix and the production process and must bear responsibility for this initial very poor performance. That said, in month three, the production manager has achieved modest favourable mix and yield variances ($100 and $50), maintaining the improving trend that started in month two. His very poor initial performance may, in part, have been the result of an inadequate induction process or could have reflected a conscious attempt to improve the quality of the output by increasing the quality of the mix. It may also be possible that certain customers requested a different shade of green requiring a change in the mix of blue and yellow paint.

Whatever the background, the very poor yield performance in January suggests that his changes to the mix had very unfortunate consequences in terms of productivity.

Quality

The managing director will have been concerned in January and February that the increasing sales and customer satisfaction levels reported by the sales director may have been bought at a high price.

The comment of the sales director however that sales continue to rise suggests that the new production manager – after some initial costly experimentation - has managed to identify a new mix that is both cost efficient and very appealing to customers.

Overall

There was cause for concern in January and February over the performance of both new appointments.

The performance of the purchasing manager still continues to be of concern but is on an improving trend, which, if maintained, should ensure that costs are brought fully under control.

The production manager, after a very worrying start, appears now to be delivering green paint using a recipe that is both economical and popular with customers.

(b) **Variance calculations**

Material price variance

	Standard	Actual	Difference	Actual quantity	Variance
Blue paint	$2.5	$2.6	–0.1	1000	100 (A)
Yellow paint	$3.0	$3.1	–0.1	4000	400 (A)
Bonding agent	$10.0	$9.9	0.1	500	50 (F)
					450 (A)

Note: Compare the standard prices with the actual prices and multiply the difference by the actual amounts bought

Material mix variance

Standard Mix

a. Blue paint:	5500 × 0.2 = 1100 litres
b. Yellow paint:	5500 × 0.7 = 3850 litres
c. Bonding agent	5500 × 0.1 = 550 litres

Actual mix	Difference	Standard price	Variance
1000 litres	100 litres @	$2.5 =	$250 (F)
4000 litres	150 litres @	$3.0 =	$450 (A)
500 litres	50 litres @	$10.0 =	$500 (F)
5500			$300 (F)

Note

(1) Calculate the proportions that make up the standard mix.

(2 : 7: 1) = 0.2 / 0.7 / 0.1.

(2) Apply these proportions to the purchases made in April of 5500 litres to give the standard cost of a standard mix.

(3) Compare the results with the actual mix and × the difference by the standard price to give the mix variance.

Material yield variance

5000 – 4950 = 50 litres × $4 per litre = $200 (F)

Note

(1) Calculate standard cost of 1 litre of green paint mix ($36 ÷ 9 litres = $4 per litre)

(2) Calculate conversion factor (converts standard **input** of 10 litres to standard **output** of 9 litres) i.e. 9 ÷ 10 = 0.9.

(3) Calculate the standard output that **should have been achieved** from the material input (5500 litres × 0.9 = 4950 litres)

(4) Compare the **actual** production of 5000 litres with the standard production of 4950 litres they should have achieved and × the difference by the standard price of $4.0 per litre. (5000 – 4950 = 50 litres × $4 per litre = $200 (F)

Actual production was 5000 litres of green paint

The actual production of 5000 litres should have cost 5000 × $4.0 = $20,000

The overall usage variance was therefore $20,000 – $19,950 = $50 (F)

There are three reasons for the favourable $50 variance:

	$
The price variance	450 (A)
The mix variance	300 (F)
The yield variance	200 (F)
Total variance	50 (F)

INSPECTION DEPARTMENT

Answers

(a) **Idle time variance**

	Hrs	Hrs	Hrs
Expected idle time			
8,600 hrs x 20%	1,720		
8,600 hrs x 20%		1,680	
8,600 hrs x 20%			1,780
Actual idle time	1,700	1,200	1,400
	20F	480F	380F
x Std enhanced rate	x 7.50	x 7.50	x 7.50
	$150 F	$3,600 F	$2,850 F

Efficiency variances

	Hrs	Hrs	Hrs
Std hrs of actual output	6,600	6,700	6,800
Actual productive hrs worked			
8,600 - 1,700	6,900		
8,400 - 1,200		7,200	
8,900 - 1,400			7,500
	300A	500A	700A
x Std enhanced rate	x 7.50	x 7.50	x 7.50
	$2,250 A	$3,750 A	$5,250 A

Rate variance

December

AHSR 8,600 hrs × $6/hr = 51,600

AHAR = 53,320

$1,720 A Rate

January

AHSR	8,400 hrs	×	$6/hr	=	50,400	
AHAR						$4,200 A Rate
				=	54,600	

February

AHSR	8,900 hrs	×	$6/hr	=	53,400	
AHAR						$4,450 A Rate
				=	57,850	

Labour rate variance

This calculates the difference between the standard cost per hour ($6) and the actual cost per hour. The variance is adverse for each of the three months indicating that labour cost more than was expected.

Labour productive efficiency variance

This calculates if production took more or less hours than expected and is based on the hours worked. The efficiency variances are adverse for each month indicating that production took longer than was expected.

Excess idle time variance

This is the difference between the expected idle time of 20% and the actual idle time. The variance is favourable for each month indicating that the actual idle time is less than 20%.

(b) **Idle Time**

20F / 1,720	480F / 1,680	380F / 1,780
=1.2%F	=28.6%F	=21.3%F

Efficiency

300A	500A	700A
6,600	6,700	6,800
=4.5%A	=7.5%A	=10.3%A

Rate

1,720A	4,200A	4,450A
51,600	50,400	50,400
=3.3%A	=8.3%A	=8.3%A

SUCCESS SERVICES CO

Answers

(a) **Financial analysis**

This data prompts a number of comments.

Turnover. This is up substantially, an increase over the previous year of 44%. The new MD has clearly had a significant impact. How has this been achieved?

Profit. This is also up, by 16%. However, net profits have grown at a much slower rate than sales and this is reflected in the sharply reduced net profit margin of 20.1%, compared with 25% in the previous year. It appears that the increased turnover may have been "bought" via price reductions and lower margins or a combination of lower prices and increased costs – perhaps increased expenditure on marketing and advertising.

Gearing. Interest cover was 5X but has fallen to just 3X. If the company has borrowed at a variable rate it is now substantially more vulnerable to interest rate rises.

Average receivables days are up by 12 days – indicating reduced efficiency in chasing up outstanding debts and / or the granting of more generous payment terms to encourage prospective customers.

Overall, significant growth is being achieved – but at the expense of margins, interest cover and extended credit. This is a potentially worrying trend.

(b) **Non-financial information**

Financial indicators tell us where the company has been – not necessarily where it is going. They are inevitably backward looking. Furthermore, financial indicators are poor at identifying why performance has improved or declined – they show effects but not causes.

Non financial measures, such as those in the Balanced Scorecard, can provide a better guide to future performance since they measure attributes which are essential to the long term success of a business – e.g. customer satisfaction, new product development, product quality, employee satisfaction and training etc.

Customer perspective is aimed at seeing the business through the eyes of its customers. It uses measures that are judged critical to increasing customer satisfaction.

The Internal perspective considers those key internal processes which the business must master if it is to satisfy customers' needs and flourish. It asks what are the core competencies and critical technologies that are essential to securing market leadership.

Innovation and learning focuses on whether the business can continue to develop and deliver value to its customers. It typically includes measures such as speed to market and employee retention rates.

(c) **Performance of the business**

Customer perspective

Customer numbers

The number of customers has increased by nearly 50%. This is a dramatic increase and suggests that there has been a major promotional drive to recruit new customers. The cost of such promotion may account for part of the reduction in the net profit margin. This recruitment drive may have included some form of new customer incentives such as reduced prices for a limited period and may also have included a relaxation of payment terms

% of sales from new software products

This metric also reflects a substantial increase, of over 50%, and implies that substantially increased resource has been devoted to new product development. This focus on new development may well have increased costs but has the potential to lay the foundations for a sustainable increase in sales.

% on-time installation of new products

This metric shows a sharp and worrying fall in the proportion of products that are delivered on time, implying that the increased effort and cost expended on promotion and developing new software products may be being compromised by a failure to meet promised delivery dates.

Average value of software sales

The average value of software sales has fallen by over 20%. The mix of sales may have changed or, perhaps more likely in view of the reduced margin data, there may have been price reductions to increase sales volume.

% customers who complained

This metric, showing a tripling in the rate of complaints, suggests that there has been a major failure to meet customer requirements. This data should prompt an urgent review of both product development procedures and customer relationships with a view to:

A identifying what went wrong and the steps needed to prevent a recurrence of the development / installation problems and

B establishing the general level of customer satisfaction and seeking to repair any damaged relationships

Internal perspective

The launch of two new products – from a zero base in the previous year – suggests that significant effort has gone into new product launches in the current year.

The two products could have been under development for some time or they could have been initiated and launched within the current year. The launch of these new products – if they were not thoroughly tested to ensure they were bug free – could have been a major contributor to the dramatic increase in the level of customer complaints. If it is found that the new products were a significant contributor to customer complaints the procedures for testing and launch of new products will need to be reviewed.

The tender success rate has increased by just over 50%. This could reflect a number of factors such as better understanding of customer requirements which has been successfully translated into product specifications or – much less encouraging - a decision to tender at lower prices or to offer more challenging delivery dates. The latter interpretation appears more likely in the light of the deterioration in service levels suggested by other indicators.

Learning and growth perspective

Programmer output has increased sharply – by some 14%. This has been accompanied however by a worrying 33% increase in the number of bugs per 1000 lines of code. Has the company been selling products that were released prematurely – hence the customer complaints?

The 40%+ fall in the number of development staff who have completed a development course and the 16% deterioration in the employee retention rate is also indicative of increased pressure to "get product out of the door".

This perspective suggests that product quality – and customer satisfaction – is taking second place to a sales drive.

Overall, the company appears to have made a major change in direction under its new MD. Priority appears to have been given to short term sales and profit growth at the expense of customers, product quality, staff, margins, interest cover and liquidity.

The financial data shows growth but has some worrying features – margins, gearing and liquidity.

The balanced scorecard data reveals a dramatic deterioration in service quality and customer and staff satisfaction which suggests that the sales and profit growth is likely to be short lived. Urgent action is required by Michael Speed to ensure that much greater emphasis is given to product quality and customer satisfaction – this may mean longer development times and a reduced rate of sales growth but this is a price that is worth paying.

KDS

Answers

(a) **Divisional administrator's proposal**

Effect on 20X5 ROI

It will have been assumed in arriving at the 31/12/X5 net assets that the debt will have been paid. Reversing this assumption has the effect of increasing liabilities and has no effect on assets, as cash is excluded. Thus net assets will be reduced by $90,000 (to $4,310,000).

Whether the $2,000 late payment penalty is accounted for in 20X5 or 20X6 will depend to some extent on the company's accounting policy. The accruals concept would, however, lean towards it being accounted for in 20X5. Thus operating profits would be reduced by $2,000 (to $647,000).

The new ROI would thus be 647 ÷ 4,310 × 100 = 15.01%

Thus the target will have been achieved and bonuses paid. This is, of course, no indication of improved performance, but simply an arithmetical anomaly arising as a result of one side of the transaction being ignored in the calculation. In fact, the finance cost of the late payment is extremely high.

Longer term effects

There would be no quantifiable long-term effects, although relationships with the supplier may be adversely affected by the late payment.

The works manager's proposal

Effect on 20X5 ROI

Assuming no depreciation charge in 20X5, net assets would be increased by the cost of the new assets, $320,000 (to $4,720,000), and operating profits would be unaffected.

The new ROI would thus be 649 ÷ 4,720 × 100 = 13.75%

This represents a reduction of ROI in the short term.

Longer term effects

In 20X6 and beyond, the full impact of the cost savings and depreciation charge would be felt – operating profits would be increased by a net $(76,000 – 40,000) = $36,000. Net assets value will be increased, but the increase will be smaller each year as the asset is depreciated.

In 20X6, the equipment's own ROI would be

36 ÷ (320 – 40) × 100 = 12.86%

This will still not help the division to achieve its target of 15%, although it does exceed the company's cost of capital and thus may be desirable overall.

However, by the end of 20X7, the equipment WDV will be $(320,000 – 80,000) = $240,000, giving a ROI of 15%, exactly on target. As it increases above this level it will help the division to achieve its overall target.

This illustrates one of the major problems with using book values for assets in performance measures – as the assets get older, they appear to give better performance. This can have the effect of deterring managers from replacing assets even though this may be of benefit in the long term through cost savings (as above), increased productivity etc.

(b) Residual income (RI) is an absolute measure of performance, and is arrived at by deducting a notional interest charge at the company's cost of capital on the net assets. Appraising the two divisions' performance forecasts under this method would have the following results:

	20X5 operating profit	**Interest charge (12% net assets)**	**Residual income**
	$	$	$
Division K	649,000	528,000	121,000
Division D	120,000	57,600	62,400

In summary, RI has advantages and disadvantages over ROI as a performance measure, and both suffer from common valuation problems. One of these can be used as part of a package of performance indicators – market share, productivity, employee satisfaction, technological advancement, etc – but neither is perfect in isolation.

The performance rankings of the two divisions are now apparently reversed. However, the RIs of the two divisions are not directly comparable – whilst Division K has produced nearly twice the level of RI than that of Division D, the net asset base required to do this is over nine times as large. RI cannot be meaningfully used to compare investments of differing sizes, as ROI can.

One could also question the use of the company's average cost of money in computing the notional interest charge. The two divisions have been set a target well above this - this may be because they are considered riskier than average. If 15% had been used in the computation, Division K would have negative RI, whilst Division D has positive RI - reflecting the same information as the ROI, that K is not achieving its target return.

The RI uses the same principles for establishing profit and asset values as the ROI, and thus shares the same problems. As assets get older and their WDV falls, the imputed interest falls and RI rises.

However, RI can be of greater benefit than ROI in management decision making. Management may only feel inclined to undertake new investment if doing so improves their performance measure. For example, Division D currently enjoys a ROI of 25% and its manager may only consider new projects that give a return at least as good as this (although this may depend upon the particular structure of the bonus scheme - a fixed bonus provided the target of 15% is reached may not provoke such an attitude).

However, the RI measure will improve with new investment, i.e. increase, provided the investment's returns are at least covering the rate used in computing the notional interest (12% or 15%). This will ensure that projects that are worthwhile from the company's point of view will also be seen as such by the divisional manager (goal congruence).

(c) Financial measures taken in isolation are unlikely to tell the whole story of a division's or company's performance. They must be put into context, taking account of the circumstances in which they were achieved – new products being introduced, market changes, technological changes, competitors' moves, availability of resources, etc.

For example, one might question why the two divisions in KDS are apparently performing at such different levels. Whilst quality of management may well be a contributory factor, it is unlikely to explain a difference of over 10 percentage points in ROI.

The age profile of assets used should be considered, as discussed above. Division K may have recently invested in new machinery, possibly in response to technological advances. Not to do so would put them at a disadvantage over their competitors, and thus is for long-term benefit. The industry of the much smaller Division D may be more static, requiring less asset changes.

Performance relative to the market and competitors should be considered (market share, product leadership, etc) and the degree of innovation achieved. Level of complaints received may also be monitored.

Consider the performance of a manager – labour turnover, staff morale, managers' relationships with both subordinates and superiors. The level of job satisfaction felt by employees at all levels is an important consideration in the plan for achievement of company objectives.

SATELLITE NAVIGATION SYSTEMS

Answers

(a)

Report

To Operations Manager

From Management Accountant

Date May 2005

Subject Performance of S Inc for four months to 31 December

Production and sales

Production and sales were 1,100 units in September and October, 950 units in November and 900 units in December. There has thus been a marked decline over the four-month period. This good performance in the first two months and poor performance in the latter two months may be due to a seasonal variation. If this is the case, it would be good for the budget to reflect the expected seasonal variation, rather than just being a flat 1,000 units per month.

Tutorial note: The output was calculated by taking the standard cost of actual output and dividing by the standard cost per system, i.e. $1,276,000/$1,160 = 1,100 units, $1,102,000/$1,160 = 950 units and $1,044,000/$1,160 = 900 units.

Materials

The material price variance was favourable for the first two months, and then very adverse for November and December. This was possibly due to the exchange rate movement if the systems are imported. The effect of the exchange rate variations should be quantified. Any remaining adverse variances may be due to inefficient purchasing by the purchasing manager. It should be investigated as to whether there are alternative suppliers for the systems.

The material usage variance was adverse in every month, but was particularly bad in October and even worse in December. In October the variance was $7,200 A and as the material cost was $400 per unit, this meant that an extra $7,200/$400 = 18 units were used on a production of 1,100 units. In December, the variance was $16,000/ $400 = 40 extra units on production of 900 units. This variance could possibly be due to the large batch of systems which did not have the correct adaptors. The variance needs careful investigation in order to find out where the excess units were used, which systems and which teams of fitters were involved.

Labour

The labour rate variance was adverse in September and October and substantially adverse in November and December. Expressing the variances as percentages, for September the standard labour cost was $320 x 1,100 units = $352,000 and thus the variance was $4,200 A/$352,000 = 1.1% A. In November the variance was $5,500 A/$352,000 = 1.6% A. These minor variances could be explained by more overtime than expected being worked, especially as production was high in the first two months. Then things were much worse in the latter two months, for November the variance was $23,100 A/($320 per unit x 950 units) = 7.6% A and in December the variance was $24,000 A/($320 per unit x 900 units) = 8.3%. These substantial variances are almost certainly due to higher wage rates being offered in order to retain staff and lower the labour turnover. It would be very useful to have information on the number of staff leaving the business. Overtime is unlikely to be the cause for the variances in November and December as production was lower than budget.

The labour efficiency variance was $16,000 favourable in September ($16,000/$352,000 = 4.5% F), zero in October and $32,000 adverse in November and December ($32,000 A/$320 per unit x 950 units) = 10.5% A, and $32,000 A/$320 per unit x 900 units) = 11.1% A). It would be expected that some of this variance was due to the large batch of systems which did not have the correct adaptors. This problem was not apparent until fitting was attempted, thus involving the fitters in extra work. If this were the case then we would expect the labour efficiency variance to tie up with the material usage variance, but it does not. We are also told that there is a fluctuation of ± 25% in the fitting times, so even the substantial variances for November and December fall within this range and thus might not represent inefficiency, but simply the fitting of a higher proportion of more labour intensive systems.

It would be useful to have information on the standard times for different systems and the numbers of the different systems, instead of treating all systems alike. The high labour turnover also means that experienced workers are leaving and that new workers are constantly having to be trained. The efficiency of the new workers would be poor to start off with.

Variable overheads

The variable overhead efficiency variance is based on labour hours and thus simply moves in line with the labour efficiency variance.

The expenditure variance was $7,000 A in September, improved to $2,000 A in October and then $2,000 F in November. It was zero in December. For this variance to have any meaning it must be sub-analysed into its different components in order to determine which ones are being overspent and which ones underspent.

Taking the variable overheads as a whole, the variance gets worse as production levels fall, perhaps indicating that the variable overheads are not entirely variable but may include a fixed element.

Fixed overheads

The fixed overhead volume variance simply reflects the better than expected production in the first two months and the worse than expected production in the latter two months. The fixed overhead volume variance has no significance as it does not represent a cash flow (if we make more or fewer units than expected then the fixed overheads do not change), but is simply a mathematical device to reconcile budgeted profit with actual profit in an absorption costing system.

The fixed overhead expenditure variance is $5,000 A, $10,000 A, $20,000 A and $20,000 A over the four months and thus shows a worsening pattern, but again in order to understand where things are going wrong we need to sub-analyse the fixed overhead into their different components. We have been told that rent, rates insurance and computing costs have risen in price noticeably; these costs may be regarded as uncontrollable. Managers' attention should be devoted to investigating the controllable costs and reducing any overspend.

Conclusion

Overall the actual cost was 4.4% worse than expected (($4,906,201 – $4,698,000)/$4,698,000). Whilst this variance might not be regarded as significant, the individual variances in many cases are much bigger and should be investigated. There is a marked decline in performance in November and December. It is important that the individual variances are investigated and their causes understood so that future performance improves.

(b)

	September	October	November	December
	$	$	$	$
Standard cost of actual output	1,276,000	1,276,000	1,102,000	1,044,000
Standard cost per unit	1,160	1,160	1,160	1,160
Actual units of output	1,100	1,100	950	900
Standard material usage (x $400)	440,000	440,000	380,000	360,000
Price % variance	1.25 F	0.76 F	2.51 A	2.87 A
Usage % variance	0.09 A	1.6 A	0.21 A	4.4 A

Percentage variance chart for September to December

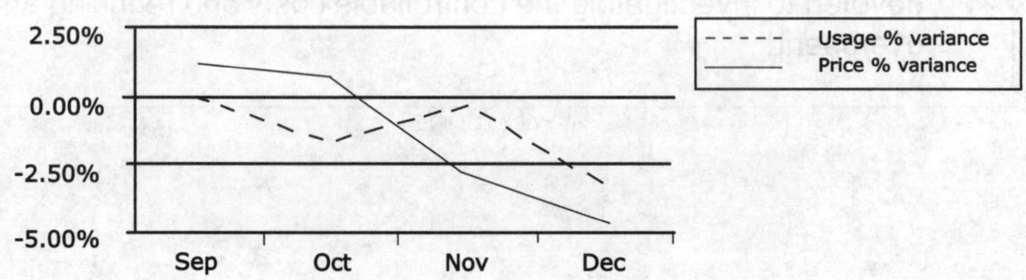

The percentage variance chart can be used to monitor the trend of variances. Significant variances may be identified by setting a control limit. If variances exceed the control limit then action is taken. Alternatively variances which show a worrying trend, such as the material usage variance for S limited, may be investigated before the variance exceeds the control limit.

Index

Index